SCHAUM'S OUTLINE OF

THEORY AND PROBLEMS

OF

PROGRAMMING
WITH
PASCAL

•

WITH EMPHASIS ON TURBO PASCAL AND
WITH FEATURES OF STANDARD ANSI PASCAL

Second Edition

•

BYRON S. GOTTFRIED, Ph.D.
Professor of Industrial Engineering
University of Pittsburgh

SCHAUM'S OUTLINE SERIES
McGRAW-HILL, INC.

New York St. Louis San Francisco Auckland Bogotá Caracas
Lisbon London Madrid Mexico City Milan Montreal
New Delhi San Juan Singapore
Sydney Tokyo Toronto

To Marcia, Sharon, Gail and Susan

BYRON S. GOTTFRIED is a Professor of Industrial Engineering and Academic Director of the Freshman Engineering Program at the University of Pittsburgh. He received his Ph.D. from Case-Western Reserve University in 1962 and has been a member of the Pitt faculty since 1970. His primary interests are in the modeling and simulation of industrial processes. Dr. Gottfried also has active interests in computer graphics and computer programming languages. He is the author of several books, including *Programming with Structured BASIC*, *Programming with C* and *Programming with Pascal* in the Schaum's Outline Series.

 This book is printed on recycled paper containing a minimum of 50% total recycled fiber with 10% postconsumer de-inked fiber. Soybean based inks are used on the cover and text.

Turbo Pascal is a registered trademark of Borland International, Inc.
MS-DOS is a registered trademark of Microsoft Corporation.

Schaum's Outline of Theory and Problems of
PROGRAMMING WITH PASCAL

1 2 3 4 5 6 7 8 9 10 11 12 13 14 15 16 17 18 19 20 BAW BAW 9 8 7 6 5 4 3

ISBN 0-07-023924-X

Sponsoring Editor: John Aliano
Production Supervisor: Leroy Young
Editing Supervisor: Maureen Walker
Cover design by Amy E. Becker

Gottfried, Byron S., date
    Schaum's outline of theory and problems of programming
  with PASCAL – 2nd ed.
      p.   cm. – (Schaum's outline series)
    Includes index.
    ISBN 0-07-023924-X
    1. Pascal (Computer program language) I. Title. II. Title:
    Theory and problems of programming with PASCAL.
    QA76.73.P2G68 1993
    005.13'3 – dc20   93-4710
                               CIP

Preface

Pascal has become the language of choice for introductory classes in computer programming at most colleges and universities. Many high schools and community colleges also offer introductory or secondary programming courses in Pascal.

There are several reasons for Pascal's popularity. First, Pascal was specifically designed to promote an orderly, disciplined approach to computer programming. Its use therefore encourages the development of programs that are logical, well organized, clearly written and relatively free of errors. Moreover, the language is available for practically any computer, whether it be a large mainframe, a minicomputer or an inexpensive desktop computer. In fact, most instructional uses of Pascal are now carried out on personal computers.

This book offers instruction in computer programming using the commonly used features of Pascal. *In this second edition, emphasis is placed on Borland International's Turbo Pascal, though the features of standard ANSI Pascal are also discussed.* Important differences between the two, such as the handling of strings, packed arrays and conformant array parameters, are thoroughly discussed and illustrated. The emphasis, however, is on programming fundamentals, not on details. Hence, many of Turbo Pascal's special features are not discussed.

The book continues in the tradition of other programming texts in the Schaum's Outline Series by presenting complete and understandable explanations, supplemented by a large number of illustrative examples. In addition, the book presents an orderly approach to programming, stressing the importance of clarity, legibility and efficiency in program development. The reader is therefore exposed to the principles of good programming practice as well as the specific rules of Pascal.

The style of writing has been kept elementary, so that the book can be used by a wide reader audience ranging from high-school students to practicing professionals. The book is particularly well suited for advanced secondary or beginning college-level students, as a textbook for an introductory programming course, as a supplementary text, or as an effective self-study guide.

For the most part, the required mathematical level does not go beyond high-school algebra. Much of the material requires no mathematical background at all.

The material is presented in such a manner that the reader can write complete, though elementary, Pascal programs and run them concurrently with reading the text material. This will greatly enhance the beginning programmer's self-confidence and stimulate interest in the subject. (It should be recognized that computer programming is a skill, much like creative writing or playing a musical instrument. Such skills cannot be acquired simply by reading a textbook!)

A large number of examples are included as an integral part of the text. These include several comprehensive programming examples as well as simple drill-type problems. These examples should be studied carefully as the reader progresses through each chapter and begins to write his or her own programs.

Sets of review questions, drill problems and programming problems are also included at the end of each chapter. The review questions enable readers to test their recall of the material presented within each chapter. They also provided an effective chapter summary. Most of the drill problems and programming problems require no special mathematical or technical background. Serious students should solve as many of these problems as possible. (Answers to most of the drill problems are provided at the end of the text.) When using this book in a programming course, the instructor may wish to supplement the programming problems with additional programming assignments that reflect particular disciplinary interests.

The principal features of the language are summarized in Appendixes A – H at the end of the book. This material should be used frequently for ready reference and quick recall. It will be particularly useful when writing or debugging a new program.

Finally, the readers who complete this book will have had a solid exposure to general programming concepts as well as the specific rules of Pascal. From this, they should have acquired some realistic understanding of the capabilities and limitations of computers. They should also be able to program a computer to carry out specific tasks of their own choosing. And they may very well experience some of the excitement and exhilaration of being a part of the current computer revolution, which appears to be a major factor in the reshaping of modern post-industrial societies.

BYRON S. GOTTFRIED

Contents

Complete Programming Examples

The programming examples are listed in the order in which they first appear within the text. The examples vary from very simple to moderately complex. Multiple versions are presented for some of the programs.

1. *Area of a Circle* - Examples 1.6 - 1.15
2. *Roots of a Quadratic Equation* - Examples 5.2 - 5.5, 5.8
3. *Evaluating a Polynomial* - Example 5.7
4. *Averaging a List of Numbers* - Examples 6.4, 6.5, 6.8
5. *Repeated Averaging of a List of Numbers* - Example 6.9
6. *Compound Interest Factors* - Example 6.10
7. *Encoding Characters* - Example 6.13
8. *Solution of an Algebraic Equation* - Example 6.14
9. *Calculating Depreciation* - Examples 6.17, 7.12
10. *Averaging a List of Nonnegative Numbers* - Examples 6.22, 7.8
11. *Maximum of Three Integers* - Examples 7.3, 7.4, 7.7
12. *Search for a Maximum* - Example 7.14
13. *Calculating Factorials* - Examples 7.17, 7.19
14. *Simulation of a Game of Chance (Shooting Craps)* - Example 7.18
15. *Printing Backward* - Example 7.20
16. *The Towers of Hanoi* - Examples 7.22, 8.11
17. *Number of Days Between Two Dates* - Example 8.10
18. *Deviations About an Average* - Example 9.4
19. *Reordering a List of Numbers* - Example 9.5
20. *Names and Addresses* - Examples 9.8, 9.9
21. *Table Manipulation* - Example 9.12
22. *Adding Two Tables of Numbers* - Examples 9.17, 9.35
23. *A Pig Latin Generator* - Example 9.28
24. *A Customer Billing System* - Example 10.21
25. *Inventory Control* - Example 10.28
26. *Creating a File of Customer Records* - Examples 11.7, 11.8, 11.9
27. *Creating a File of Squares and Square Roots* - Example 11.10
28. *Reading a File of Customer Records* - Example 11.11
29. *Reading a File of Squares and Square Roots* - Example 11.12
30. *Copying a File* - Example 11.13
31. *Appending to a File* - Example 11.14
32. *Updating a File* - Example 11.15
33. *Updating a Customer Billing System* - Example 11.16
34. *Transferring Data Between Text Files* - Example 11.18
35. *Entering and Saving a Text File* - Example 11.19
36. *Encoding and Decoding Text* - Example 11.20
37. *Printing Output Data* - Example 11.21
38. *Analyzing a Line of Text* - Example 12.16
39. *Number of Vowels in a Line of Text* - Example 12.19
40. *Creating a Linked List* - Example 13.8
41. *Processing a Linked List* - Example 13.9

Chapter 1

Introductory Concepts

This book offers instruction in computer programming using a disciplined, structured programming language called Pascal. We will see how a problem that is initially described in vague terms can be analyzed, outlined and finally transformed into a well-organized Pascal program. These concepts are demonstrated in detail by the many sample problems that are included in the text.

1.1 INTRODUCTION TO COMPUTERS

Today's computers come in many different forms. They range from massive, multipurpose *mainframes* and *supercomputers* to desktop-size *personal computers*. Between these extremes is a vast middle ground of *minicomputers* and *workstations*. Large minicomputers approach mainframes in computing power, whereas workstations are powerful personal computers.

Mainframes and large minicomputers are used by many businesses, universities, hospitals and government agencies to carry out sophisticated scientific and business calculations. These computers are expensive (large computers can cost millions of dollars) and may require a sizable staff of supporting personnel and a special, carefully controlled environment.

Personal computers, on the other hand, are small and inexpensive. In fact, portable, battery-powered personal computers smaller than a typewriter are now available. Personal computers are widely used in most schools and businesses, and they are rapidly becoming common household items. Students typically use personal computers when learning to program with Pascal.

Fig. 1.1 shows a student using a personal computer.

Fig. 1.1

1

Despite their small size and low cost, modern personal computers approach small minicomputers in computing power. They are now used for many applications that formerly required larger, more expensive computers. Moreover, their performance continues to improve dramatically as their cost continues to drop. The design of a personal computer permits a high level of interaction between the user and the computer. Most applications (e.g., word processors, graphics programs, spreadsheets and database management programs) are specifically designed to take advantage of this feature, thus providing the skilled user with a wide variety of creative tools to write, draw or carry out numerical computations. Applications involving high-resolution graphics are particularly common.

Many organizations connect personal computers to larger computers or to other personal computers, thus permitting their use either as stand-alone devices or as terminals within a computer *network*. Connections over telephone lines are particularly common. When viewed in this context, we see that personal computers often *complement*, rather than *replace*, the use of larger computers.

1.2 COMPUTER CHARACTERISTICS

All digital computers, regardless of their size, are basically electronic devices that can transmit, store, and manipulate *information* (i.e., *data*). Several different types of data can be processed by a computer. These include *numeric data*, *character data* (names, addresses, etc.), *graphic data* (charts, drawings, photographs, etc.), and *sound* (music, speech patterns, etc.). The two most common types, from the standpoint of a beginning programmer, are numeric data and character data. Scientific and technical applications are concerned primarily with numeric data, whereas business applications usually require processing of both numeric and character data.

To process a particular set of data, the computer must be given an appropriate set of instructions called a *program*. These instructions are entered into the computer and then stored in a portion of the computer's *memory*.

A stored program can be *executed* at any time. This causes the following things to happen.

1.   A set of information, called the *input data*, will be entered into the computer (from the keyboard, a floppy disk, etc.) and stored in a portion of the computer's memory.

2.   The input data will be processed to produce certain desired results, known as the *output data*.

3.   The output data, and perhaps some of the input data, will be printed onto a sheet of paper or displayed on a *monitor* (a television receiver specially designed to display computer output).

This three-step procedure can be repeated many times if desired, thus causing a large quantity of data to be processed in rapid sequence. It should be understood, however, that each of these steps, particularly steps 2 and 3, can be lengthy and complicated.

EXAMPLE 1.1

A computer has been programmed to calculate the area of a circle using the formula $a = \pi r^2$, given a numeric value for the radius r as input data. The following steps are required.

1.   Read the numeric value for the radius of the circle.

2.   Calculate the value of the area using the above formula. This value will be stored, along with the input data, in the computer's memory.

3.   Print (display) the values of the radius and the corresponding area.

4.   Stop.

Each of these steps will require one or more instructions in a computer program.

The foregoing discussion illustrates two important characteristics of a digital computer: *memory* and *capability to be programmed*. A third important characteristic is *speed and reliability*. We will say more about memory, speed, and reliability in the next few paragraphs. Programmability will be discussed at length throughout the remainder of this book.

Memory

Every piece of information stored within the computer's memory is encoded as some unique combination of zeros and ones. These zeros and ones are called *bits* (*bi*nary dig*its*). Each bit is represented by an electronic device that is, in some sense, either "off" (zero) or "on" (one).

Small computers have memories that are organized into 8-bit multiples called *bytes*, as illustrated in Fig. 1.2. Notice that the individual bits are numbered, beginning with 0 (for the rightmost bit) and extending to 7 (the leftmost bit). Normally, a single character (e.g., a letter, a single digit or a punctuation symbol) will occupy one byte of memory. An instruction may occupy 1, 2 or 3 bytes. A single numeric quantity may occupy 1 to 8 bytes, depending on its *precision* (i.e., the number of significant figures) and its *type* (integer, floating-point, etc.).

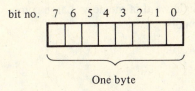

One byte

Fig. 1.2

The size of a computer's memory is usually expressed as some multiple of $2^{10} = 1024$ bytes. This is referred to as 1K. Small computers have memories whose sizes typically range from 64K to several megabytes, where 1 megabyte (1M) is equivalent to $2^{10} \times 2^{10} = 1024$K bytes.

EXAMPLE 1.2

The memory of a small personal computer has a capacity of 256K bytes. Thus, as many as $256 \times 1024 = 262{,}144$ characters and/or instructions can be stored in the computer's memory. If the entire memory is used to represent character data (which is actually quite unlikely), then over 3200 names and addresses can be stored within the computer at any one time, assuming 80 characters for each name and address.

If the memory is used to represent numeric data rather than names and addresses, then over 65,000 individual numbers can be stored at any one time, assuming each numeric quantity requires 4 bytes of memory.

One 32-bit word

Fig. 1.3

Large computers have memories that are organized into *words* rather than bytes. Each word will consist of a relatively large number of bits—typically 32 or 36. The bit-wise organization of a 32-bit word is illustrated in Fig. 1.3. Notice that the bits are numbered, beginning with 0 (for the rightmost bit) and extending to 31 (the leftmost bit).

Fig. 1.4 shows the same 32-bit word organized into 4 consecutive bytes. The bytes are numbered in the same manner as the individual bits, ranging from 0 (for the rightmost byte) to 3 (the leftmost byte).

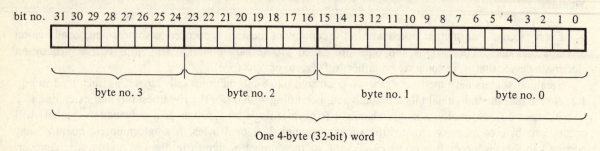

One 4-byte (32-bit) word

Fig. 1.4

The use of a 32- or a 36-bit word permits one numeric quantity, or a small *group* of characters (typically 4 or 5), to be represented within a single word of memory. Large computers commonly have several million words (i.e., several megawords) of memory.

EXAMPLE 1.3

The memory of a large computer has a capacity of 2M (2048K) words, which is equivalent to 2048 x 1024 = 2,097,152 words. If the entire memory is used to represent numeric data (which is unlikely), then more than 2 million numbers can be stored within the computer at any one time, assuming each numeric quantity requires one word of memory.

If the memory is used to represent characters rather than numeric data, then about 8 million characters can be stored at any one time, based upon 4 characters per word. This is more than enough memory to store the contents of an entire book.

Most computers also employ *auxiliary storage devices* (e.g., magnetic tapes, disks, optical memory devices) in addition to their primary memories. These devices typically range from 20 or 40 megabytes for a small computer to several hundred megawords for a large computer. Moreover, they allow information to be recorded permanently, since they can often be physically disconnected from the computer and stored when not in use. However, the access time (i.e., the time required to store or retrieve information) is considerably greater for these auxiliary devices than for the computer's primary memory.

Speed and Reliability

Because of its extremely high speed, a computer can carry out calculations within minutes that might require many days, and perhaps even months or years, if carried out by hand. For example, the end-of-semester grades for all students in a large university can typically be processed in just a few minutes on a large computer.

The time required to carry out simple computational tasks, such as adding two numbers, is usually expressed in terms of *microseconds* (1 μsec = 10^{-6} sec) or *nanoseconds* (1 *n*sec = 10^{-3} μsec = 10^{-9} sec). Thus, if a computer can add two numbers in 10 nanoseconds (typical of a modern medium-speed computer), 100 million (10^8) additions will be carried out in one second.

This very high speed is accompanied by an equally high level of reliability. Thus, computers never make mistakes of their own accord. Highly publicized "computer errors," such as a person's receiving a tax refund of several million dollars, are the result of programming errors or data entry errors rather than errors caused by the computer itself.

1.3 MODES OF OPERATION

There are two different ways that a large computer can be shared by many different users. These are the *batch mode* and the *interactive mode*. Each has its own advantages for addressing certain types of problems.

Batch Processing

In *batch processing*, a number of jobs are entered into the computer, stored internally, and then processed sequentially. (A *job* refers to a computer program and its associated sets of input data.) After the job is processed, the output, along with a listing of the computer program, is printed on multiple sheets of paper by a high-speed printer. Typically, the user will pick up the printed output at some convenient time after the job has been processed.

In *classical batch processing*, the program and the data are recorded on *punched cards*. This information is read into the computer by means of a mechanical card reader and then processed. In the early days of computing, all jobs were processed in this manner. Fortunately, this mode of operation is now obsolete.

Modern batch processing is generally tied into a timesharing system (see below). Thus, the program and the data are typed into the computer via a *timesharing terminal* or a personal computer acting as a terminal. The information is then stored within the computer's memory and processed in its proper sequence. This form of batch processing is preferable to classical batch processing, since it eliminates the need for punched cards and allows the input information (program and data) to be edited while it is being entered.

Large quantities of information (both programs and data) can be transmitted into and out of the computer very quickly in batch processing. Furthermore, the user need not be present while the job is being processed. Therefore, this mode of operation is well-suited to jobs that require large amounts of computer time or are physically lengthy. On the other hand, the total time required for a job to be processed in this manner may vary from several minutes to several hours, even though the job may have required only a second or two of actual computer time. (Each job must wait its turn before it can be read, processed, and printed out.) Thus, batch processing is undesirable when processing small, simple jobs that must be returned as quickly as possible (as, for example, when learning computer programming).

Timesharing

Timesharing allows many different users to use a single computer simultaneously. Generally, the host computer is a mainframe or a large minicomputer. The various users communicate with the computer through their own individual terminals. In a modern timesharing network, personal computers are often used as timesharing terminals. Since the host computer operates much faster than a human sitting at a terminal, one large computer can support many terminals at essentially the same time. Therefore, each user will be unaware of the presence of any other users and will seem to have the host computer at his or her own disposal.

An individual timesharing terminal may be wired directly to the host computer, or it may be connected to the computer over telephone lines, a microwave circuit, or even an earth satellite. Thus, the terminal can be located far—perhaps hundreds of miles—from its host computer. Systems in which personal computers are connected to large mainframes over telephone lines are particularly common. Such systems make use of *modems* (i.e., *mo*dulator/*dem*odulator devices) to convert the digitized computer signals into analog telephone signals and vice versa. Through such an arrangement a person working at home, on his or her own personal computer, can easily access a remote computer at school or at the office.

Timesharing is best suited for processing relatively simple jobs that do not require extensive data transmission or large amounts of computer time. Many applications that arise in schools and commercial offices have these characteristics. Such applications can be processed quickly, easily, and at minimum expense using timesharing.

EXAMPLE 1.4

A major university has a computer timesharing capability consisting of 200 hard-wired timesharing terminals and 80 additional telephone connections. The timesharing terminals are located at various places around the campus and are wired directly to a large mainframe computer. Each terminal is able to transmit information to or from the central computer at a maximum speed of 960 characters per second.

The telephone connections allow students who are not on campus to connect their personal computers to the central computer. Each personal computer can transmit data to or from the central computer at a maximum speed of 240 characters per second. Thus, all 280 terminals and personal computers can interact with the central computer at the same time, though each student will be unaware that others are simultaneously sharing the computer.

Interactive Computing

Interactive computing is a type of computing environment that originated with commercial timesharing systems and has been refined by the widespread use of personal computers. In an interactive computing environment, the user and the computer interact with each other during the computational session. Thus, the user may periodically be asked to provide certain information that will determine what subsequent actions are to be taken by the computer and vice versa.

EXAMPLE 1.5

A student wishes to use a personal computer to calculate the radius of a circle whose area has a value of 100. A program is available that will calculate the area of a circle, given the radius. (Note that this is just the opposite of what the student wishes to do.) This program isn't exactly what is needed, but it does allow the student to obtain an answer by trial and error. The procedure will be to guess a value for the radius and then calculate a corresponding area. This trial-and-error procedure continues until the student has found a value for the radius that yields an area sufficiently close to 100.

Once the program execution begins, the message

```
Radius = ?
```

is displayed. The student then enters a value for the radius. Let us assume that the student enters a value of 5 for the radius. The computer will respond by displaying

```
Area = 78.5398
```

```
Do you wish to repeat the calculation?
```

The student then types either yes or no. If the student types yes, the message

```
Radius = ?
```

again appears, and the entire procedure is repeated. If the student types no, the message

```
Goodbye
```

is displayed and the computation is terminated.

Shown below is a printed copy of the information displayed during a typical interactive session using the program described above. In this session, an approximate value of $r = 5.6$ was determined after only three calculations. The information typed by the student is underlined.

```
Radius = ? 5
Area = 78.5398

Do you wish to repeat the calculation? yes

Radius = ? 6
Area = 113.097

Do you wish to repeat the calculation? yes

Radius = ? 5.6
Area = 98.5204

Do you wish to repeat the calculation? no

Goodbye
```

Notice the manner in which the student and the computer appear to be conversing with one another. Also, note that the student waits until he or she sees the calculated value of the area before deciding whether or not to carry out another calculation. If another calculation is initiated, the new value for the radius supplied by the student will depend on the previously calculated results.

Programs designed for interactive computing environments are sometimes said to be *conversational* in nature. Computerized games are excellent examples of such interactive applications. These include fast-action, graphical arcade games, even though the user's responses may be reflexive rather than numeric or verbal.

1.4 TYPES OF PROGRAMMING LANGUAGES

Many different languages can be used to program a computer. The most basic of these is *machine language*—a collection of very detailed, cryptic instructions that control the computer's internal circuitry. This is the natural dialect of the computer. Very few computer programs are actually written in machine language, however, for two significant reasons: first, because machine language is very cumbersome to work with and second, because every different type of computer has its own unique instruction set. Thus, a machine-language program written for one type of computer cannot be run on another type of computer without significant alterations.

Usually, a computer program will be written in some *high-level* language whose instruction set is more compatible with human languages and human thought processes. Most of these are *general-purpose* languages such as Pascal. (Some other popular general-purpose languages are C, Fortran and BASIC.) There are also various *special-purpose* languages that are specifically designed for a particular type of application. Some common examples are CSMP and SIMAN, which are special-purpose *simulation* languages, and LISP, a *list-processing* language that is widely used for artificial intelligence applications.

As a rule, a single instruction in a high-level language will be equivalent to several instructions in machine language. This greatly simplifies the task of writing complete, correct programs. Furthermore, the rules for programming in a particular high-level language are much the same for all computers, so that a program written for one computer can generally be run on many different computers with little or no alteration. Thus, we see that a high-level language offers three significant advantages over machine language: *simplicity, uniformity* and *portability* (i.e., machine independence).

A program that is written in a high-level language must, however, be translated into machine language before it can be executed. This is known as *compilation* or *interpretation*, depending on how it is carried out. (Compilers translate the entire program into machine language before executing any of the instructions. Interpreters, on the other hand, proceed through a program by translating and then executing single instructions or small groups of instructions.) In either case, the translation is carried out automatically within the computer. In fact, inexperienced programmers may not even be aware that this process is taking place, since they typically see only their original high-level program, the input data, and the calculated results. Most implementations of Pascal operate as compilers.

A compiler or interpreter is itself a computer program. It accepts a program written in a high-level language (e.g., Pascal) as input, and generates a corresponding machine-language program as output. The original high-level program is called the *source* program, and the resulting machine-language program is called the *object* program. Every computer must have its own compiler or interpreter for a particular high-level language.

It is generally more convenient to develop a new program using an interpreter rather than a compiler. Once an error-free program has been developed, however, a compiled version will normally execute much faster than an interpreted version. The reasons for this are beyond the scope of our present discussion.

1.5 INTRODUCTION TO PASCAL

Pascal is a general-purpose, high-level programming language that has been derived from Algol-60. Its instructions are made up of algebraic-like expressions and certain English words such as BEGIN, END, READ, WRITE, IF, THEN, REPEAT, WHILE, DO, etc. In this respect Pascal resembles many other high-level languages. Pascal also contains some unique features, however, that have been specifically designed to encourage the use of *structured programming*—an orderly, disciplined approach toward programming that promotes clear, efficient, error-free programs. For this reason, many educators and professional programmers favor the use of Pascal over other general-purpose languages.

Pascal was named in honor of Blaise Pascal (1623-1662), the brilliant French scientist and mathematician whose many accomplishments include the invention of the world's first mechanical calculating machine.

History of Pascal

Pascal was originally developed in the early 1970s by Niklaus Wirth at the Technical University in Zurich, Switzerland. The original purpose was to develop a disciplined, high-level language for teaching structured programming. Wirth's original language definition is sometimes referred to as *standard Pascal* or *standard Pascal as defined by Jensen and Wirth*.[*] There is, however, some ambiguity in the term "standard Pascal," as there are now several different standards. In the United States, an official standard has been defined jointly by the American National Standards Institute (ANSI) and the Institute of Electrical and Electronics Engineers (IEEE).[**] This official standard is often referred to as ANSI Pascal.

---

[*]K. Jensen and N. Wirth, Pascal User Manual and Report, 2d edition, Springer-Verlag, 1974.

[**]American National Standard Pascal Computer Programming Language, ANSI/IEEE 770X3.97-1983, Institute of Electrical and Electronics Engineers, New York, 1983.

In 1983 Borland International, a small computer software company, began marketing an inexpensive Pascal compiler called *Turbo Pascal*, for use on personal computers. Turbo Pascal was an instant success, because of its low cost and its ease of use. As Turbo Pascal continued to evolve, a complete programming environment, including an editor and an interactive debugger, was created around the language. Today Turbo Pascal is the dominant implementation of Pascal used with personal computers. It is widely used both as a teaching language and as a powerful general-purpose language for many different kinds of applications.

This book is concerned with the commonly used features of the Pascal language, as implemented both in Turbo Pascal and in ANSI Pascal.

Structure of a Pascal Program

Every Pascal program contains a header and a block. The *header* begins with the word PROGRAM, followed by some additional information that may be required. Usually, this part of the program is only one line long.

The *block* has two main parts—the declaration part and the statement part. The *declaration part* defines the various data items that are used within the program. The *statement part* contains the actual statements that cause actions to be taken. At least one statement must be present in every Pascal program.

This overall program structure is outlined below in greater detail.

1. Header

2. Block, consisting of

   (*a*) Declarations, which include

   > Labels
   > Constants
   > Type definitions
   > Variables
   > Procedures and functions

   (*b*) Statements

Each of these program components will be discussed in much greater detail later in this book. Only the overview is important for now. It should be understood that all of the declaration items need not be present in any single Pascal program. Those items that are present, however, must appear in the order shown above.

EXAMPLE 1.6 Area of a circle

Here is an elementary Pascal program, called `circle`, that reads in the radius of a circle, calculates its area and then writes out (i.e., displays) the area.

```
PROGRAM circle;                          (* HEADER *)

VAR area,radius : real;                  (* VARIABLE DECLARATION *)

BEGIN
    read(radius);                        (* STATEMENT *)
    area := 3.14159*sqr(radius);         (* STATEMENT *)
    writeln(area)                        (* STATEMENT *)
END.
```

The principal components of this program have been separated and labeled in order to emphasize the overall program organization. Normally, a program this simple will not include this many comments. Rather, it might appear as shown below.

```
PROGRAM circle;

(* AREA OF A CIRCLE *)

VAR area,radius : real;

BEGIN
    read(radius);
    area := 3.14159*sqr(radius);
    writeln(area)
END.
```

The following features should be pointed out in the above program.

1. Some of the words are capitalized. These are *reserved words* (or *keywords*) that have special predefined meanings. (More about this later.)

2. The first line contains the program name (`circle`). This is the program *header*.

3. The second line is a *comment* that identifies the purpose of the program. Comments can always be recognized because they are enclosed in special symbols, such as (`*  .  .  .  *`).

4. The three indented lines between `BEGIN` and `END` are the program *statements*. They cause a value for the radius to be entered into the computer, a value for the area to be calculated, and the value of the area to be displayed. Indenting these statements is not essential but is strongly recommended as a matter of good programming practice. (This is the type of disciplined program development that Pascal is designed to encourage.)

5. The numerical values for the radius and the area are represented by the symbolic names `radius` and `area`. These symbolic names are called *variables*. They are defined (declared) in the third line of the program.

6. The symbolic name `sqr` in line 6 is a *standard function* that is used to compute the square of the radius.

7. Finally, notice the punctuation at the end of each line. Most lines end with semicolons; some have no punctuation and the last line ends with a period. This is a part of Pascal's syntax. We will say more about punctuation in later sections of this book.

1.6 SOME SIMPLE PASCAL PROGRAMS

In this section we present several Pascal programs that illustrate some commonly used features of the language. All of the programs are extensions of Example 1.6; that is, each program calculates the area of a circle, or the areas of several circles. Each program illustrates a somewhat different approach to this problem. All of the programs are written in Turbo Pascal.

You should not attempt to understand the syntactic details of these examples, though experienced programmers will recognize features similar to those found in other general-purpose programming languages. Beginners should focus their attention only on the overall program logic. The details will be provided later in this book.

EXAMPLE 1.7 Area of a Circle

Here is a variation of the program given in Example 1.6 for calculating the area of a circle.

```
PROGRAM circle;

(* AREA OF A CIRCLE - VERSION 2 *)

CONST pi = 3.14159;
VAR radius,area : real;

BEGIN
   write('radius = ');
   read(radius);
   area := pi*sqr(radius);
   writeln('area =',area)
END.
```

This program contains a *constant identifier*, `pi`, that represents the numerical value 3.14159. In addition, when this program is executed it *prompts* the user for the value of the radius (by displaying `radius = `) and then provides a *label* with the value of the area (by displaying `area = `).

The interactive dialog resulting from a typical program execution is shown below. The user's response to the input prompt is underlined, for clarity.

```
radius = 3
area = 2.8274310000E+01
```

Notice that Turbo Pascal generates numerical output in scientific form. Thus, the calculated value for the area is 2.827431×10^1, which is equivalent to 28.27431. We will see another way to format numerical output in later examples.

EXAMPLE 1.8 Area of a Circle using a Function

Here is another variation of the program shown in Examples 1.6 and 1.7. This program illustrates the use of a *function* to calculate and return a value. When executed, this program behaves in the same manner as the program shown in Example 1.7

```
PROGRAM circle;

(* AREA OF A CIRCLE - VERSION 3 *)

VAR radius,area : real;

FUNCTION funct(r : real) : real;
CONST pi = 3.14159;
BEGIN
   funct := pi*sqr(r)
END;
```

```
BEGIN
   write('radius = ');
   read(radius);
   area := funct(radius);
   writeln('area =',area)
END.
```

In this program a separate programmer-defined function, called `funct`, is used to carry out the actual calculations. Within this function, `r` is a *parameter* that represents the value of the radius supplied to `funct` from the main program block. The function name, `funct`, represents the calculated result (i.e., the area).

A reference to the function appears in the main block, within the statement

```
area := funct(radius);
```

This statement causes the value of `radius` to be transferred to `funct`. The value returned by `funct` is then assigned to `area`. The use of functions will be discussed in detail in Chap. 7.

EXAMPLE 1.9 Area of a Circle using a Procedure

In this example we rewrite the previous program using a *procedure* rather than a function.

```
PROGRAM circle;

(* AREA OF A CIRCLE - VERSION 4 *)

VAR radius,area : real;

PROCEDURE calc(VAR r,a : real);
CONST pi = 3.14159;
BEGIN
   a := pi*sqr(r)
END;

BEGIN
   write('radius = ');
   read(radius);
   calc(radius,area);
   writeln('area =',area)
END.
```

The actual calculations are now carried out in the procedure named `calc`. Within this procedure, `r` and `a` are parameters that represent the value of the radius and the area, respectively. In contrast to a function, note that the procedure name (`calc`) does not represent a calculated quantity.

The procedure is referenced within the main block, with the statement

```
calc(radius,area);
```

This statement causes the known value of `radius` to be transferred to `calc` and the newly calculated value of `area` to be returned. We will discuss the use of procedures in detail within Chap. 7.

When the program is executed, the resulting interactive dialog and the calculated results are indistinguishable from those shown earlier, in Example 1.7.

EXAMPLE 1.10 Area of a Circle with Error Checking

Now consider a variation of the program shown in Example 1.8.

```
PROGRAM circle;

(* AREA OF A CIRCLE - VERSION 5 *)

VAR radius,area : real;

FUNCTION funct(r : real) : real;
CONST pi = 3.14159;
BEGIN
   funct := pi*sqr(r)
END;

BEGIN
   write('radius = ');
   read(radius);
   IF radius < 0 THEN area := 0
                 ELSE area := funct(radius);
   writeln('area =',area)
END.
```

This program again calculates the area of a circle, using the function `funct` and the constant identifier `pi`, as in Example 1.8. Now, however, we have added a simple error-correction routine, which tests to see if the value of the radius is less than zero. (Mathematically, a negative value for the radius does not make any sense.) The test is carried out within the main block, using an IF - THEN - ELSE statement (see Chap. 6). Thus, if `radius` has a negative value, a value of zero is assigned to `area`; otherwise, the value for `area` is calculated within `funct`, as before.

EXAMPLE 1.11 Areas of Several Circles

The following program expands the previous example by calculating the areas of several circles.

```
PROGRAM circle;

(* AREA OF A CIRCLE - VERSION 6 *)

VAR radius,area : real;
    i,n : integer;

FUNCTION funct(r : real) : real;
CONST pi = 3.14159;
BEGIN
   funct := pi*sqr(r)
END;

BEGIN
   write('How many circles? ');
   read(n);
   writeln;
```

```
      FOR i := 1 TO n DO
         BEGIN
            write('radius = ');
            read(radius);
            IF radius < 0 THEN area := 0
                          ELSE area := funct(radius);
            writeln('area = ',area:4:1);
            writeln
         END
END.
```

In this program the total number of circles, represented by the variable n, must be entered into the computer before any calculations are carried out. The FOR structure then creates a *loop* that calculates all of the areas. The statements within the loop are executed repeatedly, once for each circle (see Chap. 6).

The variable i is used as a counter within the loop. Its value will increase by 1 during each pass through the loop, beginning with 1 and ending with n. Thus, the beginning and ending values for i determine the number of passes through the loop.

The term `area:4:1` within the first `writeln` statement specifies that the current value for area will be displayed as a fixed-point quantity (without an exponent) within a field of four characters, with one digit to the right of the decimal point.

When the program is executed it generates an interactive dialog, as shown below. The user's responses are underlined.

```
How many circles? 3

radius = 3
area = 28.3

radius = 4
area = 50.3

radius = 5
area = 78.5
```

EXAMPLE 1.12 Areas of an Unspecified Number of Circles using WHILE - DO

The previous program can be improved by processing an unspecified number of circles, where the calculations continue until a value of zero is entered for the radius. This avoids the need to count, and then specify, the number of circles in advance. This feature is especially helpful when there are many sets of data to be processed.

```
PROGRAM circle;

(* AREA OF A CIRCLE - VERSION 7 *)

VAR radius,area : real;

FUNCTION funct(r : real) : real;
CONST pi = 3.14159;
BEGIN
   funct := pi*sqr(r)
END;
```

```
BEGIN
   writeln('To STOP, enter 0 for the radius');
   writeln;
   write('radius = ');
   read(radius);

   WHILE radius <> 0 DO
      BEGIN
         IF radius < 0 THEN area := 0
                       ELSE area := funct(radius);
         writeln('area = ',area:4:1);
         writeln;
         write('radius = ');
         read(radius)
      END;

   writeln;
   writeln('Goodbye, have a NICE DAY!')
END.
```

This program uses a WHILE - DO structure in place of the FOR structure shown in the last example. The WHILE - DO structure creates a loop that continues to execute as long as the value assigned to radius is not zero. Note that the initial value for the radius must be specified before entering the WHILE - DO structure. Also, note that this program will display a message at the beginning of the program execution, indicating how to end the computation.

The dialog resulting from a typical execution of this program is shown below. Once again, the user's responses are underlined.

```
To STOP, enter 0 for the radius

radius = 3
area = 28.3

radius = 4
area = 50.3

radius = 5
area = 78.5

radius = 0

Goodbye, have a NICE DAY!
```

EXAMPLE 1.13 Areas of an Unspecified Number of Circles using REPEAT - UNTIL

Pascal includes a third type of looping structure, called REPEAT - UNTIL. This structure is similar to WHILE - DO except that the logical test appears at the *end* of the structure rather than the beginning. Here is a variation of the previous program that uses REPEAT - UNTIL rather than WHILE - DO.

```
PROGRAM circle;

(* AREA OF A CIRCLE - VERSION 8 *)

VAR radius,area : real;

FUNCTION funct(r : real) : real;
CONST pi = 3.14159;
BEGIN
    funct := pi*sqr(r)
END;

BEGIN
    writeln('To STOP, enter 0 for the radius');
    writeln;
    write('radius = ');
    read(radius);

    REPEAT
        IF radius < 0 THEN area := 0
                      ELSE area := funct(radius);
        writeln('area = ',area:4:1);
        writeln;
        write('radius = ');
        read(radius)
    UNTIL radius = 0;

    writeln;
    writeln('Goodbye, have a NICE DAY!')
END.
```

When this program is executed, the resulting output is identical to that shown in the last example.

EXAMPLE 1.14 Calculating and Storing the Areas of Several Circles

Some problems require that a series of calculated results be stored within the computer, perhaps for recall in a later calculation. The corresponding input data may also be stored internally, along with the calculated results. This can be accomplished through the use of *arrays*.

The following program utilizes two arrays, called `radius` and `area`, to store the radius and the area for as many as 100 different circles. Each array can be thought of as a list of numbers. The individual numbers within each list are referred to as *array elements*. These elements are numbered, beginning with 1. Thus, the radius of the first circle will be stored within the array element `radius[1]`, the radius of the second circle will be stored within `radius[2]`, and so on. Similarly, the corresponding areas will be stored in `area[1]`, `area[2]`, etc.

Here is the complete program.

```
PROGRAM circle;

(* AREA OF A CIRCLE - VERSION 9 *)
```

```
    VAR radius,area : ARRAY [1..100] OF real;
        i, n : integer;


    FUNCTION funct(r : real) : real;
    CONST pi = 3.14159;
    BEGIN
        funct := pi*sqr(r)
    END;



BEGIN
    writeln('To STOP, enter 0 for the radius');
    writeln;
    i := 1;
    write('radius = ');
    read(radius[i]);

    (* enter the radii and calculate the areas *)
    WHILE radius[i] <> 0 DO
        BEGIN
            IF radius[i] < 0 THEN area[i] := 0
                            ELSE area[i] := funct(radius[i]);

            i := i+1;
            write('radius = ');
            read(radius[i])
        END;

    n := i-1;    (* tag the highest value of i *)

    writeln;
    writeln('Summary of Results');
    writeln;

    (* display the results *)
    FOR i := 1 TO n DO
        BEGIN
            writeln('i = ',i:1,'   Radius = ',radius[i]:3:1,
                            '   Area = ',area[i]:4:1)
        END;

    writeln;
    writeln('Goodbye, have a NICE DAY!')
END.
```

An unspecified number of radii will be entered into the computer, as in the last few examples. As each new value is entered (i.e., as the *i*th value is entered), it is stored within `radius[i]`. Its corresponding area is then calculated and stored within `area[i]`. This process will continue until all of the radii have been entered (that is, until a value of zero is entered for the radius). The entire set of stored values (i.e., the array elements whose values are nonzero) will then be displayed. Note that none of the output will be displayed until all of the data have been entered and all of the calculations have been carried out.

When the program is executed it results in an interactive dialog, such as that shown below. The user's responses are once again underlined.

```
To STOP, enter 0 for the radius

radius = 3
radius = 4
radius = 5
radius = 0

Summary of Results

i = 1   Radius = 3.0   Area = 28.3
i = 2   Radius = 4.0   Area = 50.3
i = 3   Radius = 5.0   Area = 78.5

Goodbye, have a NICE DAY!
```

This simple program does not make any use of the values that have been stored within the arrays. Its only purpose is to demonstrate the mechanics of utilizing arrays within a program. In a more complex example, we might want to determine an average value for the areas, and then compare each individual area with the average. To do this, we would have to recall the individual areas (the individual array elements area[1], area[2], . . ., etc.) after all of the areas have been calculated.

The use of arrays is discussed in Chap. 9.

EXAMPLE 1.15 Calculating and Storing the Areas of Several Circles

Here is a more sophisticated approach to the problem described in the previous example.

```
PROGRAM circle;

(* AREA OF A CIRCLE - VERSION 10 *)
TYPE circdata = RECORD
                   id : string;
                   radius : real;
                   area : real
               END;

VAR c : ARRAY [1..100] OF circdata;
    i, n : integer;


FUNCTION funct(r : real) : real;
CONST pi = 3.14159;
BEGIN
   funct := pi*sqr(r)
END;
```

```
  BEGIN
     writeln('To STOP, enter END for the identifier');
     writeln;

     (* enter the first identifier *)
     i := 1;
     write('identifier = ');
     readln(c[i].id);

     (* enter the radius, calculate the area and enter the next identifier *)
     WHILE NOT((UpCase(c[i].id[1]) = 'E') AND
               (UpCase(c[i].id[2]) = 'N') AND
               (UpCase(c[i].id[3]) = 'D')) DO
        BEGIN
           write('radius = ');
           readln(c[i].radius);
           IF c[i].radius < 0 THEN
              c[i].area := 0
           ELSE
              c[i].area := funct(c[i].radius);

           i := i+1;
           writeln;
           write('identifier = ');
           readln(c[i].id);
        END;

     n := i-1;     (* tag the highest value of i *)

     writeln;
     writeln('Summary of Results');
     writeln;

     (* display the results *)
     FOR i := 1 TO n DO
        BEGIN
           writeln('i = ',i:1,'    ',c[i].id:5,'   Radius = ',c[i].radius:3:1,
                                 '   Area = ',c[i].area:4:1)
        END;

     writeln;
     writeln('Goodbye, have a NICE DAY!')
  END.
```

In this program we enter a one-word *identifier*, followed by a value of the radius, for each circle. The characters that make up the identifier are stored within an array called `text`. Collectively, these characters are referred to as a *string* (see Chap. 2). In this program, the maximum size of each string is 255 characters, by default.

The identifier, the radius and the corresponding area of each circle are defined as the components of a *record* (see Chap. 10). We then define `c` as an array of records. That is, each element of `c` will be a record containing a string identifier, a radius and an area. For example, `c[1].id` refers to the identifier for the first circle, `c[1].radius` refers to the radius of the first circle and `c[1].area` refers to the area of the first circle.

When the program is executed, a string is entered for each circle, followed by the value of the radius. This infirmation is stored within `c[i].id` and `c[i].radius`. The corresponding area is then calculated and stored in `c[i].area`. The procedure continues until the string END is entered. All of the information stored within the array elements (i.e., the identifier, the radius and the area for each circle) will then be displayed, and the execution will stop.

Execution of this program results in an interactive dialog, such as that shown below. Note that the user's responses are once again underlined.

```
To STOP, enter END for the identifier

identifier = RED
radius = 3

identifier = WHITE
radius = 4

identifier = BLUE
radius = 5

identifier = END

Summary of Results

i = 1      RED    Radius = 3.0    Area = 28.3
i = 2    WHITE    Radius = 4.0    Area = 50.3
i = 3     BLUE    Radius = 5.0    Area = 78.5

Goodbye, have a NICE DAY!
```

1.7 DESIRABLE PROGRAM CHARACTERISTICS

Before concluding this chapter let us briefly examine some important characteristics of well-written computer programs. These characteristics apply to programs that are written in *any* programming language, not just Pascal. They can provide us with a useful set of guidelines later in this book, when we start writing our own Pascal programs.

1. *Integrity*. This refers to the accuracy of the calculations. It should be clear that all other program enhancements will be meaningless if the calculations are not carried out correctly. Thus, the integrity of the calculations is an absolute necessity in any computer program.

2. *Clarity* refers to the overall readability of the program, with particular emphasis on its underlying logic. If a program is written clearly, it should be possible for another programmer to follow the program logic without undue effort. (It should also be possible for the original author to follow his or her own program after being away from the program for an extended period of time.) One of the objectives in the design of Pascal is the development of clear, readable programs through a disciplined approach to programming.

3. *Simplicity*. The clarity and accuracy of a program are usually enhanced by keeping things as simple as possible, consistent with the overall program objectives. In fact, it may be desirable to sacrifice a certain amount of computational efficiency in order to maintain a relatively simple, straightforward program structure.

4. *Efficiency* is concerned with execution speed and efficient memory utilization. These are generally important goals, though they should not be obtained at the expense of clarity or simplicity. Many

complex programs require a tradeoff between these characteristics. In such situations, experience and common sense are key factors.

5. *Modularity*. Many programs can be decomposed into a series of identifiable subtasks. It is good programming practice to implement each of these subtasks as a separate program module. (In Pascal, such modules are referred to as *procedures* and *functions*.) The use of a modular programming structure enhances the accuracy and clarity of a program, and it facilitates future program alterations.

6. *Generality*. Usually we will want a program to be as general as possible, within reasonable limits. For example, we may design a program to read in the values of certain key parameters rather than placing fixed values into the program. As a rule, a considerable amount of generality can be obtained with very little additional programming effort.

Review Questions

1.1   What is a mainframe computer? Where can mainframes be found? What are they generally used for?

1.2   What is a personal computer? How do personal computers differ from mainframe computers?

1.3   What is a supercomputer? A minicomputer? A workstation? How do these computers differ from one another? How do they differ from mainframes and personal computers?

1.4   Name four different types of data.

1.5   What is meant by a computer program? What, in general, happens when a computer program is executed?

1.6   What is computer memory? What kinds of information are stored in a computer's memory?

1.7   What is a bit? What is a byte? What is the difference between a byte and a word of memory?

1.8   What terms are used to describe the size of a computer's memory? What are some typical memory sizes?

1.9   Name some typical auxiliary storage devices. How do devices of this type differ from the computer's main memory?

1.10   What time units are used to express the speed with which elementary tasks are carried out by a computer?

1.11   What is the difference between batch processing and timesharing? What are the relative advantages and disadvantages of each?

1.12   What is meant by interactive computing? For what types of applications is interactive computing best suited?

1.13   What is machine language? How does machine language differ from high-level languages?

1.14   Name some commonly used high-level languages. What are the advantages of using high-level languages?

1.15   What is meant by compilation? What is meant by interpretation? How do these two processes differ?

1.16   What is a source program? An object program? Why are these concepts important?

1.17   What is meant by structured programming?

1.18 Who was Blaise Pascal? For what was he noted?

1.19 By whom was the Pascal language first developed? What was its original purpose?

1.20 Name the groups responsible for defining a Pascal standard within the United States.

1.21 What is Turbo Pascal? By whom is it distributed? Why is it important?

1.22 What two major program components must be present in every Pascal program? What is the purpose of each component?

1.23 What are the two main parts of the block? What is the purpose of each part?

1.24 What are reserved words (or keywords)?

1.25 What are standard functions?

1.26 Why are some of the statements within a Pascal program indented?

1.27 Summarize the meaning of each of the following program characteristics: integrity, clarity, simplicity, efficiency, modularity and generality. Why is each of these characteristics important?

Problems

1.28 Determine the purpose of each of the following Pascal programs.

(a)
```
PROGRAM greeting;

BEGIN
    writeln('Welcome to the Wonderful');
    writeln;
    writeln('World of Computing!')
END.
```

(b)
```
PROGRAM triangle;

VAR base,height,area : real;

BEGIN
    write('base = ');
    read(base);
    write('height = ');
    read(height);
    area := (base*height)/2;
    writeln('area = ',area)
END.
```

(c) PROGRAM payroll;

```
CONST rate = 0.14;
VAR gross,tax,net : real;

BEGIN
   write('Gross income: ');
   read(gross);
   tax := rate*gross;
   net := gross-tax;
   write(gross,tax,net)
END.
```

(d) PROGRAM smallest;

```
VAR a,b : integer;

BEGIN
   write('Please enter the first number: ');
   read(a);
   write('Please enter the second number: ');
   read(b);
   IF a <= b THEN writeln('The smaller number is: ', a)
             ELSE writeln('The smaller number is: ', b)
END.
```

(e) PROGRAM smallest;

```
VAR a,b,min : integer;

FUNCTION smaller(a,b : integer): integer;
BEGIN
   IF a <= b THEN smaller := a
             ELSE smaller := b
END;

BEGIN
   write('Please enter the first number: ');
   read(a);
   write('Please enter the second number: ');
   read(b);
   min := smaller(a,b);
   writeln('The smaller number is: ', min)
END.
```

(f) PROGRAM smallest;

```
VAR a,b,min : integer;

PROCEDURE smaller(VAR a,b,c : integer);
BEGIN
   IF a <= b THEN c := a
             ELSE c := b
END;
```

```
        BEGIN
           write('Please enter the first number: ');
           read(a);
           write('Please enter the second number: ');
           read(b);
           smaller(a,b,min);
           writeln('The smaller number is: ', min)
        END.


(g)  PROGRAM smallest;

     VAR i,n,a,b,min : integer;

     PROCEDURE smaller(VAR a,b,c : integer);
     BEGIN
        IF a <= b THEN c := a
                  ELSE c := b
     END;

     BEGIN
        write('How many pairs of numbers? ');
        read(n);

        FOR i := 1 TO n DO
          BEGIN
             writeln;
             write('Please enter the first number: ');
             read(a);
             write('Please enter the second number: ');
             read(b);
             smaller(a,b,min);
             writeln('The smaller number is: ', min)
          END
     END.


(h)  PROGRAM smallest;

     VAR a,b,min : integer;

     PROCEDURE smaller(VAR a,b,c : integer);
     BEGIN
        IF a <= b THEN c := a
                  ELSE c := b
     END;

     BEGIN
        writeln('To STOP, enter 0 for each number');
        writeln;

        write('Please enter the first number: ');
        read(a);
        write('Please enter the second number: ');
        read(b);
```

```
        WHILE ((a <> 0) OR (b <> 0)) DO
            BEGIN
                smaller(a,b,min);
                writeln('The smaller number is: ', min);

                writeln;
                write('Please enter the first number: ');
                read(a);
                write('Please enter the second number: ');
                read(b)
            END
    END.



(i)    PROGRAM smallest;

    VAR n,i : integer;
    VAR a,b,min : ARRAY [1..100] OF integer;

    PROCEDURE smaller(VAR a,b,c : integer);
    BEGIN
        IF a <= b THEN c := a
                  ELSE c := b
    END;

    BEGIN
        writeln('To STOP, enter 0 for each number');
        writeln;

        i := 1;
        write('Please enter the first number: ');
        read(a[i]);
        write('Please enter the second number: ');
        read(b[i]);

        WHILE ((a[i] <> 0) OR (b[i] <> 0)) DO
            BEGIN
                smaller(a[i],b[i],min[i]);

                i := i+1;
                writeln;
                write('Please enter the first number: ');
                read(a[i]);
                write('Please enter the second number: ');
                read(b[i])
            END;

        n := i-1;
        writeln;
        writeln('Summary of Results');
        writeln;
```

```
FOR i := 1 TO n DO
   BEGIN
      write('i = ',i,'   a = ',a[i]);
      writeln('   b = ',b[i],'   min = ',min[i])
   END
END.
```

1.29 Refer once again to the Pascal programs presented in the previous problem. Determine, as best you can, the purpose of each line within each of the programs.

Chapter 2

Pascal Fundamentals

This chapter is concerned with the basic elements that are used to construct simple Pascal statements. These elements include the Pascal character set, reserved words, identifiers, numbers, strings, constants, variables and expressions. We will see how these basic elements can be combined to form simple but complete Pascal statements. Some attention will also be given to the different kinds of statements that are available, their constituent elements and their respective purposes.

Some of this material is rather detailed and therefore somewhat difficult to absorb, particularly by an inexperienced programmer. Remember, however, that the present purpose of this material is to introduce certain basic concepts and provide some necessary definitions for the topics that follow in the next few chapters. Therefore, when reading this chapter for the first time, you need only acquire a general familiarity with the individual topics. A more detailed understanding will come later, from repeated references to this material in subsequent chapters.

2.1 THE PASCAL CHARACTER SET

Pascal uses the letters A-Z (both upper and lower case), the digits 0-9, and certain *special symbols* as building blocks to form basic program elements (e.g., numbers, identifiers, expressions, etc.). The special symbols are listed below.

+	.	<	(
−	:	<=	)
*	;	>	[
/	,	>=	]
:=	'	<>	{
=	^	..	}

Note that some of the special symbols consist of two separate, consecutive characters.

Some versions of Pascal, including Turbo Pascal, allow the symbols (* and *) to be used instead of { and } and the symbols (. and .) may be used in place of [and]. Turbo Pascal also utilizes the special symbols @, $ and #.

2.2 RESERVED WORDS

There are certain *reserved words* that have a predefined meaning in Pascal. These reserved words can be used only for their intended purpose. They cannot be arbitrarily redefined by the programmer.

The *standard* reserved words are

AND	END	MOD	REPEAT
ARRAY	FILE	NIL	SET
BEGIN	FOR	NOT	THEN
CASE	FORWARD	OF	TO
CONST	FUNCTION	OR	TYPE
DIV	GOTO	PACKED	UNTIL
DO	IF	PROCEDURE	VAR
DOWNTO	IN	PROGRAM	WHILE
ELSE	LABEL	RECORD	WITH

Most implementations of Pascal include additional reserved words. Turbo Pascal, for example, includes the following additional reserved words.

ASM	IMPLEMENTATION		OBJECT	STRING
CONSTRUCTOR	INLINE	SHL	UNTIL	DESTRUCTOR
INTERFACE	SHR	UNIT	USES	XOR

Within a Pascal program it is customary to display the reserved words in either boldface or uppercase letters. We will use uppercase letters throughout this text.

2.3 IDENTIFIERS

An *identifier* is a name that is given to some program element, such as a constant, a variable, a procedure or a program. Identifiers consist of letters or digits, in any order, except that *the first character must be a letter*. Both upper and lowercase letters are permitted. We will use only lowercase letters for identifiers, however, in order to distinguish them from reserved words (which are shown in uppercase).

EXAMPLE 2.1

The following names are valid identifiers.

x	y12	sum	temperature
names	area	taxrate	table1

The following names are not valid identifiers for the reasons stated.

c_max	Characters other than letters and digits are not allowed.
4th	The first character must be a letter.
array	ARRAY is a reserved word (see Section 2.2).
last word	Blank spaces are not allowed (remember that a blank space is a character).

An identifier can be arbitrarily long, although some implementations of Pascal recognize only the first eight characters. In such situations the remaining characters are carried along for the convenience of the programmer. Turbo Pascal recognizes the first 63 characters of an identifier.

EXAMPLE 2.2

The identifiers `filemanager` and `filemanagement` are both grammatically valid. The computer may be unable to distinguish between them, however, because the first eight letters are the same for each identifier. Therefore, only one of these identifiers should be used in a single Pascal program (unless, of course, it is known that this particular implementation of Pascal has no restriction on significant identifier length).

As a rule, an identifier should contain enough characters so that its meaning is readily apparent. On the other hand, an excessive number of characters should be avoided.

EXAMPLE 2.3

A Pascal program is being written to calculate the future value of an investment. The identifiers `value` or `futurevalue` would probably be appropriate symbolic names. However, `v` or `fv` would probably be too brief, since the intended purpose of these identifiers is not clear. On the other hand, a particularly lengthy identifier such as `futurevalueofaninvestment` would be unsatisfactory because it is too long and cumbersome.

2.4 STANDARD IDENTIFIERS

Pascal contains a number of *standard identifiers* that have certain predefined meanings. The most common standard identifiers are

abs	false	pred	succ
arctan	input	read	text
boolean	integer	readln	true
char	ln	real	trunc
chr	maxint	reset	unpack
cos	new	rewrite	write
dispose	odd	round	writeln
eof	ord	sin	
eoln	output	sqr	
exp	pack	sqrt	

Most implementations of Pascal include additional standard identifiers. Consult your programmer's reference manual to determine exactly what standard identifiers are available for your particular version of the language.

In contrast to reserved words (which can never be redefined), standard identifiers *can* be redefined by the programmer. This is accomplished by means of appropriate declarations and definitions, as explained later in this text. In most situations, however, it is good practice to use the standard identifiers only for their predefined purposes. This is particularly true of programs that are written by beginning programmers. Thus, standard identifiers should be treated in the same manner as reserved words in elementary programming situations.

2.5 NUMBERS

Numbers can be written several different ways in Pascal. In particular, a number can include a sign, a decimal point and an *exponent* (or *scale factor*) if desired. The following rules apply to all numbers.

1. Commas and blank spaces cannot be included within the number.

2. The number can be preceded by a plus (+) or a minus (–) sign if desired. If a sign does not appear, the number will be assumed to be positive.

3. Numbers cannot exceed specified maximum and minimum values. These values depend upon both the *type* of number and the particular version of Pascal being used.

Integer numbers

An *integer number* contains neither a decimal point nor an exponent. Thus, an integer number is simply a sequence of digits, preceded (optionally) by a sign.

EXAMPLE 2.4

Several valid integer numbers are shown below.

0	1	+1	–1
743	–5280	60000000	–999999

The following integer numbers are written incorrectly for the reasons stated.

123,456	Commas are not allowed.
36.	A decimal point cannot appear within an integer number.
10 20 30	Blank spaces are not allowed.

The magnitude of an integer number can range from zero to some maximum value that varies from one version of Pascal to another. In Turbo Pascal, integer numbers may range from 0 to 2,147,483,647 (negative numbers may range from –2,147,483,648 to –1). Larger or smaller ranges can also be selected, depending on the particular type of integer (Turbo Pascal includes several different types of integers). Consult your programmer's reference manual to determine the appropriate maximum value for your particular version of Pascal.

Real numbers

A *real number* must contain either a decimal point or an exponent (or both). *If a decimal point is included, it must appear between two digits.* Thus, a real number cannot begin or end with a decimal point. If a decimal point is not included within the number, it will be assumed to be positioned to the right of the last digit.

EXAMPLE 2.5

Several valid real numbers are shown below.

0.0	1.0	–0.2	827.602
50000.0	–0.000743	12.3	–315.0066

The following real numbers are not written correctly, for the reasons stated.

6.	A digit must be present on each side of the decimal point.
1,000.0	Commas are not allowed.

| .333333 | A digit must be present on each side of the decimal point. |
| 50 | Either a decimal point or an exponent must be present. |

An exponent (scale factor) can be included to shift the location of the decimal point. This is essentially the same as scientific notation except that the base 10 is replaced by the letter E (or e). Thus, the number 1.2×10^{-3} would be written as 1.2E-3 or 1.2e-3. The exponent itself must be either a positive or a negative integer.

EXAMPLE 2.6

The quantity 3×10^{10} could be represented in Pascal by any of the following real numbers.

3.0E+10	3.0E10	3e+10	3E10
0.3E+11	0.3e11	30.0E+9	·30e9

Similarly, the quantity -5.026×10^{-17} can be represented by any of the following real numbers.

−5.026E−17	−0.5026E−16	−50.26e−18	−0.0005026e−13

EXAMPLE 2.7

The following are valid real numbers with exponents.

2E−8	−0.006e−5	1.6667E+8	+0.12121212e12

The following real numbers are *not* valid for the reasons stated.

3.E+10	A digit must be present on each side of the decimal point.
8e2.3	The *exponent* must be an integer (it cannot contain a decimal point).
.3333e−3	A digit must be present on each side of the decimal point.
3E 10	Blank spaces are not allowed.

Real numbers have a much greater range than integer numbers. In Turbo Pascal, the magnitude of a real number can range from a minimum value of approximately 2.9E−39 to a maximum of approximately 1.7E+38. Larger or smaller ranges can also be selected, depending on the particular type of real number (Turbo Pascal supports several different types of real numbers). In addition, the number 0.0 (which is less than 2.9E−39) is also a valid real number. Consult the programmer's reference manual for the ranges that are appropriate for your particular version of Pascal.

The number of significant figures in a real number will also vary, depending on the type of real number selected. Generally a real number will allow at least seven or eight significant digits, which is adequate for most applications. Higher-precision values can also be selected if necessary.

It should be understood, however, that integer numbers are *exact quantities* whereas real numbers are *approximations*. Thus, the real number 1.0 might actually be represented within the computer's memory as 0.99999999..., even though it might be displayed as 1.0. Therefore real numbers should not be used for certain kinds of operations, such as counting, indexing, etc., for which integral numerical values are required. We will discuss this point at greater length in Chap. 6.

2.6 STRINGS

A *string* is a sequence of characters (i.e., letters, digits and special characters) enclosed by apostrophes. Both uppercase and lowercase letters can be used.

EXAMPLE 2.8

Several valid strings are shown below.

```
'RED'           'Washington, D.C. 20005'      '123-45-6789'
'$19.95'        'THE CORRECT ANSWER IS:'      '2*(I+3)/J'
```

The maximum number of characters that can be included in a string will vary from one version of Pascal to another. Most versions, including Turbo Pascal, allow maximum string lengths of at least 255 characters. This maximum string size is more than adequate for most purposes.

If a string includes an apostrophe, the apostrophe must be entered *twice*. Only one apostrophe will appear, however, when the string is displayed. Thus, a single apostrophe is interpreted as a string delimiter, whereas a repeated apostrophe is interpreted as a single apostrophe within the string.

EXAMPLE 2.9

A Pascal program contains the following string.

```
'PLEASE DON''T VERB YOUR NOUNS'
```

Notice the repeated apostrophe in the word *don't*. If the program causes the string to be printed or displayed, however, it will appear as it should; namely,

```
PLEASE DON'T VERB YOUR NOUNS
```

Strings are normally used in `write` and `writeln` statements to label output. We will discuss this further in Chap. 4.

2.7 DATA TYPES

One of the most important and interesting characteristics of Pascal is its ability to support many different types of data. These include *simple* data types, *string* data types, *structured* data types and *pointer* data types.

Simple-type data are single items (numbers, characters, etc.) that are associated with single identifiers on a one-to-one basis. Actually there are several different simple data types. These include the four *standard data types*—integer, real, char and boolean—and the *user-defined* simple types, which include *subrange types* and *enumerated types*. The standard data types will be discussed thoroughly in the next chapter. User-defined data types will be considered in Chap. 8.

String-type data represent strings of characters. Each single string-type data item will represent one entire string. This data type is not found in all versions of Pascal, though it is included in Turbo Pascal.

Structured-type data consist of multiple data items that are related to one another in some specified manner. Each group of data items is associated with a particular identifier. The individual data items within each group can also be associated with corresponding individual identifiers. There are four types of structured data in Pascal: arrays, records, sets and files.

Pointer-type data are used to construct dynamic structured data types. A simple description of their characteristics and use is beyond the scope of the present discussion (see Chap. 13).

The various data types are summarized below for your convenience.

1. Simple-type data
   (*a*) Standard data types
   (*i*) integer
   (*ii*) real
   (*iii*) char
   (*iv*) boolean
   (*b*) User-defined data types
   (*i*) enumerated
   (*ii*) subrange

2. String-type data

3. Structured-type data
   (*a*) Arrays
   (*b*) Records
   (*c*) Sets
   (*d*) Files

4. Pointer-type data

For now we will be concerned only with simple-type data and string-type data. These two data types are sometimes referred to collectively as *scalar-type data*. Structured-type data and pointer-type data will be discussed in later chapters of this book.

2.8 CONSTANTS

It is often convenient to associate a simple data item, such as a numerical value or a string, with an identifier, thus providing a name for the data item. The identifier is called a *constant* if the data item is assigned permanently (i.e., if the data item remains the same throughout the program).

A constant must always be *defined* before it can appear in a Pascal statement. This definition serves two purposes—it establishes that the identifier is a constant, and it associates a data item with the constant. The type of the constant will implicitly be determined by the data item.

The general form of a constant definition is expressed as

```
CONST name = value
```

where *name* is an identifier that represents the constant name, and *value* is the actual data item that is assigned to name.

EXAMPLE 2.10

A Pascal program requires frequent use of the numerical value 0.1666667. It may therefore be convenient to introduce a constant called fraction, which can be used in place of the actual number. This constant can be defined by writing

```
CONST fraction = 0.1666667;
```

Subsequent references to the identifier `fraction` will be equivalent to referencing the actual number. Note that `fraction` is considered to be a real constant, since it is associated with a real number.

EXAMPLE 2.11

Now suppose that a Pascal program makes frequent use of the string

```
The Super-Duper Computer Company
```

in order to generate report headings. This string can conveniently be represented as a constant called `title`. To do so, we write

```
CONST title = 'The Super-Duper Computer Company';
```

at the beginning of the program. If we should want to display the actual string at some other point in the program, we merely refer to the identifier `title` in the appropriate output statement. (Input/output operations will be discussed in Chap. 4.)

In this example `title` is considered to be a string-type constant, since it is associated with a string.

2.9 VARIABLES

An identifier whose value is allowed to change during the execution of a program is called a *variable*. Every variable must be individually *declared* (i.e., *defined*) before it can be used in a program. The variable declaration establishes the fact that the identifier is a variable (rather than a constant, etc.) and specifies the type of the variable. Unlike a constant definition, however, a variable declaration does *not* associate a data item (e.g., a numerical value or a string) with a variable.

The general form of a variable declaration is

```
VAR name1, name2, . . . , namen : type
```

where *name1, name2,* etc. are identifiers that represent individual variable names, and *type* refers to the data type of the variables. Note that several variables can be included in the same variable declaration provided they are all of the same type.

EXAMPLE 2.12

A Pascal program contains the integer variables `row` and `column`, the real variable `value`, and the char variable `flag`. The program would therefore contain the following declarations.

```
VAR row,column : integer;
    value : real;
    name : string;
    flag : char;
```

The appropriate data items would then be assigned to these variables at later points in the program. Remember that some versions of Pascal do not support string-type data.

EXAMPLE 2.13

Now suppose the program contains the constants described in Examples 2.10 and 2.11 and the variables described in Example 2.12. Here is the complete list of declarations.

```
CONST fraction = 0.1666667;
      title = 'The Super-Duper Computer Company'
VAR row,column : integer;
    value : real;
    name : string;
    flag : char;
```

Remember that the constant definitions must precede the variable declarations (see Section 1.5).

2.10 EXPRESSIONS

An *expression* is a collection of *operands* (i.e., numbers, constants, variables, etc.), joined together by certain *operators*, to form an algebraic-like term that represents a *value* (i.e., a simple data item). There are two types of expressions in Pascal: *numerical expressions* and *boolean expressions*. A numerical expression represents a numerical value, whereas a boolean expression represents a logical condition which is either true or false.

EXAMPLE 2.14

A typical numerical expression is shown below.

```
(b*b-4*a*c)/(2*a)
```

The identifiers a, b and c and the numbers 4 and 2 are called *operands*; and the symbols *, – and / are the corresponding *operators* (which represent multiplication, subtraction and division, respectively). The parentheses are used to specify the order in which the operations are carried out. The entire expression represents a number. Thus, if a, b and c represent the values 1, 2 and 3, respectively, the expression will represent the value -4.

When constructing a numerical expression, care must be taken to distinguish between integer and real quantities. This is true of the operators and operands as well as the expression itself. We will say more about this in the next chapter.

EXAMPLE 2.15

Here is an example of a boolean (logical) expression.

```
pay < 1000.0
```

In this expression pay is a variable of type real, 1000.0 is a real number and the symbol < is a *boolean operator*. (Note that pay and 1000.0 are *operands* in this boolean expression.) The expression will have the value true if pay represents a value that is less than 1000.0; otherwise the expression will have the value false.

Boolean expressions are used in various control structures, such as the IF — THEN structure shown below.

```
IF pay < 1000.0 THEN writeln(employeenumber);
```

This structure will cause the value of the variable `employeenumber` to be written out if the value of `pay` is less than 1000.0.

We will discuss the use of boolean expressions within control structures in much greater detail in Chapter 6.

All expressions must satisfy the following general conditions.

1. Two consecutive operators are not permitted. However, parentheses can be used to separate two operators that would otherwise be consecutive. (Remember that parentheses must always be used in *pairs*.)

2. An expression can consist of a single identifier that is used as a constant or a variable.

3. A function name (i.e., a function *reference*) can be used in place of a constant or a variable identifier within an expression (more about this in Section 2.12).

2.11 STATEMENTS

A Pascal *statement* is an instruction, or a group of instructions, that causes the computer to carry out certain actions. There are two basic types of statements in Pascal: *simple* and *structured*. Simple statements are essentially single, unconditional instructions that perform one of the following tasks.

1. Assign a data item to a variable. (An *assignment statement*.)

2. Access a self-contained computational module. (A *procedure reference*.)

3. Transfer program control to another part of the program. (The GOTO statement.)

EXAMPLE 2.16

A typical assignment statement is shown below.

```
tax := 0.14*gross;
```

In this example it is assumed that `tax` and `gross` are both variables of type real. Also, it is assumed that a real value has been assigned to `gross`. (This value may have been read into the computer, or it may have been calculated earlier in the program.) The assignment statement causes the value of `gross` to be multiplied by 0.14 and the product assigned to the variable `tax`.

Notice that the symbol used for assignment is `:=` (not =, as in most other programming languages). Also, note that the right-hand side of the statement (i.e., `0.14*gross`) is a *numerical expression*, as described in the previous section.

EXAMPLE 2.17

Here is a typical GOTO statement.

```
GOTO 100;
```

Thus, the next statement to be executed will be the statement that is labeled `100`.

Use of the GOTO statement is discouraged in Pascal. We will say more about this in Chap. 6.

We will say more about simple statements that access procedures in the next section.

Pascal recognizes several different types of structured statements. These include

1.   Compound statements, which consist of a sequence of two or more consecutive statements.

2.   Repetitive statements, which involve the repeated execution of several simple statements.

3.   Conditional statements, in which one or more simple statements are executed only if some specified logical condition is satisfied.

EXAMPLE 2.18

A typical compound statement, taken from Example 1.6, is shown below.

```
BEGIN
    read(radius);
    area := 3.14159*sqr(radius);
    writeln(area)
END
```

Notice that the simple statements that make up the compound statement are enclosed by the keywords BEGIN and END. Also, note that the simple statements are separated from one another by semicolons.

EXAMPLE 2.19

Here is a typical repetitive statement.

```
FOR count := 1 TO 100 DO write(count);
```

This statement will be executed 100 times. Each time the statement is executed, the current value of the variable count will be displayed. Thus, the statement will cause the values

```
1   2   3   . . .   100
```

to appear on the output device.

EXAMPLE 2.20

A typical conditional statement is shown below.

```
IF pay < 1000.0 THEN write('group 1') ELSE write('group 2');
```

This statement causes the message group 1 to be displayed if the variable pay represents a value that is less than 1000.0. If pay has a value that is greater than or equal to 1000.0, the message group 2 will appear instead.

Structured statements will be discussed in much greater detail in Chap. 6. For now, you should be concerned only with an overview of the general concepts.

2.12 PROCEDURES AND FUNCTIONS

Procedures and functions are self-contained program elements, sometimes referred to as *modules*, that carry out designated actions. These modules can be accessed from anywhere within a program. Moreover, if the same module is accessed from several different points, the module can be supplied with different information (i.e., different values for the required data items) at each access point.

When a module is accessed, the information provided is processed by the action statements within the module. Usually, this will cause new information to be generated. This information is then returned to the point at which the module was last accessed, and the program continues to execute from that point.

The information that is passed to a module is provided as a list of data items (i.e., constants, variables, expressions, etc.), called *parameters*. These parameters are separated by commas and enclosed in parentheses, immediately after the module name. Certain of the parameters can also be used to represent any new information that is generated within the module. Thus, the parameters may represent information being returned by a module as well as information supplied to the module.

Pascal supports both *standard* and *user-defined* procedures and functions. We will be concerned only with standard procedures and standard functions for the time being. These program elements are included in the Pascal library, which is a part of the language. A complete discussion of user-defined procedures and functions will be presented in Chap. 7.

All procedures have the following general characteristics.

1. A procedure is accessed by a simple statement consisting of the procedure name, followed by an (optional) list of parameters.

2. The parameters may represent both information supplied to the procedure and information returned by the procedure.

3. Any number of data items can be transferred between a procedure and its reference point.

EXAMPLE 2.21

The `write` statement is actually a reference (i.e., an access) to a standard Pascal procedure. Thus, the statement

```
write(a,b,c);
```

will cause the values of the parameters a, b and c to be displayed.

Note that the parameters in this example all represent information being supplied *to* the procedure; no new information is returned.

Now suppose a Pascal program contained the following two `write` statements. (Assume that these two statements appear in different places within the program.)

```
write(a,b,c);
        .
        .
        .
write(x,y,z);
```

The first statement would cause the values of the variables a, b and c to be displayed, whereas the second statement (which is identical to the first except for the parameters) would output the values of the variables x, y and z.

All functions have the following general characteristics.

1. A function is accessed by specifying its name within an expression, as though it were an ordinary variable, followed by an (optional) list of parameters.

2. The function name can be followed by an (optional) list of parameters. Normally, these parameters will be used only to transfer information *to* the function from its reference point.

3. The function will return a single data item. This data item will be represented by the function name itself.

4. A function must be of the correct data type for the expression in which it is accessed.

EXAMPLE 2.22

Consider once again the statement

```
area := 3.14159*sqr(radius);
```

The right-hand side is a numerical expression in which the value of the variable `radius` is passed to the standard function `sqr`. This function returns the value of the radius squared. The value of the radius squared is then multiplied by 3.14159, and the result is assigned to the variable `area`.

Note that `radius` is a parameter that represents a data item supplied *to* the standard function. The data item that is returned by the function is represented by the function name, `sqr`. Also, note that the type of the function is numeric (specifically, real); this specification is required if the function appears within a numerical expression.

We will say much more about procedures and functions in Chap. 7. For now we need only be concerned with the general information presented above. This information will allow us to understand the material that is discussed in the next chapter.

2.13 PASCAL SYNTAX DIAGRAMS

Before leaving this chapter, it is appropriate to discuss a method that is commonly used to represent the *syntactical* (i.e., the grammatical) constructs in Pascal. This involves the use of graphical syntax diagrams, such as that shown in the following example.

EXAMPLE 2.23

Fig. 2.1 shows a Pascal syntax diagram that explains the manner in which an identifier can be constructed.

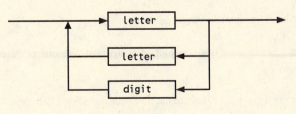

Fig. 2.1

This diagram shows that an identifier must begin with a letter, as indicated by the uppermost box containing the word *letter*. Following this box is a straight path with two optional return loops. Each return loop contains a box representing a type of character that can be included within the identifier name. Since the return loops contain the words *letter* and *digit*, respectively, we conclude that an identifier must begin with a letter, followed by any number of letters and digits, in any order.

Syntax diagrams can become quite complex, even for relatively simple constructs. Therefore many beginning programmers choose not to use them. They do, however, provide a precise definition of Pascal syntax.

Review Questions

2.1   What does the Pascal character set consist of?

2.2   What are the Pascal reserved words? How can the reserved words be identified within this textbook?

2.3   What are Pascal identifiers? What does an identifier consist of?

2.4   How many characters can be included in an identifier? Are all of these characters equally significant?

2.5   What is meant by a standard identifier?

2.6   How do standard identifiers differ from reserved words?

2.7   Summarize the general rules for writing numbers in Pascal.

2.8   What special rules apply to integer numbers?

2.9   How can the largest permissible integer number be determined for each particular computer?

2.10   Describe two different ways that real numbers can be written. Summarize the rules that apply in each case.

2.11   What is the purpose of the exponent in a real number?

2.12   Describe the differences between real and integer numbers. Under what circumstances should each type of number be used?

2.13   What is a string? What characters can be included within a string?

2.14   What restrictions apply to maximum string length?

2.15   How can an apostrophe (') be included within a string?

2.16   Name four different types of data that are supported by most versions of Pascal. Are all of these data types standardized?

2.17   What is meant by simple-type data? What are the four standard simple data types?

2.18   What is meant by user-defined simple types? How do these data types differ from the standard data types?

2.19   What is meant by string-type data? Is this data type found in all versions of Pascal?

2.20   What is meant by structured-type data? How do structured-type data differ from simple-type data?

2.21   Name four different structured data types.

2.22   What is a constant? What must be done before a constant can be used within a Pascal statement?

2.23   How is the type of a constant determined?

2.24   What is a variable? In what way does a variable differ from a constant?

2.25   Summarize the rules for declaring the data types of variables.

2.26   What is an expression? What types of expressions are supported by Pascal? How do they differ?

2.27   What is an operand? What is an operator? How are operands and operators used in an expression?

2.28   Summarize the general conditions that must be satisfied by all expressions.

2.29   What is a statement? What are the two basic types of statements in Pascal? How do they differ?

2.30   Name three different tasks that can be performed by simple statements.

2.31   What is the purpose of the assignment statement? What type of statement is this?

2.32   Name three different types of structured statements.

2.33   What is a procedure? What is a function? How do procedures and functions differ from each other?

2.34   What is a module? What is the relationship between a module, a procedure and a function?

2.35   What happens when a module is accessed?

2.36   What is meant by parameters? What is their purpose?

2.37   Name two general classes of procedures and functions.

2.38   Summarize the general characteristics of procedures.

2.39   Summarize the general characteristics of functions.

2.40   What is the significance of a function name? How does this differ from a procedure name?

2.41   What is meant by a syntactical construct? How are syntactical constructs represented in Pascal?

Problems

2.42   Determine which of the following are valid identifiers.

(a)	record1	(e)	name and address
(b)	file2	(f)	employee_number
(c)	file	(g)	123-45-6789
(d)	name		

2.43   Determine which of the following are valid numbers. If a number is valid, specify whether it is integer or real.

(a)	0.5	(f)	40–55
(b)	27,822	(g)	12E12
(c)	+93e12	(h)	131072
(d)	–4.083e–67	(i)	1.31072e5
(e)	1.		

2.44   Determine which of the following are valid strings.

(a)	'8:15 P.M.'	(e)	'Chapter 3 (Cont''d)'
(b)	"red, white and blue"	(f)	'1.30172e5'
(c)	'Don't snore in class!'	(g)	'NEW YORK, NY 10020'
(d)	'Name:	(h)	'The price is $56.50'

2.45   Write a set of constant definitions that will associate each of the following identifiers with its corresponding constant value.

Identifier	*Constant Value*
month	july
fica	123-45-6789
price	$95.00
gross	2500.00
partno	48837
bound	0.00391

2.46   Write a set of variable declarations that will associate each of the following identifiers with its corresponding data type.

Identifier	*Data Type*
period	char
terminal	boolean
status	char
index	integer
row	integer
customer	string
clearance	real

2.47 Specify the type of each of the following expressions. Identify any expression that is not written correctly.

(*a*) `counter := 87`

(*b*) `value`

(*c*) `sqr(first+second+third)`

(*d*) `cost <= 100`

(*e*) `2*-x+y`

(*f*) `factor1*(sum1+sum2)/factor2`

(*g*) `color = 'blue'`

(*h*) `maximum = 100`

2.48 Specify which of the following statements are simple and which are complex. Identify the type of each statement.

(*a*) `net := gross-(fedtax+statetax+citytax);`

(*b*)
```
BEGIN
    tax := fedtax+statetax+citytax;
    net := gross-tax
END
```

(*c*) `FOR counter := start TO finish DO write(counter);`

(*d*) `IF counter < finish THEN counter := counter+1;`

(*e*) `root := sqrt(a+b+c+d);`

(*f*) `write('root=',root);`

(*g*) `GOTO 17;`

(*h*) `new := new+old;`

2.49 Which statements in Prob. 2.48 access procedures? Which include function references?

Chapter 3

Scalar-Type Data

Now that we are familiar with Pascal data types, we can consider applications of scalar-type data in greater detail. In particular, we will consider the uses of the standard (or built-in) simple data types that are included as a part of the Pascal language. These data types include integer, real, char and boolean data. We will also consider the string data type that is defined in Turbo Pascal. The operators and standard functions that can be used with each of these data types will be discussed in detail. The chapter also includes additional information on expressions and their use in assignment statements.

Three of the standard data types, integer, char and boolean, are often referred to as *ordinal* data types, since the corresponding data items are members of an ordered, finite set. User-defined simple-type data (i.e., enumerated and subrange data) also fall into this category (see Chap. 8). Note, however, that real-type data, though ordered, are not finite in number. Hence real-type data are not included within this category.

3.1 INTEGER-TYPE DATA

Integer-type data are whole-number (integer) quantities. Included within this category are integer-type constants, variables, functions and expressions. We have already discussed the rules for writing integer numbers and for defining or declaring integer constants and variables. We will now concentrate on the operators that can be used with integer-type data, and then consider the rules for writing integer-type expressions.

Collectively, the operators that are used to carry out numerical-type operations are called *arithmetic operators*. There are six arithmetic operators that can be used with integer-type operands. Five of these will produce an integer-type result (i.e., an integer-type *resultant*); the sixth will produce a quantity of type real. These operators are summarized below.

Arithmetic Operator	Purpose	Type of Operands	Type of Resultant
+	addition	integer	integer
−	subtraction	integer	integer
*	multiplication	integer	integer
/	division	integer	real
DIV	truncated division	integer	integer
MOD	remainder after division	integer	integer

Notice that the division operator (/) will result in a real quantity, even though the operands are integer. Also, notice that there is no exponentiation operator (Pascal does not support an exponentiation operator).

44

EXAMPLE 3.1

Suppose that a and b are integer-type variables that have been assigned the values 13 and 5, respectively. Several simple integer expressions, and their resulting values, are shown below.

Expression	Value
a+b	18
a−b	8
a*b	65
a DIV b	2
a MOD b	3
a/b	2.6

There are certain rules that must be observed when using these operators to form numerical expressions. Some of the more common rules, which apply to expressions involving only two integer operands, are given below (others will be discussed in Section 3.8).

1. The resultant will be positive if both operands are of the same sign. Otherwise, the resultant will be negative.

2. The two division operators (/ and DIV) and the MOD operator require that the second operand be nonzero.

3. Use of the DIV operator with a negative operand will result in truncation toward zero; i.e., the resultant will be smaller in magnitude than the true quotient.

4. According to the ANSI standard, the second operand cannot be negative when using the MOD operator. However, many implementations of Pascal do allow this operand to be negative. In such cases the sign of the resultant will be determined so that the condition

        a = (a DIV b) + (a MOD b)

is always satisfied, regardless of the signs of the individual operands. Turbo Pascal follows this convention.

EXAMPLE 3.2

Suppose that i and j are integer-type variables whose assigned values are 11 and −3, respectively. Several integer expressions and their corresponding values are given below.

Expression	Value
i+j	8
i−j	14
i*j	−33
i DIV j	−3
i MOD j	2 (nonstandard)
i/j	−3.6666667

If i had been assigned a value of −11 and j had been assigned 3, then we would have

Expression	Value
i DIV j	−3
i MOD j	−2 (nonstandard)
i/j	−3.6666667

Finally, if i and j were both assigned negative values (−11 and −3, respectively), then we would obtain

Expression	Value
i DIV j	3
i MOD j	−2 (nonstandard)
i/j	3.66667

Note that the condition

$$i = (i \text{ DIV } j)*j + (i \text{ MOD } j)$$

is satisfied in each of the above situations. Many versions of Pascal, including Turbo Pascal, follow this convention.

3.2 REAL-TYPE DATA

Real-type data are data items that represent real numerical quantities. These include real-type constants, variables, functions and expressions.

There are four arithmetic operators that can be used with real-type operands. They are

Arithmetic Operator	Purpose	Type of Operands	Type of Resultant
+	addition	real	real
−	subtraction	real	real
*	multiplication	real	real
/	division	real	real

These operators can be used with integer-type operands to obtain integer-type resultants. Note, however, that the DIV and MOD operators cannot be used with real-type data. Also, we again remark that there is no exponentiation operator in Pascal.

EXAMPLE 3.3

Suppose that v1 and v2 are real-type variables whose assigned values are 12.5 and 0.5, respectively. Several real expressions, and their resulting values, are shown below.

Expression	Value
v1+v2	13.0
v1−v2	12.0
v1*v2	6.25
v1/v2	25.0

There are certain rules that must be followed when forming numerical expressions with real-type data. Three of the most common rules, which apply to expressions containing only two operands, are summarized below. Several other rules are presented in Section 3.8.

1. The resultant will be positive if both operands are of the same sign. Otherwise the resultant will be negative.

2. The division operator (/) requires that the second operand be nonzero.

3. If one operand is of type integer and the other is of type real, then the resulting value will always be of type real.

EXAMPLE 3.4

Let r1 and r2 be real variables whose assigned values are −0.66 and 4.50. Several real expressions and their corresponding values are given below.

Expression	*Value*
r1+r2	3.84
r1−r2	−5.16
r1*r2	−2.97
r1/r2	−0.1466667

EXAMPLE 3.5

Suppose that i is an integer-type variable that has been assigned a value of −2, and r is a real-type variable that has been assigned a value of 1.2. Then the expression

```
3*i*r
```

will represent the real value −7.2, since $3 \times (-2) \times 1.2 = -7.2$.

3.3 CHAR-TYPE DATA

Char-type data are single-character strings; i.e., single characters enclosed in apostrophes. This data-type also includes identifiers that represent single-character constants, char-type variables and certain char-type functions.

The complete set of characters that can be used with char-type data will vary from one version of Pascal to another. Most versions of Pascal permit any of the displayable characters defined within the ASCII character set (see below).

EXAMPLE 3.6

The following are acceptable char-type data items.

```
'P'        '5'        't'        '*'        ' '        ''''
```

The last data item represents a single apostrophe, as explained in Section 2.6.

Most computers, and virtually all PCs, make use of the ASCII character set (i.e., the American Standard Code for Information Interchange), in which each individual character is numerically encoded with its own unique 7-bit combination (hence a total of $2^7 = 128$ different characters). Thus, the characters are *ordered* as well as encoded. In particular, the digits are ordered consecutively in their proper numerical sequence (0-9), and the letters are arranged consecutively in their proper alphabetical order. This allows char-type data items that represent ASCII characters to be compared with one another, based upon their relative order within the character set.

Table 3-1 contains the ASCII character set, showing the decimal equivalent of the 7 bits that represent each character. Notice that the digits precede the letters, and the uppercase letters precede the lowercase letters in numerical order. Also, note that there are small groups of special characters separating the digits, the uppercase letters and the lowercase letters.

Table 3-1   The ASCII Character Set

ASCII Value	Character	ASCII Value	Character	ASCII Value	Character	ASCII Value	Character
0	NUL	32	(blank)	64	@	96	`
1	SOH	33	!	65	A	97	a
2	STX	34	"	66	B	98	b
3	ETX	35	#	67	C	99	c
4	EOT	36	$	68	D	100	d
5	ENQ	37	%	69	E	101	e
6	ACK	38	&	70	F	102	f
7	BEL	39	'	71	G	103	g
8	BS	40	(	72	H	104	h
9	HT	41	)	73	I	105	i
10	LF	42	*	74	J	106	j
11	VT	43	+	75	K	107	k
12	FF	44	,	76	L	108	l
13	CR	45	−	77	M	109	m
14	SO	46	.	78	N	110	n
15	SI	47	/	79	O	111	o
16	DLE	48	0	80	P	112	p
17	DC1	49	1	81	Q	113	q
18	DC2	50	2	82	R	114	r
19	DC3	51	3	83	S	115	s
20	DC4	52	4	84	T	116	t
21	NAK	53	5	85	U	117	u
22	SYN	54	6	86	V	118	v
23	ETB	55	7	87	W	119	w
24	CAN	56	8	88	X	120	x
25	EM	57	9	89	Y	121	y
26	SUB	58	:	90	Z	122	z
27	ESC	59	;	91	[	123	{
28	FS	60	<	92	\	124		
29	GS	61	=	93	]	125	}
30	RS	62	>	94	^	126	~
31	US	63	?	95	_	127	DEL

The first 32 characters and the last character are control characters. Usually, they are not displayed. However, some versions of Pascal (some computers) support special graphics characters for these ASCII values. For example, 001 may represent the character ☺, 002 may represent ☻, and so on.

EXAMPLE 3.7

Table 3-1 shows that the letter A is encoded as (decimal) 65 in the ASCII character set, and the letter B is encoded as 66. Since 65 is less than 66, A is considered to precede B. Similarly, A precedes a because 65 is less than 97; and 0 precedes 1 because 48 is less than 49.

Arithmetic operators cannot be used with char-type data, since char-type data items do not represent numerical quantities. Char-type data can be *compared*, however, using the *relational operators* described in the next section.

It should be understood that char-type digits and integer quantities are represented altogether differently inside the computer. Beginning programmers should be careful not to confuse them.

3.4 BOOLEAN-TYPE DATA

Boolean-type data are truth values that are either true or false. This category includes boolean-type constants, variables, functions and expressions. The two values that apply to boolean-type data (`true` and `false`) represent an ordered set, with `false` preceding `true` (`false` is encoded as 0 and `true` is encoded as 1).

Boolean-type expressions are formed by combining operands of the same type with *relational operators*. These operators represent various conditions of equality and/or inequality. There are seven relational operators in Pascal, though we will consider only six of them in this chapter. They are

Relational Operator	Meaning
=	equal to
<>	not equal to
<	less than
<=	less than or equal to
>	greater than
>=	greater than or equal to

The seventh relational operator, IN, will be discussed in Chap. 12.

These six operators can be used with operands of any type other than boolean. When used with nonnumerical operands, the inequalities refer to the order in which the operands are encoded.

EXAMPLE 3.8

Here are some simple boolean expressions involving numerical operands.

Expression	Value
2 = 3	false
2 < 3	true
0.6 >= 1.5	false

Expression	Value
0.6 >= -1.5	true
-4 <> 4	true
1.7 <= -2.2	false

EXAMPLE 3.9

Suppose that i and j are integer-type variables that have been assigned the values of 3 and −5, respectively. Several boolean expressions involving the use of these variables are shown below.

Expression	Value
i <= 10	true
i+j > 0	false
(i−j) < (i+j)	false
i−3 = j+5	true
2*i >= i DIV 2	true
(i DIV 2) >= (j+6)	false

Notice that the operands can be constants, variables or expressions.

EXAMPLE 3.10

Suppose that ch1 and ch2 are char-type variables that have been assigned the characters 'P' and 'T', respectively. Several boolean expressions involving the use of these variables are shown below.

Expression	Value
ch1 = ch2	false
ch2 = 'T'	true
ch1 = 'p'	false
ch1 < ch2	true (because 'P' precedes 'T')
ch2 > 'A'	true (because 'T' succeeds 'A')
'W' <> ch1	true

Pascal also contains three *logical operators*. Two of these operators allow boolean-type operands to be combined to form boolean-type expressions; the third is used to *negate* (i.e., to *reverse*) the value of a boolean operand.

The logical operators are

Operator	Meaning
OR	Expression will be true if either operand is true or if both operands are true.
AND	Expression will be true only if both operands are true.
NOT	This operator is used as a *prefix* to negate a boolean operand.

To avoid ambiguities in the order in which the logical operations are carried out, the boolean operands should be enclosed in parentheses.

EXAMPLE 3.11

Suppose that n is an integer-type variable that has been assigned the value 10 and s is a char-type variable that represents the character 'A'. Several boolean expressions involving the use of these variables are shown below.

Expression	*Value*
(n > 0) AND (n < 20)	true
(n > 0) AND (n < 5)	false
(n > 0) OR (n < 5)	true
(n < 0) OR (n > 20)	false
(n = 10) AND (s = 'A')	true
(n <> 5) OR (s >= 'A')	true

EXAMPLE 3.12

Suppose that the boolean expression j > 6 is true. Then the expression

        NOT (j > 6)

will be false. Also, the expression

        NOT (j <= 6)

will be true, since (j <= 6) will be false.

EXAMPLE 3.13

Now suppose that the char-type variable ch represents the character 'G'. Then the expression ch > 'A' will be true, and the expression

        NOT (ch > 'A')

will be false. Also, the expression ch = 'A' will be false, so that the expression

        NOT (ch = 'A')

will be true.

Turbo Pascal contains several additional relational and logical operators. However, a description of these operators or their uses is beyond the level of our present discussion.

We will see how boolean expressions are used in Pascal programs when we reach Chapter 6.

3.5 STRING-TYPE DATA

String-type data are multicharacter strings, i.e., sequences of characters enclosed in apostrophes. String-type data may also include identifiers that represent string constants, string-type variables and certain string-type expressions. This data type is not included in all versions of Pascal, though it is included in many, including Turbo Pascal.

Typically, a string-type data item may contain as many as 255 characters. This value varies from one version of Pascal to another. Single-character strings (i.e., char-type data items) may also be defined as string-type data.

String-type data items can be combined back-to-back (i.e., *concatenated*). The concatenation operator (+) is used for this purpose.

EXAMPLE 3.14

Suppose that `str1`, `str2` and `str3` are string-type variables that represent the strings `'RED'`, `'WHITE'` and `'BLUE'`, respectively. Then the concatenation expression

```
str1+', '+str2+' and '+str3
```

will represent the string

```
RED, WHITE and BLUE
```

Notice that we have concatenated three string variables and two string constants into a single combined string.

String-type data items can be compared with one another to determine their relative ordering with respect to their encoded characters. It is also possible to compare a char-type data item with a string-type data item. The relational operators (=, <>, <, <=, >, >=) are used to compare strings.

Two strings will be considered equal (equivalent) if they are of the same length and the respective characters are the same. Otherwise, the value of the expression will be based upon the first dissimilar pair of corresponding characters.

EXAMPLE 3.15

Here are some boolean expressions involving string-type data.

Expression	*Value*
`'cat' < 'dog'`	true
`'cat' < 'car'`	false
`'cat' = 'CAT'`	false
`'cat' < 'cats'`	true
`'black' < 'brown'`	true
`'black' < 'blue'`	true

Note that the comparisons are case-sensitive.

3.6 STANDARD CONSTANTS

Pascal includes three standard identifiers that represent constants. They are `maxint`, `true` and `false`. The first of these, `maxint`, specifies the largest value that may be assumed by an integer-type quantity. The two remaining constants, `true` and `false`, represent the two values that may be assigned to a boolean-type data item. (Remember that `true` and `false` represent an ordered set, with `false` preceding `true`.)

3.7 STANDARD FUNCTIONS

Pascal also contains a number of *standard functions* that are used with various simple data-types. (Standard functions are also referred to as *intrinsic* or *built-in* functions.) Some of these functions accept one type of parameter and return a value of the same type, while others accept a parameter of one type and return a value of a different type. Several of the more common functions are summarized in Table 3-2 below.

Table 3-2   Some Common Standard Functions

Function	Purpose	Type of Parameter (x)	Type of Result
abs(x)	Compute the absolute value of x.	integer or real	same as x
arctan(x)	Compute the arctangent of x.	integer or real	real
chr(x)	Determine the character represented by x.	integer	char
cos(x)	Compute the cosine of x (x in radians).	integer or real	real
exp(x)	Compute e^x, where e=2.7182818... is the base of the natural (Naperian) system of logarithms.	integer or real	real
ln(x)	Compute the natural logarithm of x (x > 0).	integer or real	real
odd(x)	Determine if x is odd or even. (Return a value of true if x is odd, false otherwise.)	integer	boolean
ord(x)	Determine the (decimal) integer that is used to encode the character x.	char	integer
pred(x)	Determine the predecessor of x.	integer, char or boolean	same as x
round(x)	Round x (determine the closest integer).	real	integer
sin(x)	Compute the sine of x (x in radians).	integer or real	real
sqr(x)	Compute the square of x.	integer or real	same as x
sqrt(x)	Compute the square root of x (x >= 0).	integer or real	real
succ(x)	Determine the successor to x.	integer, char or boolean	same as x
trunc(x)	Truncate x (i.e., drop the decimal part of x).	real	integer

The purpose of most of the functions presented above should be readily apparent. There are a few, however, whose purpose may be less obvious. Their use is illustrated in the following examples.

EXAMPLE 3.16

The function `abs(x)` computes the absolute value of the number represented by the parameter `x`. Thus, if `diff` is a real-type variable that has been assigned a value of −0.003, then the function `abs(diff)` will return a value of 0.003 when it is accessed. (Note that `diff` is a parameter in the function access.)

EXAMPLE 3.17

The functions `chr` and `ord` are used to determine the relationship between any Pascal character and its corresponding integer code. Thus, if a computer uses the ASCII code,

```
chr(65)='A'          ord('A')=65
chr(112)='p'         ord('p')=112
chr(53)='5'          ord('5')=53
```

and so on. Note that

```
ord('A')=ord(chr(65))=65
```

and

```
chr(65)=chr(ord('A'))='A'
```

etc.

EXAMPLE 3.18

Since integer, char and boolean-type data all represent ordered sets, we can determine the predecessor or successor of any data item within one of these sets (or in any user-defined ordered set) with the functions `pred` and `succ`. Thus,

```
pred(3)=2            succ(3)=4              (integer-type data)
pred('e')='d'        succ('e')='f'          (char-type data)
pred(true)=false     succ(false)=true       (boolean-type data)
```

Also, note that the ASCII character set satisfies conditions such as

```
pred('e')=chr(ord('e')-1)
```

and

```
succ('e')=chr(ord('e')+1).
```

Remember that the functions `pred` and `succ` do not apply to real-type data.

EXAMPLE 3.19

The functions `round` and `trunc` can accept both positive and negative real-type numbers. Negative numbers are treated as though they were positive numbers, with the minus sign added after the rounding or truncation has been carried out. Thus,

```
round(2.3)=2        trunc(2.3)=2
round(3.7)=4        trunc(3.7)=3
round(-1.8)=-2      trunc(-1.8)=-1
round(-6.1)=-6      trunc(-6.1)=-6
```

Many of these standard functions can be used with other data types (i.e., nonstandard, user-defined data types.). We will mention such applications as the need arises later in this text.

Most implementations of Pascal include additional standard functions. Turbo Pascal, for example, supports many standard functions, including those shown in Table 3-3.

Table 3-3   Some Standard Functions Supported by Turbo Pascal

Function	Purpose	Type of Parameter (x)	Type of Result
concat(x1,x2,x3,...)	Concatenate two or more strings.	string	string
copy(x,y,z)	Copy z characters from string x, beginning with character number y.	string, integer, integer	string
frac(x)	Determine the fractional part of x.	real	real
int(x)	Determine the integer part of x.	real	real
length(x)	Determine the number of characters in string (x).	string	integer
pi	Return the value of π ($\pi = 3.14159265\ldots$).	(none)	real
pos(x, y)	Determine the location of string x within string y.	string, string	integer

Remember that the parameters in a function reference can be constants, variables, expressions or references to other functions. The only restriction is that the parameters be of the proper type. We will say more about parameters in Chap. 7, where we consider the subject of procedures and functions in greater detail.

EXAMPLE 3.20

Suppose that str1 and str2 are string-type variables that represent the strings 'baseball' and 'football', respectively. Several expressions that make use of standard Turbo Pascal string functions are shown below and on the next page.

Expression	Result
concat(str1,' or ',str2)	baseball or football
copy(str1,2,3)	ase
length(str2)	8

Expression	Result
pos('ball',str2)	5
pos('base',str2)	0 ('base' is not present within str2)

EXAMPLE 3.21

Suppose that x and y are real-type variables that represent the values 2.7 and −5.8, respectively. Several expressions that make use of standard Turbo Pascal functions are shown below.

Expression	Value
frac(x)	0.7
frac(y)	−0.8
int(x)	2.0
int(y)	−5.0

There are two additional commonly used standard functions, eoln and eof, that are used with data files. These functions will be described in Chap. 4.

3.8 MORE ABOUT EXPRESSIONS

An expression can sometimes become quite complex, owing to the presence of multiple operators within the expression. In such cases it becomes necessary to specify the order in which the various operations are carried out. This order may be determined by the natural *operator precedence*, which is included within the Pascal language. The precedence groups are tabulated below, from highest to lowest.

Precedence	Operator(s)						
1 (highest)		NOT					
2	*	/	DIV	MOD	AND		
3		+	−	OR			
4 (lowest)	=	<>	<	<=	>	>=	IN

Within a given precedence group the operations are carried out as they are encountered, reading from left to right.

EXAMPLE 3.22

The numerical expression

    a−b/c*sqrt(d)

is equivalent to the algebraic formula

$$a - [(b/c) \times \sqrt{d}].$$

Thus, if the variables a, b, c and d have been assigned the values 1, 2, 3 and 4, respectively, the expression would represent the value −0.33333333, since

$$1 - [(2/3) \times \sqrt{4}\,] = 1 - (4/3) = -1/3.$$

Notice that the division is carried out first, since this operation falls within a higher precedence group than subtraction. The resulting quotient is then multiplied by 4 (left-to right rule within a precedence group). Finally, this product is subtracted from the value of the first variable.

The natural operator precedence can be altered through the use of parentheses, thus allowing the operations within an expression to be carried out in any desired order. In fact, the parentheses can be *nested*, one pair within another. In such cases the innermost operations are carried out first, then the next innermost operations, and so on.

EXAMPLE 3.23

The numerical expression

```
(a-b)/(c*sqrt(d))
```

is equivalent to the algebraic formula

$$(a - b) / (c \times \sqrt{d}\,).$$

Thus, if the variables a, b, c and d have been assigned the values 1, 2, 3 and 4, respectively, the expression would represent the value -0.1666667, since $(1 - 2) / (3 \times \sqrt{4}\,) = -1/6 = -0.1666667$. (Compare with the result obtained in Example 3.22.)

EXAMPLE 3.24

Consider the boolean expression

```
(x > 0) OR (y < 10)
```

This expression will be true if x has been assigned a value greater than zero or if y has been assigned a value less than 10 (or both). If neither condition has been satisfied, then the expression will be false.

Note that the parentheses are required within this expression. Without the parentheses, Pascal would attempt to evaluate the expression incorrectly, as

```
x > (0 OR y) < 10
```

EXAMPLE 3.25

Here is a numerical expression that involves the integer-type variables a, b and c.

```
2*((a MOD 5)*(4+(b-3)/sqr(c+2)))
```

If a, b and c have been assigned the values 8, 15 and –4, respectively, then the expression would be evaluated as

```
2*((3)*(4+12/sqr(-2))) = 2*(3*(4+12/4)) = 2*(3*(4+3)) = 42
```

Sometimes it is a good idea to use parentheses to clarify an expression, even though the parentheses may not be required. On the other hand, the use of overly complex expressions should be avoided if at all possible, as such expressions are a frequent source of error (the last example contains an expression of this type).

Finally, the following grammatical rules (in addition to those stated in Sections 3.1 and 3.2) must always be observed when constructing numerical and boolean expressions.

1. *Undefined identifiers cannot appear within an expression*. (In other words, each identifier must be assigned a value before it can appear within an expression.)

2. *Preceding an identifier with a minus sign is equivalent to multiplication by* -1. Thus, $-a*b$ is equivalent to $-1*a*b$.

3. *Arithmetic operators cannot appear consecutively*. Hence, the expression $a*-b$ is not allowed, but $a*(-b)$ is permitted.

4. *Arithmetic operations cannot be implied*. Thus, the expression $2(x+y)$ is incorrect, but the expression $2*(x+y)$ is valid (note that an asterisk is missing from the first expression).

5. *Arithmetic operations cannot be carried out on char- or boolean-type data*. Therefore expressions such as

      'A'+'B'   and   (n > 0) + (n < 20)

    are not allowed. (Note, however, that implementations of Pascal that support string concatenation, such as Turbo Pascal, *do* permit concatenation of char-type data. Hence, the expression 'A'+'B' *would* be permitted in these implementations.)

6. *There cannot be an imbalance of parentheses*. In other words, the number of left parentheses must be the same as the number of right parentheses.

3.9 THE ASSIGNMENT STATEMENT

We have already seen that the *assignment statement* is a type of simple statement that is used to assign a data item to a variable. This statement is written in the form

```
variable := data item
```

The data item can be a single item (e.g., a constant, another variable, or a function reference), or it can be an expression. The data item must, however, be of the same *type* as the variable to which it is assigned. (There is one exception to this rule: an integer data item can be assigned to a real variable.)

A semicolon usually appears at the end of a Pascal statement that is followed by another Pascal statement. This semicolon is not a part of the statement itself but is a *separator* that distinguishes the end of the current statement from the beginning of the next statement.

EXAMPLE 3.26

A typical assignment is shown below.

```
area := 3.14159*sqr(radius);
```

This statement causes the value of the expression

```
3.14159*sqr(radius)
```

to be assigned to the variable `area`. Thus, if `radius` has been assigned a value of 10.0, `area` will be assigned a value of 314.159.

Remember that the semicolon at the end of the statement is a separator; it is not a part of the statement proper.

Numerical-type assignment statements frequently look like algebraic equations. This need not always be true, however, as illustrated in the next example.

EXAMPLE 3.27

Consider the assignment statement

```
count := count+1;
```

This statement causes the current value of the integer-type variable `count` to be increased by 1. (This is called *incrementing*.) Algebraically, this statement would make no sense. It is entirely logical, however, when viewed in terms of its intended purpose.

Assignment statements need not be restricted to numerical data, as shown in the following examples.

EXAMPLE 3.28

Suppose that `state` is a char-type variable. The assignment statement

```
state := 'S';
```

will cause the character S to be assigned to `state`.

EXAMPLE 3.29

Suppose that `city` is a string-type variable in a Turbo Pascal program. The assignment statement

```
city := 'San Francisco'
```

will cause the string `'San Francisco'` to be assigned to `city`.

EXAMPLE 3.30

Suppose that `flag` is a boolean variable, and `x` and `y` are integer variables. Then the assignment statement

```
flag := (x > 0) OR (y < 10);
```

will cause `flag` to be assigned either the value `true` or the value `false`, as determined by the boolean expression. Thus, `flag` will be assigned the value `true` if `x` is greater than zero or if `y` is less than 10 (or both); otherwise, `flag` will be assigned the value `false`.

Review Questions

3.1   What are scalar-type data?

3.2   What are the standard simple data types?

3.3   What are ordinal data types? What relationship do ordinal data types have to standard simple-type data?

3.4   What do integer-type data represent?

3.5   What are *arithmetic operators*? Which arithmetic operators can be used with integer-type data? What is the purpose of each of these operators?

3.6   How does the division operator (/) differ from the truncated division operator (DIV) when using integer-type operands?

3.7   Summarize the rules for using an arithmetic operator with two integer-type operands. In particular, summarize the restrictions that apply to the use of the two division operators (/ and DIV) and the MOD operator.

3.8   What do real-type data represent?

3.9   Which arithmetic operators can be used with real-type data? What is the purpose of each of these operators?

3.10   Summarize the rules for using an arithmetic operator with two real-type operands.

3.11   What type of resultant is obtained if an arithmetic operator is used with one integer-type operand and one real-type operand?

3.12   What do char-type data represent? Which characters can be used with char-type data?

3.13   What is meant by the ASCII character set? How widely used is this character set?

3.14   In what general order are the characters arranged within the ASCII character set?

3.15   What type of operations can be carried out on char-type data? Which operators are used?

3.16   What do boolean-type data represent?

3.17   How are boolean-type data items ordered?

3.18   What are *relational operators*? What is the purpose of each of these operators? With what types of operands can they be used? What type of resultant is obtained in each case?

3.19   What is the interpretation of an inequality-type relational operator being used with char-type operands?

3.20   What are *logical operators*? What is the purpose of each of these operators? With what type of operand can they be used? What type of resultant is obtained?

3.21   What do string-type data represent? Are string-type data supported in all versions of Pascal?

3.22   What operations can be carried out on string-type data?

3.23   What three standard constants are included in Pascal? What type of data item is each constant? What is the purpose of each constant?

3.24   What are *standard functions*? By what other names are they known?

3.25   What is the purpose of the `abs` function? With what types of parameters is it used? What type of resultant is obtained?

3.26   What is the purpose of the `chr` and `ord` functions? With what types of parameters are they used? What type of resultant is obtained in each case?

3.27   What is the purpose of the `pred` and `succ` functions? With what types of parameters are they used? What type of resultant is obtained in each case?

3.28   When using the ASCII character set, what relationships exist between the `chr` and `ord` functions and the `pred` and `succ` functions? Why are these relationships not valid for *all* character sets?

3.29   What is the purpose of the `round` and `trunc` functions? With what types of parameters are they used? What type of resultant is obtained in each case?

3.30   How are negative parameters treated by the `round` and `trunc` functions?

3.31   What is the purpose of the `concat` and `copy` functions? With what types of parameters are they used? What type of resultant is obtained in each case?

3.32   What is the purpose of the `length` and `pos` functions? With what types of parameters are they used? What type of resultant is obtained in each case?

3.33   Explain what is meant by operator precedence, and summarize its structure.

3.34   In what order are the operations within a precedence group carried out?

3.35   How can the natural operator precedence be altered?

3.36   In what order are the operations carried out within an expression that contains nested parentheses?

3.37   Under what circumstances should parentheses be included within an expression? Under what circumstances should they be avoided?

3.38   Summarize the rules that must be observed when constructing numerical and boolean expressions.

3.39   What is the purpose of the assignment statement? What restrictions apply to the *type* of data that is assigned to a variable?

3.40   What is the purpose of the semicolon that appears at the end of most assignment statements? Is the semicolon actually a part of the statement?

3.41   Is there a relationship between a numerical-type assignment statement and an algebraic equation?

Problems

3.42 Suppose a, b, c, d and e are numeric-type variables that have been assigned the following values.

Variable	Type	Value
a	integer	8
b	integer	5
c	real	4.3
d	real	0.8
e	real	−2.2

These variables are used in the following numerical expressions. Determine the type of each expression and the value that it represents.

(a)	`(b-a)/sqr(d-e)`		(f)	`trunc(3*sqrt(abs(d+e)))`
(b)	`round((c+d)/e)`		(g)	`frac(d+e)`
(c)	`(a DIV b)/(a MOD b)`		(h)	`int(d+e)`
(d)	`(a-2*b)*trunc(3*c-d+2*e)`		(i)	`round(pi)`
(e)	`0.01*(a-b)`			

3.43 Suppose that the variables `f11`, `f12` and `f13` are string-type variables that represent the strings `'vanilla'`, `'chocolate'` and `strawberry'`, respectively. Determine the value of each of the following string expressions.

(a)	`f11+f12+f13`		(e)	`pos('berry',f13)`
(b)	`f11+', '+f12+' and '+f13`		(f)	`pos('berry',f11)`
(c)	`length(f12)`		(g)	`copy(f12,4,5)`
(d)	`concat(copy(f12,1,5),copy(f13,6,5))`			

3.44 Several boolean expressions are shown below. Determine the value that is represented by each expression. Assume that the variables a, b, c, d and e have the same values as in Prob. 3.42 and that y and n are char-type variables that have been assigned the characters `'Y'` and `'N'`, respectively.

(a)	`c < d+e`		(e)	`true OR false`
(b)	`(y = 'Y') AND (n = 'N')`		(f)	`NOT (y < 'z')`
(c)	`trunc(c+d) <= 10.0`		(g)	`(a >= 100) AND (b <= maxint)`
(d)	`(a = 8) OR (b = 8)`		(h)	`odd(a-b)`

3.45 Evaluate each of the following expressions. Assume that the characters are members of the ASCII character set.

(a)	`abs(-4.667)`		(d)	`pred(10)`
(b)	`chr(67)`		(e)	`pred('e')`
(c)	`ord('e')`		(f)	`pred(true)`

(g)	succ('10')	(o)	round(-2.8)
(h)	succ('e')	(p)	trunc(2.2)
(i)	succ(false)	(q)	trunc(2.8)
(j)	odd(10)	(r)	trunc(-2.2)
(k)	odd(15)	(s)	trunc(-2.8)
(l)	round(2.2)	(t)	chr(ord('8')+4)
(m)	round(2.8)	(u)	ord(pred('A'))
(n)	round(-2.2)	(v)	chr(ord('g'))

3.46 Several numerical and boolean expressions are shown below. Some are written incorrectly. Determine which are incorrect and identify all errors.

(a)	sum DIV 0.005	(h)	slope <> m*x+b
(b)	200*sum	(i)	sqrt(a+b) < succ('G')
(c)	'100'+'27'+440'	(j)	(a+abs(c1+c2)/((c1+c3)*(c2+c3))
(d)	true = false	(k)	2*maxint+3
(e)	(a-b)/(2g+7)	(l)	round(a*-b)
(f)	'D'=pred('E')	(m)	odd(12.82)-6.6
(g)	value = 0.0 OR count < 100	(n)	-b+sqrt(sqr(b)-4*a*c)/(2*a)

3.47 A Pascal program includes the following variables.

Variable	Data Type
gross	real
net	real
tax	real
name	string
employee	integer
status	char
sex	char
exempt	boolean

Show how these variables are declared within the program.

Chapter 4

Data Input and Output

This chapter is concerned with methods for entering data into the computer and transferring data out of the computer. These two essential activities are commonly referred to as *input/output* operations. They can be carried out very easily in Pascal, using the special input/output statements that are included as a part of the language. Once we have learned how to carry out these operations we will be able to write a variety of complete, though simple, Pascal programs.

4.1 INPUT AND OUTPUT FILES

Let us first consider the manner in which data are transferred into and out of the computer.

Input data are generally typed directly into the computer from the keyboard. The data items are considered to be members of an *input file*. These data items are assumed to be arranged sequentially within the file, in the order specified by the program. Moreover, the data items will be grouped into logical *lines*, where each line corresponds to one line of data typed from the keyboard.

Output data are placed in an *output file,* which is essentially a mirror image of the input file. The output data items are arranged sequentially, in the order specified by the program. The data items may be grouped into logical lines, which correspond to physical lines of output when the data are printed or displayed.

It should be understood that the input and output files are not permanent files. Hence, they are not stored on an auxiliary storage device. Moreover, these files are maintained within the computer as separate entities —they are not a part of a Pascal program. However, in ANSI Pascal the input and output files are *associated* with a Pascal program by including them as parameters within the program header.

EXAMPLE 4.1

A Pascal program contains the following program header.

```
PROGRAM payroll(input,output);
```

The header specifies that the name of the program is `payroll`, and that the program utilizes both input and output files.

A program need not utilize both an input and an output file though most programs do so, since most programs accept input data and generate output data when they are executed.

EXAMPLE 4.2

A Pascal program called `primes` is used to generate the first twelve prime numbers. This program includes the following header.

```
PROGRAM primes(output);
```

This program utilizes only an output file, since it does not require any input data. If the program were modified, however, so that it would generate the first n prime numbers, where n is an input quantity, then the program header would have to be changed to

```
PROGRAM primes(input,output);
```

Such a modification would be a good idea in any event, since the program would then be much more general.

Some versions of Pascal automatically associate input files with input data entered from the keyboard, and output files with output data directed to a display device (typically, a monitor). In such situations, the input and output files need *not* be specified as parameters in the program header. Turbo Pascal operates in this manner. We will follows this convention through the remainder of this book.

EXAMPLE 4.3

If the programs referred to in Examples 4.1 and 4.2 were written in Turbo Pascal, it would not be necessary to include the parameters input and output in the program header. Hence, the headers can simply be written as

```
PROGRAM payroll;
```

and

```
PROGRAM primes;
```

The programs will still run correctly, however, if the parameters input and output *are* included within the header.

4.2 THE READ STATEMENT

The read statement is used to read data items from the input data file and assign them to integer, real, char or string-type variables. The statement is written as

```
read(input variables)
```

where the input variables are separated by commas. (*Note*: boolean-type variables *cannot* be included in the list of input variables.)

EXAMPLE 4.4

Here is a typical read statement.

```
read(a,b,c);
```

This statement causes three data items to be read from the input file and assigned to the variables a, b and c, respectively.

The data items are read from the input file and assigned to their respective variables in the same order that they are specified by the read statement. Each variable must be of the same *type* as its corresponding data item. (*Exception*: an integer number can be assigned to a real-type variable.) Each data item can be read only once.

EXAMPLE 4.5

A portion of a Pascal program is shown below.

```
VAR a,b : real;
    i,j : integer;
      .
      .
      .
  read(a,b,i,j);
```

The read statement will cause two real numbers and two integer numbers to be read from the input file and assigned to the variables a, b, i and j, respectively.

Some care must be given to the spacing of the input data items. Numerical data items must be separated from one another by blank spaces or by end-of-line designations. To be more precise, if a numerical data item follows another data item it must be *preceded* by one or more blank spaces or end-of-line designations. Real numbers can be written with or without an exponent. Moreover, real numbers that represent integral quantities (e.g., 1.0) can be written as integers (e.g., 1). Any number may be preceded by a plus or a minus sign provided there is no space between the sign and the number.

EXAMPLE 4.6

Consider once again the portion of the Pascal program shown in the last example, i.e.,

```
VAR a,b : real;
    i,j : integer;
      .
      .
      .
  read(a,b,i,j);
```

Suppose the variables are to be assigned the following values.

Variable	Value
a	12,500
b	−14.8
i	5
j	−9

The data items could be entered into the input file as follows.

```
12500.0 −14.8 5 −9
```

Alternatively, the data items might be entered in either of the following formats:

```
12500 −14.8 5 −9

+1.25e4 −1.48e1 +5 −9
```

Char-type data must be treated somewhat differently, since all characters are significant. In particular, a char-type data item must not be enclosed in apostrophes. Also, a char-type data item cannot be separated from the preceding data item by a blank space or an end-of-line designation, since the separator will be interpreted (incorrectly) as the data item. An end-of-line designation will be interpreted as a blank space if assigned to a char-type variable.

EXAMPLE 4.7

Here is a portion of a Pascal program that reads char-type data.

```
VAR c1,c2,c3 : char;
      .
      .
      .
read(c1,c2,c3);
```

Suppose the char variables are to be assigned the following values.

Variable	Value
c1	X
c2	Y
c3	Z

The data items would then be entered into the input file consecutively, without intervening spaces, as follows.

```
XYZ
```

If one read statement is followed by another, the second read statement begins where the first read statement ended. More precisely, the second read statement will begin by reading the data item following the last data item that was read by the previous read statement. Thus, a new read statement does *not* necessarily begin by reading a new line of data.

EXAMPLE 4.8

Let us again consider the the Pascal program described in Examples 4.5 and 4.6. Now suppose that the read statement is replaced by the following two statements.

```
read(a,b);
read(i,j);
```

The input file need not be changed, since the first read statement would read the first three values on the line, and the second read statement would read the last three values.

Suppose the variables are to be assigned the following values.

Variable	Value	Variable	Value
a	12,500	i	5
b	−14.8	j	−9

Then the data items might be entered into the input file as follows.

```
12500.0 -14.8 5 -9
```

In principle, there is no problem in entering mixed data types (e.g., real-, integer- and char-type data) with one `read` statement. In practice, however, some compilers experience difficulty with mixed numerical and char-type data items. In such cases in may be better to place the numerical data items on one line and the char-type data on another and then enter the data using two `readln` statements (see below).

In ANSI Pascal, strings must be entered on a character-by-character basis. Some type of looping action is required to do this, as discussed in Chap. 6. However, Turbo Pascal allows an entire string to be entered as a single entity, using a `read` statement.

EXAMPLE 4.9

A portion of a Turbo Pascal program is shown below.

```
VAR name : string;
    .
    .
    .
read(name);
```

This statement will cause a string of characters to be read into the computer and assigned to `name`. Note that the string is not restricted to any particular length (though the string length cannot exceed the maximum size that is permitted by the compiler, typically 255 characters).

When a string and several other data items are entered using a single `read` statement, the original string and any succeeding data items will be combined into a single string. This composite string will then be assigned to the string variable. In such cases, it is advisable to place the string on a separate line and enter it into the computer using a `readln` statement, as described in Section 4.3.

EXAMPLE 4.10

A portion of a Turbo Pascal program is shown below.

```
VAR name : string;
    gross,net : real;
    .
    .
    .
read(name,gross,net);
```

Now suppose the actual data items are `'Smith'`, 1200 and 800, respectively. If the data items are entered into the computer in the following order,

```
Smith 1200 800
```

then `name` will be assigned the string `'Smith 1200 800'` whereas `gross` and `net` will remain unassigned. This is, of course, incorrect (see Example 4.13 below for a correct solution to this problem).

4.3 THE READLN STATEMENT

The readln statement, like the read statement, is used to read data items from the input file and assign them to integer, real, char or string-type variables. This statement is written in the form

```
readln(input variables)
```

The difference between the two statements is that the readln statement causes the *following* (not the current) read or readln statement to begin by reading a new line of data, whereas the read statement will allow the following read or readln statement to begin on the same line.

EXAMPLE 4.11

A portion of a Pascal program is shown below.

```
VAR p1,p2,p3,p4 : integer;
  .
  .
  .
read(p1,p2);
read(p3,p4);
```

Suppose that the input file contained the following eight numbers, arranged in two lines.

```
1   2   3   4
5   6   7   8
```

The read statements would cause the numbers 1, 2, 3 and 4 to be assigned to the variables p1, p2, p3 and p4, respectively.

If the read statements were replaced with readln statements, i.e.,

```
VAR p1,p2,p3,p4 : integer;
  .
  .
  .
readln(p1,p2);
readln(p3,p4);
```

then the variables p1 and p2 would still be assigned the values 1 and 2, but p3 and p4 would be assigned the values 5 and 6, from the second line of input data.

Note that it is the *first* readln statement that causes the values for p3 and p4 to be read from the second line of input data.

If a readln statement is *preceded* by a read statement, then the readln statement will begin to read where the previous read statement ended. Thus, *the readln statement does not necessarily begin by reading a new line of data*. The readln statement behaves the same as the read statement in this respect.

EXAMPLE 4.12

Now suppose that the read statements in Example 4.11 are written as

```
read(p1,p2);
readln(p3,p4);
```

The variables p1, p2, p3 and p4 would be assigned the values 1, 2, 3 and 4, respectively, since the `readln` statement would begin by reading the third value in the first line of data.

The `readln` statement is convenient for reading data on a line-by-line basis, as is common in some applications.

EXAMPLE 4.13

A Pascal program contains the following three `readln` statements.

```
readln(a,b);
readln(c,d);
readln(e,f);
```

Suppose that the variables are all of type integer and the input file contains the numbers

```
1   2   3
4   5   6
7   8   9
```

Then the values 4 and 5 will be assigned to the variables c and d, and the values 7 and 8 will be assigned to e and f.

It is not clear what values will be assigned to a and b, since it is not known where the first `readln` statement will begin. If the statement begins at the start of the line, then the values 1 and 2 will be assigned to a and b. But if this statement is preceded by a `read` statement, such as

```
read(x);
```

then x will be assigned the value 1 and a and b will be assigned the values 2 and 3, respectively.

In Turbo Pascal, it is often convenient to read an entire string with a single `readln` statement. In such situations, it is advisable to place the string on a separate line, to avoid the possibility of its being improperly combined with other data items.

EXAMPLE 4.14

A portion of a Turbo Pascal program is shown below.

```
VAR name : string;
    gross,net : real;
        .

        .

        .

readln(name);
readln(gross,net);
```

Now suppose the actual data items are `'Smith'`, 1200 and 800, respectively. Suppose the data items are entered into the computer into the following order, as in Example 4.10:

```
Smith 1200 800
```

Then `name` will be *incorrectly* assigned the string `'Smith 1200 800'` while `gross` and `net` will remain unassigned. However, if the string and the numerical data items are placed on separate lines, e.g.,

```
Smith
1200 800
```

then `name` will be assigned the string `'Smith'`, `gross` will be assigned the value 1200 and `net` will be assigned 800, as desired.

Before leaving this example it should be noted that the two `readln` statements can be replaced by

```
readln(name);
read(gross,net);
```

However, the statements

```
read(name);
readln(gross,net);
```

will *not* work (why not?).

4.4 THE EOLN AND EOF FUNCTIONS

Pascal includes two standard functions, `eoln` and `eof`, that are useful when reading input data. The first of these, `eoln`, returns the boolean value `true` if an end-of-line designation has been detected on the line being read. Otherwise it returns the value `false`.

The value of `eoln` is automatically reset to `false` whenever a new line of input is started, provided the new line is not empty (i.e., provided the new line contains at least one data item). Thus this function allows us to read an unspecified number of data items from any one line by reading data from the same line until `eoln` returns the value `true`. We can then repeat this procedure for the next line of data, and so on. The exact manner in which this is accomplished will be described (see Examples 7.20 and 9.8).

The `eof` function is used to detect the end of an input file (i.e., an end-of-file designation). This function returns the boolean value `true` when an end-of-file designation has been detected; otherwise it returns the value `false`. Use of the `eof` function will be illustrated in Chap. 11 (see Examples 11.11 and 11.12).

The `eof` function is often used in conjunction with the `eoln` function to read an unspecified number of data items from an input file. The end of each line can be detected by means of the `eoln` function, and the end of the file (i.e., the end of the last line) can be determined by using the `eof` function. We will see how this is accomplished in Chap. 11 (see Section 11.6, particularly Examples 11.18 and 11.19).

4.5 THE WRITE STATEMENT

The `write` statement is used to write data items to the output file. This statement is written as

```
write(output data items)
```

The output data items can be strings, numerical constants, variables or expressions. In ANSI Pascal, these variables and expressions may be of type integer, real, char or boolean. (Note that boolean data items *can* be written out but string-type variables *cannot* be written out using ANSI Pascal.) The data items must be separated by commas if there are more than one. Each string must be enclosed within apostrophes, as described in Section 2.6.

EXAMPLE 4.15

Here is a typical `write` statement.

```
write('x=',x);
```

This statement causes the value of the numeric-type variable `x` to be written to the output file, with a corresponding label. Thus, if `x` represents the value 123.456, then the following output will be written to the output file. (The exact appearance may differ somewhat from one version of Pascal to another.)

```
x= 1.2345600000E+02
```

Similarly, the `write` statement

```
write('sum=',a+b);
```

causes the value of the numerical expression `a+b` to be written to the output file, with a corresponding label. Thus, if `a` and `b` represent the values 3 and –1, respectively, the `write` statement will produce the following output.

```
sum=2
```

Real numbers can be displayed in several different ways, though the default (standard) format is scientific notation, as illustrated in the above example. Boolean data items will be represented by the standard identifiers `true` or `false`, depending on their values.

Most versions of Pascal utilize a standard *field width* (i.e., number of spaces) to represent integer, real and boolean data items. This field width will be different for each data type. Moreover, the field width that is used for a given type of data will vary from one version of Pascal to another. Typically, integer data might have a standard field width of 8, real data might have a standard field width of 14 and boolean data might have a standard field width of 6. If the field is wider than necessary (as is often the case), then the data item is placed within the right portion of the field. This results in one or more leading blank spaces, as illustrated in the previous example. String and char-type data items are generally displayed with field widths exactly equal to the number of characters in the corresponding data items. Hence there will be no leading or trailing blank spaces, unless they are included as a part of the actual data.

In Turbo Pascal, real numbers are displayed in scientific notation with a field width of 17 characters including sign, decimal point and exponent. A single blank space will precede a positive real number. Integer, char, boolean and string data items are displayed with variable field widths equal to the actual number of characters required to display the quantity.

EXAMPLE 4.16

A Pascal program contains the following `write` statement.

```
write('RED',' WHITE',' BLUE');
```

This statement will generate the following line of output.

```
RED WHITE BLUE
```

Notice that the blank spaces separating the individual words are included within the last two strings. If the write statement had not included these blanks, i.e.,

```
write('RED','WHITE','BLUE');
```

then the resulting output data would appear as an unbroken sequence of letters, i.e.,

```
REDWHITEBLUE
```

If one write statement is followed by another, then the second write statement will begin where the first one ended. In other words, the initial data item that is written by the second write statement will begin on the current line, immediately after the last data item that was written by the previous write statement. Therefore, *a new write statement does not necessarily generate a new line of output data.*

EXAMPLE 4.17

A portion of a Pascal program is shown below.

```
VAR a,b : real;
    i,j : integer;
    p,q : char;
      .
      .
      .
write(' a=',a,' b=',b,' i=',i);
write(' j=',j,' p=',p,' q=',q);
```

Suppose that the variables have been assigned the following values.

Variable	Value
a	12500.0
b	−14.8
i	5
j	−9
p	X
q	Y

In ANSI Pascal, the resulting output data might appear on one line, as

```
a= 1.2500000E+04 b=−1.4800000E+01 i=        5 j=        −9 p=X q=Y
```

In Turbo Pascal, the output would appear somewhat differently as

```
a= 1.2500000000E+04 b=−1.4800000000E+01 i=5 j=−9 p=X q=Y
```

Turbo Pascal can write the strings that are represented by string variables, just as it can read entire strings and assign them to string variables.

EXAMPLE 4.18

A Turbo Pascal program contains the statement

```
write('Name: ',customer);
```

Suppose `customer` is a string-type variable that has been assigned the string `'William Brown'`. Then execution of the program will result in the following output:

```
Name: William Brown
```

4.6 THE WRITELN STATEMENT

The `writeln` statement is identical to the `write` statement, except that the `writeln` statement results in an end-of-line designation being written after the last data item. Therefore any *subsequent* `write` or `writeln` statement will begin a new line of output.

The statement is written as

```
writeln(output data items)
```

where the output data items can be strings, numerical constants, variables or expressions, as in the `write` statement.

EXAMPLE 4.19

Suppose that the `write` statements in Example 4.17 are replaced with `writeln` statements, i.e.,

```
VAR a,b : real;
    i,j : integer;
    p,q : char;
     .
     .
     .
writeln(' a=',a,' b=',b,' i=',i);
writeln(' j=',j,' p=',p,' q=',q);
```

Two lines of output will now be generated. In Turbo Pascal, they will appear as

```
a= 1.2500000000E+04 b=-1.4800000000E+01 i=5
j=-9 p=X q=Y
```

It is the *first* `writeln` statement that causes the original single line of output to be broken up into two lines. The *second* `writeln` statement begins writing where the first statement left off (at the beginning of the second line). Therefore, the statements

```
writeln(' a=',a,' b=',b,' i=',i);
write(' j=',j,' p=',p,' q=',q);
```

will produce the same two lines of output shown above, but the statements

```
write(' a=',a,' b=',b,' i=',i);
writeln(' j=',j,' p=',p,' q=',q);
```

will generate the *single* line of output shown in Example 4.17.

An *empty* writeln statement can be used to generate a blank line, as illustrated in Example 4.20.

EXAMPLE 4.20

Consider the following three writeln statements:

```
writeln('line one');
writeln;
writeln('line two');
```

These statements will generate three lines of output (including one blank line), as shown below:

```
line one

line two
```

If the empty writeln statement were not present the blank line would not appear, and the two printed lines would be spaced closer together, i.e.,

```
line one
line two
```

4.7 FORMATTED OUTPUT

Output data can usually be made more legible by altering the field widths associated with numerical and boolean-type data. This can easily be accomplished by adding certain *format* features within the write and writeln statements. In particular, each integer, real or boolean item in a write or writeln statement is followed by a colon and a positive integer quantity which indicates the field width. The integer quantity can be expressed as a constant, a variable or an expression.

EXAMPLE 4.21

A Pascal program contains the following write statement.

```
write('The answer is',sum : 4);
```

Suppose that sum is an integer-type variable whose assigned value is −16. Then the integer quantity will be written out using a four-character field, resulting in the following output:

```
The answer is -16
```

Notice the blank space preceding the minus sign. This is a part of the four-character field.

EXAMPLE 4.22

Now suppose that the `write` statement in the above example is changed to read

```
write('The answer is',sum : j+2);
```

If `j` is an integer-type variable that has been assigned the value 3, then the field associated with `sum` will be five characters wide and the output will appear as

```
The answer is  -16
```

Notice that *two* blank spaces now precede the minus sign.

The specified field width is interpreted as the *minimum* field width associated with the data item. If the field width is too large, then the data item is shifted to the right portion of the field, resulting in one or more leading blank spaces. On the other hand, additional space will automatically be added if the field width is too small, thus preventing a part of the data item from being truncated.

EXAMPLE 4.23

Returning to Example 4.21, suppose that `sum` had been assigned a value of 3. Then the output would appear as

```
The answer is   3
```

Notice that the number has been placed within the right portion of the field, resulting in three leading spaces between "is" and "3."

On the other hand, if `sum` had been assigned a value of 1000, then the output would appear as

```
The answer is1000
```

The 4-digit number now fills the entire field.

Now suppose that the value −30000 had been assigned to `sum`. The resulting output would be

```
The answer is-30000
```

Two additional spaces have now been added to the output field to accommodate the 5-digit number and its sign.

A real-type number can be written in a more conventional form (without the exponent) if a second format term is included. Thus the complete format designation for a real number is a colon, followed by an integer indicating the total field width, followed by another colon, followed by another integer indicating the number of places to the right of the decimal point. The decimal part of the number will automatically be rounded when appropriate.

EXAMPLE 4.24

Suppose that `root` is a real-type variable that has been assigned the value 17487.266. This number can be written out in several different ways. The results obtained using Turbo Pascal are shown below.

Writeln Statement	*Resulting Output*
`writeln('root=',root);`	`root= 1.7487266000E+04`
`writeln('root=',root : 12);`	`root= 1.74873E+04`
`writeln('root=',root : 18);`	`root=   1.7487266000E+04`
`writeln('root=',root : 10 : 3);`	`root= 17487.266`
`writeln('root=',root : 8 : 1);`	`root= 17487.3`

ANSI Pascal also includes the `page` statement. This is a standard procedure that causes the next output item to be displayed at the top of a new page.

EXAMPLE 4.25

Suppose a Pascal program contains the following three statements.

```
writeln(a,b,c);
page;
writeln(x,y,z);
```

If the program is run on a mainframe computer using a line printer as a primary output device, these statements will cause the values of the variables a, b and c to be printed on one line, followed by the values of the variables x, y and z on another line. The `page` statement will cause the second line of output to appear at the top of a new page.

Turbo Pascal, and many other versions of Pascal intended for use on personal computers or workstations, do not recognize the `page` statement. In such cases the `page` statement is simply ignored if it is present. On some interactive systems, however, the `page` statement may cause the screen to be cleared.

4.8 CLOSING REMARKS

Before leaving this chapter, a few general remarks about the `read`, `readln`, `write`, `writeln` and `page` statements are in order.

First, these statements are actually *standard procedures* that are included as a part of the Pascal language. We have already discussed the use of the various standard procedures, and the manner in which they are accessed, in Sections 2.11 and 2.12. The reader is again reminded that the access to a standard procedure is considered to be a type of simple statement. It is in this sense that we refer to the use of these procedures as *statements*.

Second, it should be understood that these statements actually represent a simple subset of Pascal's input/output capability. We will consider the topic of input/output operations in greater generality when we study files in Chap. 11

Finally, remember that the details associated with the `read`, `readln`, `write` and `writeln` statements tend to be system-dependent, so that their behavior may vary from one version of Pascal to another. In particular, the appearance of output data may not be exactly the same in all versions of Pascal.

The basic input/output operations described in this chapter, together with the material covered in earlier chapters, provide us with the ability to write complete, though simple, Pascal programs. We have already seen several complete Pascal programs in Chap. 1 (see Examples 1.6 through 1.15). The next chapter will contain instructions for organizing, writing and running such programs.

Review Questions

4.1   What is an input file? Where do the input data items come from?

4.2   What is an output file? Where are the output data items displayed?

4.3   How are the data items arranged within an input or an output file?

4.4   How are the input and output files referred to in an ANSI Pascal program? How do these rules differ in Turbo Pascal?

4.5   What is the purpose of the `read` statement?

4.6   In what sense must the data items in the input file correspond to the variables in the `read` statement?

4.7   Summarize the rules for separating numerical data items within the input file. Summarize the rules for char-type data items.

4.8   Can boolean-type data be processed with a `read` statement?

4.9   How are data items read from the input file when one `read` statement follows another?

4.10   How are strings entered in an ANSI Pascal program? How can they be entered in Turbo Pascal? What possible problem might be encountered when entering a string followed by other data items on the same line?

4.11   What is the purpose of the `readln` statement? How does this statement differ from the `read` statement?

4.12   What happens when a `readln` statement is preceded by a `read` statement? What happens when a `read` statement is preceded by a `readln` statement?

4.13   What is the purpose of the `eoln` function? What type of information is provided by this function?

4.14   What is the purpose of the `eof` function? What type of information is provided by this function? How does this function differ from the `eoln` function?

4.15   In general terms, how can the `eoln` and `eof` functions be used to read an unspecified number of data items from an input file?

4.16   What is the purpose of the `write` statement? What data types can be included in this statement?

4.17   Can strings be included within a `write` statement? Can numerical constants be included? Can expressions be included? Compare with the `read` statement. Answer both for ANSI Pascal and Turbo Pascal.

4.18   How are real numbers normally displayed when written out by a `write` statement? Answer both for ANSI Pascal and Turbo Pascal.

4.19   Can boolean-type data be processed with the `write` statement? Compare with the `read` statement.

4.20   What is meant by a field width? What are the default field widths for your particular version of Pascal?

4.21   How are data items written to the output file when one `write` statement follows another?

4.22   What is the purpose of the `writeln` statement? How does this statement differ from the `write` statement?

4.23   What happens when a `writeln` statement is preceded by a `write` statement? What happens when a `write` statement is preceded by a `writeln` statement?

4.24   Why might an empty `writeln` statement be included in a Pascal program? What type of statement would the empty `writeln` statement most likely follow?

4.25   How can the default field width be altered in the output file? To what types of data does this apply?

4.26   What happens if an output field is wider than necessary for a given data item? What happens if the output field is too narrow?

4.27   How can a real number be displayed in nonscientific form (i.e., without an exponent)?

4.28   Suppose that a real number is displayed in nonscientific form and the field is not wide enough for the entire decimal part of the number. Will the decimal be rounded or truncated?

4.29   What is the purpose of the `page` statement? Is this statement recognized by all versions of Pascal?

4.30   Do the `read`, `readln`, `write` and `writeln` statements behave in exactly the same manner in all versions of Pascal? Explain.

Problems

4.31   The skeletal outline of a complete Pascal program is shown below. Explain what the program does, in terms of data input and output. Assume the program is written in ANSI Pascal.

```
PROGRAM sample;
CONST factor = 12345;
      flag = 'entry point';
VAR i1,i2 : integer;
    r1,r2,r3 : real;
    c1,c2 : char;
    b1 : boolean;
BEGIN
    readln(c1,c2,i1,i2,r1,r2,r3);
    . . .
    writeln(' i1=',i1:4, ' i2=',i2:4);
    writeln;
    writeln(' r1=',r1:10:2, ' r2=',r2:10:2, ' r3=',r3:12:4);
    writeln;
    write(' First char is ',c1,' Second char is ',c2);
    write(' Test status: ',b1:5);
END.
```

4.32   The following problem situations refer to the constants and variables defined in the preceding problem. Write an appropriate statement, or group of statements, for each situation.

(*a*)   Read the values for i1, r3 and c2 from one line of data.

(*b*)   Read the values for i1, r1, r2 and c1 from one line, followed by the values of i2, r3 and c2 from another line.

(*c*)   Write the values for the two constants on one line, followed by the values for all of the variables on another line. Do not label the output, but leave a blank space between the two constants. Also, place two blank lines between the two lines of output (i.e., triple-space the output).

(*d*)   Write the values of the two constants on one line, followed by the values of i1, r1, r2 and c1 on another line, followed by the values of i2, r3, b1 and c2 on another line. Double-space the output. Label all of the output items.

(*e*)   Repeat the previous problem. This time do not label the output data but format them as follows:

> integer: 5 characters
> real: 10 characters, with 3 digits to the right of the decimal point (no exponent)
> boolean: 7 characters

Also, precede each string or char-type data item with one blank space.

4.33   Suppose an input file contains the following two lines of data.

```
10   0.005   4.66E12ABC
-817  2.7E-3  XYZ
```

What values will be assigned to the variables given in Prob. 4.32(*b*)?

4.34   Suppose an input file contains the following three lines of data.

```
10   0.005
4.66E12  ABC
-63   17.7  75
```

What values will be assigned to the variables given in Prob. 4.32(*b*)?

4.35   Suppose the variables listed in Prob. 4.31 have been assigned the following values.

Variable	Value	Variable	Value
i1	−630	r3	0.000185
i2	375	c1	$
r1	20.8	c2	5
r2	−477300.0	b1	false

Show how the data will appear in the output file if the data items are displayed in the manner described in Prob. 4.32(*c*).

4.36　Repeat Prob. 4.35, assuming that the output data are displayed in the manner described in Prob. 4.32(*d*).

4.37　Repeat Prob. 4.35, assuming that the output data are displayed in the manner described in Prob. 4.32(*e*).

4.38　Here is a portion of a Pascal program.

```
PROGRAM sample2;
VAR a,b,c,d : integer
BEGIN
   . . .
   readln(a,b,c,d);
   . . .
   writeln(5*(a+b)/2 : c+2, 10*(a-b)/2 : c+d-1);
. . .
END.
```

Suppose the input file contains the following data:

```
   3    5    4    1
```

What output will be generated by this program? Asssume the program is written in ANSI Pascal.

4.39　The skeletal outline of a Turbo Pascal program is shown below.

```
PROGRAM example;
CONST flag = 'red';
      factor = 0.005;
VAR str1,str2 : string;
    i1,i2,i3 : integer;
    r1,r2 : real;
    c1,c2,c3,c4 : char;
BEGIN
   . . .
   readln(str1);
   readln(str2);
   readln(i1,i2,i3);
   readln(r1,r2);
   read(c1,c2,c3,c4);
   . . .
   writeln(flag,factor);
   writeln;
   writeln(str1);
   writeln(str2);
   write(i1,i2,i3);
   writeln(r1,r2);
   writeln;
   write(c1,c2,c3,c4);
   . . .
END.
```

In general terms, how must the input data items be entered? How will the output data items appear? Will the output items be separate and distinct from one another?

4.40 Each of the following problems shows a set of data within an input data file. In each case, what values will be assigned to the variables in Prob. 4.39?

(a)   Smith, Robert
       New York, NY
       1   2   3
       4   5
       blue   green

(b)   red
       green
       1
       2
       3
       4
       5
       b
       l
       u
       e

(c)   red   green   1   2   3   4   5   blue

(d)   red
       green
       1   2   3
       4   5   blue
       yellow

4.41 How will the output generated in Prob. 4.39 appear, assuming that the variables have been assigned the following values?

Variable	Value	Variable	Value
str1	San Francisco	c1	P
str2	California	c2	I
i1	100	c3	N
i2	−200	c4	K
i3	−300		
r1	400.444		
r2	−500.555		

4.42 Suppose the output statements in Prob. 4.39 are replaced with those shown below.

```
writeln('flag=',flag,' factor=',factor:6:3);
writeln;
write('City: ',str1);
writeln('   State: ',str2);
```

```
writeln;
write('i1=',i1:4,' i2=',i2:4);
writeln(' i3=',i3:4,' r1=',r1:6:1,' r2=',r2:6:1);
writeln;
write('color=',c1,c2,c3,c4);
```

How will the output appear, assuming the variables are assigned the values shown in the preceding problem?

4.43 The following problem situations refer to the constants and variables defined in Prob. 4.39. Write an appropriate statement, or group of statements, for each situation.

(*a*)   Read each string from a separate line. Then read all of the numerical data items from an additional line.

(*b*)   Read each string from a separate line. Then read the values of i1, r2, c3 and c4 from an additional line.

(*c*)   Read the integer data items from one line, the real data items from another line and the char-type data items from a third line.

(*d*)   Read each data item from a separate line.

(*e*)   Write the values for the two constants and all of the variables on one line. Do not label the output, but place at least one blank space between each data item.

(*f*)   Repeat the previous problem, with the numerical data items formatted as follows.

      integer: 4 characters
      real: 8 characters, with 2 digits to the right of the decimal point (no exponent)

(*g*)   Write the values for the two constants on one line, followed by the values of the char-type variables on another line, followed by the the values of the numerical variables on a third line. Do not label the output, but place at least one blank space between each data item. Also, leave a blank line between each line of printed output (i.e., double space the output).

(*h*)   Repeat the previous problem. This time label each constant and each numerical value. Write the char-type data as successive characters, without intervening spaces. Precede these characters with a single label.

(*i*)   Write the values of flag, i1, r1, c1 and c2 on one line, followed by the values of factor, i2, i3, r2, c3, and c4 on another line. Do not label the output, but place at least one blank space between each data item. Leave two blank lines between the lines of output.

(*j*)   Repeat the previous problem, with the numerical data formatted as follows:

      integer: 5 characters
      real: 7 characters, with 2 digits to the right of the decimal point (no exponent)

(*k*)   Write the values for both constants and all of the variables. Write each data item on a separate line. Label all of the data items. Format the numerical data as follows:

integer: 4 characters
real: 12 characters, with an exponent

4.44   A portion of a Turbo Pascal program is shown below.

```
PROGRAM example2;
VAR w,x,y,z : integer;
BEGIN
   . . .
   readln(w,x,y,z);
   . . .
   writeln('SUM=',x+y+z : w,' PRODUCT=',x*y*z : w+3);
   . . .
END.
```

Suppose the input file contains the following values.

3   10   20   30

What will the output will look like?

Chapter 5

Creating and Running a Pascal Program

By now we have learned enough about Pascal to write complete, though simple, Pascal programs. We therefore pause briefly from our coverage of new features and devote some attention to the planning, writing and execution of a Pascal program. We will also consider methods for detecting and correcting the different types of errors that can occur in improperly written programs.

Our attention will be directed primarily toward the use of Borland International's Turbo Pascal on an IBM-compatible personal computer. We emphasize this particular version of Pascal because of its widespread popularity and because it is representative of contemporary Pascal usage on many different computers.

5.1 PLANNING A PASCAL PROGRAM

When developing a new program, the overall program strategy should be completely planned out before beginning any detailed programming. This allows you to concentrate on the general program logic, without being concerned with the syntactic details of the individual instructions. Once the overall program strategy has been clearly established, the details associated with the individual program statements can be considered. This approach is generally referred to as "top-down" programming. With large programs, this entire process might be repeated several times, with more programming detail added at each stage.

Top-down program organization is normally carried out by developing an informal outline, consisting of phrases or sentences that are part English and part Pascal. In its initial stages the amount of actual Pascal is minimal, consisting only of various keywords that define major program components (e.g., PROGRAM, BEGIN, END). The descriptive English material is then inserted between these keywords, often in the form of program comments. The resulting outline is often referred to as *pseudo code*.

EXAMPLE 5.1 Roots of a Quadratic Equation

Suppose we wish to calculate the roots of the quadratic equation $ax^2 + bx + c = 0$, using the well-known formulas

$$x_1 = \frac{-b + \sqrt{b^2 - 4ac}}{2a} \qquad \text{and} \qquad x_2 = \frac{-b - \sqrt{b^2 - 4ac}}{2a}$$

where the values of a, b and c are known. Let us assume that the values of a, b and c are such that $b^2 - 4ac$ will always be positive. Therefore we need not worry about attempting to calculate the square root of a negative number.

We will enter the values for a, b and c interactively. That is, each numerical value will be entered in response to an appropriate on-screen prompt. We will also label the output, so that the meaning of each value is clearly understood.

The overall steps to be followed are as follows:

1. Declare a, b, c, x_1 and x_2 to be real-type variables.
2. Read numeric values for a, b and c.

3.   Calculate a value for $\sqrt{b^2 - 4ac}$

4.   Calculate values for x_1 and x_2, using the above formulas.

5.   Display the values for x_1 and x_2.

Each of these steps appears very simple when viewed from the top. However, some of these steps can be broken down further to facilitate the actual programming. In particular, the data input step involves an interactive dialog generated by pairs of read and write statements (see Example 1.7). The remaining steps can be written in terms of Pascal keywords interspersed with descriptive English phrases.

Here is a different form of the outline, written as pseudo code. Notice the introduction of an additional variable, root. Also, note the use of the Turbo Pascal functions sqr and sqrt.

```
PROGRAM roots

(* declare a, b, c, x1, x2 and root to be real-type variables *)

BEGIN
    (* generate (write) a prompt for a *)
    (* read a value for a *)

    (* generate (write) a prompt for b *)
    (* read a value for b *)

    (* generate (write) a prompt for c *)
    (* read a value for c *)

    (* Evaluate sqrt(sqr(b)-4*a*c) and assign to root *)

    (* Calculate values for x1 and x2 using the formulas *)
    (*    x1 := (-b + root) / (2*a)    *)
    (*    x2 := (-b - root) / (2*a)    *)

    (* Display (writeln) the values for x1 and x2, with appropriate labels *)
END.
```

Since this problem is particularly simple, the pseudo code does not require any additional refinement. If this were a more complex problem, however, we might write a more detailed version of the pseudo code, showing a finer breakdown of the overall program logic.

We will consider the detailed development and implementation of this program in Examples 3.2, 3.3 and 3.4.

Another method that can be used to develop a Pascal program is the "bottom-up" approach. This method may be useful for programs that make use of independent program modules (i.e., user-defined procedures and functions; see Chap. 7). The bottom-up approach involves the detailed development of these program modules early in the overall planning process. The overall program development is then based upon the known characteristics of these individual modules.

In practice, we often use both approaches: top-down for the overall program planning, and bottom-up with respect to independent program modules. Note, however, that the individual modules may themselves be developed using the top-down approach.

5.2 WRITING A PASCAL PROGRAM

Once an overall program strategy has been formulated and a program outline has been written, attention can be given to the detailed development of the actual Pascal program. At this point the emphasis becomes one of translating each step of the program outline (or each portion of the pseudo code) into one or more equivalent Pascal statements. This should be a straightforward activity provided the overall program strategy has been thought through carefully and in enough detail.

When writing a complete Pascal program there are, however, some additional points that must be kept in mind. First, the various declarations and definitions must be entered in the proper order. Second, some care must be given to the design of the user interface (though this issue should first be addressed in the program planning phase). And finally, attention must be given to certain aspects of programming style that are concerned with program organization, clarity and legibility. Let us consider each of these topics in some detail.

In Section 1.5 we presented an outline showing the overall structure of a Pascal program. This outline is repeated below, followed by some explanatory comments.

1. Header

2. Block, consisting of

    (*a*) Declarations, which include

           Labels
           Constants
           Type definitions
           Variables
           Procedures and functions

    (*b*) Statements

Recall that the header is a one-line item, beginning with the word PROGRAM and followed by the program title. In some versions of Pascal (e.g., ANSI Pascal, but not Turbo Pascal) the program title will be followed by references to any input and output files, enclosed in parentheses and separated by commas.

The program block consists of a declarations part and an action-statement part. The declarations must appear in the order given, though all of these declaration types need not appear in any single program. In fact, constants and variables are the only types of declarations that have been considered so far. For now, the important point to remember is that constant definitions must precede variable declarations.

The action statements can be written in many different ways. The only firm requirement is that all of the action statements be embedded within one overall compound statement (i.e., BEGIN . . . END). Thus, every program must include one BEGIN . . . END sequence. Other compound statements can be embedded within this overall compound statement, as required. Each compound statement can include a variety of individual action statements or groups of statements. (More about this in the next chapter.)

Some care must be given to the matter of punctuation, particularly the use of the semicolon. In particular, the following rules must be observed.

1. In Pascal, the semicolon is used as a statement *separator* (not a statement *terminator*). Hence it is used between successive statements and declarations, rather than as an ending for every particular statement and declaration.

2. Special rules apply to BEGIN and END. These keywords are actually *brackets* that indicate the beginning and end of a compound statement. Therefore BEGIN need not be followed by a semicolon, and END need not be preceded by a semicolon.

3. An unnecessary semicolon (e.g., preceding an END bracket) will be interpreted as a *null statement* (i.e., an empty statement). Usually this will not have any noticeable effect on the execution of the program, though there are certain situations in which the program logic could be unintentionally altered. Therefore, unnecessary semicolons should be avoided.

4. Every complete program must be terminated by a period. Thus, the final END bracket must be followed by a period.

Consult the Pascal syntax diagrams at the end of this book for precise information concerning the punctuation required by specific statements.

EXAMPLE 5.2 Roots of a Quadratic Equation

Presented below is a complete Turbo Pascal program corresponding to the outline and pseudo code presented in Example 5.1.

```
PROGRAM roots;

(* REAL ROOTS OF A QUADRATIC EQUATION *)

VAR a,b,c,root,x1,x2 : real;

BEGIN
   (* read input data *)

   write('a = ');
   read(a);
   write('b = ');
   read(b);
   write('c = ');
   read(c);

   (* calculate roots *)

   root := sqrt(sqr(b)-4*a*c);
   x1 := (-b+root)/(2*a);
   x2 := (-b-root)/(2*a);

   (* display output *)

   writeln;
   writeln('x1 = ',x1:6:2,'     x2 = ',x2:6:2)
END.
```

Notice that the declarations and statements are separated by semicolons, with the semicolons appearing at the end of each line as needed. BEGIN is not followed by a semicolon and END is not preceded by a semicolon, since these two keywords serve as brackets that define the beginning and the end of the single compound statement. Note the period at the end of the program, as required. Finally, notice the liberal use of comments, which identify each group of statements in accordance with its logical function.

There are some other desirable features that could be added to this program. For example, we might want to execute the program repetitively, for several different sets of input data. Or, we might have added error traps, preventing the user from processing input data resulting in negative values of $b^2 - 4ac$. We will see how such features can be added as we progress through the remaining chapters of this book.

You should understand that there is more to writing a complete Pascal program than simply arranging the individual declarations and statements in the right order and then punctuating them correctly. Attention should also be given to the inclusion of certain subjective features that will improve the readability of the program and its resulting output. These features include the logical sequencing of the statements, the use of indentation, the use of comments, the generation of prompts for input data and the display of clearly labeled output.

The logical sequencing of the statements within the program is, to a large extent, determined by the underlying logic of the program. Often, however, there are several different ways to sequence certain statements without altering the program logic. This is particularly true of more complex programs that involve the use of conditional or repeated program segments. In such cases, the sequencing of certain statements, or groups of statements, can have a major effect on the logical clarity of the program. Therefore it is important that the statements be sequenced in the most effective manner. We will say more about this in the next chapter, where we discuss the various types of conditional and repetitive features that are available in Pascal.

The use of indentation is closely related to the sequencing of groups of statements within a program. Whereas sequencing affects the *order* in which a group of statements is carried out, indentation illustrates the *subordinate nature* of individual statements within a group. The advantages of indentation are readily apparent, even in the simple programs presented earlier in this book. This will become even more apparent later, as we encounter Pascal programs whose structure is more complex.

Comments should always be included within a Pascal program. The more complicated the program, the more useful are the comments. If written intelligently, a few well-placed comments can provide an overview of the general program logic. Comments can also delineate major segments of a program, identify certain key items within the program and provide other useful information about the program. (Such comments can be of great use to the person who wrote the program as well as to other persons trying to read and understand the program, since a programmer may not remember all of the details of his or her own program over an extended period of time. This is especially true of long, complicated programs.) The comments placed within a program need not always be extensive; a few well-placed comments can often greatly clarify an otherwise obscure program.

Another important characteristic of a well-written program is its ability to generate clear, legible prompts for input data and to display clearly labeled output. We have illustrated this idea in the examples encountered earlier in this book, and we will continue to do so in later examples.

5.3 ENTERING THE PROGRAM INTO THE COMPUTER

Once the program has been written, it must be entered into the computer before it can be compiled and executed. In older versions of Pascal this was done by typing the program into the computer on a line-by-line basis. Editing changes were made using the backspace key for the current line being entered, or by deleting and retyping a line once it had already been entered into the computer.

Most contemporary versions of Pascal include a full-screen *editor* that is used for this purpose. The editor is generally integrated into the software environment. Thus, to access the editor, you must first enter the Pascal programming environment. The manner with which this is accomplished varies from one implementation of Pascal to another.

Consider, for example, Turbo Pascal as implemented on an IBM-compatible personal computer. To enter Turbo Pascal, simply type "turbo" at the system prompt. This will result in the full-screen display shown in Fig. 5.1.

The first line in this figure is a *menu bar*. Selecting one of the items in the menu bar (e.g., File, Edit, Search, Run, etc.) will cause a *drop-down menu* to appear, with a number of choices related to the menu bar selection. For example, the File menu includes choices that allow you to open a new program, to retrieve an old program, to save a program, to print a program listing or to exit from Turbo Pascal. We will discuss some of these menu items later in this chapter.

Usually a pointing device, such as a *mouse*, is used to select a menu item. This is accomplished by moving the cursor over the desired item and then "clicking" on the item; i.e., pressing a button on the pointing device.

The large clear space beneath the menu bar is called a *window*; it is actually an *editing area* where a new program can be entered or an existing program can be displayed. Portions of the program listed in this area can be changed, deleted, copied or moved to another part of the program. Some of these changes are made directly in the editing area, while others are made by *highlighting* (i.e., marking) a part of the program and then moving or deleting the highlighted material using the selections provided in the Edit menu.

Scroll bars are present at the right and near the bottom of the window. You can move vertically through the active program by clicking along the right scroll bar, or by dragging a small square marker up or down. Similarly, you can move horizontally across the active program by clicking along the bottom scroll bar, or by dragging a small square marker to the right or the left.

The bottom line contains a listing of certain frequently used function keys. Thus, pressing function key F1 produces extensive on-screen help. Pressing F2 saves the current program, and so on.

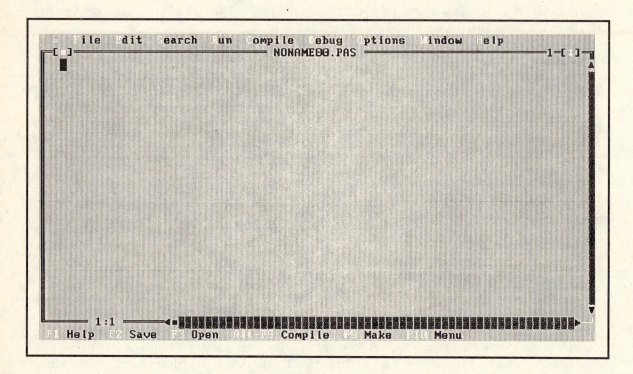

Fig. 5.1

To enter a new program in Turbo Pascal, you simply type the program into the editing area on a line-by-line basis and press the ENTER key at the end of each line. To edit a line, use the mouse or the cursor movement (arrow) keys to locate the beginning of the edit area. Then use the BACKSPACE or DELETE keys to remove unwanted characters. You may also insert additional characters, as required.

You may *delete* one or more lines simply by highlighting the lines and then selecting Cut from the Edit menu. A block of lines can be *moved* to another location using the Cut and Paste selections in the Edit menu. Similarly, a block of lines can be *copied* to another location using the Copy and Paste selections. Detailed editing instructions are provided in the Turbo Pascal User's Manual.

Once the program has been entered, it should be saved on an auxiliary memory device before it is executed. In Turbo Pascal, this is accomplished by selecting Save or Save As from the File menu, and then supplying a program name, such as ROOTS.PAS. (The extension PAS will be added automatically if an extension is not included with the file name.) Once the program has been saved and a name has been provided, it can again be saved at a later time (with, for example, any recent editing changes) simply by selecting Save from the File menu.

A program that has been saved can later be recalled by selecting Open from the File menu, and then either typing the program name or selecting the program name from a list of stored programs. A printed copy of the current program may be obtained by selecting Print from the File menu.

EXAMPLE 5.3 Roots of a Quadratic Equation

Suppose you have entered the Pascal program shown in Example 5.2 into an IBM-compatible personal computer using Turbo Pascal. After all typing corrections have been made, the screen will appear as shown in Fig. 5.2. (Some blank lines have been removed from the program listing in order to show the entire program.)

```
  File  Edit  Search  Run  Compile  Debug  Options  Window  Help
[ ]                             ROOTS.PAS                              1-[ ]
PROGRAM roots;
(* REAL ROOTS OF A QUADRATIC EQUATION *)
VAR a,b,c,root,x1,x2 : real;
BEGIN
   (* read input data *)
   write('a = ');
   read(a);
   write('b = ');
   read(b);
   write('c = ');
   read(c);

   (* calculate roots *)
   root := sqrt(sqr(b)-4*a*c);
   x1 := (-b+root)/(2*a);
   x2 := (-b-root)/(2*a);

   (* display output *)
   writeln;
   writeln('x1 = ',x1:6:2,'    x2 = ',x2:6:2)
END.
     1:1
  Help     Save     Open        Compile     Make     Menu
```

Fig. 5.2

In order to save the program, select Save or Save As from the File menu, as shown in Fig. 5.3. Once you press the ENTER key a dialog box will appear, prompting you for the name of the program being saved. You then respond by entering a program name, such as ROOTS.PAS (this is not shown). You may then conclude the session by selecting Exit from the File menu.

5.4 COMPILING AND EXECUTING THE PROGRAM

Once the program has been entered into the computer, edited and saved, it can be compiled and executed by selecting Run from the Run menu. If the program is compiled successfully it will begin execution, prompting for input as required. If the program is not compiled successfully it will display an error message, superimposed over the program listing. The error message will indicate where the error occurred as well as the type of error.

When program execution begins, a new window (called the output window) appears on the screen in place of the edit window which contained the program listing. If the program involves an interactive input dialog, it will be displayed in the output window. Once the program execution has been completed, however, the edit window will be restored, replacing the output window. Thus, the final output will not be visible. In order to see the final output (along with the interactive input dialog), select Output from the Window menu. The output window will then be superimposed over a portion of the edit window, so that the program listing (or a part of it) and the output can both be seen at the same time. This can be very helpful when debugging a program (more about this later).

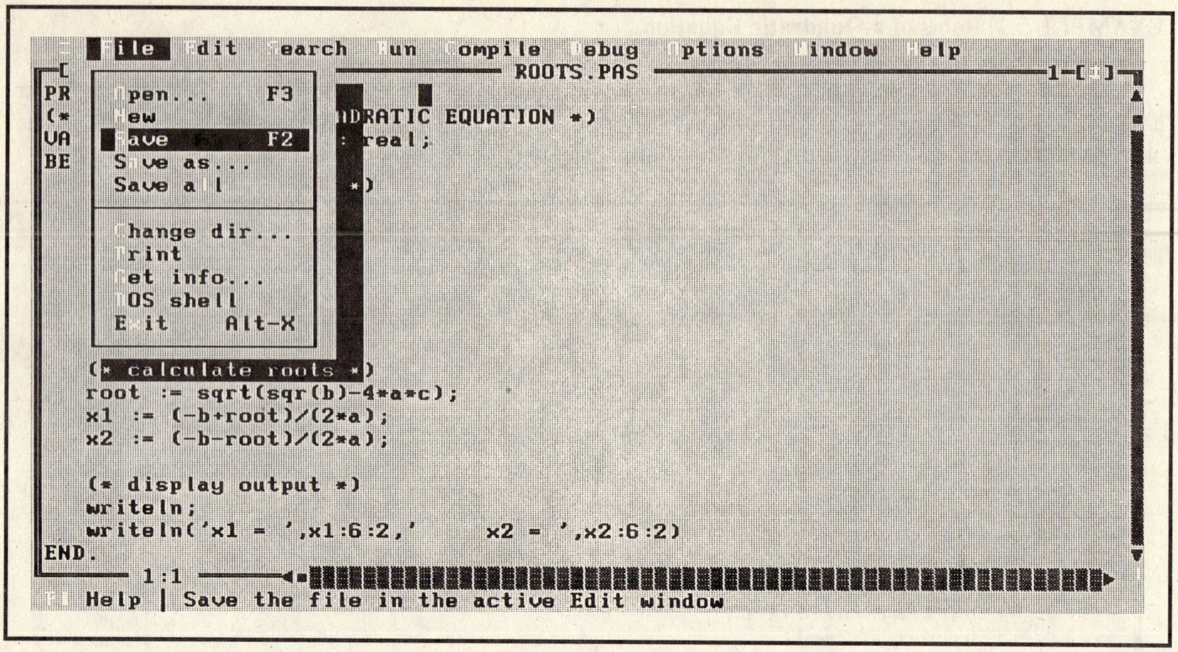

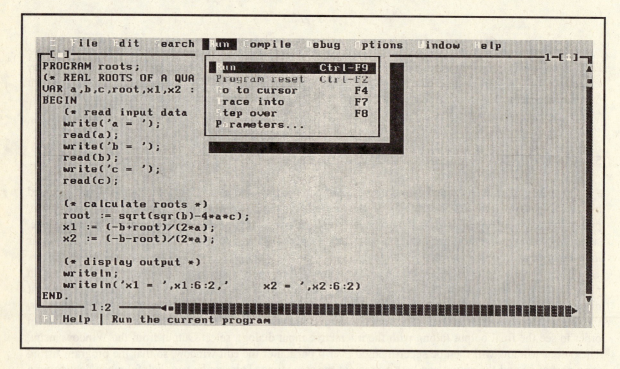

Fig. 5.3

EXAMPLE 5.4 Roots of a Quadratic Equation

Suppose you have reentered Turbo Pascal after concluding the session described in Example 5.3. You begin by loading ROOTS.PAS into the computer's memory (select Open from the File menu). In order to compile and execute the program after it has been loaded, select Run from the Run menu, as shown in Fig. 5.4.

Fig. 5.4

The edit window, containing the program listing, is replaced by the output window once the program begins to execute. This is shown in Fig. 5.5, for the input values $a = 2$, $b = 5$ and $c = 3$. When viewing Fig. 5.5 remember that the numerical values have been entered by the user, in response to the input prompts.

```
Turbo Pascal  Version 6.0  Copyright (c) 1983,90 Borland International
a = 2
b = 5
c = 3
```

Fig. 5.5

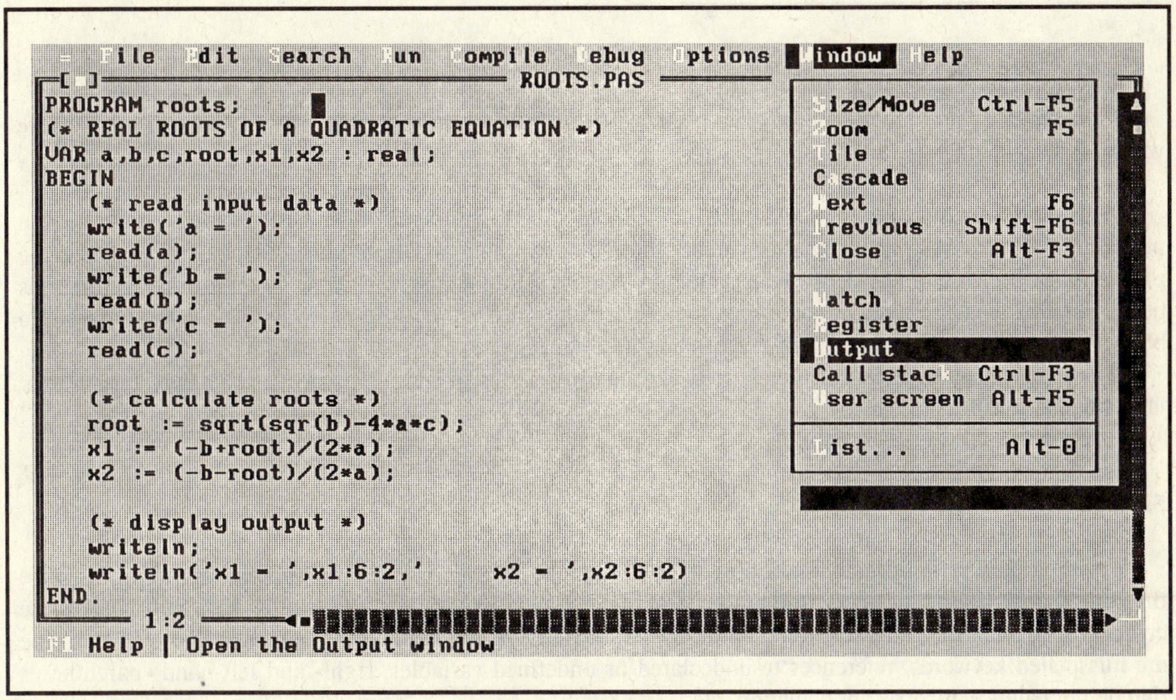

```
 ═ File Edit Search Run Compile Debug Options Window Help
 ┌[■]══════════════════════ ROOTS.PAS ═══════════┌──────────────────────┐
 PROGRAM roots;         ■                         │ Size/Move    Ctrl-F5 │
 (* REAL ROOTS OF A QUADRATIC EQUATION *)         │ Zoom            F5   │
 VAR a,b,c,root,x1,x2 : real;                     │ Tile                 │
 BEGIN                                            │ Cascade              │
    (* read input data *)                         │ Next            F6   │
    write('a = ');                                │ Previous   Shift-F6  │
    read(a);                                      │ Close        Alt-F3  │
    write('b = ');                                ├──────────────────────┤
    read(b);                                      │ Watch                │
    write('c = ');                                │ Register             │
    read(c);                                      │ Output               │
                                                  │ Call stack  Ctrl-F3  │
    (* calculate roots *)                         │ User screen  Alt-F5  │
    root := sqrt(sqr(b)-4*a*c);                   ├──────────────────────┤
    x1 := (-b+root)/(2*a);                        │ List...       Alt-0  │
    x2 := (-b-root)/(2*a);                        └──────────────────────┘

    (* display output *)
    writeln;
    writeln('x1 = ',x1:6:2,'    x2 = ',x2:6:2)
 END.
 └──── 1:2 ─────◄─█████████████████████████████████████████████████████►
  F1 Help │ Open the Output window
```

Fig. 5.6

Once the last input quantity has been entered ($c = 3$), the program resumes execution, the output window disappears and the edit window (containing the program listing) again reappears. The edit window remains on the screen when the execution ends. The calculated results (i.e., the final output) are shown in the output window. To return to the output window, select Output from the Window menu, as shown in Fig. 5.6.

Fig. 5.7 shows the output window, as it appears upon completion of the program execution (compare with Fig. 5.5, which illustrates the input phase). Thus, we see that $x_1 = -1$ and $x_2 = -1.5$ when $a = 2$, $b = 5$ and $c = 3$.

```
   ═ File  Edit  Search  Run  Compile  Debug  Options  Window  Help
                            ═ ROOTS.PAS ═                              1
 PROGRAM roots;
 (* REAL ROOTS OF A QUADRATIC EQUATION *)
 VAR a,b,c,root,x1,x2 : real;
 BEGIN
    (* read input data *)
    write('a = ');
    read(a);
    write('b = ');
    read(b);
    write('c = ');
    read(c);

    (* calculate roots *)
    root := sqrt(sqr(b)-4*a*c);
 ══[ ]════════════════════════ Output ═══════════════════════════2═[ ]═
 Turbo  Pascal   Version 6.0  Copyright (c) 1983,90 Borland International
 a = 2
 b = 5
 c = 3

 x1 =   -1.00      x2 =   -1.50
 ◄▓▓▓▓▓▓▓▓▓▓▓▓▓▓▓▓▓▓▓▓▓▓▓▓▓▓▓▓▓▓▓▓▓▓▓▓▓▓▓▓▓▓▓▓▓▓▓▓▓▓▓▓▓▓▓▓▓▓▓▓▓▓►
 F1 Help   Scroll   F10 Menu
```

Fig. 5.7

In this case, the program executed without any difficulties. Things do not always go this smoothly, however, as we will see in Examples 5.5 and 5.6.

A Turbo Pascal program can also be compiled and executed in separate steps if desired. To compile a program without subsequent execution, select the Compile command from the Compile menu. Once the program has been compiled, it can be executed by selecting Run from the Run menu. If a program that has been compiled is later altered in some way, then selecting Run from the Run menu will cause the program to be automatically recompiled and then executed, as described above.

There are other variations of the compile/execute procedures in Turbo Pascal. Consult the Turbo Pascal User's Guide for further details.

5.5 ERROR DIAGNOSTICS

Programming errors usually remain undetected until an attempt is made to compile the program. Once the compilation begins, however, the presence of *syntactic* errors will become readily apparent, since these errors will prevent the program from compiling successfully. Some particularly common errors of this type are misspelled keywords, references to undeclared or undefined variables, right- and left-hand parentheses that do not balance, incorrect punctuation, etc.

Most implementations of Pascal will generate diagnostic messages when syntactic errors are detected during compilation. The meaning of these diagnostic messages is not always straightforward, but the messages are nevertheless helpful in identifying the nature and location of the errors.

EXAMPLE 5.5 Syntactic Errors

A version of ROOTS.PAS containing several syntactic errors is shown below. (There are 5 errors; can you find them?)

```
PROGRAM roots;

(* REAL ROOTS OF A QUADRATIC EQUATION *)

VAR a,b,c,root,x1,x2 : real;

BEGIN
   (* read input data *)

   write('a = ');
   read(a);
   writr('b = ');
   read(b);
   write('c = ');
   read(c);

   (* calculate roots *)

   root = sqrt(sqr(d)-4*a*c);
   x1 := (-b+root)/(2*a);
   x2 := (-b-root)/(2*a;

   (* display output *)

   writeln
   writeln('x1 = ',x1:6:2,'    x2 = ',x2:6:2)
END.
```

When an attempt was made to compile the program in Turbo Pascal, the following error message was generated.

```
Error 3: Unknown identifier.
```

The cursor was placed at the beginning of the statement that contains the error; i.e.,

```
writr('b = ');
```

(Note that the keyword write is misspelled.)

When this error was corrected and another attempt was made to compile the program, the following error message appeared.

```
Error 91: ":=" expected.
```

Now the cursor appeared under the equal sign in the statement

```
root = sqrt(sqr(d)-4*a*c);
```

The difficulty here is the missing colon before the equal sign.

When this error was corrected and still another attempt was made to compile the program, the first error message again appeared, i.e.,

```
Error 3: Unknown identifier.
```

with the cursor under the variable d in the statement

```
root = sqrt(sqr(d)-4*a*c);
```

The problem here is the undeclared variable d, which should be the variable b.

Correcting this error and again attempting to compile resulted in the following error message:

```
Error 89: ")" expected.
```

The cursor now appeared under the semicolon at the end of the statement

```
x2 := (-b-root)/(2*a;
```

The problem here is the missing right parenthesis following the variable a.

When this error was corrected and another attempt was made to compile the program, still another error message appeared:

```
Error 85: ";" expected.
```

The cursor was positioned under the first letter (w) in the statement

```
writeln('x1 = ',x1:6:2,'      x2 = ',x2:6:2)
```

Now the problem is the missing semicolon at the end of the *preceding* writeln statement. When this problem was corrected the program compiled correctly (finally!), without any diagnostic error messages.

Execution errors are also very common. Such errors occur during the execution of programs that are free of syntactic errors. Some common execution errors are a reference to a nonexistent variable, the generation of an excessively large number (exceeding the largest permissible number that can be stored in the computer), division by zero, and attempting to compute the logarithm or the square root of a negative number. Diagnostic messages are usually generated in situations of this type, making it easy to identify and correct the sources of error. Such diagnostics are sometimes called *execution* diagnostics, to distinguish them from the *syntactic* diagnostics or *compilation* diagnostics described earlier.

EXAMPLE 5.6 Execution Errors

In this example we see what happens when we attempt to execute ROOTS.PAS after a successful compilation. We first attempt to execute the program with the values $a = 1$, $b = 2$ and $c = 3$. After all of the input data have been entered, the following message will appear:

```
    Error 207: Invalid floating point operation.
```

Also, the cursor will be positioned to the left of the statement

```
    root = sqrt(sqr(b)-4*a*c);
```

indicating that this statement is the source of error. The problem in this case is the choice of input values, which result in the value -8 for the quantity $b^2 - 4ac$. Since this value is negative, its square root cannot be calculated and the program cannot continue its execution beyond this point.

We next attempt to execute the program using the input values $a = 10^{-30}$, $b = 10^{10}$ and $c = 10^{36}$. A numerical overflow now occurs in the calculation of x_2. Hence the following message will appear:

```
    Error 25: Floating point overflow.
```

The cursor will now be positioned to the left of the statement

```
    x2 := (-b-root)/(2*a);
```

Notice that this diagnostic message does not indicate exactly where the overflow occurred. Some additional effort is required to determine that the difficulty arises in the calculation of x_2 (see Example 5.8).

5.6 LOGICAL DEBUGGING

We have just seen that syntactic errors and execution errors usually result in the generation of error messages when the program is compiled and executed. Errors of this type are usually easy to find and correct, even if the error messages are unclear. Much more subtle, however, are *logical* errors. Here the program correctly conveys the programmer's instructions, free of syntactic errors, but the programmer has supplied the computer with instructions that are logically incorrect. Such errors can be very difficult to detect, since the output resulting from a logically incorrect program may appear to be error-free. Moreover, logical errors are often hard to find even when they are known to exist (as, for example, when the computed output is obviously incorrect). Thus, a good bit of probing may be required in order to find and correct errors of this type. Such probing is known as *logical debugging*.

Detecting Errors

The first step in attacking logical errors is to find out if they are present. This can sometimes be accomplished by testing a new program with data that will yield a known answer. If the correct results are *not* obtained, then the program obviously contains errors. If the correct results *are* obtained, however, you cannot be absolutely certain that the program is error free, since some errors cause incorrect results only under certain circumstances (as, for example, with certain values of the input data or with certain program options). Therefore, a new program should receive thorough testing before it is considered to be error free. This is especially true of complicated programs or programs that will be used extensively by others.

Sometimes a calculation will have to be carried out by hand (with the aid of a calculator) in order to obtain a known answer. For some problems, however, the amount of work involved in carrying out a hand calculation is prohibitive, since a calculation that requires a few minutes of computer time may require *several weeks or months* to solve by hand. Therefore, a sample calculation cannot always be developed to test a new program. The logical debugging of such programs can be particularly difficult, though you can often detect the presence of logical errors by studying the computed results carefully to see if they are reasonable.

Correcting Errors

Once you have established that a program contains a logical error, some resourcefulness and ingenuity may be required to find the error. Error detection should always begin with a thorough review of each logical group of statements within the program. Knowing that an error exists somewhere, you can often spot the error by carefully inspecting the program. If the error cannot be found, it sometimes helps to set the program aside for a while. This is especially true if you are experiencing some fatigue or frustration; it is not unusual for a tired, tense programmer to miss an obvious error the first time around.

If you cannot locate an error by inspection, you should modify the program to print out certain intermediate results and then rerun it. This technique is referred to as *tracing*. The source of error often becomes evident once you examine these intermediate calculations carefully. In particular, you can usually identify the specific area within the program where things begin to go wrong. The greater the amount of intermediate output, the more likely you are to pinpoint the source of error.

Sometimes an error simply cannot be located, despite the most elaborate debugging techniques. On such occasions you may suspect some difficulty that is beyond your control, such as a hardware problem or an error in the Pascal compiler. In most cases, however, the problem turns out to be some subtle error in the program logic. Thus, you should resist the temptation to blame the computer and not continue to look for that elusive programming error. Although hardware problems do occur *on rare occasions*, they usually produce very bizarre results, such as the computer "dying" or spewing out unintelligible characters. Also, errors occasionally turn up in a new compiler, though they are usually detected and removed after the compiler has been in use for a short period of time.

Finally, you should recognize that some logical errors are inescapable in computer programming, though a conscientious programmer will make every attempt to minimize their occurrence. You should therefore anticipate the need for some logical debugging when writing realistic, meaningful programs.

EXAMPLE 5.7 Evaluating a Polynomial

A student has written a Turbo Pascal program to evaluate the formula

$$y = [(x-1)/x] + [(x-1)/x]^2/2 + [(x-1)/x]^3/3 + [(x-1)/x]^4/4 + [(x-1)/x]^5/5$$

To simplify the programming, the student has defined a new variable, u, as

$$u = [(x-1)/x]$$

so that the formula becomes

$$y = u + u^2/2 + u^3/3 + u^4/4 + u^5/5$$

Here is the student's Pascal program, called POLY.PAS.

```
PROGRAM poly;
(* PROGRAM TO EVALUATE AN ALGEBRAIC FORMULA *)
VAR u,x,y : real;
BEGIN
   write('x = ');
   read(x);
   u := x-1/x;
   y := u+sqr(u/2)+(u/3)*sqr(u/3)+sqr(sqr(u/4))+(u/5)*sqr(sqr(u/5));
   writeln('y = ',y)
END.
```

The student suspects that y should have a value of about 0.7 when $x = 2$. However, the following result is obtained when the program is loaded, compiled and executed using Turbo Pascal. (The user's response to the input prompt is underlined for clarity.)

```
x = 2
y =   2.2097053906E+00
```

Since the calculated value of y differs from the value expected, it is apparent that the program contains logical errors that must be found and corrected.

After inspecting the program carefully, the student realized that the first assignment statement is incorrect. The statement should have been written as

```
u := (x-1)/x;
```

The student corrected the program and reran it, again using the value of $x = 2$. The resulting output,

```
y =   5.6738377025E-01
```

indicates that a logical error is still present.

After some additional study, the student discovered that the second assignment statement is also incorrect. This statement should be written as

```
y := u + sqr(u)/2 + u*sqr(u)/3 + sqr(sqr(u))/4 + u*sqr(sqr(u))/5;
```

The program was then modified and rerun, resulting in the output

```
y =   6.8854166667E-01
```

which now appears correct, since this value is close to 0.7.

Debugging Aids

Most contemporary versions of Pascal include special debugging features that facilitate the detection of errors. For example, they may allow you to step through a program one instruction at a time. They may also allow the program to execute until it reaches certain designated places, called *breakpoints*. The execution of the program will then temporarily be suspended, revealing the values of certain program variables or expressions (called *watch variables* or *watch expressions*) at the time the execution is suspended. Or, they may allow the execution of a program to be suspended only if a watch expression becomes true. By monitoring the values of watch expressions at carefully selected breakpoints, it is easier to determine where and when an error originates.

Turbo Pascal, for example, includes several debugging features within its integrated environment. Some of these features (Trace and Step) are activated from the Run menu, as shown in Fig. 5.4. Others are selected from the Debug menu, as shown in Fig. 5.8.

EXAMPLE 5.8 Roots of a Quadratic Equation

In Example 5.6 we saw that an overflow occurred during the execution of the program ROOTS.PAS when the values $a = 10^{-30}$, $b = 10^{10}$ and $c = 10^{36}$ were entered as input data. We stated that the source of the problem was the calculation of x_2, but we did not say how this conclusion was obtained. Let us now use the Turbo Pascal debugger to establish this conclusion.

```
  ═══ File  Edit  Search  Run  Compile  █Debug  Options  Window  Help
  ┌[■]──────────────────────────────── RO
  PROGRAM roots;   █                         Evaluate/modify...   Ctrl-F4
  (* REAL ROOTS OF A QUADRATIC EQUATIO      Watches               ▶
  VAR a,b,c,root,x1,x2 : real;              █oggle breakpoint     Ctrl-F8
  BEGIN                                     Breakpoints...
     (* read input data *)
     write('a = ');
     read(a);
     write('b = ');
     read(b);
     write('c = ');
     read(c);

     (* calculate roots *)
     root := sqrt(sqr(b)-4*a*c);
     x1 := (-b+root)/(2*a);
     x2 := (-b-root)/(2*a);

     (* display output *)
     writeln;
     writeln('x1 = ',x1:6:2,'       x2 = ',x2:6:2)
  END.
  ──── 1:1 ──────◄■████████████████████████████████████████████████►
  █1 Help | Set or clear an unconditional breakpoint at the cursor position
```

Fig. 5.8

We first load ROOTS.PAS into the Turbo Pascal environment, as in Example 5.3 (see Fig. 5.2). We then activate the debugger and carry out the following steps.

1. Set (root), (-b+root), (-b-root) and (2*a) as watch expressions. This is done by selecting Watches/Add Watch from the Debug menu four different times, as illustrated in Fig. 5.9. Upon completion, the Add Watch window will list all of the current watch expressions, as shown in Fig. 5.10.

2. Set the second assignment statement (x1 := . . .) as a breakpoint. To do so, we move the cursor to this statement and then select Toggle Breakpoint from the Debug menu. The assignment statement (the breakpoint) will then be highlighted in the program listing, as shown in Fig. 5.11.

3. Select Run from the Run menu. Then enter the input values in response to the program prompts.

The program will stop at the designated breakpoint. At this point only the first assignment statement will have been executed. The current values of the watch expressions can be seen in the watch window (choose Watch from the Window menu), as shown in Fig. 5.11. From Fig. 5.11 we see that the watch expressions have the following values.

Watch Expression	*Value*
root	10000000000.0 (i.e., 10^{10})
-b+root	0
-b-root	-20000000000.0 (i.e., -2×10^{10})
2*a	2.0E-30 (i.e., 2×10^{-30})

From the current values of these watch expressions we can see that the value of x1 will be zero and the value of x2 will be -2×10^{10} divided by 2×10^{-30}, which is -1×10^{40}. The magnitude of this value exceeds 1.7×10^{38}, which is the largest permissible real number in Turbo Pascal (see Section 2.5). Hence, we see that the overflow occurs when evaluating x2. We can verify this by pressing function key F7 twice, first to assign a value to x1 and then to x2. After the second statement is executed, an overflow message appears and the program execution comes to a halt, with the cursor positioned to the left of the statement x2 := . . . . . Fig. 5.12 shows the appearance of the error message in the edit window.

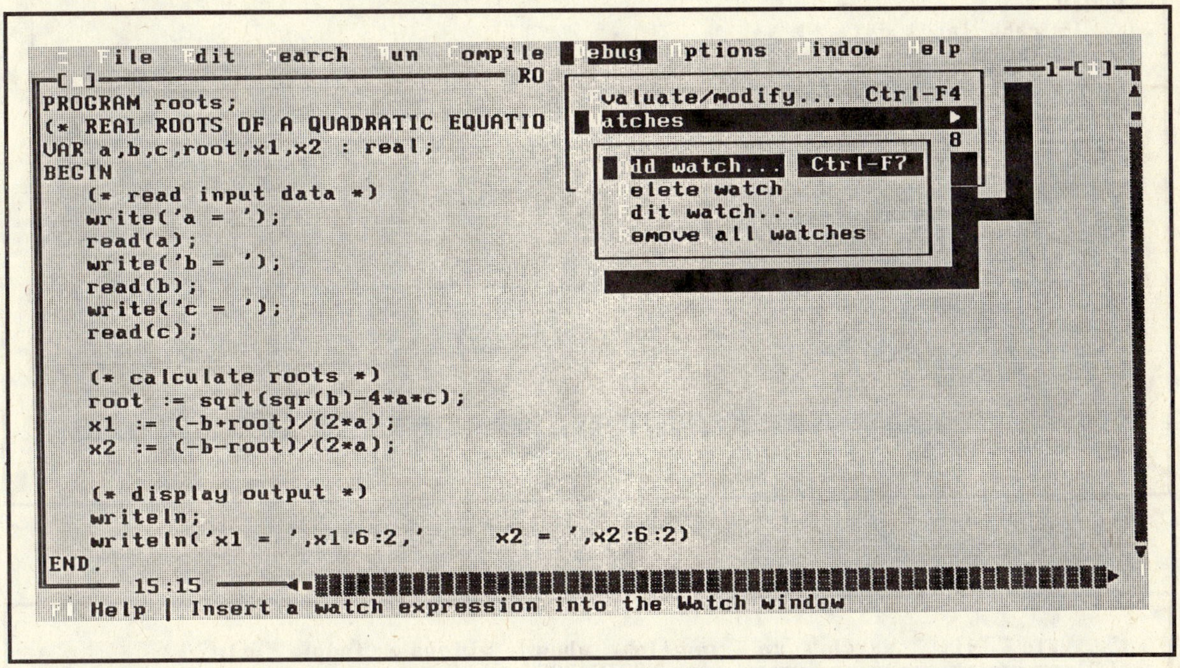

```
   File  Edit  Search  Run  Compile  Debug  Options  Window  Help
[ ]                             RO        valuate/modify...   Ctrl-F4
PROGRAM roots;                            atches                    ►
(* REAL ROOTS OF A QUADRATIC EQUATIO                              8
VAR a,b,c,root,x1,x2 : real;              dd watch...    Ctrl-F7
BEGIN                                     elete watch
   (* read input data *)                 dit watch...
   write('a = ');                         emove all watches
   read(a);
   write('b = ');
   read(b);
   write('c = ');
   read(c);

   (* calculate roots *)
   root := sqrt(sqr(b)-4*a*c);
   x1 := (-b+root)/(2*a);
   x2 := (-b-root)/(2*a);

   (* display output *)
   writeln;
   writeln('x1 = ',x1:6:2,'      x2 = ',x2:6:2)
END.
   15:15
 F1 Help | Insert a watch expression into the Watch window
```

Fig. 5.9

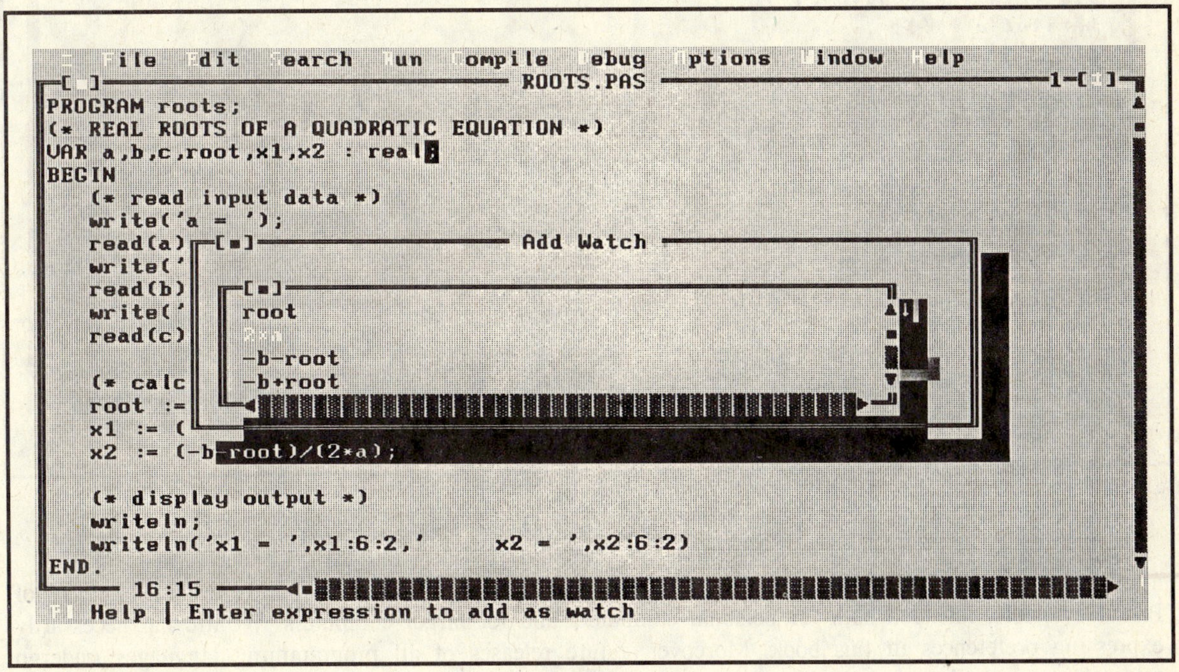

```
   File  Edit  Search  Run  Compile  Debug  Options  Window  Help
[ ]                             ROOTS.PAS
PROGRAM roots;
(* REAL ROOTS OF A QUADRATIC EQUATION *)
VAR a,b,c,root,x1,x2 : real;
BEGIN
   (* read input data *)
   write('a = ');
   read(a)  [ ]                      Add Watch
   write('
   read(b)   [ ]
   write('     root
   read(c)    2*a
              -b-root
              -b+root
   (* calc
   root :=
   x1 := (
   x2 := (-b-root)/(2*a);

   (* display output *)
   writeln;
   writeln('x1 = ',x1:6:2,'      x2 = ',x2:6:2)
END.
   16:15
 F1 Help | Enter expression to add as watch
```

Fig. 5.10

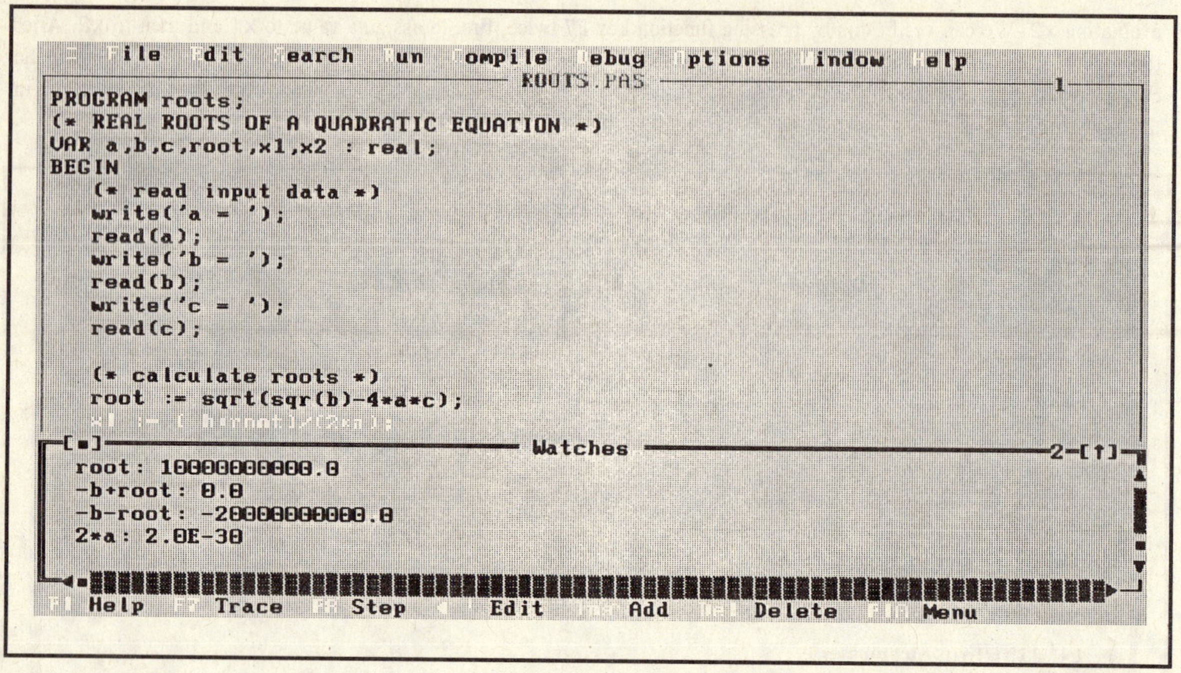

```
 ≡  File  Edit  Search  Run  Compile  Debug  Options  Window  Help
 ─────────────────────────── ROOTS.PAS ─────────────────────────1──
PROGRAM roots;
(* REAL ROOTS OF A QUADRATIC EQUATION *)
VAR a,b,c,root,x1,x2 : real;
BEGIN
   (* read input data *)
   write('a = ');
   read(a);
   write('b = ');
   read(b);
   write('c = ');
   read(c);

   (* calculate roots *)
   root := sqrt(sqr(b)-4*a*c);
   x1 := (-b+root)/(2*a);
[■]─────────────────────── Watches ──────────────────────2─[↑]─
  root: 10000000000.0
  -b+root: 0.0
  -b-root: -20000000000.0
  2*a: 2.0E-30

 F1 Help  F7 Trace  F8 Step  ◄┘ Edit  Ins Add  Del Delete  F10 Menu
```

Fig. 5.11

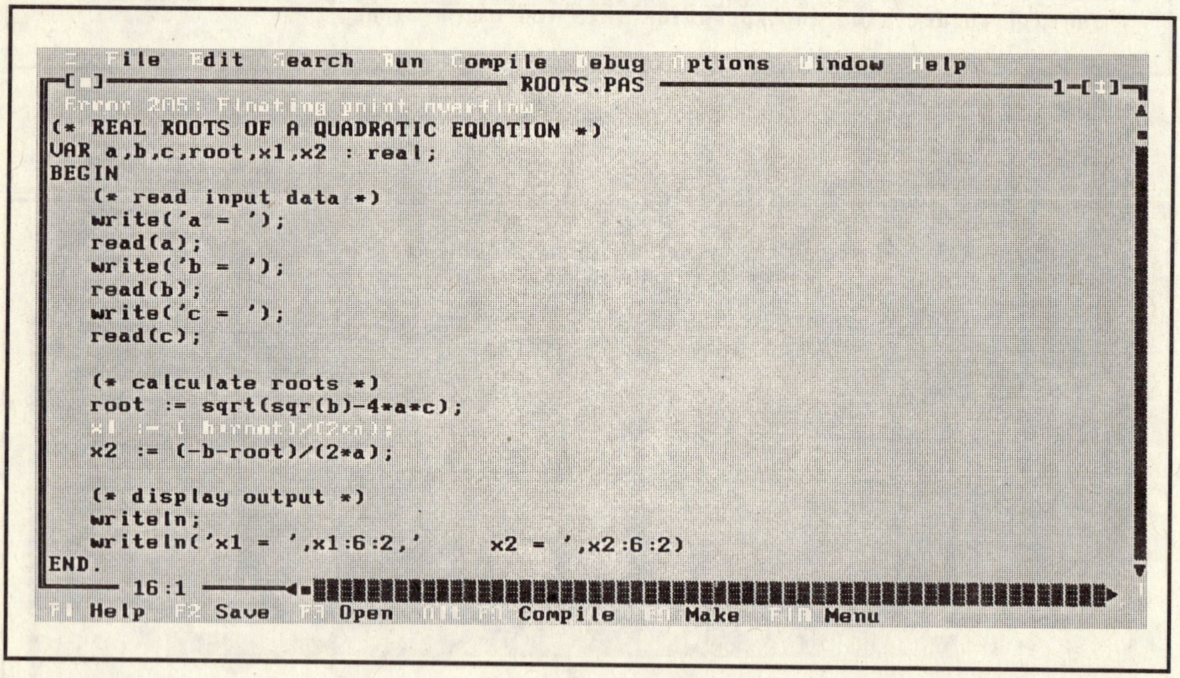

```
 ≡  File  Edit  Search  Run  Compile  Debug  Options  Window  Help
─[■]──────────────────────── ROOTS.PAS ──────────────────────1─[↕]─
Error 205: Floating point overflow.
(* REAL ROOTS OF A QUADRATIC EQUATION *)
VAR a,b,c,root,x1,x2 : real;
BEGIN
   (* read input data *)
   write('a = ');
   read(a);
   write('b = ');
   read(b);
   write('c = ');
   read(c);

   (* calculate roots *)
   root := sqrt(sqr(b)-4*a*c);
   x1 := (-b+root)/(2*a);
   x2 := (-b-root)/(2*a);

   (* display output *)
   writeln;
   writeln('x1 = ',x1:6:2,'     x2 = ',x2:6:2)
END.
──── 16:1 ────
 F1 Help  F2 Save  F3 Open  Alt-F9 Compile  F9 Make  F10 Menu
```

Fig. 5.12

Finally, it should be understood that there are many high-quality, contemporary implementations of Pascal available, intended both for personal computers and for larger computers. We are not necessarily expressing preferences in this book. Moreover, future releases of all programming languages undergo refinements as the languages continue to evolve. Thus, some of the details presented in this chapter will undoubtedly change in the years ahead.

Review Questions

5.1   What is meant by "top-down" programming? What are its advantages? How is it carried out?

5.2   What is pseudo code?

5.3   What is meant by "bottom-up" programming? How does it differ from top-down programming?

5.4   Summarize the overall structure of a Pascal program.

5.5   How is the semicolon used in Pascal? Where must it appear?

5.6   What is the purpose of BEGIN and END? What punctuation is associated with these two keywords?

5.7   What special punctuation mark must appear at the end of every Pascal program?

5.8   How much flexibility is permitted in the logical sequencing of the statements within a Pascal program? Explain.

5.9   Why are some statements or groups of statements indented within a Pascal program? Is this indentation essential? Is it desirable? Explain.

5.10   What are the reasons for placing comments within a Pascal program? How extensive should these comments be?

5.11   Describe the use of the write statement in conjunction with data input.

5.12   What are menu bars? What are drop-down menus? How can menu bars and drop-down menus be accessed?

5.13   What is the difference between compilation and execution of a Pascal program?

5.14   What is a syntactic error? What is an execution error? How do syntactic errors and execution errors differ?

5.15   Name some common syntactic errors. Name some common execution errors.

5.16   What is a logical error? How do logical errors differ from syntactic and execution errors?

5.17   What are diagnostic messages?

5.18   What is the difference between syntactic diagnostics and execution diagnostics? Name some situations in which each type of diagnostic message would be generated.

5.19   What is meant by logical debugging? Name some logical debugging procedures.

5.20   What is meant by tracing? In what way is tracing useful?

5.21   What are breakpoints? What are watch expressions? What useful purposes are served by breakpoints and watch expressions?

5.22   In Turbo Pascal, what features are provided by the Run menu? What features are provided by the Debug menu? What features are provided by the Window menu?

5.23   In Turbo Pascal, how can the current values of the watch expressions be viewed when the program reaches a breakpoint? How can the final output be viewed upon completion of the program execution?

Problems

The following questions are concerned with information gathering rather than actual problem solving.

5.24 If personal computers are used at your particular school or office, obtain answers to the following questions.

(*a*) Exactly what equipment is available (printers, auxiliary memory devices, etc.)?

(*b*) What operating system is available?

(*c*) How are programs saved, displayed, and transferred from one memory device to another?

(*d*) What version of Pascal is available on your computer? How is it accessed?

(*e*) How is the editor accessed? How are normal editing functions (e.g., insert, delete, etc.) carried out?

(*f*) How is an existing Pascal program loaded into the computer's memory? How is a program listed? How is a program saved? How is a program compiled and executed?

5.25 If timesharing is used at your particular school or office, obtain answers to the following questions.

(*a*) Are video display terminals (monitors) available? Are hard-copy terminals available?

(*b*) How is a terminal turned on or off?

(*c*) How is a single character deleted from a typed line before it is transmitted to the computer? How is an entire line deleted?

(*d*) How is a typed line transmitted to the computer?

(*e*) Can a hard copy of your timesharing session be obtained? If so, how?

(*f*) Is a telephone dial-up required to establish a connection with the computer? If so, what is the dial-up procedure?

(*g*) How do you log on and log off your computer?

(*h*) Can your timesharing terminal be operated in a local mode (i.e., as a stand-alone device, independent of the host computer)? If so, how is this done?

(*i*) How is Pascal accessed?

(*j*) What editor or editors are available on your system? How are normal editing functions (e.g., insert, delete, etc.) carried out?

(*k*) How is an existing Pascal program loaded into the computer's memory? How is a program listed? How is a program saved? How is a program executed?

(*l*) How much does it cost to use your particular timesharing system?

Programming Problems

5.26	Enter the program given in Example 1.6 into the computer, making any necessary modifications that may be required by your particular version of Pascal. Be sure to correct any typing errors. List the program, correct any apparent errors, and save it when you are sure it is correct. Compile the program, then execute the program using several different values for the radius. Verify that the computed answers are correct by comparing them with hand calculations.

5.27	Enter, edit and execute the programs given in Examples 1.7 and 1.10. Verify that they run correctly with your particular version of Pascal.

5.28	Enter, edit and execute a few of the programs given in Prob. 1.28. Verify that they run correctly with your particular version of Pascal.

5.29	Example 5.2 presents a Pascal program for determining the real roots of a quadratic equation. Enter this program into the computer and save it. Then execute the program using several different sets of input data. Verify that the calculated results are correct by comparing them with hand calculations.

5.30	Repeat Prob. 5.29 using input data that will generate execution diagnostics, as illustrated in Example 5.6. Be sure you understand the cause and the meaning of each diagnostic message.

5.31	Write an interactive Pascal program for each of the following problem situations. Enter each program into the computer, being sure to correct any typing errors. Compile, save and execute the program. Repeat as often as necessary in order to obtain an error-free program.

(a)	Display HELLO! in the middle of a line.

(b)	Have the computer print

```
Hi, What's your name?
```

on one line. The user then enters his or her name immediately after the question mark. The computer then skips two lines and prints the following two lines.

```
Welcome, (name)!
Let's be friends!
```

(c)	Convert a temperature reading in Fahrenheit degrees to Celsius, using the formula

$$^oC = (5 / 9) (^oF - 32)$$

Test the program with the following values: 68, 150, 212, 0, −22, −200 (degrees Fahrenheit).

(d)	Determine how much money (in dollars) is in a piggy bank that contains n_1 half-dollars, n_2 quarters, n_3 dimes, n_4 nickels and n_5 pennies. Use the following values to test your program: $n_1 = 11, n_2 = 7, n_3 = 3, n_4 = 12, n_5 = 17$ (Answer: 8.32 dollars).

(e)	Calculate the volume and area of a sphere using the expressions

$$V = 4\pi r^3 / 3? \quad A = 4\pi r^2$$

Test the program using the following values for the radius (r): 6, 12.2, 0.2.

(*f*)   Calculate the mass of air in an automobile tire, using the formula

$$PV = 0.37m(T + 460)$$

where P = pressure, pounds (force) per square inch
       V = volume, cubic feet
       m = mass of air, pounds
       T = temperature, $^\circ F$

If an automobile tire containing 2 cubic feet of air is inflated to 28 pounds per square inch at room temperature (70 $^\circ F$), how much air is in the tire?

(*g*)   If *a*, *b* and *c* represent the three sides of a triangle, then the area of the triangle is

$$A = \sqrt{s(s-a)(s-b)(s-c)}$$

where $s = (a + b + c) / 2$. Also, the radius of the *largest inscribed* (inner) circle is given by

$$r_i = A / s$$

and the radius of the *smallest circumscribed* (outer) circle is

$$r_c = abc / (4 A)$$

Calculate the area of the triangle, the area of the largest inscribed circle and the area of the smallest circumscribed circle for each of the following sets of data:

a:	11.88	5.55	10.00	13.75	12.00	20.42	7.17	173.67
b:	8.06	4.54	10.00	9.89	8.00	27.24	2.97	87.38
c:	12.75	7.56	10.00	11.42	12.00	31.59	6.66	139.01

(*h*)   Suppose that *P* dollars are invested at an annual interest rate of *i* (expressed as a decimal). If the interest is reinvested, after *n* years the total amount of money, *F*, can be determined as follows:

$$F = P (1+i)^n.$$

This is known as the *law of compound interest*.
        If $5000 is invested at 6%, compounded annually, how much money will have accumulated after 10 years?
        If the interest is compounded quarterly rather than annually, the above equation must be changed to read

$$F = P (1+i/4)^{4n}$$

If the same $5000 is invested at the rate of 6%, compounded quarterly, how much will have accumulated after 10 years? Compare this answer with the result obtained earlier, for interest compounded annually.

(*i*)   The increase in population of a bacteria culture with time is directly proportional to the size of the population. Thus, the larger the population, the faster the bacteria will increase in number. Mathematically, the population at any time can be expressed as

$$P = P_0[1 + ct + (ct)^2/2 + (ct)^3/6 + \cdots + (ct)^n/n!]$$

where t = time in hours beyond a reference time
P_0 = bacteria population at the reference time
P = bacteria population at time t
c = an experimental constant

Calculate the population multiplication factor (P/P_0) at 2, 5, 10, 20 and 50 hours beyond the reference time, assuming $c = 0.0289$. Include the first 10 terms of the series (i.e., let $n = 9$).

(j) Read a five-letter word into the computer, then encode the word on a letter-by-letter basis by subtracting 30 from the numerical value that is used to represent each letter. Thus, if the ASCII character set is being used, the letter a (which is represented by the value 97) would become a C (represented by 67), and so on. *Hint*: Note that C = chr(ord(a)−30).

Display both the original and the encoded versions of the word. Test the program with the following words: white, roses, Japan, zebra.

(k) Read into the computer a five-letter word that has been encoded using the scheme described above. Decode the word by reversing the above procedure. Then display both the encoded and the decoded versions of the word.

Chapter 6

Control Structures

In all of the Pascal programs that we have encountered so far each instruction was executed once and once only, in the same order that it appeared within the program. Programs of this type are unrealistically simple since they do not include any logical control structures, such as tests to determine if certain conditions are true or false, the repeated execution of groups of statements, or the selection of one group of statements out of several different possibilities. Yet most programs that are of practical interest make extensive use of such features. Thus, we must learn to utilize logical control structures in our programs so that we can consider more interesting and realistic problem situations.

For example, many programs require that a group of consecutive instructions be executed repeatedly, until some logical condition has been satisfied. Generally the required number of repetitions will not be known in advance. This type of repetition is known as *conditional looping*. A related operation is *unconditional looping* (or just plain *looping*), in which the execution of a group of consecutive instructions is repeated some specified number of times. Another situation that arises frequently is the need to carry out a logical test, and then take some particular action which depends upon the outcome of that test. This is known as *conditional execution*. And finally, there is a special kind of conditional execution in which a particular group of statements is chosen from several available groups. This is sometimes referred to as *selection*.

All of these operations can easily be carried out in Pascal. We will see how this is accomplished in this chapter. The use of this material will open the door to a much broader and more interesting class of programming problems.

6.1 PRELIMINARIES

Before considering the details of the Pascal control structures, let us review certain concepts that were presented in Chaps. 2 and 3. These concepts must be used in conjunction with the control structures; hence their understanding is essential before we can proceed further.

First, recall that a boolean expression represents a condition that is either true or false (see Section 2.10). Boolean expressions are formed by combining operands of the same type (any type *other than boolean*) with one of the seven *relational operators*: =, <>, <, <=, >, >=, and IN (see Section 3.4). So far we have discussed only the first six relational operators; the seventh (IN) will be deferred until we reach Chap. 12.

EXAMPLE 6.1

Several boolean expressions are shown below.

```
count <= 100
sqrt(a+b+c) > 0.005
answer = 0
balance >= cutoff
ch1 < 'T'
```

The first four expressions involve numerical operands. Their meaning should be readily apparent.

In the last expression, `ch1` is assumed to be a char-type variable. This expression will be true if the character represented by ch1 "comes before" T in the character set; i.e., if `ord(ch1) < ord('T')`. Otherwise, the expression will be false.

In addition to the relational operators, Pascal contains three *logical operators* (OR, AND and NOT) that are used with boolean operands (Section 3.4). The first two (OR and AND) are used to combine boolean operands to form logical expressions; the third (NOT) is a prefix that is used to negate a boolean operand.

EXAMPLE 6.2

Here are some boolean expressions that illustrate the use of the logical operators.

```
(count <= 100) AND (ch1 <> '*')
(balance < 1000.0) OR (status = 'R')
(answer < 0) OR ((answer > 5.0) AND (answer < 10.0))
(pay >= 1000.0) AND (NOT single)
```

Note that ch1 and status are assumed to be char-type variables in these examples, and single is assumed to be boolean. The remaining variables are assumed to be numeric (either integer or real).

Also, notice that the boolean operands are enclosed in parentheses, to avoid any ambiguities in the order in which the operations are carried out.

Recall also that there are two basic types of statements in Pascal—*simple* and *structured* (see Section 2.11). Simple statements refer to assignment statements, procedure references and the GOTO statement. We have already discussed assignment statements and procedure references in Sections 2.11 and 2.12; the GOTO statement will be discussed at the end of this chapter.

Of greater importance at this time are structured statements, since most of the Pascal control structures fall into this category. We will present a detailed discussion of each of these control structures later in this chapter. For now, however, let us recall our earlier discussion of one type of structured statement—the compound statement.

A *compound statement* consists of a sequence of two or more consecutive statements, enclosed within the keywords BEGIN and END and separated by semicolons. The individual statements that make up the compound statement can be simple or structured. Thus, individual structured statements (i.e., control structures) can be included within a compound statement. Moreover, one compound statement can be embedded within another.

EXAMPLE 6.3

Here is an elementary compound statement which we have seen before.

```
BEGIN
    read(radius);
    area := 3.14159*sqr(radius);
    write(radius,area)
END
```

Here is a more complex compound statement.

```
BEGIN
   sum := 0;
   FOR count := 1 TO n DO
      BEGIN
          read(x);
          sum := sum+x
      END;
   write(' sum = ',sum)
END
```

Notice that the second compound statement includes the FOR – TO control structure. (We will discuss the details of this control structure later in this chapter.) Also, notice that a smaller compound statement is embedded within the FOR control structure. Thus we see an example of a compound statement embedded within a control structure that is included within another compound statement.

The control structures presented in this chapter will make extensive use of both boolean expressions and compound statements.

6.2 THE WHILE – DO STRUCTURE

The WHILE – DO structure is a repetitive control structure that is used to carry out conditional looping. The general form of this structure is

WHILE *boolean expression* DO *statement*

The statement part of the structure will be executed repeatedly, as long as the boolean expression remains true. This statement can be simple or structured, though it is usually a compound statement that includes some feature which may alter the value of the boolean expression.

Suppose, for example, that we wanted to write out the digits 1, 2, . . . , 20, with one digit on each line. This could be accomplished with the following WHILE – DO structure.

```
digit := 1;
WHILE digit <= 20 DO
   BEGIN
       writeln(digit);
       digit := digit + 1
   END;
```

where digit is assumed to be an integer-type variable. We therefore begin with a value of digit = 1. We proceed to write out the current value of digit, increase its value by 1, and then repeat the cycle. This process is continued as long as (i.e., WHILE) the value assigned to digit does not exceed 20.

The net effect of this WHILE – DO structure is that the process of writing and incrementing will be repeated 20 times, resulting in 20 successive lines of output. Each line will contain a successive integer value, beginning with 1 and ending with 20.

Similarly, suppose that we wanted to determine the sum of the first n digits, where n is a known integer-type variable. This could be accomplished by writing

```
sum := 0;
digit := 1;
WHILE digit <= n DO
   BEGIN
      sum := sum + digit;
      digit := digit + 1
   END;
```

or, equivalently,

```
sum := 0;
digit := 1;
WHILE digit < n+1 DO
   BEGIN
      sum := sum + digit;
      digit := succ(digit)
   END;
```

where sum and digit (as well as n) are assumed to be integer-type variables.

In either case, we begin with a value of sum = 0, and then proceed to add successive values of digit to sum. The process of adding the current value of digit to sum and then increasing the value of digit by 1 will continue as long as (i.e., WHILE) the current value of digit is less than n + 1. At the conclusion of this process, sum will represent the sum of the first n digits; i.e., $1 + 2 + 3 + \ldots + n$.

The WHILE – DO structure is used extensively in Pascal, as there are many programming applications that require this type of conditional looping capability. We will see many sample programs that utilize the WHILE – DO structure throughout this text.

EXAMPLE 6.4 Averaging a List of Numbers

Let us use the WHILE – DO structure to obtain the average of a list of n numbers. Our strategy will be based upon the use of a partial sum that is initially set equal to zero, and is then updated as each new number is read into the computer. Thus, the problem very naturally lends itself to the use of repetition.

The actual calculations can be carried out in the following manner.

1. Assign a value of 1 to the integer variable count. (This variable will be used as a loop counter.)

2. Assign a value of 0 to the real variable sum.

3. Read in the value for n.

4. Do the following steps repeatedly, as long as the counter does not exceed n (i.e., while the value of count is less than n + 1).

    (*a*) Read in one of the numbers in the list. (Each number will be represented by the real variable x.)

    (*b*) Add the number to the value of sum.

    (*c*) Increase the value of count by 1.

5. Divide the value of sum by n to obtain the desired average.

6. Write out the calculated value for the average.

Note that this program is nothing more than an extension of the logic discussed above, with the addition of input and output statements.

The actual Pascal program is shown on the next page.

```
PROGRAM average1;

(* calculate the average of n numbers using a WHILE - DO structure. *)

VAR n,count : integer;
    x,sum,average : real;

BEGIN   (* action statements *)
   count := 1;
   sum := 0;
   write('How many numbers? ');
   readln(n);
   WHILE count < n+1 DO
   BEGIN
      write('x = ');
      read(x);
      sum := sum+x;
      count := count+1
   END;    (* count < n+1 *)
   average := sum/n;
   writeln('The average is ',average)
END.
```

Notice that the WHILE – DO structure contains a compound statement which, among other things, causes the value of count to increase. Eventually, this will cause the boolean expression

```
count < n+1
```

to become false, thus terminating the loop.

Also, note that the loop will not be executed at all if n is assigned a value that is less than 1. Physically, of course, it would not make any sense to do this.

Finally, notice that the innermost compound statement is indented within the WHILE – DO structure. This causes the physical extent of the WHILE – DO structure to be readily identifiable.

6.3 THE REPEAT – UNTIL STRUCTURE

The REPEAT – UNTIL structure is another repetitive control structure that is used to carry out conditional looping. It is similar to the WHILE – DO structure, and in some respects these two control structures complement one another.

The general form of the REPEAT – UNTIL structure is

```
REPEAT sequence of statements UNTIL boolean expression
```

The sequence of statements will be executed repeatedly, until the boolean expression becomes true. Note that the sequence of statements will always be executed at least once, since the boolean expression is not tested until the *end* of the control structure. (This is in contrast to the WHILE – DO structure, where the boolean expression is tested at the *beginning* of the control structure. The WHILE – DO structure will not be executed at all if the boolean expression is initially false.)

Note that this structure may consist of a *sequence* of statements, whereas the WHILE – DO structure permits only one statement (though it can be compound). The REPEAT – UNTIL sequence need *not* be included within BEGIN and END. Thus, the keywords REPEAT and UNTIL act as brackets that indicate the beginning and the end of the statement sequence. It is possible, of course, to include a compound statement or another control structure within this sequence. In addition, the sequence of statements will usually include some feature that will alter the value of the boolean expression.

To illustrate the use of the REPEAT – UNTIL structure, consider once again the problem of writing out the digits 1, 2, . . . ,20, with one digit on each line. We have already seen how this can be accomplished using the WHILE – DO structure (see Section 6.2). Now let us utilize the REPEAT – UNTIL structure for the same purpose.

```
digit := 1;
REPEAT
    writeln(digit);
    digit := digit + 1
UNTIL digit > 20;
```

Again, `digit` is assumed to be an integer-type variable.

We again begin with a value of `digit` = 1, and then proceed to write out the current value of `digit`, increase its value by 1, and then repeat the cycle. The process is continued UNTIL the current value of `digit` (which was just increased in value) exceeds 20.

The net effect of this REPEAT – UNTIL structure will be indistinguishable from the corresponding WHILE – DO structure presented in the last section. Thus, 20 successive lines of output will be generated, with each line showing a successive integer value.

Now let us consider the use of a REPEAT – UNTIL structure to determine the sum of the first n digits, where n is a known, integer-type variable (see Section 6.2). The required structure is

```
sum := 0;
digit := 1;
REPEAT
    sum := sum + digit;
    digit := succ(digit)
UNTIL digit > n;
```

Again, `sum` and `digit` (as well as n) are assumed to be integer-type variables.

In this case we begin with a value of `sum` = 0, and then proceed to add successive values of `digit` to `sum`. The process of adding the current value of `digit` to `sum` and then increasing the value of `digit` by 1 will continue UNTIL the current value of `digit` exceeds n. At this time, `sum` will represent the sum of the first n digits; i.e., $1 + 2 + 3 + \ldots + n$.

The REPEAT – UNTIL structure, like the WHILE – DO structure, is used extensively in Pascal. Sometimes the choice of one structure over the other is simply a matter of personal preference. In other applications, however, the choice is influenced by the desirability of testing the boolean expression either at the beginning or at the end of the control structure.

EXAMPLE 6.5 Averaging a List of Numbers

Now let us use the REPEAT – UNTIL structure to obtain the average of a list of n numbers. This is the same problem that we considered in Example 6.4, using WHILE – DO. Our approach will therefore be similar to that used in Example 6.4, making allowances for the different control structure.

The actual calculations can be carried out as follows.

1.   Assign a value of 1 to the integer variable `count`. (This variable will be used as a loop counter.)

2.   Assign a value of 0 to the real variable `sum`.

3.   Read in the value for n.

4.   Repeat the following steps, until the counter exceeds n.

(*a*) Read in one of the numbers in the list. (Each number will be represented by the real variable x.)

(*b*) Add this number to the value of sum.

(*c*) Increase the value of count by 1.

5. Divide the value of sum by n to obtain the desired average.

6. Write out the calculated value for the average.

Note the similarity between this outline and that presented in Example 6.4.

The corresponding Pascal program is shown below.

```
PROGRAM average2;

(* calculate the average of n numbers using a REPEAT - UNTIL structure. *)

VAR n,count : integer;
    x,sum,average : real;

BEGIN   (* action statements *)
   count := 1;
   sum := 0;
   write('How many numbers? ');
   readln(n);
   REPEAT
      write('x = ');
      read(x);
      sum := sum+x;
      count := count+1
   UNTIL count > n;
   average := sum/n;
   writeln('The average is ',average)
END.
```

Notice that the sequence of statements contained within the REPEAT – UNTIL structure includes a statement that causes the value of count to increase. Eventually, this causes the boolean expression

```
count > n
```

to become true, thus terminating the loop.

It should be understood that this loop will always be executed at least once, since the value of the boolean expression is not tested until the end of the loop.

Finally, observe that the sequence of statements included within the REPEAT – UNTIL structure is indented so that the physical extent of the structure can easily be identified.

This example should be carefully compared with Example 6.4. Either structure (WHILE – DO or REPEAT – UNTIL) is equally valid for this particular problem. In many situations, however, the nature of the problem will suggest a preference for one of these two structures.

6.4 THE FOR STRUCTURE

The FOR structure is used to carry out unconditional looping in Pascal. That is, this structure allows some action to be repeated a specified number of times.

The FOR structure has two different forms. The more common form is

```
FOR control variable := value1 TO value2 DO statement
```

The statement part of the structure can be either simple or structured, though it is typically a compound statement that may include other control structures. This statement will be executed for each of several consecutive values assigned to the control variable. The number of values assigned to the control variable therefore determines the number of times the statement will be executed.

The control variable must be a simple-type variable of any type other than real. Typically, it will be either an integer variable or a user-defined variable. (We will discuss user-defined variables in Chap. 8. For now, we will confine our discussion to integer-type control variables.) Initially, the control variable is assigned the value specified by *value1*. The control variable automatically takes on its next successive value each time the statement is repeated, until it finally takes on the value specified by *value2*. If the control variable is an integer-type variable, then it will automatically increase by 1 each time the statement is executed; hence, the statement will be executed (*value2–value1+1*) times.

To illustrate the use of the FOR structure, let us again consider the problem of writing out the first 20 positive integers, with one integer on each line. (We have already seen how to do this using the WHILE – DO structure in Section 6.2, and with the REPEAT – UNTIL structure in Section 6.3.) We require only a single FOR – TO statement to carry out this task. In particular, we can write

```
FOR digit := 1 TO 20 DO writeln(digit);
```

where `digit` is assumed to be an integer-type variable.

In this example `digit` takes on the successive values 1, 2, . . . ,20, thus causing the loop to be executed 20 times. During each pass, the current value of `digit` will be written out on a separate line, as required.

Similarly, the problem of determining the sum of the first n digits can be expressed as

```
sum := 0;
FOR digit := 1 TO n DO sum := sum + digit;
```

Here we begin by assigning a value of 0 to `sum`. Each pass through the loop then causes the current value of `digit` to be added to `sum`. Therefore, `sum` will represent the desired value $1 + 2 + 3 + . . . + n$ after the loop has been executed n times.

Notice how much easier it has been to use the FOR structure than the WHILE – DO or the REPEAT – UNTIL structures for these problems (see Sections 6.2 and 6.3). This is usually the case when the required number of passes through the loop is known in advance.

There are a few rules that must be adhered to when writing a FOR statement. Specifically, the values of *value1* and *value2* can be expressed as constants, variables or expressions. However, these values must be of the same data type as the control variable. Also, the value of *value1* must be less than *value2* if the statement is to be executed more than once. (If *value1* and *value2* are equal, the statement will be executed only once; if *value1* is greater than *value2*, the statement will not be executed at all.)

EXAMPLE 6.6

The use of the FOR structure is really less complicated than it first appears, as illustrated below.

The first example contains a compound statement that is executed n times. (Note that n is an integer-type variable whose value is assumed to be known, and that x is a real-type variable.) During each pass through the loop a new number (i.e., a new value for x) is read into the computer and added to `sum`. The sum of all n numbers is then written out, after the loop has been completed.

```
sum := 0;
FOR count := 1 TO n DO
    BEGIN
        write('x = ');
        readln(x);
        sum := sum+x
    END;
writeln('sum=',sum);
```

In the second example the initial and final values of the control variable are given by an integer-type variable and an integer-type expression, respectively. Notice that the compound statement is now spread out over several lines, with appropriate indentation. (This is the preferred format.)

```
sum :=0;
FOR count := n TO (3*n+1) DO
    BEGIN
        write('x = ');
        readln(x);
        sum := sum+x
    END;
writeln('sum=',sum);
```

The second form of the FOR structure is similar to the first, except for the use of the keyword DOWNTO in place of TO. Thus, the FOR structure can be written as

```
FOR control variable := value1 DOWNTO value2 DO statement
```

The action taken by this form of the FOR structure is similar to the first form, except that the control variable is evaluated backward rather than forward. Thus, if the control variable is an integer-type variable it will automatically *decrease* by 1, from `value1` to `value2`, during successive passes through the loop. Therefore `value1` should be greater than `value2`. (If the two values are equal, the statement will be executed only once; and if `value1` is less than `value2`, the statement will not be executed at all.)

EXAMPLE 6.7

Here is an illustration of the second form of the FOR structure.

```
FOR i := 0 DOWNTO -12 DO
    BEGIN
        z := 2*i+5;
        writeln('i=',i,'   z=',z)
    END;
```

This example will cause 13 lines of text to be printed. Each line will contain the current value of the integer variable `i`, followed by the corresponding value of the formula $z = 2i+5$. Notice that the successive values of `i` will decrease, from `i` = 0 on the first line, to `i` = -12 on the last line.

It should be understood that `value1` and `value2` are evaluated only once, before the first pass through the loop. Therefore the reader should not attempt to change either of these values within the loop. Also, the reader is cautioned against using the control variable once the FOR structure has terminated, since it will normally be undefined.

EXAMPLE 6.8 Averaging a List of Numbers

Let us return to the problem of averaging a list of numbers, which we considered in Examples 6.4 and 6.5. Now, however, we will use the FOR structure to carry out the looping action.

The calculations will be carried out in the following manner.

1.   Assign a value of 0 to the real variable `sum`.

2.   Read in the value for `n`.

3. Do the following steps n times (i.e., for successive values of the control variable count ranging from 1 to n).

    (*a*) Read in the next number in the list. (Each number will be represented by the real variable x.)

    (*b*) Add this number to the value of sum.

4. Divide the value of sum by n to obtain the desired average.

5. Write out the calculated value for the average.

Note the similarity between this outline and the two earlier outlines, given in Examples 6.4 and 6.5.

The complete Pascal program is shown below.

```
PROGRAM average3;

(* calculate the average of n numbers using a FOR structure. *)

VAR n,count : integer;
    x,sum,average : real;

BEGIN   (* action statements *)
   sum := 0;
   write('How many numbers? ');
   readln(n);
   FOR count := 1 TO n DO
      BEGIN
         write('x = ');
         read(x);
         sum := sum+x
      END;
   average := sum/n;
   writeln('The average is ',average)
END.
```

Notice that the control variable count is initially assigned a value of 1. This value increases by 1 each time the loop is executed, until count finally takes on a value of n. Thus, the loop will be executed exactly n times. Also, observe that the sequence of statements included within the FOR structure is indented. This permits the physical extent of the structure to be easily identified.

The reader should compare this approach to the problem with those given in Examples 6.4 and 6.5. The use of the FOR structure is better suited to this particular problem than either the WHILE – DO structure or the REPEAT – UNTIL structure, since the number of passes through the loop is known in advance. There are many problems, however, for which this is not true (see Example 6.22 and Prob. 6.45 at the end of this chapter). In such cases the WHILE – DO or REPEAT – UNTIL structures may be more appropriate. Thus, the reader should not attempt to draw general conclusions about the relative utility of these control structures; each application must be evaluated on its own merits.

6.5 NESTED CONTROL STRUCTURES

Control structures can be *nested* (i.e., embedded), one within another. The inner and outer structures need not be of the same type. It is essential, however, that one structure be completely embedded within the other. In other words, there can be no overlap.

EXAMPLE 6.9 Repeated Averaging of a List of Numbers

Suppose that we want to calculate the average of several consecutive lists of numbers. If we know in advance how many lists are to be averaged, then we can use a FOR structure to control the number of times the averaging loop is executed. The actual averaging can be accomplished using any one of the three repetition structures (WHILE – DO, REPEAT – UNTIL or FOR), as illustrated in Examples 6.4, 6.5 and 6.8.

Let us arbitrarily use the REPEAT – UNTIL structure to carry out the averaging, as in Example 6.5. Thus, we will proceed in the following manner.

1.   Read in a value for `loopmax`, an integer quantity that indicates the number of lists that will be averaged.

2.   Repeatedly read in a list of numbers and determine its average (i.e., calculate an average for successive values of the control variable loop ranging from 1 to `loopmax`). Follow the steps given in Example 6.5 to calculate each average.

Here is the actual Pascal program.

```
PROGRAM average4;

(* calculate the average of n numbers repeatedly, using nested loops *)

VAR loop,loopmax,n,count : integer;
    x,sum,average : real;

BEGIN   (* action statements *)
   write('How many lists? ');
   readln(loopmax);
   FOR loop := 1 TO loopmax DO
      BEGIN
         count := 1;
         sum := 0;
         write('List number ',loop,'   How many numbers? ');
         readln(n);
         REPEAT
            write('x = ');
            read(x);
            sum := sum+x;
            count := count+1
         UNTIL count > n;
         average := sum/n;
         writeln('List number ',loop,'   The average is ',average);
         writeln
      END      (* loop *)
END.
```

Notice the manner in which the REPEAT – UNTIL structure is nested within the FOR structure. (This is easy to see, because of the indentation.) Thus the entire averaging procedure will be completely executed during each pass through the outer loop.

Many applications require the use of nested FOR structures. In such situations each FOR structure must utilize a different control variable. (Remember also that each inner FOR structure must be completely embedded within the next outermost FOR structure.) This is illustrated in the next example.

EXAMPLE 6.10 Compound Interest Factors

Suppose a given sum of money, P, is invested for n years at an interest rate of i percent, compounded annually. The amount of money that will have accumulated after n years, F, can be determined by the well-known formula (the so-called *law of compound interest*)

$$F = P\,(1 + i\,/\,100)^n$$

The ratio F/P is often tabulated as a function of the interest rate and the number of years. Thus the future value, F, can be determined as the product of the present value, P, and the tabulated value F/P; i.e.,

$$F = P \times (F/P)$$

Let us generate a table of compound interest factors for interest rates of 5, 6, 7, 8, 9, 10, 11 and 12 percent, and for periods of 1 through 20 years. To do so, we will utilize a nested loop structure, with an outer loop to generate successive rows for $n = 1$ to 20, and an inner loop to generate the columns within each row for $i = 5, 6, \ldots, 12$.

We begin by defining the following variables.

`factor` = a real variable that represents the calculated value of F/P

i = an integer variable that represents the interest rate, expressed as a percentage

n = an integer variable that represents the number of years

The computation will proceed as follows.

1. Write out a heading containing n and the various interest rates.

2. Do the following for consecutive values of n ranging from 1 to 20.

    (*a*) Write the current value of n.

    (*b*) Within each row, do the following for consecutive values of i ranging from 5 to 12.

        (*i*)   Calculate the value of F/P and assign it to `factor`.

        (*ii*) Write out the current value of `factor`.

    (*c*) Skip to the next line (with an empty writeln statement).

Here is the complete Pascal program.

```
PROGRAM compoundinterest;

(* generate a table of compound interest factors *)

VAR i,n  : integer;
    factor : real;
BEGIN   (* action statements *)
    write('  n     5%        6%        7%        8%');
    writeln('      9%       10%       11%       12%');
    writeln;
    FOR n := 1 TO 20 DO
       BEGIN                   (* generate successive rows *)
          write(n:3);
          FOR i := 5 TO 12 DO
             BEGIN                (* generate entries within each row *)
                factor := exp(n*ln(1+0.01*i));
                write(factor:9:5)
             END;
          writeln
       END
END.
```

Note that this program does not require any input data. Also, notice the manner in which the program uses nested FOR-type structures. In particular, observe that the inner structure is completely embedded in the outer structure and that each structure has its own control variable.

The output generated by this program is shown below.

n	5%	6%	7%	8%	9%	10%	11%	12%
1	1.05000	1.06000	1.07000	1.08000	1.09000	1.10000	1.11000	1.12000
2	1.10250	1.12360	1.14490	1.16640	1.18810	1.21000	1.23210	1.25440
3	1.15763	1.19102	1.22504	1.25971	1.29503	1.33100	1.36763	1.40493
4	1.21551	1.26248	1.31080	1.36049	1.41158	1.46410	1.51807	1.57352
5	1.27628	1.33823	1.40255	1.46933	1.53862	1.61051	1.68506	1.76234
6	1.34010	1.41852	1.50073	1.58687	1.67710	1.77156	1.87041	1.97382
7	1.40710	1.50363	1.60578	1.71382	1.82804	1.94872	2.07616	2.21068
8	1.47746	1.59385	1.71819	1.85093	1.99256	2.14359	2.30454	2.47596
9	1.55133	1.68948	1.83846	1.99900	2.17189	2.35795	2.55804	2.77308
10	1.62889	1.79085	1.96715	2.15892	2.36736	2.59374	2.83942	3.10585
11	1.71034	1.89830	2.10485	2.33164	2.58043	2.85312	3.15176	3.47855
12	1.79586	2.01220	2.25219	2.51817	2.81266	3.13843	3.49845	3.89598
13	1.88565	2.13293	2.40985	2.71962	3.06580	3.45227	3.88328	4.36349
14	1.97993	2.26090	2.57853	2.93719	3.34173	3.79750	4.31044	4.88711
15	2.07893	2.39656	2.75903	3.17217	3.64248	4.17725	4.78459	5.47357
16	2.18287	2.54035	2.95216	3.42594	3.97031	4.59497	5.31089	6.13039
17	2.29202	2.69277	3.15882	3.70002	4.32763	5.05447	5.89509	6.86604
18	2.40662	2.85434	3.37993	3.99602	4.71712	5.55992	6.54355	7.68997
19	2.52695	3.02560	3.61653	4.31570	5.14166	6.11591	7.26334	8.61276
20	2.65330	3.20714	3.86968	4.66096	5.60441	6.72750	8.06231	9.64629

The generality of this program can be increased considerably by allowing the values of n to range from 1 to nmax and by allowing the values of i to range from i1 to i2 in increments of i3, where nmax, i1, i2 and i3 are input quantities. You are encouraged to make this modification as a programming exercise.

6.6 THE IF STRUCTURE

The IF structure is a conditional control structure that allows some action to be taken only if a given logical condition has a specified value (either true or false).

This structure has two different forms. The simpler form is

```
IF boolean expression THEN statement
```

This structure is often referred to as the IF – THEN structure. The statement-part of the structure will be executed if and only if the boolean expression is true. If the boolean statement is false, then the statement-part of the structure will be ignored. The statement itself can be either simple or structured, though it is often a compound statement.

EXAMPLE 6.11

Some examples of the IF – THEN structure are shown below.

```
IF count <= 100 THEN count := count+1;

IF tag = '*' THEN BEGIN writeln(accountno); credit := 0 END;
```

```
IF test THEN BEGIN
                x := 100;
                test := false
           END;


IF (balance < 1000.0) OR (status = 'R') THEN writeln(balance);
```

In the first example, the integer variable `count` will be increased by 1 if its current value does not exceed 100. The second example causes the value of `accountno` to be displayed, and a value of 0 to be assigned to `credit` if an `'*'` has been assigned to the char-type variable `tag`. Notice that this example includes a compound statement.

The third example includes both a boolean variable (`test`) and a compound statement. If `test` is originally true, then a value of 100 is assigned to `x` and `test` is set to false.

In the last example, the value of `balance` is written out if its value is less than 1000.0 or if the char-type variable `status` represents the character `'R'` (or both).

Finally, notice that there are no semicolons included in the IF – THEN structure, except within the compound statements.

The second form of the IF structure is

IF *boolean expression* THEN *statement1* ELSE *statement2*

This is frequently referred to as the IF – THEN – ELSE structure. In this case, *statement1* will be executed if the boolean expression is true; otherwise, *statement2* will be executed. Notice that one statement or the other is always executed (but never both statements). Again, the individual statements may be either simple or structured, and are often compound statements.

Semicolons should not appear in an IF – THEN – ELSE structure, except as separators within a compound statement. Beginners sometimes make the mistake of placing a semicolon before the keyword ELSE. This should be avoided, as it will result in a compilation error.

EXAMPLE 6.12

Here are several examples illustrating the use of the IF – THEN – ELSE structure.

```
IF status='S' THEN tax := 0.20*pay ELSE tax := 0.14*pay;

IF tag = '*' THEN BEGIN writeln(accountno); credit := 0 END
           ELSE credit := 1000;

IF circle THEN BEGIN
                readln(radius);
                area := 3.141593*sqr(radius);
                writeln(' Area of circle=',area)
           END
        ELSE BEGIN
                readln(length, width);
                area := length*width;
                writeln(' Area of rectangle=',area)
           END;
```

In the first example the value of `tax` is determined in one of two possible ways, depending on the value that is assigned to the char-type variable `status`.

The second example looks for certain "tagged" accounts. If an account is tagged (i.e., if an ' * ' is assigned to the char-type variable `tag`), then the account number is displayed and the credit limit is set to zero; otherwise the credit limit is set at 1000.

The third example shows how an area can be calculated for either of two different geometries. If the boolean-type variable `circle` is true, then the radius of a circle is read into the computer, the area is calculated and then displayed. If `circle` is false, then the length and width of a rectangle are read into the computer, the area is calculated and then displayed.

Notice once again that there are no semicolons in the IF – THEN – ELSE structure, except as separators in the compound statements.

IF structures can be nested within one another, just as any other control structure. Some of the forms that nested IF structures can take on are shown below.

The most general form of two-layer nesting is

```
IF be1 THEN IF be2 THEN s1 ELSE s2
        ELSE IF be3 THEN s3 ELSE s4
```

where *be1*, *be2* and *be3* represent boolean expressions, and *s1*, *s2*, *s3* and *s4* represent statements. In this situation, one complete IF – THEN – ELSE structure will be executed if *be1* is true, and another will be executed if *be1* is false. It is, of course, possible that *s1*, *s2*, *s3* and *s4* will contain other IF – THEN – ELSE structures. We would then have multi-layer nesting.

Some other forms of two-layer nesting are

```
IF be1 THEN s1
        ELSE IF be2 THEN s2 ELSE s3

IF be1 THEN IF be2 THEN s1 ELSE s2
        ELSE s3

IF be1 THEN IF be2 THEN s1 ELSE s2
```

In each of the first two cases, the subordinate nature of the inner IF – THEN – ELSE structure is indicated by the line on which it is written. In the last case, however, it is not clear which boolean expression is associated with the ELSE clause. The answer is *be2*. Thus, this last example is equivalent to

```
IF be1 THEN BEGIN
            IF be2 THEN s1 ELSE s2
        END
```

If we should want to associate the ELSE clause with *be1* rather than *be2*, we could write

```
IF be1 THEN BEGIN
            IF be2 THEN s1
        END
    ELSE s2
```

or

```
IF be1 THEN BEGIN IF be2 THEN s1 END
    ELSE s2
```

Clearly, this type of nesting must be carried out carefully in order to avoid possible ambiguities.

EXAMPLE 6.13 Encoding Characters

Let us write a simple Pascal program that will read in an ASCII character and then display an encoded character in its place. If the character is a letter or a digit, then replace it with the next character in the sequence, except that Z should be replaced by A, z by a, and 9 by 0. Thus 1 becomes 2, C becomes D, p becomes q, and so on. Any character other than a letter or a digit should be replaced by an asterisk (*). Continue the computation until an asterisk is entered as the input character. (The asterisk should be interpreted as a stopping condition.)

In order to outline the program, let us define the following variables.

  charin = a char-type variable that represents the input character

charout = a char-type variable that represents the output character

    flag = a boolean variable that indicates whether or not to continue the looping action.

The computation will proceed as follows.

1. Assign a value of true to flag.

2. Repeat the following steps until the value of flag becomes false.

    (a) Read in a value for charin

    (b) If charin represents an asterisk (*), set flag to false. Otherwise, determine if charin represents a letter or a digit.

        (i) If charin represents a letter or a digit, set charout to its appropriate value.

        (ii) If charin represents some other character, let charout represent an asterisk (*).

        (iii) Display the newly assigned value of charout.

The corresponding Pascal program is shown below.

```
PROGRAM charactercode;

(* REPLACE INPUT CHARACTERS WITH EQUIVALENT ENCODED CHARACTERS *)

VAR charin,charout : char;
    flag : boolean;

BEGIN
    flag := true;
    REPEAT
        write(' Enter character: ');
        readln(charin);
        IF charin = '*'    (* stopping criterion *)
            THEN flag := false
            ELSE BEGIN      (* character replacement *)
                    IF ((charin >= '0') AND (charin < '9')) OR
                       ((charin >= 'A') AND (charin < 'Z')) OR
                       ((charin >= 'a') AND (charin < 'z'))
                    THEN charout := succ(charin)
                    ELSE IF charin = '9'
                            THEN charout := '0'
                            ELSE IF charin = 'Z'
                                    THEN charout := 'A'
                                    ELSE IF charin = 'z'
                                            THEN charout := 'a'
                                            ELSE charout := '*';
                    writeln('   New character: ',charout);
                    writeln
                END
    UNTIL flag = false
END.
```

Notice that the program contains several IF – THEN – ELSE statements, with multiple levels of nesting. Also, notice that we have chosen to use the REPEAT – UNTIL structure to carry out the looping action. We could just as easily have selected WHILE – DO.

Execution of this program generates the following representative output. The user's responses are underlined.

```
Enter character: f
   New character: g

Enter character: z
   New character: a

Enter character: P
   New character: Q

Enter character: 5
   New character: 6

Enter character: 9
   New character: 0

Enter character: ?
   New character: *

Enter character: *
```

EXAMPLE 6.14 Solution of an Algebraic Equation

For those of you who are mathematically inclined, this example illustrates how computers are used to solve algebraic equations that cannot be solved by more elementary methods. Consider, for example, the equation

$$x^5 + 3x^2 - 10 = 0$$

This equation cannot be rearranged to yield an exact solution for x. Hence we will determine the solution by a repeated trial-and-error procedure (i.e., an *iterative* procedure) that successively refines an initially crude guess.

We begin by rearranging the equation into the form

$$x = (10 - 3x^2)^{1/5}$$

Our procedure will then be to guess a value for x, substitute this value into the right-hand side of the rearranged equation and thus calculate a new value for x. If this new value is equal to the old value (or very nearly so), then we will have obtained the solution to the equation. Otherwise, this new value will be substituted into the right-hand side, and still another value obtained for x, and so on. This procedure will continue until either the successive values of x have become sufficiently close (i.e., until the computation has *converged*), or a specified number of iterations has been exceeded (thus preventing the computation from continuing indefinitely in the event that the computed results do not converge).

To see how the method works, suppose we choose an initial value of $x = 1.0$. Substituting this value into the right-hand side of the equation, we obtain

$$x = [10 - 3(1.0)^2]^{1/5} = 1.47577$$

We then substitute this new value of x into the equation, resulting in

$$x = [10 - 3(1.47577)^2]^{1/5} = 1.28225$$

Continuing the procedure, we obtain

$$x = [10 - 3(1.28225)^2]^{1/5} = 1.38344$$
$$x = [10 - 3(1.38344)^2]^{1/5} = 1.33613$$

and so on. Notice that the successive values of x appear to be converging to some final answer.

The success of the method depends on the value chosen for the initial guess. If this value is too large in magnitude, then the quantity in brackets will be negative, and a negative number cannot be raised to a fractional power. Therefore we should test for a negative value of $10 - 3x^2$ whenever we substitute a new value of x into the right-hand side.

In order to write a program outline, let us define the following symbols.

count = an iteration counter (count will increase by one unit at each successive iteration)

guess = the value of x substituted into the right-hand side of the equation

root = the newly calculated value of x

test = the quantity $(10 - 3x^2)$

error = the absolute difference between root and guess

flag = a boolean variable that signifies whether or not to continue the iteration

The computation will continue until one of the following conditions is satisfied.

1. The value of error becomes less than 0.00001 (in which case we will have obtained a converged solution).
2. Fifty iterations have been completed (i.e., count = 50).
3. test takes on a negative value (in which case the computation cannot be continued).

We will monitor the progress of the computation by writing out each successive value of root.

We can now write the following program outline.

1. Initialize the variables flag and count (assign true to flag, and 0 to count).

2. Read in a value for the initial guess (guess).

3. Carry out the following looping procedure, while flag remains true.

   (a) Increment the counter (increase its value by 1).

   (b) Assign false to flag if the new value of the counter equals 50. (This signifies the last pass through the loop.)

   (c) Evaluate test. If this value is positive, proceed as follows.

       (i) Calculate a new value for root; then write out the current value for count, followed by the current value for root.

       (ii) Evaluate error (the absolute difference between root and guess). If this value is greater than 0.00001, then assign the value of root to guess and proceed with another iteration. Otherwise write out the current values of root and count, and set flag to false (the current value of root will be considered to be the desired solution).

   (d) If the value of test is not positive, then the computation cannot proceed. Hence, write an appropriate error message ("Numbers out of range") and set flag to false.

4. Upon completion of the looping action, write an appropriate error message ("Convergence not obtained") if count has a value of 50 and the value of error is greater than 0.00001.

Now let us express the program outline in the form of pseudo code, in order to simplify the transition from a general outline to a working Pascal program.

```
PROGRAM equation;

(* variable declarations *)

BEGIN

(* initialize flag and count *)

(* read guess *)
```

```
        WHILE flag DO
           BEGIN

              (* increment count *)

              IF count = 50 THEN flag := false;

              (* evaluate test *)

              IF test > 0 THEN BEGIN (* another iteration *)

                              (* evaluate root *)

                              (* write count and root *)

                              (* evaluate error *)

                          IF error > 0.00001 THEN guess := root
                                              ELSE BEGIN

                                                       flag := false;

                                                       (* write final answer -
                                                            root and count *)

                                                   END

                        END
                 ELSE BEGIN
                          flag := false;

                          (* write error message *)

                      END
           END;

           IF (count = 50) AND (error > 0.00001) THEN    (* write error message *)
        END.
```

Here is the complete Pascal program.

```
        PROGRAM equation;

        (* DETERMINE THE ROOTS OF AN ALGEBRAIC EQUATION
           USING AN ITERATIVE PROCEDURE *)

        VAR count : integer;
            guess,root,test,error : real;
            flag : boolean;
        BEGIN
           flag := true;    (* Initialize *)
           count := 0;
           write(' Initial guess= ');    (* Begin input routine *)
           readln(guess);
           writeln;
```

(Program continues on next page)

```
        WHILE flag DO    (* Begin main loop *)
            BEGIN
                count := count+1;
                IF count = 50 THEN flag := false;
                test := 10-3*sqr(guess);

                IF test > 0
                    THEN BEGIN   (* Another iteration *)
                            root := exp(0.2*ln(test));
                            write(' Iteration number ',count:2);
                            writeln('   x= ',root:7:5);
                            error := abs(root-guess);
                            IF error > 0.00001
                                THEN guess := root
                                ELSE BEGIN   (* Write final answer *)
                                        flag := false;
                                        writeln;
                                        write(' Root= ',root:7:5);
                                        writeln('   No. of iterations= ',count:2)
                                    END
                        END
                    ELSE BEGIN   (* Error message *)
                            flag := false;
                            writeln;
                            write(' Numbers out of range - ');
                            writeln('try again using another initial guess')
                        END
            END;

        IF (count = 50) AND (error > 0.00001) (* Error message *)
            THEN BEGIN
                    writeln;
                    writeln(' Convergence not obtained after 50 iterations')
                END
    END.
```

The program includes a number of control structures, some of which are nested. In particular, the actual iteration is controlled by a WHILE – DO structure, though a REPEAT – UNTIL structure could have been used instead. In addition, several IF – THEN and IF – THEN – ELSE structures are included within the program.

Notice the statement

```
    root := exp(0.2*ln(test))
```

near the middle of the program. This statement is required in order to raise the value of test to the 1/5 power. (Remember that Pascal does not include an exponentiation operator.) Thus, we obtain the natural log of test, multiply by 0.2, and then raise e to a power equal to the resulting product.

The output that is generated for an initial guess of x = 1 is shown below. (The user's responses are underlined.) Notice that the computation has converged to the solution x = 1.35196 after 16 iterations. The output shows the successive values of x becoming closer and closer, leading to the final converged solution.

```
Initial guess= 1

Iteration number  1   x=  1.47577
```

```
Iteration number  2   x=  1.28225
Iteration number  3   x=  1.38344
Iteration number  4   x=  1.33613
Iteration number  5   x=  1.35952
Iteration number  6   x=  1.34826
Iteration number  7   x=  1.35375
Iteration number  8   x=  1.35109
Iteration number  9   x=  1.35238
Iteration number 10   x=  1.35175
Iteration number 11   x=  1.35206
Iteration number 12   x=  1.35191
Iteration number 13   x=  1.35198
Iteration number 14   x=  1.35195
Iteration number 15   x=  1.35196
Iteration number 16   x=  1.35196

Root= 1.35196   No. of iterations= 16
```

Now suppose that a value of $x = 10$ is selected as an initial guess. This value generates a negative value for test in the first iteration. Therefore the output would appear as follows.

```
Initial guess= 10

Numbers out of range - try again using another initial guess
```

It is interesting to see what happens when the initial guess is once again chosen as $x = 1$, but the maximum number of iterations is changed from 50 to 10. Try this yourself and notice what happens.

6.7 THE CASE STRUCTURE

The CASE structure is a conditional control structure that allows some particular group of statements to be chosen from several available groups. The selection will be based upon the current value of an expression, referred to as the *selector*.

The general form of the CASE structure is

```
CASE expression OF
      case label list1 : statement1;
      case label list2 : statement2;
                .
                .
                .
      case label listn : statementn
END
```

The expression can be any simple-type expression other than real. It often takes the form of a single simple-type variable.

Each of the case labels represents one of the permissible values of the expression. Thus, if the expression is of type integer, the case labels would represent integer values that fall within the permissible range. The case labels need not appear in any particular order, though each of the case labels must be unique. Moreover, each label can appear in only one list. (*Note*: these labels are referred to as *case labels* to distinguish them from a different type of label, which we will discuss in the next section.)

The statements can be either simple or structured. The use of compound statements is quite common. Null (empty) statements are also permitted, to indicate that no action is to be taken for certain values of the selector. The statements need not be unique (that is, the same statement may be used with two or more lists of case labels).

A statement will be executed if (and only if) one of its corresponding case labels matches the current value of the expression. Thus, the current value of the expression determines which of the statements will be executed. If the current value of the expression does not match any of the labels, then the action will be ignored (in Turbo Pascal) or undefined (ANSI Pascal).

EXAMPLE 6.15

A typical CASE structure involving the use of a char-type selector is illustrated below.

```
VAR choice : char;

. . . . .

CASE choice OF
    'R' : writeln(' RED ');
    'W' : writeln(' WHITE ');
    'B' : writeln(' BLUE ')
END;
```

In this example RED will be displayed if R is assigned to choice, WHITE will appear if W is assigned to choice, and BLUE will be displayed if B is assigned to choice. No output will be generated if choice is assigned some character other than R, W or B.

Here is another typical CASE structure, involving the use of a numerical expression as a selector.

```
VAR x,y : real;

. . . . .

CASE trunc(x/10) OF
    1 : y := y+5;
  3,5 : y := y-2;
    6 : y := 2*(y+1);
  2,4 : ;
    9 : y := 0
END;
```

In this example the value of x/10 is truncated and hence converted to an integer. If this integer (the selector) equals 1, then y will be increased by 5. Similarly, y will be decreased by 2 if the selector equals either 3 or 5; y will be assigned the value of 2*(y+1) if the selector equals 6; and it will be assigned 0 if the selector equals 9. The value of y will remain unchanged if the selector equals 2 or 4. The action will be undefined for all other values of the selector.

Some versions of Pascal allow a clause that specifies what action is to be taken if the value of the selector does not match any of the case labels. In Turbo Pascal, for example, an ELSE clause can be included as a part of the CASE structure.

EXAMPLE 6.16

Here is a variation of the first CASE structure shown in the previous example, as it might appear in Turbo Pascal.

```
    VAR choice : char;

    . . . . .

    CASE choice OF
        'R' : writeln(' RED ');
        'W' : writeln(' WHITE ');
        'B' : writeln(' BLUE ')
    ELSE
        writeln(' ERROR - Please try again ')
    END;
```

Now RED will be displayed if R is assigned to choice, WHITE will appear if W is assigned to choice, and BLUE will be displayed if B is assigned to choice, as before. However, if a character other than R, W or B is assigned to choice, the message ERROR - Please try again will be displayed.

In a practical sense, the CASE structure may be thought of as an alternative to the use of nested IF – THEN – ELSE structures. However, it can only replace those IF – THEN – ELSE structures that test for equalities. In such situations, the use of the CASE structure is usually more convenient. It is particularly convenient for creating responses to menu selections, as seen in the following example.

EXAMPLE 6.17 Calculating Depreciation

Let us consider how to calculate the yearly depreciation for some depreciable item (e.g., a building, a machine, etc.). There are three commonly used methods for calculating depreciation, known as the *straight-line* method, the *double declining balance* method, and the *sum-of-the-years'-digits* method. We wish to write a Pascal program that will allow us to select any one of these methods for each set of calculations.

The computation will begin by reading in the original (undepreciated) value of the item, the life of the item (i.e., the number of years over which it will be depreciated) and an integer that indicates which method will be used. The yearly depreciation and the remaining (undepreciated) value of the item will then be calculated and displayed for each year.

The straight-line method is the easiest to use. In this method the original value of the item is divided by its life (total number of years). The resulting quotient will be the amount by which the item depreciates each year. For example, if an $8000 item is to be depreciated over 10 years, then the annual depreciation would be $8000/10 = $800, so that the item would decrease by $800 each year. Notice that the annual depreciation is the same each year.

When using the double declining balance method, the value of the item will decrease by a constant *percentage* each year. (Hence the actual amount of the depreciation, in dollars, will vary from one year to the next.) To obtain the depreciation factor we divide 2 by the life of the item. This factor is multiplied by the value of the item *at the beginning of each year* (not the *original* value of the item) to obtain the annual depreciation.

Suppose, for example, that we wish to depreciate an $8000 item over 10 years, using the double declining balance method. The depreciation factor will be 2/10 = 0.20. Hence the depreciation for the first year will be 0.20 × $8000 = $1600. The second year's depreciation will be 0.20 × ($8000 - $1600) = 0.20 × $6400 = $1280; the third year's depreciation will be 0.20 × $5120 = $1024; and so on.

In the sum-of-the-years'-digits method the value of the item will decrease by a percentage that is different each year. The depreciation factor will be a fraction whose denominator is the sum of the digits from 1 to n, where n represents the life of the item. (For a 10-year lifetime, the denominator will be $1 + 2 + 3 + . . . + 10 = 55$.) For the first year the numerator will be n, for the second year it will be $(n-1)$, for the third year $(n-2)$, and so on. The yearly depreciation is obtained by multiplying the depreciation factor by the *original* value of the item.

To see how the sum-of-the-years'-digits method works, we again depreciate an $8000 item over 10 years. The depreciation for the first year will be $(10/55) × $8000 = 1454.55; for the second year it will be $(9/55) × $8000 = 1309.09, and so on.

Now let us define the following symbols.

val = the value of the item

tag = the original value of the item (i.e., the original value of val)

deprec = the annual depreciation

n = the number of years over which the item will be depreciated

year = a counter ranging from 1 to n

choice = an integer indicating which method to use

flag = a boolean variable indicating whether or not to perform another set of calculations

Our Pascal program will follow the outline presented below.

1. Declare all variables.

2. Assign the value true to flag.

3. Repeat all of the following steps, until flag becomes false.

(*a*) Read a value for choice (either 1, 2, 3 or 4, indicating what kind of calculation is to be carried out).

(*b*) If choice is not assigned a value of 4, then read values for val and n.

(*c*) If choice is assigned a value of 1, 2 or 3, calculate the yearly depreciation and the new value of the item by the appropriate method (determined by the value of choice), and display the results on a year-by-year basis. Otherwise (choice=4), set flag to false, display a message and end the computation.

Now let's express this outline in pseudo code.

```
PROGRAM depreciation1;

(* variable declarations *)

BEGIN

(* initialize flag *)

    REPEAT

        (* read choice *)

        IF choice <> 4 THEN (* read val and n *)

        CASE choice OF
            1 : BEGIN

                    (* write heading: Straight-Line Method *)

                    deprec := val/n;
                    FOR year := 1 TO n DO
                        BEGIN
                            val := val-deprec;

                            (* write year, deprec, val *)

                        END

                END;
            2 : BEGIN

                    (* write heading: Double Declining Balance Method *)

                    FOR year := 1 TO n DO
                        BEGIN
                            deprec := 2*val/n;
                            val := val-deprec;
```

```
                        (* write year, deprec, val *)

                    END
                END;
            3 : BEGIN

                    (* write heading: Sum-of-the-Years'-Digits Method *)

                    tag := val;
                    FOR year := 1 TO n DO
                        BEGIN
                            deprec := (n-year+1)*tag/(n*(n+1)/2);
                            val := val-deprec;

                            (* write year, deprec, val *)

                        END
                END;
            4 : BEGIN

                    (* write message *)

                    flag := false;
                END
        END
    UNTIL flag = false
END.
```

Most of the pseudo code is straightforward, though a few comments are in order. First, we see that a REPEAT – UNTIL structure is used to repeat the entire set of calculations. Within this overall structure, the CASE structure is used to select a particular depreciation method. Each depreciation method uses a FOR structure to loop through the entire n-year lifetime of the item.

The calculation of the depreciation for the sum-of-the-years'-digits method appears somewhat obscure. In particular, the term (n-year+1) in the numerator requires some explanation. This quantity is used to count backward (from n down to 1), as year progresses forward (from 1 to n). These declining values are required by the sum-of-the-years'-digits method. We could have set up a backward-counting loop instead (i.e., FOR year := n DOWNTO 1 DO), but then we would have required an additional forward-counting loop to display the yearly depreciations in the proper order.

At this point it is not difficult to write a complete Pascal program, as shown below.

```
PROGRAM depreciation1;

(* CALCULATE DEPRECIATION INTERACTIVELY,
   USING ONE OF THREE POSSIBLE METHODS *)

VAR n,choice,year : integer;
    val,deprec,tag : real;
    flag : boolean;

BEGIN   (* action statements *)
    flag := true;
    REPEAT    (* Begin input routine *)
        writeln;
        writeln;
        write(' Method: (1-SL  2-DDB  3-SYD  4-End) ');
        readln(choice);
        IF choice <> 4 THEN
        BEGIN
            write(' Original value: ');
```

```
            readln(val);
            write(' Number of years: ');
            readln(n);
            writeln
        END;

        CASE choice OF

            1 : BEGIN   (* SL *)
                    writeln(' Straight-Line Method');
                    writeln;
                    deprec := val/n;
                    FOR year := 1 TO n DO
                        BEGIN
                            val := val-deprec;
                            write(' End of Year ',year:2);
                            write('   Depreciation: ',deprec:5:0);
                            writeln('   Current Value: ',val:6:0)
                        END
                END;

            2 : BEGIN   (* DDB *)
                    writeln(' Double Declining Balance Method');
                    writeln;
                    FOR year := 1 TO n DO
                        BEGIN
                            deprec := 2*val/n;
                            val := val-deprec;
                            write(' End of Year ',year:2);
                            write('   Depreciation: ',deprec:5:0);
                            writeln('   Current Value: ',val:6:0)
                        END
                END;

            3 : BEGIN   (* SYD *)
                    writeln(' Sum-of-the-Years''-Digits Method');
                    writeln;
                    tag := val;
                    FOR year := 1 TO n DO
                        BEGIN
                            deprec := (n-year+1)*tag/(n*(n+1)/2);
                            val := val-deprec;
                            write(' End of Year ',year:2);
                            write('   Depreciation: ',deprec:5:0);
                            writeln('   Current Value: ',val:6:0)
                        END
                END;

            4 : BEGIN   (* end computation *)
                    writeln(' Bye, have a nice day!');
                    flag := false;
                END
        END   (* choice *)
    UNTIL flag = false
END.
```

The program generates a menu with four choices, to calculate the depreciation using one of the three methods or to end the computation. The computer will continue to accept new sets of input data, and carry out the appropriate calculations for each data set, until a value of 4 is selected from the menu.

Some representative output is shown below. In each case, an $8000 item is depreciated over a 10-year period, using one of the three methods. The computation is then terminated in response to the last menu selection. The user's responses are underlined for clarity.

```
Method: (1-SL  2-DDB  3-SYD  4-End) 1
Original value: 8000
Number of years: 10

Straight-Line Method

End of Year  1     Depreciation:     800.   Current Value:     7200.
End of Year  2     Depreciation:     800.   Current Value:     6400.
End of Year  3     Depreciation:     800.   Current Value:     5600.
End of Year  4     Depreciation:     800.   Current Value:     4800.
End of Year  5     Depreciation:     800.   Current Value:     4000.
End of Year  6     Depreciation:     800.   Current Value:     3200.
End of Year  7     Depreciation:     800.   Current Value:     2400.
End of Year  8     Depreciation:     800.   Current Value:     1600.
End of Year  9     Depreciation:     800.   Current Value:     800.
End of Year 10     Depreciation:     800.   Current Value:     0.


Method: (1-SL  2-DDB  3-SYD  4-End) 2
Original value: 8000
Number of years: 10

Double Declining Balance Method

End of Year  1     Depreciation:    1600.   Current Value:     6400.
End of Year  2     Depreciation:    1280.   Current Value:     5120.
End of Year  3     Depreciation:    1024.   Current Value:     4096.
End of Year  4     Depreciation:     819.   Current Value:     3277.
End of Year  5     Depreciation:     655.   Current Value:     2621.
End of Year  6     Depreciation:     524.   Current Value:     2097.
End of Year  7     Depreciation:     419.   Current Value:     1678.
End of Year  8     Depreciation:     336.   Current Value:     1342.
End of Year  9     Depreciation:     268.   Current Value:     1074.
End of Year 10     Depreciation:     215.   Current Value:     859.


Method: (1-SL  2-DDB  3-SYD  4-End) 3
Original value: 8000
Number of years: 10

Sum-of-the-Years'-Digits Method

End of Year  1     Depreciation:    1455.   Current Value:     6545.
End of Year  2     Depreciation:    1309.   Current Value:     5236.
End of Year  3     Depreciation:    1164.   Current Value:     4073.
```

```
End of Year  4      Depreciation:      1018.  Current Value:      3055.
End of Year  5      Depreciation:       873.  Current Value:      2182.
End of Year  6      Depreciation:       727.  Current Value:      1455.
End of Year  7      Depreciation:       582.  Current Value:       873.
End of Year  8      Depreciation:       436.  Current Value:       436.
End of Year  9      Depreciation:       291.  Current Value:       145.
End of Year 10      Depreciation:       145.  Current Value:         0.


Method: (1-SL  2-DDB  3-SYD  4-End) 4
Bye, have a nice day!
```

Notice that the last two methods result in a large annual depreciation during the early years, but a very small annual depreciation in the last few years of the item's lifetime. Also, we see that the item has a value of zero at the end of its lifetime when using the first and third methods, but a small value remains undepreciated when using the double declining balance method.

6.8 THE GOTO STATEMENT

The GOTO statement is a simple-type statement that is used to alter the sequence of program execution by transferring control (i.e., by *jumping*) to some remote part of the program. The form of the GOTO statement is

```
GOTO statement label
```

where *statement label* represents a positive integer, not greater than 9999.

EXAMPLE 6.18

Several typical GOTO statements are shown below.

```
GOTO 100;

IF flag THEN GOTO 9999;

IF sum > 100.0 THEN
    BEGIN
        writeln(sum);
        GOTO 35
    END;

IF char = '*' THEN GOTO 200 ELSE GOTO 300;
```

Each statement label must be declared before it can be utilized within a program. (Recall that the label declarations must *precede* the constant and variable declarations, as described in Sections 1.5 and 5.2.) Label declarations are of the form

```
LABEL statement label1, statement label2, . . .
```

where *statement label1, statement label2*, etc. represent the individual statement labels. (Note the distinction between *statement* labels and *case* labels, discussed in the last section. In particular, note that statement labels are restricted to positive integers whereas case labels are not so restricted, and that statement labels must be declared before they can be used whereas case labels are not declared.)

EXAMPLE 6.19

Here is a portion of a Pascal program that contains a label declaration.

```
PROGRAM sample;
LABEL 100,200,300;
CONST factor = 0.5;
VAR a,b,c : real;
```

Notice that the label declaration follows the program statement and precedes the constant definition, as required.

Labeled statements are written in the form

statement label : *statement*

Such statements may precede or follow their corresponding GOTO statements.

EXAMPLE 6.20

Several Pascal statements are shown below. Each contains a statement label.

```
10 : readln(a,b,c);

20 : FOR count := 1 TO n DO
        BEGIN
           . . . . .
        END;

99 : BEGIN
        writeln(sum);
        IF flag THEN writeln(x,y,z);
        writeln
     END;
```

Execution of the GOTO statement causes the program to transfer control to the corresponding labeled statement. Thus, the labeled statement will be the next statement to be executed.

A program may contain several different GOTO statements that transfer control to the same place (i.e., to the same remote statement) within the program. However, each labeled statement must have its own unique label (thus, no two "target" statements can have the same label).

EXAMPLE 6.21

A portion of a Pascal program is shown below.

```
PROGRAM sample;
LABEL 10,20;
CONST . . .;
VAR   . . .;
BEGIN
   . . . . .
  10 : readln(a,b,c);
         . . . . . .
        IF a <= 0 THEN GOTO 20;
         . . . . .
        GOTO 10;
         . . . . .
        IF flag THEN GOTO 20;
         . . . . .
  20 : writeln(x,y,z);
         . . . . .
END.
```

Notice that control can be transferred to statement 20 from two different places within the program. Both transfers are conditional; i.e., dependent upon some boolean expression being true.

In general, programs of this type should be avoided in Pascal. In fact, many of Pascal's features are specifically designed to eliminate the need for this type of program logic. (More about this later.)

Some care must be exercised when using the GOTO statement with compound statements. Control can be transferred *out of* or *within* a compound statement, and control can be transferred to the *beginning* of a compound statement. However, control *cannot* be transferred *into* a compound statement. Moreover, if control is transferred internally to the END of a compound statement (i.e., if the keyword END is labeled), then the label must be preceded by an empty (null) statement. This is accomplished by placing a semicolon at the end of the statement that precedes END.

Similar restrictions apply to the use of the GOTO statement with other control structures. Thus, control can be transferred within or out of a control structure, but not into a control structure.

Remember that the use of the GOTO statement is discouraged in Pascal, since it alters the clear, sequential flow of logic that is characteristic of the language. In fact, some programmers advocate a total ban on the GOTO statement, though this is a bit extreme. There is widespread agreement, however, that the GOTO statement should be used very sparingly, and only when it is awkward to use another control structure. Actually, such situations are quite rare.

In practice, the GOTO statement is sometimes included in an IF structure to transfer control (conditionally) toward the end of a program. (The WHILE - DO and REPEAT - UNTIL structures are preferred for situations that require a transfer of control toward the beginning of a program.) Usually, such moves are made in conjunction with some *global* type of strategy (e.g., jumping to the end of the program if an input quantity is negative). On the other hand, a program should not under any circumstances include a large number of *localized* jumps, as this is precisely the type of sloppy program structure that Pascal was designed to avoid.

EXAMPLE 6.22 Averaging a List of Nonnegative Numbers

Let us again consider the problem of averaging a list of numbers, as in Examples 6.4, 6.5 and 6.8. Now, however, suppose that the length of the list is not known in advance. Rather, we will continue to read and sum successive input quantities, until a negative value is read into the computer. This negative number will be interpreted as a stopping criterion and will not be included in the average.

The calculations will be carried out in the following manner.

1. Assign a value of 0 to the integer variable `count`.

2. Assign a value of 0 to the real variable `sum`.

3. Assign the value `true` to the boolean variable `flag`.

4. Do the following steps repeatedly, while `flag` remains true.

    (*a*) Read in one of the numbers in the list. (Each number will be represented by the real variable `x`.)

    (*b*) If the value of `x` is negative, GOTO step 5 below. Otherwise, add the value of `x` to `sum` and increase the value of `count` by 1.

5. Divide `sum` by `count` to obtain the desired average.

6. Write out the values of `count` and `sum`.

The corresponding Pascal program is shown below.

```
PROGRAM average5;

(* CALCULATE THE AVERAGE OF A LIST OF NUMBERS
   USING THE WHILE - DO STRUCTURE AND A GOTO STATEMENT *)

LABEL 10;

VAR count : integer;
    x,sum,average : real;
    flag : boolean;

BEGIN   (* action statements *)
    count := 0;
    sum := 0;
    flag := true;
    writeln('To STOP, enter a negative number');
    WHILE flag DO
        BEGIN
            write('x = ');
            read(x);
            IF x < 0 THEN GOTO 10;
            sum := sum+x;
            count := count+1
        END;
10 : average := sum/count;
    writeln('The average of ',count:5,' numbers is ',average)
END.
```

Notice that `flag` remains true throughout this program. Thus, the repetition will continue indefinitely, until a negative value of `x` is entered into the computer. Once a negative value for `x` is detected, control is transferred out of the loop, to statement 10. The desired average is then calculated and written out.

You should try to program this problem without the use of the GOTO statement (see Problem 6.45 at the end of this chapter). Such a program can be written, but it is somewhat more awkward than with the GOTO statement.

Review Questions

6.1   What is meant by repetition?

6.2   What is conditional looping? What is unconditional looping? In what ways do conditional looping and unconditional looping differ from one another?

6.3   What is meant by conditional execution?

6.4   What is meant by selection?

6.5   What values can be represented by a boolean expression?

6.6   Summarize the rules associated with boolean expressions.

6.7   Summarize the differences between relational operators and logical operators. What types of operands are used with each type of operator?

6.8   What is the difference between simple and structured statements?

6.9   Name three different kinds of simple statements.

6.10   Summarize the syntactical rules associated with compound statements.

6.11   What is the purpose of the WHILE – DO structure? Where is the boolean expression evaluated? What is the minimum number of times the WHILE – DO structure will be executed?

6.12   How is execution of the WHILE – DO structure terminated?

6.13   Summarize the syntactical rules associated with the WHILE – DO structure.

6.14   What is the purpose of the REPEAT – UNTIL structure? How does it differ from the WHILE – DO structure?

6.15   What is the minimum number of times the REPEAT – UNTIL structure will be executed. Compare with the WHILE – DO structure and explain the reason for the differences.

6.16   Summarize the syntactical rules associated with the REPEAT – UNTIL structure. Compare with the WHILE – DO structure.

6.17   What is the purpose of the FOR structure? How does it differ from the WHILE – DO and the REPEAT – UNTIL structures?

6.18   How many times will a FOR structure be executed? Compare with the WHILE – DO and the REPEAT – UNTIL structures.

6.19   What is the purpose of the control variable in a FOR structure? What type of variable can this be?

6.20   Describe the two different forms of the FOR structure. What is the purpose of each?

6.21   Summarize the syntactical rules associated with FOR structures.

6.22   What rules apply to the nesting of control structures? Can one type of control structure be embedded within another?

6.23   What is the purpose of the IF structure? In what way is this structure fundamentally different from WHILE – DO, REPEAT – UNTIL and FOR?

6.24   Describe the two different forms of the IF structure. Fundamentally, how do they differ?

6.25   Summarize the syntactical rules associated with IF structures.

6.26   How are nested IF structures interpreted? In particular, how is the structure

         IF *be1* THEN IF *be2* THEN *s1* ELSE *s2*

interpreted? Which boolean expression is associated with the ELSE clause?

6.27   What is the purpose of the CASE structure? How does this structure differ from the other structures described in this chapter?

6.28   What is a selector? What purpose does it serve?

6.29   What values can be assigned to the case labels?

6.30   What happens when the value of the selector is the same as one of the labels? What happens when the value of the selector is not the same as any of the case labels?

6.31   Summarize the syntactical rules associated with the CASE structure. Can two or more labels be associated with one statement?

6.32   What additional selection features are available in Turbo Pascal?

6.33   Compare the use of the CASE structure with the use of nested IF – THEN – ELSE structures. Which is more convenient?

6.34   What is the purpose of the GOTO statement? Is this a simple or a structured statement?

6.35   Summarize the syntactical rules associated with statement labels. What values can be used as statement labels? How are they declared? How is a statement label associated with a remote ("target") statement?

6.36   Compare the syntax associated with statement labels with that of case labels. Note all differences.

6.37   Describe the restrictions that apply to the use of the GOTO statement with compound statements. Do these same restrictions apply when using the GOTO statement with other control structures?

6.38   Why is the use of the GOTO statement discouraged in Pascal? Under what conditions might the GOTO statement be helpful? What type of usage should be avoided, and why? Discuss thoroughly.

Problems

6.39   Determine the value of each of the following boolean expressions, assuming the identifiers are constants whose values are as follows: f = 300, p = –0.001, q = 0.001, c = '5'.

(a) 2*f >= 500

(f) (p = abs(q)) OR (c > 4)

(b) abs(p) = abs(q)

(g) sqr(p) < sqrt(q)

(c) c = 5

(h) (q < 0) OR ((f > 0) AND (f < 100))

(d) p + q > 0

(i) NOT (c < '7')

(e) (abs(p) = q) AND (c > '4')

6.40 Several control structures are outlined below. Some are written incorrectly. Identify all errors.

(a)
```
VAR result : real;
    . . . . .
    WHILE result > 0 DO
       BEGIN
          . . . . .
       END;
```

(f)
```
VAR a,b,c,d : integer;
    . . . . .
    FOR a := b DOWNTO d D
       BEGIN
          . . . . .
          FOR c := b TO d DO
             BEGIN
                . . . . .
             END
    END;
```

(b)
```
VAR a,b,c,d : integer;
    . . . . .
    REPEAT
       . . . . .
    UNTIL (a+b) > (2*c-d);
```

(c)
```
VAR x,n1,n2 : real;
    . . . . .
    FOR x := n1 TO n2 DO
       BEGIN
          . . . . .
       END;
```

(g)
```
VAR a,b,c,d : integer;
    . . . . .
    FOR b := a TO c DO
       BEGIN
          . . . . .
          FOR d := a TO b DO
             BEGIN
                . . . . .
             END
    END;
```

(d)
```
VAR x : char;
    . . . . .
    FOR x := 'z' DOWNTO 'a' DO
       BEGIN
          . . . . .
       END;
```

(e)
```
VAR a,b,c : integer;
    . . . . .
    FOR a := b TO c DO
       BEGIN
          . . . . .
       END;
```

(h)
```
VAR i,j : integer;
    x : real;
    flag : boolean;
    . . . . .
IF i < 0 THEN IF j > 10 THEN flag := true
                ELSE flag := false ELSE x := -0.1;
```

```
(i)  VAR flag : boolean;
          c : char;
     . . . .
     flag := true;
     WHILE flag DO
        BEGIN
           . . . . .
           REPEAT
              . . . . .
              read(c);
              IF c = '*' THEN flag := false;
              . . . . .
           UNTIL NOT flag
        END;


(j)  VAR x,y : real;
     . . . . .
     CASE sqr(x) OF
          1.0 : y := x;
          4.0 : y := 2*x;
          9.0 : y := 3*x;
         16.0 : y := 4*x
     END;


(k)  LABEL 10;
     VAR c : char;
        . . . . . .
     read(c);
     . . . . .
     IF c = '*' THEN GOTO 10;
     . . . . .
     WHILE c <> '*' DO
        BEGIN
           . . . . .
     10 : write(c);
           . . . . .
        END;


(l)  LABEL 1,2,3;
     VAR i : integer;
        . . . . .
     CASE i OF
        1 : BEGIN . . . GOTO 3 . . . END;
        2 : BEGIN . . . GOTO 3 . . . END;
        3 : BEGIN . . . END
     END;
```

6.41 Write a loop that will calculate the sum of each third integer, beginning with $i = 2$ (i.e., calculate the sum $2 + 5 + 8 + 11 + \cdots$) for all values of i that are less than 100. Write the loop three different ways:

(a)   using a WHILE - DO structure

(b)   using a REPEAT - UNTIL structure

(c)   using a FOR structure

6.42   Write a CASE structure that will examine the value of a char-type variable called `color` and print one of the following messages, depending on the character assigned to `color`.

(a)   RED, if either r or R is assigned to `color`

(b)   GREEN, if either g or G is assigned to `color`

(c)   BLUE, if either b or B is assigned to `color`

(d)   BLACK, if `color` is assigned any other character

6.43   Describe the output that is generated by each of the following Pascal programs.

(a)
```
PROGRAM sample;
VAR i,x : integer;
BEGIN
    i := 0;
    x := 0;
    WHILE i < 20 DO
        BEGIN
            IF (i MOD 5) = 0 THEN
                BEGIN
                    x := x + i;
                    write(x:3)
                END;
            i := i + 1
        END;
    writeln;
    writeln('x =',x:3)
END.
```

(b)
```
PROGRAM sample;
VAR i,x : integer;
BEGIN
    i := 0;
    x := 0;
    REPEAT
        IF (i MOD 5) = 0 THEN
            BEGIN
                x := x + 1;
                write(x:3)
            END;
        i := i + 1
    UNTIL i >= 20;
    writeln;
    writeln('x =',x:3)
END.
```

(c)
```
PROGRAM sample;
VAR i,x : integer;
BEGIN
    i := 0;
    x := 0;
    FOR i := 1 TO 20 DO
       BEGIN
          IF (i MOD 5) = 0 THEN
             BEGIN
                x := x + 1;
                write(x:3)
             END
       END;
    writeln;
    writeln('x =',x:3)
END.
```

(d)
```
PROGRAM sample;
VAR i,x : integer;
BEGIN
    i := 0;
    x := 0;
    FOR i := 1 TO 10 DO
       BEGIN
          IF (i MOD 2) = 1
             THEN
                x := x + i
             ELSE
                x := x - 1;
          write(x:3)
       END;
    writeln;
    writeln('x =',x:3)
END.
```

(e)
```
PROGRAM sample;
VAR i,j,x : integer;
BEGIN
    i := 1;
    x := 0;
    WHILE i < 5 DO
       BEGIN
          FOR j := 1 TO i DO
             BEGIN
                x := x + (i + j - 1);
                write(x:3)
             END;
          i := i + 1
       END;
    writeln;
    writeln('x =',x:3)
END.
```

```
(f)    PROGRAM sample;
       VAR i,j,x : integer;
       BEGIN
          x := 0;
          FOR i := 1 TO 5 DO
             BEGIN
                j := 1;
                WHILE j < i DO
                   BEGIN
                      x := x + (i + j - 1);
                      write(x:3);
                      j := j + 1
                   END
             END;
          writeln;
          writeln('x =',x:3)
       END.

(g)    PROGRAM sample;
       VAR i,j,x : integer;
       BEGIN
          i := 1;
          x := 0;
          WHILE i < 5 DO
             BEGIN
                j := 0;
                REPEAT
                   x := x + (i + j - 1);
                   write(x:3);
                   j := j + 1
                UNTIL j = i;
                i := i + 1
             END;
          writeln;
          writeln('x =',x:3)
       END.

(h)    PROGRAM sample;
       VAR i,j,k,x : integer;
       BEGIN
          x := 0;
          FOR i := 0 TO 4 DO
             FOR j := 0 TO i-1 DO
                BEGIN
                   k := (i + j - 1);
                   IF (k MOD 2) = 0
                      THEN x := x + k
                      ELSE IF (k MOD 3) = 0
                              THEN x := x + k - 2;
                   write(x:3);
                END;
          writeln;
          writeln('x =',x:3)
       END.
(i)    PROGRAM sample;
       VAR i,j,k,x : integer;
```

```
BEGIN
   x := 0;
   FOR i := 0 TO 4 DO
      FOR j := 0 TO i-1 DO
         BEGIN
            CASE (i+j-1) OF
               -1,0 : x := x + 1;
               1,2,3 : x := x + 2
               ELSE   x := x + 3
            END;
            write(x:3)
         END;
   writeln;
   writeln('x =',x:3)
END.
```

Programming Problems

6.44 Compile and execute the programs given in Examples 6.4, 6.5 and 6.8 using the following 10 numbers:

27.5	87.0
13.4	39.9
53.8	47.7
29.2	8.1
74.5	63.2

6.45 Modify the program given in Example 6.22, which averages a list of numbers whose length is unspecified, so that the GOTO statement is eliminated. Write the new program two different ways:

(*a*) Using a WHILE – DO structure

(*b*) Using a REPEAT – UNTIL structure

Test each version of the program using the data presented in the last problem.

6.46 Rewrite the depreciation program given in Example 6.17 to use the IF – THEN – ELSE structure instead of the CASE structure. Test the program using the data given in Example 6.17. Which version do you prefer? Why?

6.47 The equation

$$x^5 + 3x^2 - 10 = 0$$

which was presented in Example 6.14, can be rearranged into the form

$$x = \sqrt{(10 - x^5)/3}$$

Rewrite the Pascal program presented in Example 6.14 to make use of the above form of the equation. Run the program and compare the calculated results with those presented in Example 6.14. Why are the results different? (Do computers ever make mistakes?)

6.48 Modify the program given in Example 6.14, which solves for the roots of an algebraic equation, so that the WHILE – DO structure is replaced by a REPEAT – UNTIL structure. Which structure is best suited for this particular problem?

6.49 Modify the program given in Example 6.14, which solves for the roots of an algebraic equation, so that the WHILE – DO structure is replaced by a FOR – TO structure. Compare the use of the FOR – TO, WHILE – DO and REPEAT – UNTIL structures. Which version do you prefer, and why?

6.50 Write a complete Pascal program for each of the problems presented below. Use the most natural type of control structure for each problem. Begin with a detailed outline, then rewrite the outline in pseudo code if the translation into a working Pascal program is not entirely clear. Be sure to use good programming style (comments, indentation, etc.).

(a) Calculate the *weighted average* of a list of n numbers, using the formula

$$x_{avg} = f_1 x_1 + f_2 x_2 + \cdots + f_n x_n$$

where the *f*s are fractional weighting factors, i.e.,

$$0 <= f_i < 1 \quad \text{and} \quad f_1 + f_2 + \cdots + f_n = 1.$$

Test your program with the following data:

i = 1	f = 0.06	x = 27.5
2	0.08	13.4
3	0.08	53.8
4	0.10	29.2
5	0.10	74.5
6	0.10	87.0
7	0.12	39.9
8	0.12	47.7
9	0.12	8.1
10	0.12	63.2

(b) Calculate the cumulative product of a list of *n* numbers. Test your program with the following set of data (*n* = 6): 6.2, 12.3, 5.0, 18.8, 7.1, 12.8.

(c) Calculate the *geometric average* of a list of numbers, using the formula

$$x_{avg} = [x_1 x_2 x_3 \ldots x_n]^{1/n}$$

Test your program using the data given in part (b) above. Compare the results obtained with the arithmetic average of the same data. Which average is larger?

(d) Determine the roots of the quadratic equation

$$ax^2 + bx + c = 0$$

using the well-known quadratic formula

$$\frac{-b \pm \sqrt{b^2 - 4ac}}{2a}$$

(see Example 5.8). Allow for the possibility that one of the constants has a value of zero, and that the quantity $b^2 - 4ac$ is less than or equal to zero. Test the program using the following sets of data:

$a = 2$	$b = 6$	$c = 1$
3	3	0
1	3	1
0	12	−3
3	6	3
2	−4	3

(e) The *Fibonacci numbers* are members of an interesting sequence in which each number is equal to the sum of the previous 2 numbers. In other words,

$$F_i = F_{i-1} + F_{i-2}$$

where F_i refers to the ith Fibonacci number. The first two Fibonacci numbers are, by definition, equal to 1; i.e., $F_1 = F_2 = 1$. Thus,

$$F_3 = F_2 + F_1 = 1 + 1 = 2$$
$$F_4 = F_3 + F_2 = 2 + 1 = 3$$
$$F_5 = F_4 + F_3 = 3 + 2 = 5$$

and so on.

Write a program that will determine and display the first n Fibonacci numbers. Test the program with $n = 23$.

(f) A *prime number* is a positive integer quantity that is evenly divisible (without a remainder) only by 1 or by itself.

Calculate and tabulate the first n prime numbers. (*Hint*: a number, n, will be a prime if the quotients $n/2$, $n/3$, $n/4$, . . .,n/sqrt(n) are all nonzero.) Test your program by calculating the first 100 prime numbers.

(g) Write a conversational-style program that will read in a positive integer value and determine the following:

(i)　If the integer is a prime number.

(ii)　If the integer is a Fibonacci number.

Write the program in such a manner that it will execute repeatedly (loop), until a zero value is detected for the input quantity. Test the program with several integer values of your choice.

(h) Calculate the sum of the first n odd integers (i.e., $1 + 3 + 5 + \cdots + 2*n-1$). Test the program by calculating the first 100 odd integers (note that the last integer will be 199).

(*i*) The sine of x can be calculated approximately by summing the first n terms of the infinite series

$$\sin x = x - x^3/3! + x^5/5! - x^7/7! + \cdots$$

where x is expressed in radians.

Write a Pascal program that will read in a value for x and then calculate its sine. Write the program two different ways:

1. Sum the first n terms, where n is a positive integer that is read into the computer along with the numerical value for x.

2. Continue adding successive terms in the series until the value of term becomes smaller (in magnitude) than 10^{-5}.

Test the program for $x = 1$, $x = 2$ and $x = -3$. In each case write out the number of terms used to obtain the final answer.

(*j*) Suppose that P dollars are borrowed from a bank, with the understanding that A dollars will be repaid each month until the entire loan has been repaid. Part of the monthly payment will be interest, calculated as i percent of the current unpaid balance. The remainder of the monthly payment will be applied toward the unpaid balance.

Write a Pascal program that will determine the following information:

(1) The amount of interest paid each month.

(2) The amount of money applied toward the unpaid balance each month.

(3) The cumulative amount of interest that has been paid at the end of each month.

(4) The amount of the loan that is still unpaid at the end of each month.

(5) The number of monthly payments required to repay the entire loan.

(6) The amount of the last payment (since it will probably be less than A).

Test your program using the following data: $P = \$40{,}000$; $A = \$2{,}000$; $i = 1\%$ per month.

(*k*) A class of students earned the following grades for the 6 examinations taken in a Pascal programming course.

Student Name	Student Number	Exam Scores (Percent)					
Adams	10001	45	80	80	95	55	75
Brown	10002	60	50	70	75	55	80
Davis	10003	40	30	10	45	60	55
Fisher	10004	0	5	5	0	10	5
Hamilton	10005	90	85	100	95	90	90
Jones	10006	95	90	80	95	85	80
Ludwig	10007	35	50	55	65	45	70
Osborne	10008	75	60	75	60	70	80
Prince	10009	85	75	60	85	90	100
Richards	10010	50	60	50	35	65	70
Smith	10011	70	60	75	70	55	75
Thomas	10012	10	25	35	20	30	10
Wolfe	10013	25	40	65	75	85	95
Zorba	10014	65	80	70	100	60	95

Write a conversational-style Pascal program that will accept each student's number and exam grades as input, determine an average grade for each student, and then display the student number, the individual exam grades and the calculated average. Make the program as general as possible.

(*l*) Write a Turbo Pascal program that will solve the problem described in part. (*k*) above. Now, however, enter the student's name in place of each student number. Enter each name as a string and assign it to a string-type variable.

(*m*) Modify the program written for part (*k*) above to allow for unequal weighting of the individual exam grades. In particular, assume that each of the first four exams contributes 15 percent to the final score, and each of the last two exams contributes 20 percent.

(*n*) Extend the program written for part (*m*) above so that an overall class average is determined in addition to the individual student averages.

(*o*) Write a Pascal program that will allow the computer to be used as an ordinary desk calculator. Consider only the common arithmetic operations (addition, subtraction, multiplication and division). Include a memory that can store one number.

(*p*) Generate the following "pyramid" of digits, using nested loops.

```
                1
               232
              34543
             4567654
            567898765
           67890109876
          7890123210987
         890123454321098
        90123456765432109
       0123456789876543210
```

(*Do not* simply write out 10 multi-digit strings.)

(*q*) Generate a plot of the function

$$y = e^{-0.1t} \sin 0.5t$$

on a printer, using an asterisk (*) for each of the points that makes up the plot. Have the plot run vertically down the page, with one point (one asterisk) per line. (*Hint*: Each line should consist of one asterisk, preceded by an appropriate number of blank spaces. Determine the position of the asterisk using the round function.)

(*r*) Write a Pascal program that will convert a positive integer quantity to a roman numeral. Design the program so that it will execute repeatedly, until a value of zero is read in from the keyboard.

(*s*) Write an interactive Pascal program that will convert a date, entered in the form mm-dd-yy (*example*: 4-12-69), into an integer that indicates the number of days beyond January 1, 1960. To do so, make use of the following relationships:

(1) The day of the current year can be determined approximately using the following formula:
```
day := trunc(30.42*(mm - 1)) + dd
```

(2) If mm = 2 (February), *increase* the value of day by 1.

(3) If mm > 2 and mm < 8 (March, April, May, June and July), *decrease* the value of day by 1.

(4) If yy MOD 4 = 0 and mm > 2 (leap year), *increase* the value of day by 1.

(5) *Increase* the value of day by 1461 for each full 4-year cycle beyond 1-1-60.

(6) *Increase* day by 365 for each additional full year beyond the completion of the last full 4-year cycle, then add 1 (for the most recent leap year).

Test the program with today's date, or any other date of your choice.

Chapter 7

Procedures and Functions

We have already seen that Pascal programs can easily be written in a modular form, thus allowing an overall problem to be decomposed into a sequence of individual subproblems. Modularization provides two important advantages in Pascal. First, for tasks that must be accessed from more than one place within a program, modularization avoids the need for redundant (repeated) programming of essentially the same set of instructions. Rather, a program module can be defined once, and then accessed from several different places within the program. A different set of data can be processed each time the module is accessed. The use of program modules can therefore reduce the length of a program appreciably.

Of even greater significance is the logical clarity resulting from the decomposition of a program into individual, concise modules, where each module represents some well-defined part of the overall problem. Such programs are easier to write and to debug, and their logical structure is more apparent, than programs that lack this type of structure. This is particularly true of lengthy, complicated programs. Many Pascal programs are therefore modularized, even though they may not involve repeated execution of the same tasks. In fact the decomposition of a program into individual modules is generally considered to be an important part of good programming practice.

There are two types of program modules in Pascal — *procedures* and *functions*. These two types of program structures are similar, though they are accessed differently and they each exchange information in a different manner. We have already discussed the use of standard procedures (e.g., `read` and `write`) and standard functions (e.g., `sqr`) in Chap. 2. Let us now consider procedures and functions in greater detail. In particular, we will see how procedures and functions are written, how they differ from one another, and how each type of structure is properly used. We will also consider an interesting property of Pascal known as *recursion*, in which a procedure or function can successively access itself.

7.1 PROCEDURES

A *procedure* is a self-contained program structure that is included within a Pascal program. In most other programming languages, this type of a structure is known as a *subroutine*.

A procedure can be referenced simply by writing the procedure name, followed by an optional list of parameters. The parameters must be enclosed in parentheses and, if there are more than one, separated by commas. Procedure references are also known as procedure *accesses* or procedure *calls*.

When a procedure is referenced, control is automatically transferred to the beginning of the procedure. The action statements within the procedure are then executed, taking into account any special declarations that are unique to the procedure. When all of the action statements have been executed, control is automatically returned to the statement *immediately after* the procedure reference.

EXAMPLE 7.1

A Pascal program reads in three integer quantities and then determines which quantity is the largest. The program includes the procedure `maximum`, which determines the largest of the three quantities and then writes out the result. The action statements that read in the three quantities and then access the procedure are shown below.

```
BEGIN
   flag := 'Y';
   WHILE (flag = 'Y') OR (flag = 'y') DO
      BEGIN
         write('Enter three integers: ');
         readln(a,b,c);
         maximum;                    (* procedure access *)
         writeln;
         write('Again? (Y/N) ');
         readln(flag);
         writeln
      END
END.
```

When the procedure statement `maximum` is encountered, control is automatically transferred to this procedure (the procedure itself is not shown in this example). The procedure determines which of the variables a, b and c has the largest value and then writes out this result. Control is then returned to the following `readln` statement (which is also a procedure reference).

The main portion of the program will read successive sets of integers and determine the maximum of each set. The repetition, which is controlled by the WHILE – DO structure, will continue as long as the user answers Y (or y) to the prompt.

Now let us consider how the procedure itself is written. Each procedure has its own header and its own block. The header is written as

    PROCEDURE *name*

or, if *formal parameters* are included,

    PROCEDURE *name*(*formal parameters*)

We will discuss the use of formal parameters in Section 7.3.

The block consists of a declarations part (which is local to the procedure) and a group of action statements, just like the Pascal program in which the procedure is included. Thus, a procedure can be thought of as a special type of Pascal program that is embedded within another Pascal program.

EXAMPLE 7.2

Here is a procedure called `maximum` that finds the largest of three integer quantities, a, b and c, and writes out the result.

```
PROCEDURE maximum;

(* find the largest of three integer quantities *)

VAR max : integer;

BEGIN
   IF a > b THEN max := a ELSE max := b;
   IF c > max THEN max := c;
   writeln('The maximum is ',max)
END;
```

The first line, which includes the keyword PROCEDURE, is the procedure header. (Note the similarity to the program header.) This is followed by the procedure block, which consists of one variable declaration and several action statements.

Notice that this procedure requires that values for a, b and c be assigned before the procedure is accessed. Use of the procedure is compatible with the program segment shown in Example 7.1.

All procedure declarations, such as that shown in the preceding example, must be included within the calling block (or some other external block that surrounds the calling block). In particular, the procedure and function declarations must be the last items in the declarations section, following the variable declarations (see Sections 1.5 and 5.2). After a procedure has been declared it can be accessed anywhere in the action part of the block.

EXAMPLE 7.3 Largest of Three Numbers

Here is a complete Pascal program that combines the program segments shown in the previous two examples.

```pascal
PROGRAM sample;

(* determine the maximum of three integer quantities using a procedure *)

VAR a,b,c : integer;
    flag  : char;

PROCEDURE maximum;
(* find the largest of three integer quantities *)
VAR max : integer;
BEGIN
   IF a > b THEN max := a ELSE max := b;
   IF c > max THEN max := c;
   writeln('The maximum is ',max)
END;

BEGIN    (* main action block *)
   flag := 'Y';
   WHILE (flag = 'Y') OR (flag = 'y') DO
      BEGIN
         write('Enter three integers: ');
         readln(a,b,c);
         maximum;                    (* procedure access *)
         writeln;
         write('Again? (Y/N) ');
         readln(flag);
         writeln
      END
END.
```

This program repeatedly reads sets of three integers and determines the maximum of each set. The computer will continue to read and process successive sets of data as long as the most recent value for a is not zero.

Notice that the procedure is declared before it is accessed, and that the procedure declaration follows the variable declarations. (The blank lines are included only to improve the overall readability of the program.) Also, observe that the variables a, b and c, which are defined in the main part of the program, are recognized throughout the program, including the procedure. On the other hand, max is defined only within the procedure. Thus, it is not possible to make use of the variable max within the main part of the program.

The rules that govern procedure references are actually more general than the above examples indicate. We shall see shortly that a procedure can be accessed by the main program more than once. Moreover, a procedure can also be accessed by other procedures and functions.

7.2 SCOPE OF IDENTIFIERS

The constants and variables that appear within the action statements of a procedure may have been declared externally, within a program block that contains the procedure declaration, or locally, within the procedure itself. Those constants and variables that are declared within a block containing the procedure declaration can be utilized anywhere within that block, whether inside of or external to the procedure. Identifiers defined in this manner are considered to be *global* to the procedure. On the other hand, *local* constants and variables are not defined outside of the procedure and therefore cannot be utilized externally.

The *scope* of an identifier refers to the region within which the identifier is declared and can hence be utilized. This concept applies to *all* types of declarations, not just constants and variables.

EXAMPLE 7.4 Largest of Three Numbers

Let us again examine the Pascal program shown in Example 7.3.

```
PROGRAM sample;

(* determine the maximum of three integer quantities using a procedure *)

VAR a,b,c : integer;
    flag  : char;

PROCEDURE maximum;
(* find the largest of three integer quantities *)
VAR max : integer;
BEGIN
   IF a > b THEN max := a ELSE max := b;
   IF c > max THEN max := c;
   writeln('The maximum is ',max)
END;

BEGIN    (* main action block *)
    flag := 'Y';
    WHILE (flag = 'Y') OR (flag = 'y') DO
       BEGIN
          write('Enter three integers: ');
          readln(a,b,c);
          maximum;                    (* procedure access *)
          writeln;
          write('Again? (Y/N) ');
          readln(flag);
          writeln
       END
END.
```

This program contains one procedure, called maximum. The variables a, b and c are declared *outside* of this procedure and are therefore *global* to the procedure. These variables can be utilized both within and outside of the procedure, as in this example. However, the variable max is declared *within* the procedure. Thus max is *local* to the procedure, and cannot be utilized elsewhere.

In general, local identifiers are preferrable to global identifiers, provided this is not inconsistent with the overall program logic. In particular, the use of local identifiers contributes to greater program legibility. It also minimizes the likelihood of programming errors caused by incorrect or inconsistent identifier references.

On the other hand, many programs require that certain data items be recognized both within and outside of a procedure. One way to transfer such information across procedure boundaries is to make use of global identifiers, since global identifiers can be referenced wherever necessary. (Another approach is to use *parameters*, as discussed in the next section.) Thus a program might contain both local and global identifiers, depending on the logical requirements of the problem and the corresponding program structure. It is important to recognize when to use each type of identifier.

It is possible to use the same identifier to represent different entities in different portions of a program. Thus, an identifier that is declared locally within a procedure may have the same name as a global identifier that has been declared externally. In such situations, the local definition will take precedence within its scope. Outside of this scope, however, the local identifier will be undefined, so that the global definition will apply.

EXAMPLE 7.5

The skeletal portion of a Pascal program containing two procedures is shown below.

```
PROGRAM sample;

VAR a,b : integer;
    c,d : char;

PROCEDURE one;
VAR a,d : real;
BEGIN
    . . . . .
END;

PROCEDURE two;
VAR a : char;
    b : boolean;
BEGIN
    . . . . .
END;

BEGIN    (* main program - action statements *)
    . . . . .
END.
```

Procedure one contains two real, local variables: a and d. This procedure also recognizes two global variables: b, which is integer, and c, which is of type char. Procedure two recognizes the local variables a and b, which are of types char and boolean, respectively. Procedure two also recognizes the global variables c and d, which are of type char. The main block contains four local variables: a and b, which are integer, and c and d, which are of type char.

Note that several of the variable names are used differently within the procedures than in the main block. In particular, a is redefined within each procedure, and b and d are each redefined within one of the procedures. The local definitions will take precedence within their respective procedures. Within the main block, however, the the variables will be interpreted as in the original declarations.

The use of the local variables, within their respective scopes, will not alter the values that are assigned to the global variables. The fact that the local and global variables share the same names is immaterial. (As a rule, however, good programming practice would suggest that the variable names all be different unless the particular problem suggests, for some reason, that they be repeated.)

The issue of global versus local declarations applies to procedures (and functions) as well as to constants and variables. Thus, it is possible to declare a procedure (or a function) within another procedure. This feature allows procedures to be *nested*, one within another. In such situations it is important, of course, that a procedure not be accessed outside of the block that contains the procedure declaration.

EXAMPLE 7.6

Here is a skeletal outline of a Pascal program that contains nested procedures. The scope of the various procedures is indicated by indentation.

```
PROGRAM main;

   PROCEDURE one;

      PROCEDURE two;
      BEGIN             (* procedure two - action statements *)
         . . . . .
      END;

      PROCEDURE three;
      BEGIN             (* procedure three - action statements *)
         . . . . .
         two;           (* access procedure two *)
         . . . . .
      END;

   BEGIN                (* procedure one - action statements *)
      . . . . .
      two;              (* access procedure two *)
      . . . . .
      three;            (* access procedure three *)
      . . . . .
   END;                 (* end procedure one *)
BEGIN                   (* main program - action statements *)
   . . . . .
   one;                 (* access procedure one *)
   . . . . .
END.
```

In this example, procedure one is declared within the main program block, and procedures two and three are declared within procedure one. The scope of procedures two and three is therefore local to procedure one. Thus, procedures two and three can be accessed within procedure one, but not within the main action statements. Procedures two and three can also access each other. On the other hand, procedure one can be accessed by the main action statements, since it is declared within the main block.

EXAMPLE 7.7 Largest of Three Numbers

We now consider a variation of the Pascal program shown in Example 7.4. In the present example we decompose the original procedure maximum into two procedures, one nested within the other (as indicated by the indentation). The outermost procedure is still called maximum, but some of the original action statements now appear in the embedded procedure findmax.

```
      PROGRAM sample;

      (* maximum of three integer quantities using two procedures *)

      VAR a,b,c : integer;
          flag  : char;

          PROCEDURE maximum;
          (* This procedure finds the largest of three integer quantities *)
          VAR max : integer;

              PROCEDURE findmax;
              (* This is where the action is *)
              BEGIN
                  IF a > b THEN max := a ELSE max := b;
                  IF c > max THEN max := c
              END;

          BEGIN    (* back to maximum - action statements *)
              findmax;                    (* procedure access *)
              writeln('The maximum is ',max)
          END;

      BEGIN    (* main action statements *)
          flag := 'Y';
          WHILE (flag = 'Y') OR (flag = 'y') DO
              BEGIN
                  write('Enter three integers: ');
                  readln(a,b,c);
                  maximum;                (* procedure access *)
                  writeln;
                  write('Again? (Y/N) ');
                  readln(flag);
                  writeln
              END
      END.
```

Notice that findmax is declared within maximum, and maximum is declared within the main program block. Thus, findmax is local to maximum. Notice also that maximum is accessed in the main block, but findmax is accessed within maximum.

A similar situation is seen with respect to the variables a, b, c, flag and max. In particular, a, b, c and flag are global with respect to the procedures, since they are declared within the main program block. These four variables can therefore be utilized anywhere within the program. On the other hand, max is local to the procedure maximum, and can therefore be utilized only within maximum or its nested subroutine, findmax.

The concept of scope must be observed with statement labels as well as with constants, variables and procedures (and functions). In particular, a statement cannot be labeled unless the statement is included within the scope of the label declaration. Also, control cannot be transferred to a labeled statement from outside the scope of the label. However, in ANSI Pascal it is possible to transfer control to a labeled statement from anywhere within the scope of the label. Thus, control can be transferred out of an ANSI Pascal procedure (or function), provided the transfer does not go beyond the scope of the label definition. This applies even to procedures that have been nested several layers deep.

Turbo Pascal, on the other hand, is more restrictive. In Turbo Pascal, control connot be transferred out of a procedure (or function) to a label that is within an external enclosing block.

EXAMPLE 7.8 Averaging a List of Nonnegative Numbers

In Example 6.22 we saw a Pascal program that calculates the average of a list of numbers using a GOTO statement to transfer control out of a conditional loop once a negative number is read into the computer. (The negative number is intended as a stopping condition and is not included in the average.)

Let us now rewrite this program in ANSI Pascal so that the data input and data accumulation functions are handled through a procedure. We will retain the use of the GOTO statement, so that control is transferred out of the procedure once a negative number is entered into the computer. The complete ANSI Pascal program is shown below.

```
PROGRAM average6;

(* AVERAGE A LIST OF NUMBERS USING A WHILE - DO STRUCTURE
   AND A GOTO STATEMENT WITHIN A PROCEDURE *)

LABEL 10;
VAR count : integer;
    sum,average : real;

PROCEDURE enterdata;
(* read and sum successive real, positive quantities *)
VAR x : real;
    flag : boolean;
BEGIN   (* action statements *)
   flag := true;
   writeln('To STOP, enter a negative number');
   WHILE flag DO
      BEGIN
         write('x = ');
         read(x);
         IF x < 0 THEN GOTO 10;
         sum := sum+x;
         count := count+1
      END
END;

BEGIN   (* main action statements *)
     count := 0;
     sum := 0;
     enterdata;
10 : average := sum/count;
     writeln('The average of ',count:5,' numbers is ',average)
END.
```

Within this program the statement label 10 and the variables count, sum and average are declared within the main block, since these items are required both in the action part of this block and in the enclosed procedure. On the other hand, x and flag are declared locally within the procedure because these identifiers are not required outside of the procedure. Notice that control is transferred directly out of the procedure when a negative value for x is encountered.

It should be understood that the present example contains several contrivances in order to illustrate certain features. For example, this program could (and probably should) have been written without the GOTO statement. Moreover, the calculation of the average and the subsequent output statements could have been included within the procedure. This would have allowed all of the variables to be declared locally within the procedure – a generally better approach to the problem.

Finally, it should be understood that this program is not valid in Turbo Pascal because of the transfer out of procedure enterdata, to statement number 10 within the main block (i.e., the external block enclosing enterdata).

7.3 PARAMETERS

Many Pascal programs require that information be exchanged between a procedure (or a function) and the point at which the procedure (function) is referenced. One way to accomplish this is to utilize global variables, as discussed in the last section. We have also seen, however, that there are some potentially undesirable aspects to the use of global variables. For example, altering the value of a global variable within a procedure may inadvertently alter certain information outside of the procedure, and vice versa. Furthermore, the transfer of multiple data sets cannot easily be accommodated with global variables.

The use of *parameters* offers a better approach to the exchange of information between a procedure and its reference point. Each data item is transferred between an *actual parameter*, which is included within the procedure statement, and a corresponding *formal parameter*, which is defined within the procedure itself. When the procedure is accessed, the actual parameters are substituted for the formal parameters, thus creating an information exchange mechanism between the procedure and its reference point. The manner in which the information is exchanged depends, however, on the manner in which the parameters are defined and utilized.

EXAMPLE 7.9

The skeletal structure given below illustrates the simplest type of information exchange between a procedure reference and the procedure itself.

```
PROGRAM sample;

VAR a,b,c,d : real;

    PROCEDURE flash(x,y : real);
    BEGIN
        . . . . .
        (* process the values of x and y *)
        . . . . .
    END;

BEGIN
    . . . . .
    flash(a,b);
    . . . . .
    flash(c,d);
    . . . . .
END.
```

In this example the variables x and y are real-type formal parameters defined within the procedure flash. The actual parameters are the real variables a, b, c and d. We will assume that a, b, c and d have been assigned values elsewhere in the program, prior to the procedure references.

The first procedure reference causes the values of the actual parameters a and b to be transferred to the formal parameters x and y. Thus, the values of a and b are passed to procedure flash, where they are then processed. (The manner in which they are processed is immaterial in this example.)

This process is then repeated in the second procedure statement, this time transferring the values of c and d to x and y. The values of c and d are thus passed to flash, where they are processed accordingly.

Notice that we have processed two different data sets simply by accessing the same procedure twice, with a different set of actual parameters each time.

There are certain rules that must be observed in order to establish a correspondence between a procedure reference and the procedure itself (i.e., when substituting actual parameters for formal parameters). They are:

1. The number of actual parameters in the procedure reference must be the same as the number of formal parameters in the procedure definition.

2. Each actual parameter must be of the same type as its corresponding formal parameter.

3. Each actual parameter must be expressed in a manner which is consistent with its corresponding formal parameter, as determined by the *class* of the formal parameter (see below).

EXAMPLE 7.10

Consider the following skeletal program structure.

```
PROGRAM sample;
VAR a,b : integer;
    c,d : real;
    PROCEDURE flash(x : integer; y : real);
    BEGIN
       . . . . .
       (* process the values of x and y *)
       . . . . .
    END;
BEGIN
    . . . . .
    flash(a,c);
    . . . . .
    flash(b,d);
    . . . . .
END.
```

Note that each procedure reference (i.e., each procedure statement) includes two actual parameters, since two formal parameters (x and y) are defined within the procedure. Moreover, x is declared as an integer-type variable, and y is a real-type variable. Thus, each procedure reference must include one integer variable and one real variable, in that order.

A procedure can contain four different *classes* of formal parameters. They are *value parameters*, *variable parameters*, *procedure parameters* and *function parameters*. We will discuss value parameters and variable parameters at this time. The two remaining classes will be discussed later in this chapter (see Section 7.6).

Value Parameters

Value parameters can best be thought of as *input parameters* for their respective procedures. The use of a value parameter involves a transfer of value rather than an actual parameter substitution. Thus, when information is transferred between an actual parameter and a value parameter, the value of the actual parameter is assigned to the value parameter. This value can then be processed within the procedure, by referring to the value parameter. Values that are represented by value parameters *cannot*, however, be transferred in the opposite direction; i.e., from the procedure to the calling portion of the program. This is why value parameters are generally regarded as input parameters.

Value parameters are very simple to use. They are declared by simply including their names and corresponding data types within the procedure header, without any prefix (such as VAR). It is the absence of such a prefix that identifies this class of parameters, by default. Examples 7.9 and 7.10 both make use of value parameters.

You should understand that any alteration to the value of a value parameter within the procedure will not affect the value of any of the actual parameters (remember that value parameters are regarded as *input* parameters). This characteristic may limit the use of value parameters. However, value parameters are easy to use in situations that allow for a one-way transfer of information. Furthermore, since it is the *values* of the actual parameters that are transferred rather than the parameters themselves, there is considerable latitude in the manner in which the actual parameters can be written. In particular, an actual parameter may be expressed as a constant, a variable or an expression (provided the value of the parameter is of the proper data type).

EXAMPLE 7.11

Consider the following modification of the program outline shown in Example 7.10.

```
PROGRAM sample;
VAR a,b : integer;
    c,d : real;

  PROCEDURE flash(x : integer; y : real);
  BEGIN
      . . . . .
      (* process the values of x and y *)
      . . . . .
  END;

BEGIN
    . . . . .
    flash(3,a*(c+d)/b);
    . . . . .
    flash(2*(a+b),-0.5);
    . . . . .
END.
```

Notice that the formal parameters x and y, declared in procedure flash, are value parameters. (This is also true in Examples 7.9 and 7.10.) The first of these (x) is of type integer, and the second (y) is real. Therefore, each reference to flash must contain two actual parameters, the first of which must be of type integer and the second real.

The main block includes two different procedure statements (i.e., two different references to flash). Each procedure statement contains two actual parameters, the first of which is of type integer and the second real, as required. Notice that two of these parameters are written as constants, and two are written as expressions. Thus, the first procedure statement transfers the value 3 to x, and the value of the real expression a*(c+d)/b to y. Similarly, the second procedure statement transfers the value of the integer expression 2*(a+b) to x, and the value -0.5 to y.

EXAMPLE 7.12 Calculating Depreciation

Consider once again the problem described in Example 6.17 of calculating depreciation by one of three different methods. Let us now rewrite the program so that a separate procedure is used for each method. This approach offers us a cleaner way to organize the program into its logical components, retaining the logic given in Example 6.17. We will use value parameters within each procedure, since the procedures do not return any values to the main (calling) block.

Here is the complete Pascal program.

```
PROGRAM depreciation2;

(* CALCULATE DEPRECIATION BY ONE OF THREE POSSIBLE METHODS USING PROCEDURES *)

VAR years,choice : integer;
    value : real;
    flag : boolean;

  PROCEDURE straightline(n : integer; val : real);
  (* Calculate depreciation using the straight line method *)
  VAR year : integer;
      deprec : real;
  BEGIN
     writeln(' Straight-Line Method');
     writeln;
     deprec := val/n;
     FOR year := 1 TO n DO
        BEGIN
           val := val-deprec;
           write(' End of Year ',year:2);
           write('   Depreciation: ',deprec:5:0);
           writeln('   Current Value: ',val:6:0)
        END
  END;

  PROCEDURE decliningbalance(n : integer; val : real);
  (* Calculate depreciation using the double declining balance method *)
  VAR year : integer;
      deprec : real;
  BEGIN
     writeln(' Double Declining Balance Method');
     writeln;
     FOR year := 1 TO n DO
        BEGIN
           deprec := 2*val/n;
           val := val-deprec;
           write(' End of Year ',year:2);
           write('   Depreciation: ',deprec:5:0);
           writeln('   Current Value: ',val:6:0)
        END
  END;

  PROCEDURE sumofyears(n : integer; val : real);
  (* Calculate depreciation using the sum-of-the-years'-digits method *)
  VAR year : integer;
      deprec,tag : real;
  BEGIN
     writeln(' Sum-of-the-Years''-Digits Method');
     writeln;
     tag := val;
```

(Program continues on next page)

```
      FOR year := 1 TO n DO
          BEGIN
              deprec := (n-year+1)*tag/(n*(n+1)/2);
              val := val-deprec;
              write(' End of Year ',year:2);
              write('  Depreciation: ',deprec:5:0);
              writeln('   Current Value: ',val:6:0)
          END
      END;

BEGIN     (* main action block *)
    flag := true;
    REPEAT     (* Begin input routine *)
        writeln;
        writeln;
        write(' Method: (1-SL  2-DDB  3-SYD  4-End) ');
        readln(choice);
        IF choice <> 4 THEN
        BEGIN
            write(' Original value: ');
            readln(value);
            write(' Number of years: ');
            readln(years);
            writeln
        END;    (* input routine *)
        CASE choice OF
            1 : straightline(years,value);
            2 : decliningbalance(years,value);
            3 : sumofyears(years,value);
            4 : BEGIN
                    writeln(' Bye, have a nice day!');
                    flag := false
                END
        END    (* choice *)
    UNTIL flag = false
END.
```

Notice that the CASE structure is still employed, as in Example 6.17, but now the program utilizes a different procedure for each type of calculation. The procedures make use of the value parameters n and `val`, which represent the lifetime of the depreciated item and its original value, respectively. The corresponding actual parameters in the main block are `years` and `value`. Thus, when a procedure is referenced, the value of `years` is assigned to n, and the value of `value` is assigned to `val`. (We could, of course, have utilized the same variable names in both the main block and each of the procedures. This would have been simpler, though perhaps less instructive.)

Variable Parameters

We have seen that value parameters are convenient to work with in situations where information is transferred only from the procedure reference to the procedure. In many applications, however, information must be transferred in both directions between the procedure and the procedure reference. In other words, the procedure must be able to accommodate both input from and output to the calling block. Variable parameters are generally used in such situations.

When a procedure containing a variable parameter is accessed, an actual parameter in the procedure statement is substituted for the formal parameter within the procedure itself. Thus, the actual parameter will be utilized during the execution of the procedure. This contrasts with the use of a value parameter, where the *value* of the actual parameter is assigned to the formal parameter (note the distinction between *assignment* and *substitution*). It is this substitution process that allows a two-way transfer of information between the procedure reference and the procedure itself.

On the other hand, it should be pointed out that only a *variable* can be substituted for another variable. Thus, the actual parameters that are substituted for variable parameters must themselves be variables — they *cannot* be constants or expressions. We therefore have somewhat less generality in the use of variable parameters than with value parameters.

Another consequence of the substitution process is the fact that any change in the value of a variable parameter within a procedure will also change the value of the corresponding actual parameter outside of the procedure. Thus, variable parameters can affect a program globally, even though their scope is local to the procedure within which they are declared.

Variable parameters are declared within the procedure header, as are value parameters. However, variable parameter declarations must be preceded by the keyword VAR, as illustrated in the next example.

EXAMPLE 7.13

Consider once again the skeletal program structure presented in Example 7.10. If the procedure were modified to make use of variable parameters, the skeletal structure would appear as follows.

```
PROGRAM sample;
VAR a,b : integer;
    c,d : real;
    PROCEDURE flash( VAR x : integer; VAR y : real);
    BEGIN
        . . . . .
        (* process the values of x and y *)
        . . . . .
    END;

BEGIN
    . . . . .
    flash(a,c);
    . . . . .
    flash(b,d);
    . . . . .
END.
```

The first procedure statement causes the actual parameters a and c to be substituted for x and y. If the value of either x or y is altered within the procedure, then a corresponding alteration in the value of a or c will occur in the main block. Similarly, the second procedure statement results in b and d being substituted for x and y. Any alteration in the value of either x or y within the procedure will therefore cause a corresponding alteration in the value of b or d in the main block.

Note that the actual parameters agree with the corresponding formal parameters in number and in type.

EXAMPLE 7.14 Search for a Maximum

Suppose we wish to find the particular value of *x* that causes the function

$$y = x \cos (x)$$

to be maximized within the interval bounded by $x = 0$ on the left and $x = \pi$ on the right. We will require that the maximizing value of x be known quite accurately. We will also require that the search scheme be relatively efficient in the sense that the function $y = x \cos (x)$ be evaluated as few times as possible.

An obvious way to solve this problem would be to generate a large number of closely spaced trial functions (that is, evaluate the function at $x = 0$, $x = 0.0001$, $x = 0.0002, \ldots, x = 3.1415$, and $x = 3.1416$) and determine the largest of these by visual inspection. This would not be very efficient, however, and it would require human intervention to obtain the final result. Instead let us use the following *elimination scheme*, which is a highly efficient computational procedure for all functions that have only one "peak" within the search interval.

The computation will be carried out as follows. We begin with two search points at the center of the search interval, located a very small distance from each other, as shown in Fig. 7.1.

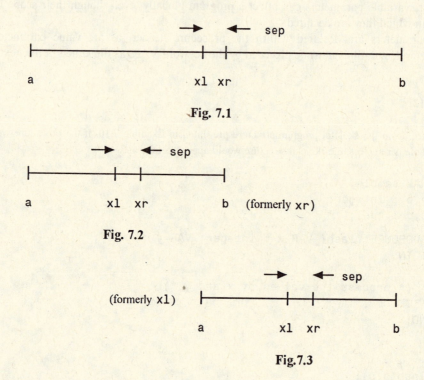

Fig. 7.1

Fig. 7.2

Fig. 7.3

The following notation is used.

> a = left end of the search interval
> $x1$ = left-hand interior search point
> xr = right-hand interior search point
> b = right end of the search interval
> sep = distance between $x1$ and xr.

If a, b and sep are known, then the interior points can be calculated as

```
x1 = a + .5*(b-a-sep)
xr = a + .5*(b-a+sep) = x1 + sep
```

Let us evaluate the function $y = x \cos (x)$ at $x1$ and at xr, and let us call these values $y1$ and yr, respectively. Suppose $y1$ turns out to be greater than yr. Then we know that the maximum will lie somewhere between a and xr. Hence we retain only that portion of the search interval which ranges from $x = a$ to $x = xr$ (we will now refer to the old point xr as b, since it is now the right end of the new search interval), and generate two *new* search points, $x1$ and xr. These points will be located at the center of the new search interval, a distance sep apart, as shown in Fig. 7.2.

On the other hand, suppose now that in our *original* search interval the value of `yr` turned out to be greater than `yl`. This would indicate that our new search interval should lie between `xl` and `b`. Hence we rename the point which was originally called `xl` to be `a`, and we generate two *new* search points, `xl` and `xr`, at the center of the new search interval, as shown in Fig. 7.3.

We continue to generate a new pair of search points at the center of each new interval, compare the respective values of `y`, and eliminate a portion of the search interval until the search interval becomes smaller than `3*sep`. Once this happens we can no longer distinguish the interior points from the boundaries. Hence the search is ended.

Each time we make a comparison between `yl` and `yr` we eliminate that portion of the search interval that contains the smaller value of `y`. If both interior values of `y` should happen to be identical (which can happen, though it is unusual), then the search procedure stops, and the maximum is assumed to occur at the center of the last two interior points.

Once the search has ended, either because the search interval has become sufficiently small or because the two interior points yield identical values of `y`, we can calculate the approximate location of the maximum as

```
xmax = .5*(xl + xr)
```

The corresponding maximum value of the function can then be obtained as `xmax cos (xmax)`.

Let us consider a program outline for the general case where `a` and `b` are input quantities but `sep` has a fixed value of 0.0001.

1. Assign a value of `sep` = 0.0001.

2. Read in the values of `a` and `b`.

3. Repeat the following until either `yl` becomes equal to `yr` (the desired maximum will be at the midpoint), or the most recent value of `(b-a)` becomes less than or equal to `3*sep`:

    (*a*) Generate the two interior points, `xl` and `xr`.

    (*b*) Calculate the corresponding values of `yl` and `yr`, and determine which is larger.

    (*c*) Reduce the search interval, by eliminating that portion that does not contain the larger value of `y`.

4. Evaluate `xmax` and `ymax`.

5. Write out the values of `xmax` and `ymax`, and stop.

Step 3 can very conveniently be packaged as a procedure. To do so, let us define the variables `a`, `b`, `xl`, `xr`, `yl` and `yr` to be variable parameters. (The values represented by these parameters will change through the course of the computation, and will be transferred back and forth between the procedure and the main block.)

```pascal
PROCEDURE reduce( VAR a,b,xl,xr,yl,yr : real);

(* Interval reduction routine *)

BEGIN
    xl := a + 0.5*(b-a-sep);
    xr := xl + sep;
    yl := xl*cos(xl);
    yr := xr*cos(xr);
    IF yl > yr THEN b := xr;    (* retain left interval *)
    IF yr > yl THEN a := xl     (* retain right interval *)
END;
```

Notice that `sep` is not declared as a parameter within the procedure. We will define `sep` as a global constant within the main block, since its value never changes. Also, notice the use of the standard function `cos` within the procedure; we will also utilize this function in the main block. Finally, observe that the interval reduction will not work properly if `yl` and `yr` are equal (which is possible but unlikely). This problem can easily be corrected, by replacing one of the `>` operators with `>=`.

It is now quite easy to write the complete program, as shown on the next page.

```
PROGRAM maximum;

(* FIND THE MAXIMUM OF A FUNCTION WITHIN A SPECIFIED INTERVAL *)

CONST sep = 0.0001;
VAR a,b,xl,xr,xmax,yl,yr,ymax : real;

    PROCEDURE reduce( VAR a,b,xl,xr,yl,yr : real);
    (* Interval reduction routine *)
    BEGIN
        xl := a + 0.5*(b-a-sep);
        xr := xl + sep;
        yl := xl*cos(xl);
        yr := xr*cos(xr);
        IF yl > yr THEN b := xr;    (* retain left interval *)
        IF yr > yl THEN a := xl     (* retain right interval *)
    END;

BEGIN     (* main action block *)
    write('a = ');
    readln(a);
    write('b = ');
    readln(b);
    REPEAT
        reduce(a,b,xl,xr,yl,yr);
    UNTIL (yl=yr) OR ( b-a <= 3*sep );
    xmax := 0.5*(xl+xr);
    ymax := xmax*cos(xmax);
    writeln;
    writeln('xmax = ',xmax:8:6,'    ymax = ',ymax:8:6)
END.
```

Execution of the program, with a = 0 and b = 3.141593, results in the following dialog (the user's responses are underlined).

```
a = 0
b = 3.141593

xmax = 0.860586    ymax = 0.561096
```

Thus, we have obtained the location and the value of the maximum within the given original interval.

7.4 FUNCTIONS

A *function* is a self-contained program structure that is in many respects similar to a procedure. (Recall our brief discussion of procedures and functions in Section 2.12.) Unlike a procedure, however, a function is used to return a single simple-type value to its reference point. Moreover, a function is referenced by specifying its name within an expression, as though it were an ordinary simple-type variable. The function name can be followed by one or more actual parameters, enclosed in parentheses and separated by commas. In most situations, the actual parameters will transfer information to value parameters within the function and can therefore be expressed as constants, variables or expressions.

EXAMPLE 7.15

Suppose that `factorial` is the name of a function that calculates the factorial of some integer quantity. (Recall that the factorial of an integer quantity, n, is defined as $n! = 1 \times 2 \times \ldots \times n$.) Then the formula

$$f = x! / a! (x - a)!$$

could be expressed in Pascal as

```
f := factorial(x)/(factorial(a)*factorial(x-a));
```

where `f`, `x` and `a` are integer-type variables.

Note the similarity between the use of this user-defined function and the use of a standard function, as described in Section 2.12.

A function definition consists of a function header and a block. The function header is written in the form

```
FUNCTION name : type
```

or, if parameters are included,

```
FUNCTION name(formal parameters) : type
```

The last item, *type*, specifies the data type of the result that is returned by the function.

Generally, the formal parameters will be value parameters rather than variable parameters. This allows the corresponding actual parameters to be expressed as constants, variables or expressions. (Remember that these parameters will provide only *input* values to the function; the single *output* value provided by the function will be represented by the function name rather than a parameter.)

The block is similar to that of a procedure, and involves the same rules of scope as a procedure. Within the block, however, the identifier that represents the function name must be assigned a value of the appropriate type, as specified in the header. This is the value that the function returns to its reference point. Values can be assigned to the function name at multiple points within the block. Once an assignment is made, however, it cannot subsequently be altered.

EXAMPLE 7.16

Here is a function called `factorial` that calculates the factorial of an integer quantity.

```
FUNCTION factorial(n : integer) : integer;
(* Calculate the factorial of n *)
VAR factor,product : integer;
BEGIN
   IF n <= 1 THEN factorial := 1
   ELSE BEGIN
           product := 1;
           FOR factor := 2 TO n DO
               product := product*factor;
           factorial := product
        END
END;
```

The first line, which contains the keyword `FUNCTION`, is the function header. Notice that the header includes a declaration of the value parameter n. Also, notice the last item on the line (`integer`), which states that the function will return an integer-type quantity.

This function accepts a value for n and then calculates the value of n! using two local integer variables, `factor` and `product`. The final result is assigned to the identifier `factorial`, which is also the function name.

Note that there are two different assignments to `factorial`, but only one of these assignments is utilized when the function is executed. The choice depends upon the value that is assigned to n. Once `factorial` is assigned a value, however, it is not altered within the function.

To amplify on this last point, consider the following (incorrect) variation of the above function.

```
FUNCTION factorial(n : integer) : integer;
(* Calculate the factorial of n *)
VAR factor : integer;
BEGIN
    factorial := 1;
    IF n > 1 THEN FOR factor := 2 TO n DO
                      factorial := factorial*factor
END;
```

On the surface this version appears more appealing than the original, since it is simpler. This version is *not* valid, however, because the value of `factorial` is altered after its initial assignment when n is greater than 1.

Functions are declared in the same manner as procedures, within the calling block or some external block that surrounds the calling block. There is no particular order with respect to functions vs. procedures. (Remember, though, that the function and procedure declarations must be the *last* declarations within the block, following any label, constant, type and variable declarations.)

EXAMPLE 7.17 Calculating Factorials

Here is a complete Pascal program that determines the factorial of a given input quantity.

```
PROGRAM factorials;

(* Calculate the factorial of an integer quantity using a function *)

VAR x : integer;

    FUNCTION factorial(n : integer) : integer;
    (* calculate the factorial of n *)
    VAR factor,product : integer;
    BEGIN
        IF n <= 1 THEN factorial := 1
                  ELSE BEGIN
                           product := 1;
                           FOR factor := 2 TO n DO
                               product := product*factor;
                           factorial := product
                       END
END;

BEGIN     (* main action block *)
    write('Enter a positive integer: ');
    readln(x);
    writeln;
    writeln('x = ',x,'   x! = ',factorial(x))
END.
```

Notice that the function `factorial` is accessed only once, in the last `writeln` statement within the main block.

When running this program some care must be given to the value that is assigned to x, since an overflow may occur if x is assigned too large a number. (Remember that factorials increase in value very quickly.) This is particularly true of some desktop computers, where the largest permissible integer quantity may be relatively limited.

Functions can be nested, one within another, in the same manner as procedures. Moreover, the nesting of functions and procedures can be interchanged. Thus, a function can be declared within a procedure that has been declared within another function, and so on.

EXAMPLE 7.18 Simulation of a Game of Chance (Shooting Craps)

Here is an interesting programming problem that makes use of a procedure with nested functions.

"Craps" is a popular dice game in which you throw a pair of dice one or more times until you either win or lose. The game can be computerized by substituting the generation of random numbers for the actual throwing of the dice.

There are two ways to win in craps. You can throw the dice once and obtain a score of either 7 or 11, or you can obtain a 4, 5, 6, 8, 9 or 10 on the first throw, and then repeat the same score on a subsequent throw before obtaining a 7. Conversely, there are two ways to lose. You can throw the dice once and obtain a 2, 3 or 12, or you can obtain a 4, 5, 6, 8, 9 or 10 on the first throw and then obtain a 7 on a subsequent throw before repeating your original score.

Let us computerize the game in a conversational manner, so that one throw of the dice will be simulated each time you depress the ENTER key. A message will then appear indicating the outcome of each throw. At the end of each game, you will be asked whether or not you want to continue to play.

Our program will require a random number generator that produces uniformly distributed random integers between one and six. (By *uniformly distributed* we mean that any number within the range is just as likely to appear as any other number.) Turbo Pascal includes a standard function, called `random`, that can generate such random integers simply by writing

```
d1 := 1 + random(6);
```

Thus, the integer variable d1 will be assigned a value of 1, 2, 3, 4, 5 or 6 with equal likelihood.

You should understand that these numbers will not really be random because the *same* sequence of numbers will always be generated for a given starting value (i.e., for the same "seed"). However, the sequence of numbers will *appear* to be random, and will have many of the statistical characteristics of numbers that are truly random. Moreover, we can generate a *different* sequence of random numbers each time we execute the program if we precede the first reference to `random` with an access to the standard procedure `randomize`. This procedure accesses the computer's internal clock to provide a different "seed" every time the program is executed.

We will not discuss the mechanics of the random number generator further, as it is well beyond the scope of this book. Its use, however, is quite simple. Thus, to simulate the throwing of a pair of dice (where each die returns a random integer between 1 and 6), we simply write

```
d1 := 1 + random(6);
d2 := 1 + random(6);
```

Let us incorporate these two statements into a separate function, called `throw`, that simulates one throw of the dice. This function can easily be written as

```
FUNCTION throw : integer;
(* Throw the dice once *)
VAR d1,d2 : integer;

BEGIN
    d1 := 1 + random(6);
    d2 := 1 + random(6);
    throw := d1 + d2
END;
```

Now let us define a procedure, called play, that simulates one complete game of craps (i.e., the dice will be thrown as many times as is necessary to establish either a win or a loss). This procedure will therefore contain function throw. The complete rules of craps will also be built into this procedure. In pseudo code, we can write this function as

```
PROCEDURE play;
(* Simulate a single game of craps *)
VAR score,tag : integer;
(* define function throw *)
BEGIN
    (* instruct the user to throw the dice *)
    score := throw;
    CASE score OF
        7,11 : BEGIN    (* win on first throw *)
                . . . . .
                (* write a message indicating a win on the first throw *)
                . . . . .
            END;
      2,3,12 : BEGIN    (* loss on first throw *)
                . . . . .
                (* write a message indicating a loss on the first throw *)
                . . . . .
            END;
  4,5,6,8,9,10 : BEGIN    (* multiple throws *)
                tag := score;
                REPEAT
                . . . . .
                (* instruct the user to throw the dice again *)
                . . . . .
                score := throw;
            UNTIL (score = tag) OR (score = 7);
            IF score = tag
                THEN BEGIN
                    . . . . .
                    (* write a message indicating a win *)
                    . . . . .
                    END
                ELSE BEGIN
                    . . . . .
                    (* write a message indicating a loss *)
                    . . . . .
                    END
            END    (* multiple throws *)
    END    (* case *)
END;
```

Finally, the main block will be used to control the execution of the game. This routine will consist of little more than a call to standard procedure `randomize`, some interactive input/output and a call to procedure `play`. (Note, however, that `play` will be defined within this block.) Thus, we can write the pseudo code as follows.

```pascal
PROGRAM craps;

(* Interactive simulation of a game of craps
   using the Turbo Pascal random number generator *)

VAR count : integer;
    n : real;
    answer : char;
    flag : boolean;
    (* define procedure play *)
BEGIN
    randomize;
    flag := true;

    (* generate a welcoming message *)

    WHILE flag DO
       BEGIN
          play;
          write('Do you want to play AGAIN? (Y/N) ');
          readln(answer);
          IF (answer = 'N') OR (answer = 'n') THEN flag := false
       END;

    (* generate a sign-off message *)

END.
```

Note that the program will be executed recursively, until the player indicates a desire to stop.

Here is the complete Pascal program.

```pascal
PROGRAM craps;

(* Interactive simulation of a game of craps
   using the Turbo Pascal random number generator *)

VAR count : integer;
    n : real;
    answer : char;
    flag : boolean;

    PROCEDURE play;
    (* Simulate a single game of craps *)
    VAR score,tag : integer;

        FUNCTION throw : integer;
        (* Throw the dice once *)
        VAR d1,d2 : integer;
```

(Program continues on next page)

```
      BEGIN    (* throw the dice once *)
         d1 := 1 + random(6);
         d2 := 1 + random(6);
         throw := d1 + d2
      END;   (* throw *)

   BEGIN    (* play one game *)
      writeln;
      writeln('Throw the dice . . .');
      readln;
      score := throw;

      CASE score OF
           7,11 : BEGIN    (* win on first throw *)

                     write(score:3,' - Congratulations!');
                     writeln('  You WIN on the first throw!');
                     writeln
                  END;

         2,3,12 : BEGIN    (* loss on first throw *)
                     write(score:3,' - Tough luck!');
                     writeln('  You LOSE on the first throw!');
                     writeln
                  END;

   4,5,6,8,9,10 : BEGIN    (* multiple throws *)
                     tag := score;
                     REPEAT
                        write(score:3);
                        writeln(' - Throw the dice again . . .');
                        readln;
                        score := throw;
                     UNTIL (score = tag) OR (score = 7);
                     IF score = tag
                        THEN BEGIN
                                write(score:3);
                                write(' - You WIN by matching');
                                writeln(' your first score');
                                writeln
                             END
                        ELSE BEGIN
                                write(score:3);
                                write(' - You LOSE by failing to');
                                writeln(' match your first score');
                                writeln
                             END
                  END    (* multiple throws *)
      END   (* case *)
   END;   (* play *)

BEGIN    (* executive routine *)
   randomize;
   flag := true;
   writeln('Welcome to the Game of CRAPS!');
```

```
        writeln;
        write('Press ENTER to begin playing');
        readln;
        WHILE flag DO
            BEGIN
                play;
                write('Do you want to play AGAIN? (Y/N) ');
                readln(answer);
                IF (answer = 'N') OR (answer = 'n') THEN flag := false
            END;
        writeln;
        writeln('Bye, come back again!')
    END.
```

When the program is executed, it generates an interactive dialog, such as that shown below. As usual, the user's responses are underlined for clarity.

```
Welcome to the Game of CRAPS!

Press ENTER to begin playing

Throw the dice . . .

   7 - Congratulations!  You WIN on the first throw!

Do you want to play AGAIN? (Y/N) y

Throw the dice . . .

   5 - Throw the dice again . . .

   6 - Throw the dice again . . .

  12 - Throw the dice again . . .

   7 - You LOSE by failing to match your first score

Do you want to play AGAIN? (Y/N) y

Throw the dice . . .

   9 - Throw the dice again . . .

   4 - Throw the dice again . . .

   9 - You WIN by matching your first score

Do you want to play AGAIN? (Y/N) y

Throw the dice . . .

   2 - Tough luck!  You LOSE on the first throw!

Do you want to play AGAIN? (Y/N) n

Bye, come back again!
```

Finally, you are cautioned against altering the value of a global variable or a variable parameter within a function, as this may have unexpected and unwanted results outside of the function. Actions of this type are referred to as *side effects* of functions. (Note that such unwanted side effects can also be generated by a procedure. Side effects are generally more dangerous with functions, however, because we tend to think of a function as returning only one value.)

7.5 RECURSION

One of the most interesting features of Pascal is the ability of a procedure or a function to call itself. This is known as *recursion*. The use of recursion is particularly convenient for those problems that can be defined in naturally recursive terms, though such problems can also be programmed using nonrecursive techniques.

Every recursive procedure or function must include a *terminating condition*. This prevents the recursion from continuing indefinitely. Generally, the terminating condition takes the form of an if-then-else statement that causes the recursion to stop if the terminating condition is satisfied. While the terminating condition remains unsatisfied, however, the procedure (or function) simply calls itself at the appropriate place, just as it would call some other procedure or function.

EXAMPLE 7.19 Calculating Factorials

In Example 7.17 we saw a program for calculating the factorial of a given input quantity, using a nonrecursive function to perform the actual calculations. Now let us see how this same calculation can be carried out using recursion.

First, notice that the factorial of a positive integer quantity, n, can be defined recursively as $n! = n \times (n-1)!$, where, by definition, $1! = 1$. These equations provide the basis for the following recursive function.

```
FUNCTION factorial(n : integer) : integer;
(* Calculate the factorial of n recursively*)
BEGIN
   IF n <= 1 THEN factorial := 1
             ELSE factorial := n*factorial(n-1)
END;
```

Notice that this function is much simpler than that presented in Example 7.17. The close correspondence between this function and the natural problem definition, in recursive terms, should be readily apparent. Also, notice that the IF - THEN clause provides a termination condition which is activated when the parameter n becomes less than or equal to 1 (n will never become less than 1 unless its original value is less than 1).

Here is the complete Pascal program. The main block is very similar to that shown in Example 7.17.

```
PROGRAM factorials;

(* CALCULATE THE FACTORIAL OF A GIVEN INTEGER QUANTITY RECURSIVELY *)

VAR x : integer;

   FUNCTION factorial(n : integer) : integer;
   (* Calculate the factorial of n recursively*)
   BEGIN
      IF n <= 1 THEN factorial := 1
                ELSE factorial := n*factorial(n-1)
   END;

BEGIN   (* main action block *)
   write('Enter a positive integer: ');
   readln(x);
   writeln;
   writeln('x = ',x,'   x! = ',factorial(x))
END.
```

Notice that the function `factorial` is accessed repeatedly; once in the main block, and (n-1) times within itself.

In some applications, the use of recursion allows multiple data items to be stored inside the computer without the need for special data structures. This is illustrated in the next example.

EXAMPLE 7.20 Printing Backward

Suppose we want to write a program that will read in a line of text whose length is unspecified until the end of the line is detected. The line of text will then be displayed in reverse order (i.e., backward).

The traditional approach to this problem is to store the characters in a list as they are read in. We would then write them out in reverse order by proceeding through the list backward, after all of the characters have been entered. In order to do this, however, we would have to create a special data structure (an *array*) to store the characters as they are entered. (We will see how this is done in Chap. 9.)

Another way to solve this problem is to use recursion, as shown below.

```
PROGRAM backward;

(* READ A LINE OF TEXT AND DISPLAY IT IN REVERSE ORDER. *)

    PROCEDURE flipit;
    (* Read single characters recursively, then display them *)
    VAR c : char;
    BEGIN
        read(c);
        IF NOT eoln THEN flipit;
        write(c)
    END;

BEGIN     (* main action block *)
    writeln('Enter a line of text, then press RETURN');
    flipit
END.
```

Procedure `flipit` is the key to the program. This procedure calls itself recursively, reading in successive characters until an end-of-line is encountered (until `eoln` is true). Notice that the recursive call precedes the `write` statement. Hence, *all* of the characters will be read in before any of them are displayed. After all of the characters have been read in, the *most recent* character will be displayed (because the most recent character corresponds to the most recent procedure call), followed by the second most recent character, and so on.

For example, if the program is executed with the following line of input,

```
NOW IS THE TIME FOR ALL GOOD MEN TO COME TO THE AID OF THEIR COUNTRY
```

the following line of output will be generated.

```
YRTNUOC RIEHT FO DIA EHT OT EMOC OT NEM DOOG LLA ROF EMIT EHT SI WON
```

If a procedure or a function containing local variables is called recursively, then a *different* set of local variables will be created during each call. The names of the local variables will, of course, be the same (as declared within the procedure or function). However, a different set of values will be associated with these variable names each time the procedure or function is activated. These values will become available as the procedure or function "unwinds," i.e., as the previous recursive calls are completed.

EXAMPLE 7.21

Consider the recursive procedure `flipit` shown in Example 7.20. This procedure includes the local char-type variable `c`. Each time the procedure is called, a different character is read in and assigned to `c`. Thus, several different characters will be associated with `c` and stored sequentially within the computer's memory. These characters will be independent of one another. They will be displayed in the desired order as the previous recursive calls are completed (which means that more recent values of `c` will already have been entered, stored and displayed).

Sometimes the use of recursion can greatly simplify a problem that might otherwise require a very complex program. The following classical example illustrates this feature exceedingly well.

EXAMPLE 7.22 The Towers of Hanoi

The Towers of Hanoi is a popular children's game involving three poles and a number of different-sized disks. Each disk has a hole in the center, allowing the disks to be stacked around the poles. Initially, the disks are stacked on the left-most pole in the order of their size, with the largest on the bottom and the smallest on the top. (See Fig. 7.4.)

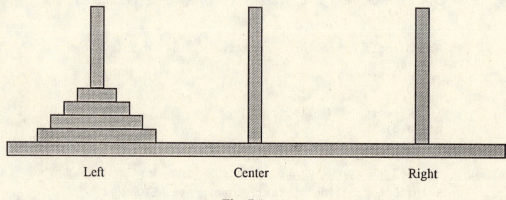

Left   Center   Right

Fig. 7.4

The object of the game is to transfer the disks from the leftmost pole to the rightmost pole, without ever placing a larger disk on top of a smaller disk. Only one disk may be moved at one time, and each disk must always be placed over one of the poles.

The general strategy is to consider one of the poles to be the origin, and another to be the destination. The third pole will be used for intermediate storage, thus allowing for the movement of the disks. Therefore, if *n* disks are initially stacked on the left pole, the problem of moving all *n* disks to the right pole can be represented in the following manner.

1. Move the top *n*−1 disks from the left pole to the middle pole, using the right pole for intermediate storage.

2. Move the remaining disk to the right pole.

3. Move the *n*−1 disks on the middle pole to the right pole, using the left pole for intermediate storage.

Thus, the problem can be expressed in recursive terms which apply for any value of *n* greater than 0. (When *n* = 1, we simply move one disk from the left pole to the right pole.)

In order to write a program for this game we first number the poles, so that left = 1, center = 2 and right = 3. We then construct a recursive procedure called `transfer` that will transfer *n* disks from one pole to another. We will refer to the poles with the integer-type variables `origin`, `destination`, and `other`. Thus, if we assign the value 1 to `origin`, 3 to `destination` and 2 to `other`, we will in effect be specifying the movement of *n* disks from pole 1 (the leftmost pole) to pole 3 (the rightmost pole), using pole 2 (the center pole) for intermediate storage. With this notation, the procedure will have the following skeletal structure.

```
PROCEDURE transfer(n,origin,destination,other : integer);

IF n>0 THEN
    (* transfer n-1 disks from the origin to the intermediate pole *)
    (* transfer the remaining disk from the origin to the destination *)
    (* transfer n-1 disks from the intermediate pole to the destination *)
END;
```

The transfer of n-1 disks can be accomplished by a recursive call to `transfer`. Thus, we can write

```
transfer(n-1,origin,other,destination)
```

for the first transfer, and

```
transfer(n-1,other,destination,origin)
```

for the second. (Note the order of the parameters in each call.) The actual movement of a disk from the origin to the destination simply requires displaying the values for `origin` and `destination`. This can be carried out by calling another procedure, called `diskmove`, which is defined within `transfer`. The complete procedure `transfer` can be written as follows.

```
PROCEDURE transfer(n,origin,destination,other : integer);

    PROCEDURE diskmove(origin,destination : integer);
    BEGIN
        writeln('Move ',origin:1,' to ',destination:1)
    END;

BEGIN
    IF n>0 THEN BEGIN
        transfer(n-1,origin,other,destination);
        diskmove(origin,destination);
        transfer(n-1,other,destination,origin)
    END
END;
```

It is now a simple matter to add the main block, which merely reads in a value for n and then initiates the computation by calling `transfer`. In this first procedure call, the actual parameters will be specified as integer numbers; i.e.,

```
transfer(n,1,3,2)
```

This specifies the transfer of all n disks from pole 1 (the origin) to pole 3 (the destination), using pole 2 for intermediate storage.

Here is the complete program.

```
PROGRAM towersofhanoi1;

(* THE TOWERS OF HANOI, USING RECURSIVE PROCEDURE CALLS *)

VAR n : integer;
```

(Program continues on next page)

```
        PROCEDURE transfer(n,origin,destination,other : integer);
        (* Transfer n disks from the origin to the destination *)

            PROCEDURE diskmove(origin,destination : integer);
            (* Move a single disk from the origin to the destination *)
            BEGIN
                writeln('Move ',origin:1,' to ',destination:1)
            END;   (* diskmove *)

        BEGIN    (* transfer *)
            IF n>0 THEN BEGIN
                            transfer(n-1,origin,other,destination);
                            diskmove(origin,destination);
                            transfer(n-1,other,destination,origin)
            END
        END;   (* transfer *)

    BEGIN      (* main action block *)
        write('Enter the number of disks -> ');
        readln(n);
        writeln;
        transfer(n,1,3,2)
    END.
```

It should be understood that a *different* set of values is defined for the value parameters n, origin, destination and other each time transfer is called. These sets of values will be stored independently of one another within the computer's memory. It is this ability to store these independent sets of values and then retrieve them at the proper time that allows the recursion to work.

When the program is executed for the case where n = 3, the following output is obtained.

```
    Enter the number of disks -> 3

    Move 1 to 3
    Move 1 to 2
    Move 3 to 2
    Move 1 to 3
    Move 2 to 1
    Move 2 to 3
    Move 1 to 3
```

You should think through this sequence of moves to verify that it is indeed correct.

In all of the recursive examples that we have seen so far, a single procedure or a single function has called itself. There is another form of recursion, called *mutual recursion*, in which one procedure (or one function) calls another, and the second procedure (or function) then calls the first. Recall, however, that a procedure or function cannot be accessed before it has been declared. Thus there is a potential problem with mutual recursion, when the first procedure (or function) calls the second before it has been declared.

Pascal solves this problem by allowing a *dummy declaration* for the second procedure (or function) to precede the first procedure (or function). This dummy declaration consists of the procedure (function) header, followed by the keyword FORWARD. The true declaration for the second procedure (function) is then written in the proper place, after the first procedure (function) declaration. It is written in the usual manner except that the formal parameter list is omitted from the header. In the case of a function, the result type is also omitted.

EXAMPLE 7.23

Here is a skeletal outline of a function that calls a procedure, which then recursively calls the function.

```
FUNCTION second(a,b : real) : real; FORWARD;    (* dummy declaration *)

PROCEDURE first(x,y : real);
VAR w : real;
BEGIN
   . . . . .
   w := second(x,y);
   . . . . .
END;

FUNCTION second;
VAR u,v : real;
BEGIN
   . . . . .
   first(u,v);
   . . . . .
   second := . . .
   . . . . .
END;
```

Notice that the dummy declaration for second is necessary so that first can access second before second has been declared. The true declaration for second then follows the declaration for first. Note that the function header in second is now abbreviated.

You should understand that the use of recursion is not necessarily the best way to approach a problem, even though the problem definition may be recursive in nature. A nonrecursive implementation may be more efficient in terms of memory utilization and execution speed. Thus, the use of recursion frequently involves a tradeoff between simplicity and performance degradation. Each problem should therefore be judged on its own individual merits.

7.6 MORE ABOUT PARAMETERS

Sometimes it is desirable for a given procedure or function to access another procedure or function that has been defined (declared) outside the scope of the given procedure or function. For example, we may wish to have procedure A make use of function B, though function B has been defined outside of procedure A. In ANSI Pascal, this may be accomplished by passing the external procedure or function (e.g., function B) to the given procedure or function (e.g., procedure A) as a parameter. Thus, ANSI Pascal supports procedure parameters and function parameters as well as value parameters and variable parameters.

The formal parameter declaration for a procedure or a function parameter is written in the form of a procedure or a function header, as illustrated below.

EXAMPLE 7.24

Consider the procedure process within an ANSI Pascal program. Suppose this function must access an externally defined real function that includes an integer-type parameter. Let us refer to this externally defined function as f. The procedure (process) might appear as follows.

```
PROCEDURE process (FUNCTION f(u : integer) : real; c1,c2 : integer);
VAR c : integer;
    x : real;
BEGIN
   FOR c := c1 TO c2 DO
      BEGIN
         x := f(c);
         writeln(' x=',x)
      END
END;
```

The main block might include the following reference to this procedure.

```
process(calc,1,100);
```

where the function `calc` is defined within the main block.

Here is a skeletal structure of the entire program.

```
PROGRAM transfer;
. . . . .
FUNCTION calc(w : integer) : real;                  (* function definition *)
. . . . .
BEGIN   (* function calc *)
   . . . . .
   calc := . . .
END;   (* calc *)


                                                    (* procedure definition *)
PROCEDURE process (FUNCTION f(u : integer) : real; c1,c2 : integer);
VAR c : integer;
    x : real;
BEGIN
   FOR c := c1 TO c2 DO
      BEGIN
         x := f(c);
         writeln(' x=',x)
      END
END;   (* process *)

BEGIN   (* main block *)
   . . . . .
   process(calc,1,100);
   . . . . .
END.
```

The formal procedure and function parameters and the actual procedure and function parameters must correspond with respect to their own parameters. This correspondence must include the number, class, and type of parameters.

ANSI Pascal does not permit *standard* procedures or *standard* functions to be passed as parameters. However, some implementations of the language do not impose this restriction.

Procedure parameters and function parameters are particularly useful when the given procedure or function accesses *different* procedures or functions (i.e., makes use of different actual parameters) at different calling points. The use of this technique is illustrated in the next two examples.

EXAMPLE 7.25

Consider once again the ANSI Pascal procedure process, defined in the last example. This procedure can be accessed several times in the main block, with a different function parameter included in each access. Thus, the main block might include the statements

```
process(calc,1,100);
. . . . .
process(flag,-10,50);
```

where the functions calc and flag are defined within the main block.

EXAMPLE 7.26

Here is an example of a function being passed to another function within an ANSI Pascal program.

```
FUNCTION sum (x : real; FUNCTION f(c : integer; x : real) : real;
                                              c1,c2 : integer) : real;

VAR c : integer;
    s : real;
BEGIN
    s := 0;
    FOR c := c1 TO c2 DO s := s + f(c,x);
    sum := s
END;
```

In this example the function sum calculates the sum of several values, where each value is determined by accessing the function f which is passed to sum as a parameter.

The main block might include several statements such as

```
value1 := sum(x,root,a,b);
. . . . .
value2 := sum(z,cube,1,n+1);
```

where root and cube are functions defined elsewhere within the program, x and z are real variables, and a, b and n are integer variables. Note that sum accepts a different actual parameter (first root, then cube) each time it is accessed.

In order to pass a procedure or function as a parameter to another procedure or function in Turbo Pascal, we must first define a procedure or function data type. (Type definitions are formally introduced and discussed in the next chapter.) The formal parameter within the receiving procedure or function is then written as a procedure-type or function-type parameter. The corresponding actual parameter can be either a procedure or function name, or a procedure- or function-type variable that has been assigned a procedure or a function name. The following example illustrates how this is done.

EXAMPLE 7.27

The outline of a Turbo Pascal program is shown below. In this program a function and a procedure are passed to procedure process at one point in the program, then a different function and a different procedure are passed to process at a different point in the program.

```
PROGRAM TurboTransfer;
{$F+}                         (* special Turbo Pascal directive *)
TYPE func = function(x : real) : real;
     proc = procedure(VAR x : real);

VAR x : real;
    f : func;
    p : proc;

FUNCTION f1(w : real) : real;
BEGIN
  . . . . .
   f1 := . . .
END;

FUNCTION f2(w : real) : real;
BEGIN
  . . . . .
   f2 := . . .
END;

PROCEDURE p1(VAR w : real);
BEGIN
  . . . . .
END;

PROCEDURE p2(VAR w : real);
BEGIN
  . . . . .
END;

PROCEDURE process(x : real; f : func; p : proc);
(* accepts a real, a function and a procedure as parameters *)
VAR z : real;
BEGIN
  . . . . .
   z := f(x);                 (* function call *)
  . . . . .
   p(z);                      (* procedure call *)
  . . . . .
END;

BEGIN   (* main action block *)
   writeln(' Please enter a real number: ');
   readln(x);
  . . . . .
   process(x,f1,p2);       (* procedure call *)
  . . . . .
   f := f2;
   p := p1;
   process(x,f,p)          (* procedure call, params written differently *)
END.
```

This program begins by defining `func` as a function data type and `proc` as a procedure data type. The variables `f` and `p` are then declared as `func`-type and `proc`-type variables, respectively. We then encounter two conventional function declarations (`f1` and `f2`), each function accepting a real parameter (`w`) and returning a real value, and two conventional procedure declarations (`p1` and `p2`), each procedure accepting a real variable parameter(w).

The last procedure declaration (`process`) includes three formal parameters: `x`, a real-type parameter, `f`, a `func`-type parameter and `p`, a `proc`-type parameter. This procedure will therefore accept a real quantity, a function and a procedure as parameters. The function passed as a parameter is accessed at some point within `process`, as seen in the outline. The procedure passed as a parameter is then accessed at some later point.

The main portion of the program accesses `process` in two different places. In each access, different actual parameters are passed to `process`. In particular, function `f1` and parameter `p2` are passed to `process` in the first access, whereas function `f2` and procedure `p1` are passed to `process` in the second access.

The actual parameters are written differently in each procedure access, simply to illustrate different options. In the first procedure access, the function and procedure names, `f1` and `p2`, are passed directly as actual parameters. In the second procedure access, the function `f2` is assigned to the `func`-type variable `f`, and the procedure `p1` is assigned to the `proc`-type variable `p`; the variables `f` and `p` are then passed as actual parameters.

Notice the symbol {$F+}, which appears in the second line of the outline. This is a Turbo Pascal *directive*; it is required in order to assign a procedure or function to a procedure- or function-type variable.

Turbo Pascal, like ANSI Pascal, does not permit standard procedures or standard functions to be passed as parameters, nor does it permit nested procedures or functions to be passed as parameters. In addition, the {$F+} directive must be included, as in the preceding example.

Review Questions

7.1   What are the advantages of program modularization? What two types of program modules are available in Pascal?

7.2   How is a procedure referenced? What other words are used to refer to a procedure reference?

7.3   Describe the grammatical structure of a procedure. How is the procedure header written?

7.4   In what part of a Pascal program must a procedure declaration appear?

7.5   What is the difference between global and local identifiers? Which is preferable and why?

7.6   What is meant by the scope of an identifier?

7.7   What is meant by nested procedures? What restriction requires particular attention when attempting to access nested procedures?

7.8   Does the concept of scope apply only to identifiers that represent constants and variables? Explain.

7.9   How do the rules of scope affect transfers of control associated with the use of the GOTO statement?

7.10   What are parameters? How are they used?

7.11   What is the difference between actual parameters and formal parameters?

7.12   Summarize the rules that must be observed when substituting actual parameters for formal parameters.

7.13   What are the four different classes of formal parameters? How do they differ?

7.14   What are value parameters? How are formal value parameters written? For what type of application are value parameters generally used?

7.15   What are variable parameters? How are formal variable parameters written? How do variable parameters differ from value parameters, in terms of

(*a*)   the way they are written

(*b*)   the way they are used

7.16   What is a function? How does a function differ from a procedure?

7.17   How is a function referenced? Compare with a procedure reference.

7.18   Describe the grammatical structure of a function. How is the function header written? How does this grammatical structure differ from that of a procedure?

7.19   Where within a Pascal program must a function declaration appear? Is there any particular ordering that must be observed between procedure declarations and function declarations?

7.20   Can functions be nested in the same manner as procedures? Can the nesting of functions and procedures be interchanged?

7.21   What is meant by the side effects associated with a function? Are procedures also susceptible to side effects?

7.22   What is meant by recursion? Is recursion an essential programming technique?

7.23   When writing a recursive procedure or function, what prevents the recursive process from continuing indefinitely?

7.24   What advantage does recursion offer with respect to the storage of multiple data items?

7.25   Suppose that a recursive procedure or function includes a set of local variables. As the procedure or function is accessed repeatedly, how are the local variables interpreted?

7.26   What is meant by mutual recursion?

7.27   When defining mutually recursive procedures (or functions), what potential problem is solved by the use of a dummy declaration? How is the dummy declaration written? What changes must be made to other declarations because of the dummy declaration?

7.28   When is it desirable to pass a procedure or a function as a parameter?

7.29   When a procedure or a function is passed as a parameter, what correspondence must be maintained between formal parameters and actual parameters?

7.30   How are formal procedure parameters and formal function parameters written in ANSI Pascal?

7.31   How are procedures or functions passed to other procedures or functions in Turbo Pascal? Compare with the method used in ANSI Pascal.

7.32   What restrictions apply when passing procedures or functions to other procedures or functions? Can standard procedures or standard functions be passed as parameters? Can nested procedures or nested functions be passed as parameters?

Problems

7.33 Several statements containing procedure and function references are outlined below. Describe the meaning of each statement. (Assume that `sample` and `sample1` are procedures, and that `demo` and `demo1` are functions. Type compatibility is assumed throughout.)

(*a*)　`sample;`

(*b*)　`sample1(a,b,c);`

(*c*)　`sample1(a+b,2*x,sqr(c));`

(*d*)　`z := demo;`

(*e*)　`z := a + 2*demo − 3;`

(*f*)　`z := demo1(a,b,c);`

(*g*)　`z := y + demo1(a+b,2*x,sqr(c));`

(*h*)　`IF demo1(a,b,c) < zstar THEN z := demo1(a,b,c);`

7.34 Describe the output that is generated by each of the following Pascal programs.

(*a*)
```
PROGRAM a;
VAR i : integer;

PROCEDURE proc1;
VAR i : integer;
BEGIN
   i := 3;
   write(i:3)
END;

BEGIN
   i := 1;
   write(i:3);
   proc1;
   write(i:3)
END.
```

(*b*)
```
PROGRAM b;
VAR i : integer;

PROCEDURE proc1;
BEGIN
   i := 3;
   write(i:3)
END;

BEGIN
   i := 1;
   write(i:3);
   proc1;
   write(i:3)
END.
```

(c)
```
PROGRAM c;
VAR i : integer;

PROCEDURE proc1(i : integer);
BEGIN
   i := 3;
   write(i:3)
END;

BEGIN
   i := 1;
   write(i:3);
   proc1(i);
   write(i:3)
END.
```

(d)
```
PROGRAM d;
VAR i : integer;

PROCEDURE proc1(VAR i : integer);
BEGIN
   i := 3;
   write(i:3)
END;

BEGIN
   i := 1;
   write(i:3);
   proc1(i);
   write(i:3)
END.
```

(e)
```
PROGRAM e;
VAR i : integer;

PROCEDURE proc1(i : integer);
BEGIN
   i := i+2;
   write(i:3)
END;

PROCEDURE proc2(i : integer);
BEGIN
   i := i+3;
   proc1(i);
   write(i:3)
END;

BEGIN
   i := 1;
   proc1(i);
   proc2(i);
   write(i:3)
END.
```

```
(f)    PROGRAM f;
       VAR i : integer;

       PROCEDURE proc2(i : integer); forward;

       PROCEDURE proc1(i : integer);
       BEGIN
          i := i+3;
          proc2(i);
          write(i:3)
       END;

       PROCEDURE proc2;
       BEGIN
          i := i+2;
          write(i:3)
       END;

       BEGIN
          i := 1;
          proc1(i);
          proc2(i);
          write(i:3)
       END.

(g)    PROGRAM g;
       VAR i : integer;

       FUNCTION fun1(i : integer) : integer;
       BEGIN
          i := i+1;
          fun1 := i
       END;

       BEGIN
          i := 2;
          write(fun1(i):3,i:3)
       END.

(h)    PROGRAM h;
       VAR i : integer;

       FUNCTION fun1 : integer;
       BEGIN
          i := i+1;
          fun1 := i
       END;

       BEGIN
          i := 2;
          write(fun1:3,i:3)
       END.
```

(*i*)   ```
PROGRAM i;
VAR j : integer;

FUNCTION fun1(i : integer) : integer;
BEGIN
    i := i+1;
    write(i:3);
    fun1 := i
END;

FUNCTION fun2(i : integer) : integer;
BEGIN
    i := i+2;
    write(i:3);
    fun2 := fun1(i)+i
END;

BEGIN
    j := 2;
    write(j:3,fun2(j):3)
END.
```

(*j*)   ```
PROGRAM j;
VAR k : integer;

PROCEDURE proc1(VAR i : integer);
BEGIN
    i := i+1;
    write(i:3)
END;

FUNCTION fun1(i : integer) : integer;
BEGIN
    i := i+2;
    proc1(i);
    write(i:3);
    fun1 := i+3
END;

BEGIN
    k := 2;
    proc1(k);
    write(k:3,fun1(k):3)
END.
```

(*k*)   ```
PROGRAM k;
VAR sum : integer;

PROCEDURE add(i : integer);
BEGIN
    sum := sum+i;
    IF i > O THEN add(i-1)
END;
```

(*Program continues on next page*)
```

```
         BEGIN
            sum := 0;
            add(5);
            writeln('sum = ',sum)
         END.
```

(*l*)   PROGRAM l;

```
      FUNCTION sum(i : integer) : integer;
      BEGIN
         IF i < 1 THEN sum := 0
                  ELSE sum := i+sum(i–2);
      END;

      BEGIN
         writeln('sum = ',sum(9))
      END.
```

(*m*)   PROGRAM m;

```
      (* ANSI Pascal *)

      VAR x : real;

      FUNCTION f1(w : real) : real;
      BEGIN
         f1 := 10*w
      END;

      FUNCTION f2(w : real) : real;
      BEGIN
         f2 := 0.1*w
      END;

      PROCEDURE p1(w : real);
      BEGIN
         writeln(w:5)
      END;

      PROCEDURE p2(w : real);
      BEGIN
         writeln(w:5:3)
      END;

      PROCEDURE p3(x : real; FUNCTION f(x : real) : real;
                            PROCEDURE p(x : real));
      VAR z : real;
      BEGIN
         z := f(x);
         p(z)
      END;
```

(Program continues on next page)

```
        BEGIN
           x := 1.5;
           p3(x,f1,p1);
           p3(x,f2,p1);
           p3(x,f2,p2);
           p3(x,f1,p2)
        END.

(n)     PROGRAM n;
        {$F+}                       (* this program is unique to Turbo Pascal *)
        TYPE func = function(x : real) : real;
             proc = procedure(VAR x : real);

        VAR x : real;
            f : func;
            p : proc;

        FUNCTION f1(w : real) : real;
        BEGIN
           f1 := frac(w)
        END;

        FUNCTION f2(w : real) : real;
        BEGIN
           f2 := int(w)
        END;

        PROCEDURE p1(VAR w : real);
        BEGIN
           w := 2*w
        END;

        PROCEDURE p2(VAR w : real);
        BEGIN
           w := w/2
        END;

        PROCEDURE process(x : real; f : func; p : proc);
        VAR z : real;
        BEGIN
           z := f(x);
           p(z);
           writeln(' z =',z:5:2)
        END;

        BEGIN
           x := 1.5;
           process(x,f1,p1);
           process(x,f1,p2);
           f := f2;
           p := p1;
           process(x,f,p);
           p := p2;
           process(x,f,p)
        END.
```

7.35 Express each of the following formulas in a recursive form.

(a) $y = (x_1 + x_2 + \cdots + x_n)$

(b) $y = 1 - x + x^2/2 - x^3/6 + x^4/24 + \cdots + (-1)^n x^n/n!$

(c) $p = (f_1 * f_2 * \cdots * f_n)$

Programming Problems

7.36 Write a procedure that will calculate the real roots of the quadratic equation

$$ax^2 + bx + c = 0$$

using the quadratic formula

$$\frac{-b \pm \sqrt{b^2 - 4ac}}{2a}$$

Assume that a, b and c are real constants whose values are given, and that x_1 and x_2 are the calculated roots. Also, assume that $b^2 > 4ac$, so that the calculated roots will always be real.

7.37 Write a complete Pascal program that will calculate the real roots of the quadratic equation

$$ax^2 + bx + c = 0$$

using the quadratic formula, as described in the previous problem. Read the coefficients a, b and c into the computer in the main action block. Then access the procedure written for the preceding problem in order to obtain the desired solution. Finally, display the values of the coefficients, followed by the calculated values of x_1 and x_2. Be sure that all of the output is clearly labeled.

Test the program using the following data.

$a = 2$	$b = 6$	$c = 1$
3	3	0
1	3	1

7.38 Modify the procedure written for Prob. 7.36 so that *all* roots of the quadratic equation

$$ax^2 + bx + c = 0$$

will be calculated, given the values of a, b and c. Note that the roots will be repeated (i.e., there will only be one real root) if $b^2 = 4ac$. Also, the roots will be complex if $b^2 < 4ac$. In this case, the real part of each root will be determined as

$$-b/2a$$

and the imaginary parts will be calculated as

$$\left\{ \pm \sqrt{(4ac - b^2)} \right\} i$$

where i represents $\sqrt{-1}$.

7.39 Modify the Pascal program written for Prob. 7.37 so that *all* roots of the quadratic equation

$$ax^2 + bx + c = 0$$

will be calculated, using the procedure written for Prob. 7.38. Be sure that all of the output is clearly labeled. Test the program using the following data.

$a = 2$	$b = 6$	$c = 1$
3	3	0
1	3	1
0	12	-3
3	6	3
2	-4	3

7.40 Write a function that will allow a real or integer-type number to be raised to an integer-type power. In other words, we wish to evaluate the formula

$$y = x^n$$

where y and x are either real or integer-type variables and n is an integer-type variable. (Assume that y and x will always be of the same type.)

7.41 Write a complete Pascal program that will read in numerical values for x and n, evaluate the formula

$$y = x^n$$

using the function written for Prob. 7.40, and then write out the calculated result. Test the program using the following data.

$x = 2$	$n = 3$	$x = 1.5$	$n = 3$
2	12	1.5	10
2	-5	1.5	-5
-3	3	0.2	3
-3	7	0.2	5
-3	-5	0.2	-5

7.42 Expand the function written for Prob. 7.40 so that x can be raised to any power, either real or integer. (*Hint*: use logarithms if the exponent is of type real. Remember to test for negative values of x.) Include this function in the program written for Prob. 7.41. Test the program using the data given in Prob. 7.41 and the following additional data.

$x = 2$	$n = 0.2$	$x = 1.5$	$n = 0.2$
2	-0.8	1.5	-0.8
-3	0.2	0.2	0.2
-3	-0.8	0.2	-0.8
		0.2	0.0

7.43 Modify the character encoding program given in Example 6.13 so that it makes use of a procedure. Compile and execute the program to be sure that it runs correctly.

7.44 Modify the program for calculating the solution of an algebraic equation, given in Example 6.14, so that each iteration is carried out within a function. Compile and execute the program to be sure that it runs correctly.

7.45 Modify the program for averaging a list of numbers, given in Example 7.8, so that it makes use of a function. Test the program using the following 10 numbers:

27.5	87.0
13.4	39.9
53.8	47.7
29.2	8.1
74.5	63.2

7.46 The program given in Example 7.14 can easily be modified to *minimize* a function of x. Such a minimization procedure can provide us with a highly effective technique for calculating the roots of a nonlinear algebraic equation. For example, suppose we want to find the particular value of x that causes some function $f(x)$ to equal zero. A typical function of this nature might be

$$f(x) = x + \cos(x) - 1 - \sin(x).$$

If we let $y(x) = f(x)^2$, then the function $y(x)$ will always be positive except for those values of x that are roots of the given function, i.e., for which $f(x)$, and hence $y(x)$, will equal zero. Therefore any value of x that causes $y(x)$ to be minimized will also be a root of the equation $f(x) = 0$.

Modify the program shown in Example 7.14 to minimize a given function. Use the program to obtain the roots of the following equations:

(a) $x + \cos(x) = 1 + \sin(x)$, $\pi/2 < x < \pi$

(b) $x^5 + 3x^2 + 10$, $0 <= x <= 3$ (see Example 6.14)

7.47 Modify the program shown in Example 7.18 so that a sequence of craps games will be simulated automatically, in a noninteractive manner. Include an integer-type counter that will determine the total number of wins, and an integer input variable whose value will specify how many games will be simulated.

Use the program to simulate some large number of games (e.g., 1000). Estimate the probability of coming out ahead when playing craps. (This value, expressed as a decimal, is equal to the number of wins divided by the total number of games played. If the probability exceeds 0.500, it favors the player; otherwise it favors the house.)

7.48 Rewrite each of the following programs so that it includes at least one procedure or function, whichever is most appropriate. Be careful with your choice of parameters.

(a) Calculate the weighted average of a list of numbers [see Prob. 6.50(a)].

(b) Calculate the cumulative product of a list of numbers [see Prob. 6.50(b)].

(c) Calculate the geometric average of a list of numbers [see Prob. 6.50(c)].

(d) Calculate and tabulate a list of prime numbers [see Prob. 6.50(f)].

(e) Compute the sine of x, using the method described in Prob. 6.50(i).

(f) Compute the repayments on a loan [see Prob. 6.50 (j)].

(g) Determine the average exam score for each student in a class, as described in Prob. 6.50(k).

7.49 Write a complete Pascal program to solve each of the problems described below. Utilize procedures and/or functions wherever appropriate. Compile and execute each program using the data given in the problem description.

(a) Suppose you place a given sum of money, A, into a savings account at the beginning of each year for n years. If the account earns interest at the rate of i percent annually, then the amount of money that will have accumulated after n years, F, is given by

$$F = A \, [(1 + i/100) + (1 + i/100)^2 + (1 + i/100)^3 + \cdots + (1 + i/100)^n]$$

Write an interactive Pascal program to determine the following.

(i) How much money will accumulate after 30 years if $1000 is deposited at the beginning of each year and the interest rate is 6 percent per year, compounded annually?

(ii) How much money must be deposited at the beginning of each year in order to accumulate $100,000 after 30 years, again assuming that the interest rate is 6 percent per year, with annual compounding?

In each case, first determine the unknown amount of money. Then create a table showing the total amount of money that will have accumulated at the end of each year. Use the function written for Prob. 7.40 to carry out the exponentiation.

(b) Modify the above program to accommodate quarterly rather than annual compounding of interest. Compare the calculated results obtained for both problems. *Hint*: the proper formula is

$$F = A \, [(1 + i/100m)^m + (1 + i/100m)^{2m} + (1 + i/100m)^{3m} + \cdots + (1 + i/100m)^{nm}]$$

where m represents the number of interest periods per year.

(c) Home mortgage costs are determined in such a manner that the borrower pays the same amount of money to the lending institution each month throughout the life of the mortgage. The fraction of the total monthly payment that is required as an interest payment on the outstanding balance of the loan varies, however, from month to month. Early in the life of the mortgage most of the monthly payment is required to pay interest, and only a small fraction of the total monthly payment is applied toward reducing the amount of the loan. Gradually, the outstanding balance becomes smaller, which causes the monthly interest payment to decrease, and the amount that is used to reduce the outstanding balance therefore increases. Hence the balance of the loan is reduced at an accelerated rate.

Typically, prospective home buyers know how much money they must borrow and the time required for repayment. They then ask a lending institution how much their monthly payment will be at the prevailing interest rate. They should also be concerned with how much of each monthly payment is charged to interest, how much total interest they have paid since they first borrowed the money, and how much money they still owe the lending institution at the end of each month.

Write a Pascal program that can be used by a lending institution to provide a potential customer with this information. Assume that the amount of the loan, the annual interest rate and the duration of the loan are specified. The amount of the monthly payment is calculated as

$$A = i \, P \, (1 + i)^n / [(1 + i)^n - 1]$$

where A = monthly payment, dollars

P = total amount of the loan, dollars

i = monthly interest rate, expressed as a decimal (e.g., express 1/2 percent as 0.005)

n = total number of monthly payments

The monthly interest payment can then be calculated from the formula

$$I = i \, B$$

where I = monthly interest payment, dollars

B = current outstanding balance, dollars

The current outstanding balance is simply equal to the original amount of the loan, less the sum of the previous payments toward principal. The monthly payment toward principal (i.e., the amount which is used to reduce the outstanding balance) is simply

$$T = A - I$$

where T = monthly payment toward principal.

Make use of the function written for Prob. 7.35 to carry out the exponentiation.

Use the program to calculate the cost of a 25-year, $50,000 mortgage at an annual interest rate of 8 percent. Then repeat the calculations for an annual interest rate of 8.5 percent. How significant is the additional 0.5 percent in the interest rate over the entire life of the mortgage?

(d) The method used to calculate the cost of a home mortgage in the previous problem is known as a *constant payment* method, since each monthly payment is the same. Suppose instead that the monthly payments were computed by the method of simple interest. That is, suppose that the same amount is applied toward reducing the loan each month. Hence

$$T = P / n$$

However, the monthly interest will depend on the amount of the outstanding balance; that is,

$$I = i B$$

Thus the total monthly payment, $A = T + I$, will decrease each month as the outstanding balance diminishes.

Write a Pascal program to calculate the cost of a home mortgage using this method of repayment. Label the output clearly. Use the program to calculate the cost of a 25-year, $50,000 loan at 8 percent annual interest. Compare the results with those obtained in Prob. 7.49(c).

(e) Suppose we are given a number of discrete points (x_1, y_1), (x_2, y_2), . . . , (x_n, y_n) which are read from a curve $y = f(x)$, where x is bounded between x_1 and x_n. We wish to approximate the area under the curve by breaking up the curve into a number of small rectangles and calculating the area of these rectangles. (This is known as the *trapezoidal rule*.) The appropriate formula is

$$A = (y_1 + y_2)(x_2 - x_1)/2 + (y_2 + y_3)(x_3 - x_2)/2 + \cdots + (y_{n-1} + y_n)(x_n - x_{n-1})/2$$

Notice that the average height of each rectangle is given by $(y_i + y_{i+1})/2$ and the width of each rectangle is equal to $(x_{i+1} - x_i)$ for $i = 1, 2, \ldots, (n-1)$.

Write a Pascal program to implement this strategy, using a function to evaluate the mathematical formula $y = f(x)$. Use the program to calculate the area under the curve $y = x^3$ between the limits $x = 1$ and $x = 4$. Solve this problem first with 16 evenly spaced points, then with 61 points, and finally with 301 points. Note that the accuracy of the solution will improve as the number of points increases. (The exact answer to this problem is 63.75.)

(f) The preceding problem describes a method known as the *trapezoidal rule* for calculating the area under a curve $y(x)$, where a set of tabulated values (x_1, y_1), (x_2, y_2), . . ., (x_n, y_n) is used to describe the curve. If the tabulated values of x are equally spaced, then the equation given in the preceding problem can be simplified to read

$$A = (y_1 + 2y_2 + 2y_3 + 2y_4 + \cdots + 2y_{n-1} + y_n) h/2$$

where h is the distance between successive values of x.

Another technique that applies when there is an even number of equally spaced intervals, i.e., an odd number of data points, is *Simpson's rule*. The computational equation for implementing Simpson's rule is

$$A = (y_1 + 4y_2 + 2y_3 + 4y_4 + 2y_5 + \cdots + 4y_{n-1} + y_n) h/3$$

For a given value of h, this method will yield a more accurate result than the trapezoidal rule. (Note that the method requires about the same amount of computational complexity as the trapezoidal rule.)

Write a Pascal program for calculating the area under a curve using either of the above techniques, assuming an odd number of equally spaced data points. Implement each method with a separate procedure, utilizing a function to evaluate $y(x)$. Use the program to calculate the area under the curve

$$y = e^{-x}$$

where x ranges from 0 to 1. Calculate the area using each method, and compare the results with the correct answer of $A = 0.7468241$.

(g)   Still another technique for calculating the area under a curve is to employ the *Monte Carlo* method, which makes use of randomly generated numbers. Suppose that the curve $y = f(x)$ is positive for any value of x between the specified lower and upper limits $x = a$ and $x = b$. Let the largest value of y within these limits be y^*. The Monte Carlo method proceeds as follows.

(*i*)   Begin with a counter set equal to zero.

(*ii*)   Generate a random number, r_x, whose value lies between a and b.

(*iii*)   Evaluate $y(r_x)$.

(*iv*)   Generate a second random number, r_y, whose value lies between 0 and y^*.

(*v*)   Compare r_y with $y(r_x)$. If r_y is less than or equal to $y(r_x)$, then this point will fall on or under the given curve. Hence the counter is incremented by 1.

(*vi*)   Repeat steps (*ii*) through (*v*) a large number of times. Each time will be called a *cycle*.

(*vii*)   When a specified number of cycles has been completed, the fraction of points which fell on or under the curve, f, is computed as the value of the counter divided by the total number of cycles. The area under the curve is then obtained as

$$A = f y^* (b - a).$$

Write a Pascal program to implement this strategy. Use this program to find the area under the curve $y = e^{-x}$ between the limits $a = 0$ and $b = 1$. Determine how many cycles are required to obtain an answer that is accurate to 3 significant figures. Compare the computer time required for this problem with the time required for the preceding problem. Which method is better?

(h)   A normally distributed random variate x, with mean μ and standard deviation σ, can be generated from the formula

$$x = \mu + \sigma \frac{\sum_{i=1}^{n} r_i - n/2}{\sqrt{n/12}}$$

where r_i is a uniformly distributed random number whose value lies between 0 and 1. A value of $n = 12$ is frequently selected when using this formula. The underlying basis for the formula is the *central limit theorem*, which states that a set of mean values of uniformly distributed random variates will be normally distributed.

Write a Pascal program that will generate a specified number of normally distributed random variates with a given mean and a given standard deviation. Let the number of random variates, the mean and the standard deviation be input parameters.

(i)   Write a Pascal program that will allow a person to play a game of tic-tac-toe against the computer. Write the program in such a manner that the computer can be either the first or the second player. If the computer is to be the first player, let the first move be generated randomly (see Example 7.18). Write out the complete status of the game after each move. Have the computer acknowledge a win by either player when it occurs.

7.50   For each of the following problems, write an interactive Pascal program that includes a recursive function.

   (a)   Determine the value of the nth Fibonacci number, F_n, where $F_n = F_{n-1} + F_{n-2}$ and $F_1 = F_2 = 1$ [see Prob. 6.50(e)]. Let the value of n be an input parameter.

   (b)   The *Legendre polynomials* can be calculated by means of the formulas $P_0 = 1$, $P_1 = x$,

   $$P_n = \frac{2n-1}{n} x P_{n-1} - \frac{n-1}{n} P_{n-2}$$

   where $n = 2, 3, 4, \ldots$ and x is any real number between -1 and 1. (Note that the Legendre polynomials are real-type quantities.) Let the values of n and x be input parameters.

Chapter 8

User-Defined Simple-Type Data

We have already seen that there are two general categories of simple-type data in Pascal. They are *standard-type* data and *user-defined* data (see Section 2.7). These two categories can be further subdivided as follows.

1. Standard-type data
   (*a*) integer
   (*b*) real
   (*c*) char
   (*d*) boolean
2. User-defined data
   (*a*) enumerated
   (*b*) subrange

The use of standard-type data has already been discussed in detail in Chap. 3. We now turn our attention to user-defined simple data types. In particular, we will consider *subrange-type* data and *enumerated-type* data. We will see how these simple data types can be declared, and how they can be utilized effectively within a Pascal program.

8.1 SUBRANGE-TYPE DATA

A *subrange* refers to some portion of the original range of an ordered, simple data type. Subrange-type data are the data items that fall within this subrange, thus forming a subset of contiguous, ordered data. The original data type is referred to as the *host* data type. Each of the data items falling within the subrange is considered to be of the host type. The name given to the subrange constitutes a new, user-defined data type.

The subrange concept can be applied to any set of ordered, simple data. This includes previously defined enumerated data (discussed in the next section) as well as three of the standard data types — integer, char and boolean. Note that real-type data *cannot* be used to define a subrange.

The association between the name of the new data type and its individual data items is established by the *type definition*. The general form of a subrange-type definition is written as

```
TYPE name = first data item..last data item
```

where *name* is the name of the subrange data type, `first data item` is the first of the ordered data items within the subrange, and `last data item` is the last of the ordered data items. The complete subrange will consist of all data items contained within these two bounds, including the bounds themselves. Note the two consecutive periods that separate the first and last data items.

EXAMPLE 8.1

Consider the following type definitions.

200

```
TYPE dayofyear = 1..365;
     counter = 1..maxint;
     caps = 'A'..'Z';
```

Here we define three different subrange types, called `dayofyear`, `counter` and `caps`, respectively. Thus, data of type `dayofyear` can take on any integer value between 1 and 365. Similarly, data of type `counter` can take on any integer value between 1 and the largest permissible integer value (see Section 3.6). Data of type `caps`, on the other hand, can take on any of the uppercase characters A through Z.

Once these new data types have been established, we can define variables that are of these data types. For example,

```
VAR day : dayofyear;
     i : counter;
     symbol : caps;
```

Thus, `day` is a variable of type `dayofyear`, `i` is a variable of type `counter` and `symbol` is a variable of type `caps`.

Since subrange-type data are always ordered, subrange variables may be used with the relational operators to form boolean expressions. They may also be used with the standard functions `pred`, `succ` and `ord`, in the same manner as other ordered simple-type data. We will see examples of this later in this chapter.

8.2 ENUMERATED-TYPE DATA

An *enumerated* data type consists of an ordered sequence of identifiers, where each identifier is interpreted as an individual data item. These data items will collectively be associated with a particular name that serves to identify the enumerated data type.

In general terms, the type definition is written as

```
TYPE name = (data item 1,data item 2,. . . .,data item n)
```

where *name* is the name of the enumerated data type, and *data item 1*, *data item 2*, etc. are the actual data items.

EXAMPLE 8.2

In this example we define an enumerated data type called `days`. The actual data items will be the days of the week; i.e., `sunday`, `monday`, `tuesday`, `wednesday`, `thursday`, `friday` and `saturday`. Thus, the type definition will be written as

```
TYPE days = (sunday,monday,tuesday,wednesday,thursday,friday,saturday);
```

Notice that the data items are enclosed in parentheses and separated by commas.

We can now define individual variables of type `days`. For example,

```
VAR offdays : days;
```

Thus, `offdays` can take on any of the values `sunday`, `monday`, . . . , `saturday`.

We can define a subrange of an enumerated data type if we wish. To do so, the enumerated type definition must precede the subrange definition, as illustrated in the next example.

EXAMPLE 8.3

Several user-defined data types are given below.

```
TYPE days = (sunday,monday,tuesday,wednesday,thursday,friday,saturday);
     weekdays = monday..friday;
     month = 1..31;
     caps = 'A'..'Z';
```

The first line repeats the enumerated type definition given in the last example. In the second line we define a subrange data type called `weekdays`, consisting of a subset of `days` (specifically, the five data items `monday`, `tuesday`, `wednesday`, `thursday` and `friday`). Note that the enumerated type definition `days` must precede the subrange definition `weekdays`.

The third line defines another subrange data type called `month`. This data type consists of the consecutive integers 1 through 31. Thus, this data type is a subset of the standard integer-data type.

Finally, the last line defines the subrange data type `caps`, which consists of the uppercase letters A through Z. Notice that this last data type is a subset of the standard char-type data.

Since enumerated-type data are defined in an ordered sequence, the relational operators may be applied to enumerated-type variables to form boolean expressions. Also, the standard functions `pred` and `succ` may be used to determine which data items precede and succeed any particular data item.

EXAMPLE 8.4

Consider the enumerated data type `days`, defined in Example 8.2. Several boolean expressions that make use of the individual data items, and their corresponding values, are shown below.

Expression	Value
sunday < tuesday	true
wednesday >= saturday	false
monday <> friday	true
pred(friday) = thursday	true
succ(friday) = saturday	true
succ(tuesday) <> pred(thursday)	false

The standard function `ord` can also be used with enumerated data. To do so, it must be understood that the first data item is assigned the ordinal number 0, the second data item is assigned the ordinal number 1, and so on. Thus, if there are n data items within an enumerated data type, the ordinal values will range from 0 to $n - 1$.

EXAMPLE 8.5

Consider once again the enumerated data type `days`, defined in Example 8.2. The following boolean expressions illustrate the relative order of the individual data items. All of the expressions are true.

```
succ(sunday)  = monday          ord(sunday)   = 0
pred(monday)  = sunday          ord(monday)   = 1
succ(monday)  = tuesday         ord(tuesday)  = 2
    . . . . .                       . . . . .
pred(friday)  = thursday        ord(saturday) = 6
succ(friday)  = saturday
pred(saturday) = friday
```

8.3 MORE ABOUT DECLARATIONS

Let us review what we have learned concerning the overall structure of a Pascal program. In particular, let us examine the declarations part of the program, since we are now able to understand the meaning of all of the constituent items. (Recall that this material has been presented earlier, in Sections 1.5 and 5.2.)

Here is the overall program structure.

1. Header

2. Block, consisting of

    (*a*) Declarations, which include

> Labels
> Constants
> Type definitions
> Variables
> Procedures and functions

    (*b*) Statements

The declarations section begins with statement labels, which are used in conjunction with the GOTO statement (see Section 6.8). This is followed by constant definitions (Section 2.8), then type definitions, as discussed in Sections 8.1 and 8.2. Then come variable declarations (Section 2.9), followed by procedure and function declarations (Sections 7.1 and 7.4).

Of particular significance is the fact that *the type definitions precede the variable declarations*. This permits variables to be declared in terms of user-defined data types as well as the standard data types. Our ability to utilize user-defined data types is thus considerably enhanced.

It is also possible to combine a subrange-type definition with a corresponding variable declaration. This is particularly convenient if the subrange type is used with only one variable declaration.

The declaration of variables whose data types are user-defined is illustrated in the next example.

EXAMPLE 8.6

Consider the following type definitions and variable declarations. (The type definitions are reproduced from Example 8.3.)

The variables workdays and holidays are of type weekdays. Hence, each of these variables can take on the values monday, tuesday, wednesday, thursday or friday. Similarly, the variable dayofmonth is of type month, and can therefore take on any of the integer values 1 through 31.

```
TYPE days = (sunday,monday,tuesday,wednesday,thursday,friday,saturday);
     weekdays = monday..friday;
     month = 1..31;
     caps = 'A'..'Z';
```

```
VAR workdays,holidays : weekdays;
    dayofmonth : month;
    hoursworked : 1..24;
    grosspay,netpay : real;
    employeenumber : 1..maxint;
```

The variable `hoursworked` is a subrange-type variable, similar to `dayofmonth`. It can take on any of the integer values 1 through 24. Note, however, that the type definition and the variable declaration are now combined. We could, of course, have replaced this single declaration with

```
TYPE hour = 1..24;
VAR hoursworked : hour;
```

though this is a bit more cumbersome.

We could also have combined the definition of the type `month` with the declaration of the variable `dayofmonth`. Thus, we could have written

```
VAR dayofmonth : 1..31;
```

Finally, the last two variable declarations establish that `grosspay` and `netpay` are real-type variables, and that `employeenumber` is a positive integer-type variable. Thus, we see variable declarations that involve standard data-types as well as user-defined data types in this example. (Note that `employeenumber` is actually a subrange-type variable, since it is restricted to the available set of positive integers.)

8.4 UTILIZING USER-DEFINED DATA

Once enumerated and subrange data have been defined, they can be used just as other simple-type data items are used within a Pascal program. This includes their use as control variables in FOR structures and as selectors in CASE structures.

EXAMPLE 8.7

Here is an example of an enumerated data type being used as a control variable in a FOR structure.

```
FOR workdays := monday TO friday DO
    BEGIN
        . . . . .
    END;
```

The control variable `workdays` is defined in Example 8.6. Hence, `workdays` will take on the value `monday` during the first pass through the loop, `tuesday` during the second pass, and so on, until `workdays` takes on the value `friday` during the last (fifth) pass.

EXAMPLE 8.8

Now consider the use of the same enumerated variable, `workdays`, as a selector in a CASE structure.

```
      CASE workdays OF
            monday    : writeln(' First workday');
            tuesday   : writeln(' Second workday');
            wednesday : writeln(' Third workday');
            thursday  : writeln(' Fourth workday');
            friday    : writeln(' Last workday')
      END;
```

A message uniquely identifying the value currently assigned to `workdays` will be displayed each time the CASE structure is encountered.

We have already seen that enumerated and subrange data can be used to create boolean-type expressions. Integer-type subrange data can also appear in integer-type expressions, following essentially the same rules as those that apply to standard integer-type data.

Both enumerated and subrange-type variables can be assigned values of an appropriate (corresponding) type. Thus, an element of an enumerated type can be assigned to an enumerated variable of the same type. Similarly, an element of a subrange can be assigned to a subrange variable of the same type.

EXAMPLE 8.9

Suppose that `holidays` is an enumerated variable, and that `hoursworked` and `employeenumber` are subrange variables, as defined in Example 8.6. Then the following assignment statements are valid.

```
      employeenumber := 12345;
      holidays := thursday;
      hoursworked := 8;
```

Enumerated-type data *cannot* be entered into the computer via a `read` or a `readln` statement. Integer or char-type subrange data *may* be entered provided the values fall within the permissible subrange. A similar restriction applies to writing out data via the `write` or `writeln` statement.

The use of enumerated-type data allows a Pascal program to be expressed in terms of variables that are closely related to the corresponding problem definition. This practice is strongly encouraged, since it promotes clarity and logical simplicity. Program debugging is also simplified.

The advantages to the use of subrange data are similar, though perhaps less dramatic. In particular, the use of subrange data simplifies the program and enhances its readability. It may also result in a modest reduction in memory requirements.

EXAMPLE 8.10 Number of Days Between Two Dates

Suppose that two different dates are entered into the computer, and we wish to determine the number of days between the two dates. One way to approach this problem is to determine the number of days from each of the specified dates to some common base date. The number of days between the two dates can then be determined as the difference in these two numbers less one.

Let us choose January 1, 1960, as the base date. If each of the dates is entered in the form `mm dd yy` (where `mm` represents an integer, `dd` and integer and `yy` an integer), then the number of days from a given date to the base date can be determined in the following manner.

1.　Determine the day of the current year approximately as

```
      n := trunc(30.42*(mm - 1)) + dd
```

2.　If mm = 2 (February), increase the value of `n` by 1

3. If mm > 2 and mm < 8 (March, April, May, June and July), *decrease* the value of n by 1

4. If yy MOD 4 = 0 and mm > 2 (leap year), increase the value of n by 1

5. Increase the value of n by 1461 for each full 4-year cycle beyond 1-1-60.

6. Increase n by 365 for each additional full year beyond the completion of the last full 4-year cycle, then add 1 for the most recent leap year.

Let us utilize a function called daysbeyond1960 to determine an appropriate value for n, given the values for mm, dd and yy. We will assume that n, mm, dd and yy are integer subrange-type variables. Here is the complete function, which is based upon the six steps described above.

```
FUNCTION daysbeyond1960(mm : month; dd : day; yy : year) : numberofdays;

(* Convert a given date (month,day,year) to the
   number of days beyond January 1, 1960. *)

VAR n : numberofdays;

BEGIN
    n := trunc(30.42*(mm-1)) + dd;
    IF mm=2 THEN n := n + 1;
    IF (mm > 2) AND (mm < 8) THEN n := n - 1;
    IF (yy MOD 4 = 0) AND (mm > 2) THEN n := n + 1;
    IF (yy-1960) DIV 4 > 0 THEN n := n + 1461*((yy-1960) DIV 4);
    IF (yy-1960) MOD 4 > 0 THEN n := n + 365*((yy-1960) MOD 4) + 1;
    daysbeyond1960 := n
END;
```

It is now a simple matter to complete the entire program. To do so, we define the integer subrange types day, month, year and numberofdays; then declare an appropriate group of subrange-type global variables (dd, mm, yy, days1 and days2). The function declaration appears next, followed by the main block which merely reads in the two dates, accesses the function for each of the dates, and then writes out the final answer.

Here is the entire program.

```
PROGRAM dates;

(* DETERMINE THE NUMBER OF DAYS BETWEEN TWO DATES *)

TYPE day = 1..31;
     month = 1..12;
     year = 1960..2100;
     numberofdays = 0..maxint;
VAR dd : day;
    mm : month;
    yy : year;
    days1,days2 : numberofdays;

FUNCTION daysbeyond1960(mm : month; dd : day; yy : year) : numberofdays;

(* Convert a given date (month,day,year) to the
   number of days beyond January 1, 1960. *)

VAR n : numberofdays;
```

(Program continues on next page)

```
    BEGIN
      n := trunc(30.42*(mm-1)) + dd;
      IF mm=2 THEN n := n + 1;
      IF (mm > 2) AND (mm < 8) THEN n := n - 1;
      IF (yy MOD 4 = 0) AND (mm > 2) THEN n := n + 1;
      IF (yy-1960) DIV 4 > 0 THEN n := n + 1461*((yy-1960) DIV 4);
      IF (yy-1960) MOD 4 > 0 THEN n := n + 365*((yy-1960) MOD 4) + 1;
      daysbeyond1960 := n
    END;

    BEGIN    (* main action block *)
      write('Enter the first date  (mm dd yyyy) :');
      readln(mm,dd,yy);
      days1 := daysbeyond1960(mm,dd,yy);
      write('Enter the second date (mm dd yyyy) :');
      readln(mm,dd,yy);
      days2 := daysbeyond1960(mm,dd,yy);
      writeln;
      writeln('There are ',days2-days1-1,' days between the two dates.')
    END.
```

In this program, the second date is assumed to be greater than the first date.

Execution of the program results in the following output, if the two input dates are December 29, 1963 and December 29, 1993. The user's responses are underlined.

```
Enter the first date  (mm dd yyyy) :12 29 1963
Enter the second date (mm dd yyyy) :12 29 1993

There are 10957 days between the two dates.
```

The previous example illustrates the use of subrange-type data in a realistic programming problem. The use of enumerated-type data is illustrated in the next example.

EXAMPLE 8.11 The Towers of Hanoi

Consider once again the recursive program presented in Example 7.22. Let us now modify the program so that enumerated-type data are used to represent the three poles. In particular, let us introduce the enumerated data type pole, whose three constituent elements are left, center and right. The complete program is shown below.

```
PROGRAM towersofhanoi2;

(* TOWERS OF HANOI, USING RECURSIVE PROCEDURE CALLS AND USER-DEFINED DATA *)

TYPE poles = (left,center,right);
     disks = 0..maxint;
VAR n : disks;

    PROCEDURE transfer(n : disks; origin,destination,other : poles);
    (* Transfer n disks from the origin to the destination *)
```

```
        PROCEDURE diskmove(origin,destination : poles);
        (* Move a single disk from the origin to the destination *)
        BEGIN
            write('Move ');
            CASE origin OF
                left   : IF destination = center
                           THEN writeln('left to center')
                           ELSE writeln('left to right');
                center : IF destination = left
                           THEN writeln('center to left')
                           ELSE writeln('center to right');
                right  : IF destination = center
                           THEN writeln('right to center')
                           ELSE writeln('right to left')
            END   (* case *)
        END;   (* diskmove *)

    BEGIN   (* transfer *)
       IF n>0 THEN BEGIN
                      transfer(n-1,origin,other,destination);
                      diskmove(origin,destination);
                      transfer(n-1,other,destination,origin)
                  END
    END;   (* transfer *)

BEGIN  (* main action block *)
   write('Enter the number of disks -> ');
   readln(n);
   writeln;
   transfer(n,left,right,center)
END.
```

This version of the program is not as clean as that presented in Example 7.22 because of the restriction on enumerated data appearing in a `write` or `writeln` statement. Hence the need for the somewhat cumbersome CASE structure in procedure `diskmove`. Otherwise, however, the program definition is more straightforward, since the individual poles can be referred to in more natural terms.

Execution of the program for the case of n = 3 results in the following output. (The user's response is again underlined.)

```
Enter the number of disks -> 3

Move left to right
Move left to center
Move right to center
Move left to right
Move center to left
Move center to right
Move left to right
```

Review Questions

8.1   What are the two general categories of simple-type data in Pascal? How can each be further subdivided?

8.2   How is subrange-type data defined?

8.3   To what types of simple data can the subrange concept be applied?

8.4   Which operators can be used with subrange-type data?

8.5   Which standard functions can be used with subrange-type data?

8.6   How is enumerated-type data defined? Compare with subrange-type data.

8.7   In what sense do enumerated-type data comprise an ordered sequence?

8.8   Which operators can be used with enumerated-type data?

8.9   Which standard functions can be used with enumerated-type data?

8.10 What items are included in the declarations part of a Pascal program? In what order must these items appear?

8.11 Under what circumstances is it advantageous to combine a subrange-type definition with a corresponding variable declaration? Can this also be done with enumerated-type data?

8.12 Can an enumerated data item be used as a control variable in a FOR structure? Can a subrange-type data item be used for this purpose?

8.13 Can an enumerated data item be used as a selector in a CASE structure? Can a subrange-type data item be used for this purpose?

8.14 What restrictions apply to the use of user-defined data items in an expression?

8.15 Can a user-defined data item appear in an assignment statement? What restrictions apply?

8.16 What restrictions apply to the use of user-defined data items in input/output statements?

8.17 What advantages are there in the use of enumerated-type data in a Pascal program? What disadvantages are there? Explain.

8.18 What advantages are there in the use of subrange-type data in a Pascal program? What disadvantages are there? Explain.

Problems

8.19 Consider the following type definition.

```
TYPE notes = (do,re,mi,fa,so,la,ti);
```

Determine the value of each of the following expressions.

(a)   re > fa   (d)   mi = succ(fa)
(b)   do <= ti   (e)   ord(do) < 1
(c)   pred(mi) = re   (f)   3 = ord(pred(fa)) + 1

8.20   Consider the following type definition.

```
TYPE cities = (Boston,Miami,Pittsburgh,Chicago,Denver,Phoenix,Seattle);
```

Determine the value of each of the following expressions.

(a)   pred(Pittsburgh)   (e)   succ(ord(Chicago))
(b)   succ(Denver)   (f)   Miami < Seattle
(c)   ord(Seattle)   (g)   Chicago < Pittsburgh
(d)   ord(succ(Chicago))

8.21   The skeletal outline of a Pascal program utilizing enumerated data is shown below.

```
PROGRAM sample1;
TYPE flavors = (vanilla,chocolate,strawberry,cherry,coconut);
     sizes = (small,medium,large);
VAR cone,dish,sundae : flavors;
    pint,quart : vanilla..strawberry;
    conesize : sizes;

BEGIN
   . . . . .
   cone := cherry;
   . . . . .
   IF quart = chocolate THEN
                         . . .
                   ELSE
                         . . . . .
   CASE conesize OF
      small  : . . .
      medium : . . .
      large  : . . .
   END;
   . . . . .
END.
```

Answer the following questions related to this outline.

(a)   What data type is associated with the variable sundae? What values can sundae take on?
(b)   What data type is associated with the variable pint? What values can pint take on?
(c)   What numerical value is associated with coconut?
(d)   Explain what happens when the assignment statement cone := cherry is executed.
(e)   Under what conditions will the ELSE clause of the IF-THEN-ELSE structure be executed?
(f)   What values can be assigned to conesize?
(g)   If conesize represents a value of 1, what action will be taken within the CASE structure?

8.22 The skeletal outline of a Pascal program utilizing enumerated data and a procedure is shown below.

```
PROGRAM sample2;
TYPE primary = (yellow,cyan,magenta);
VAR color : primary;

   PROCEDURE proc1(VAR hue : primary);
   BEGIN
      . . . . .
      IF hue = cyan THEN . . .
                    ELSE . . .
      . . . . .
   END;

BEGIN   (* main action statements *)
   . . . . .
   proc1(color);
   . . . . .
   FOR color = yellow TO magenta DO . . .
   . . . . .
END.
```

Answer the following questions related to this outline.

(a) What data type is associated with the variable color? What values can color take on?

(b) What data type is associated with the variable hue? What values can hue take on?

(c) If the value of hue is altered within proc1, will the value of color be affected?

(d) Within the main body of the program, how many passes will be made through the FOR loop?

8.23 The skeletal outline of a Pascal program utilizing subrange data is shown below. (Note that the variables d1 and d2 do *not* represent numerical quantities.)

```
PROGRAM sample3;
TYPE digits = '0'..'9';
VAR d1,d2 : digits;

BEGIN
   . . . . .
   d1 := '7';
   d2 := '9';
   . . . . .
   REPEAT
      . . . . .
      d2 := pred(d2);
      . . . . .
   UNTIL d2 = d1;
   . . . . .
END.
```

Answer the following questions related to this outline.

(a) What data items are included within the subrange?

(b)   What data type is associated with the variable d1? What values can be assigned to d1?

(c)   How many passes will be made through the REPEAT-UNTIL loop?

8.24   Write the appropriate definitions and declarations for each of the following situations.

(a)   Define an enumerated data type called `days` consisting of the data items `sun`, `mon`, `tues`, `wed`, `thurs`, `fri` and `sat`. Then declare `days1` and `days2` to be subrange variables that can be assigned the data items `mon` through `fri` and `sun` through `sat`, respectively.

(b)   Define an enumerated data type called `colors` consisting of the data items `red`, `green`, `blue`, `white` and `black`. Declare `highlight`, `foreground` and `background` to be enumerated variables of type `colors`. Then declare `main` to be a subrange variable that can be assigned the values `red` through `blue`.

(c)   Define an enumerated data type called `suits` consisting of the data items `clubs`, `diamonds`, `hearts` and `spades`, and a subrange data type called `values` consisting of the digits 1 through 12. Declare `cardtype` to be an enumerated variable of type `suits`, and `cardvalue` to be a subrange variable of type `values`. Then declare `count` and `n` to be subrange variables consisting of all permissible positive integers.

(d)   Define an enumerated data type called `wines` consisting of the data items `chablis`, `sauterne`, `rose`, `burgundy` and `chianti`. Then declare `dinner` to be an enumerated variable of type `wines`, and declare `cost` to be a real-type variable. In addition, define a function called `special` that accepts a real-type value parameter called `cost` and returns a data item of type `wines`.

Programming Problems

8.25   Modify the program shown in Example 8.10 so that it accepts the following information as input
(a)   today's date
(b)   the user's name
(c)   the user's birthdate

and then determines how many days the user has been alive. (Enter the dates in the same manner as in Example 8.10.)

8.26   Modify the program shown in Example 8.10 so that it accepts any date beyond January 1, 1960, as input, and then prints out the corresponding day of the week. *Hint:* January 1, 1960, was a Friday.

8.27   Modify the program given in Example 8.11 so that the initial stack of disks can be on *any* pole (not necessarily the left), and the final stack can be on any other pole (not necessarily the right). Specify the origin and destination poles as input parameters. Then display the moves that are required to transfer the poles from the specified origin to the specified destination.

8.28   Modify each of the following programs to make use of enumerated and/or subrange-type data. Also, include procedures and/or functions wherever appropriate.
(a)   Repeated averaging of a list of numbers (see Example 6.9).
(b)   Calculating compound interest factors (see Example 6.10).

      (*c*)   Calculating depreciation (see Example 7.12).

      (*d*)   Simulation of a game of craps (see Example 7.18).

8.29 Solve each of the following programming problems utilizing enumerated and/or subrange data wherever appropriate. Also, be sure to modularize each program by making proper use of procedures and/or functions.

      (*a*)   Calculate the first *n* Fibonacci numbers, as described in Prob. 6.50(*e*). Then determine which of these is a prime number [see Prob. 6.50(*f*)].

      (*b*)   Convert a positive integer number to a roman numeral, as described in Prob. 6.50(*q*).

      (*c*)   Program an interactive game of tic-tac-toe, as described in Prob. 7.44(*i*).

Chapter 9

Arrays

We have already mentioned the fact that Pascal supports four different categories of data types: *simple* data, *string* data (only in Turbo Pascal), *structured* data and *pointer* data. So far, however, our discussions have been confined to simple-type data. We have seen that simple-type data include the four standard data types: *integer*, *real*, *char* and *boolean* (see Chap. 3), and the two user-defined data types: *subrange* and *enumerated* (see Chap. 8). All simple-type data have the common characteristic that each variable represents a single data item.

We now turn our attention to structured-type data. In fact, each of the next four chapters will be concerned with a different type of structured data. These chapters will cover *arrays*, *records*, *files* and *sets*, respectively. All of these data types have the common characteristic that a single variable can represent multiple data items. The individual data items can also be accessed separately (though this is done in a different manner for each structured data type). Thus, structured-type data items can be manipulated collectively or individually, depending on the requirements of each particular application.

9.1 ONE-DIMENSIONAL ARRAYS

A one-dimensional array can be thought of as a list (i.e., a column) of data items, all of the same type, that are collectively referred to by the same name. Each individual array element (i.e., each of the data items) can be referred to by specifying the array name, followed by an *index* (also called a *subscript*), enclosed in square brackets. The array elements can be of any data type, as long as they are all the same. For example, if `list` is a one-dimensional array containing *n* elements, the individual array elements will be `list[1]`, `list[2]`, ..., `list[n]`, as illustrated in Fig. 9.1.

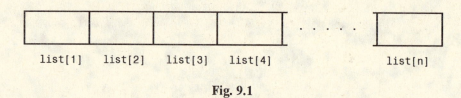

Fig. 9.1

Thus, the entire array is represented as a list of the individual array elements.

EXAMPLE 9.1

A Pascal program contains a 100-element, real-type array called `list`. Each individual element will have a value equal to 0.01 times its index value. Thus,

```
list[1] = 0.01
list[2] = 0.02
list[3] = 0.03
```

and so on.

The ith element of list can be referred to as list[i], where i is an integer-type variable. Thus, i is assigned a value of 5, then list[i] will refer to the fifth element within the array, which is list[5]. The value of this array element is 0.05.

The easiest way to define an array is to include it in a variable declaration, as follows.

```
VAR array name : ARRAY [index type] OF type
```

The index type can be an ordinal, simple type (i.e., integer, char, boolean or enumerated), or a subrange. The array itself can be of *any* type, including structured types (more about this later), though most elementary applications make use of simple-type arrays. (As a matter of practical interest, note that an array can be of type real, but its index cannot.)

EXAMPLE 9.2

A Pascal program is to include a 100-element, real-type array called list. The array declaration can be written as follows.

```
VAR list : ARRAY [1..100] OF real;
```

Alternatively, we could write

```
TYPE index = 1..100;
VAR list : ARRAY [index] OF real;
```

The first form is usually more desirable, however, because it is simpler.

Note that the array elements are of type real, but the index is a subrange of type integer.

Individual array elements can be used in expressions, assignment statements, read and write statements, etc., as though they were ordinary simple-type variables. To do so, the array element must be written as the array name, followed by an appropriate index value enclosed in square brackets. The index value can be expressed as a constant, a variable or an expression. However, the index must be of the correct type and it must fall within the correct range.

EXAMPLE 9.3

Let us again consider the one-dimensional, real array list, described in Example 9.2. Suppose we now wish to examine the value of each element of the array, and display those values that are negative. This can be accomplished with the following loop structure.

```
FOR count := 1 TO 100 DO
   IF list[count] < 0
       THEN writeln(count:3, list[count]:4:1);
```

Notice that the value of the index (i.e., the integer-type variable count) is displayed on the same line as the negative array element. Thus, if the third array element had a value of −5.0, the following output would be generated.

```
3 -5.0
```

In this example it is essential that the values of count do not fall outside the range 1..100, since the array index is undefined outside of this range. We could, however, work with a *smaller* subrange if we wish. Thus we could have written

```
FOR count := 25 TO 50 DO
   IF list[count] < 0
      THEN writeln(count:3, list[count]:4:1);
```

The use of array elements in assignment statements and in expressions must follow the same rules as with simple-type variables. Thus, if a single array element appears on either side of an assignment statement, it must be type-compatible with the other variable or expression in that statement. Also, if used within an expression, the array element must be type-compatible with the other data items that appear in the expression.

EXAMPLE 9.4 Deviations About an Average

Suppose that we want to read in a list of n real quantities and then calculate their average, as in Example 6.8. In addition to simply calculating the average, however, we will also compute the deviation of each of the numbers about the average, using the formula

```
deviation = x[i] - average
```

where x[i] represents each of the given numbers and average represents the calculated average.

Note that we are storing each of the given numbers in a one-dimensional, real-type array x. This is an essential part of this program. The reason, which must be clearly understood, is as follows.

In all of the earlier examples where we calculated the average of a list of numbers, each number was replaced by the succeeding number in the list. Hence the individual numbers were no longer available for subsequent calculations once the average had been determined. Now, however, these individual values must be retained, in order to calculate the corresponding deviations after the average has been determined. We therefore store them in the one-dimensional array x.

Let us restrict the size of x to 100 elements. However, we need not make use of all 100 elements. Rather, we shall specify the actual number of elements by assigning a positive integer quantity (not exceeding 100) to the variable n.

Here is the complete Pascal program.

```
PROGRAM deviations;

(* READ IN A LIST OF n NUMBERS, CALCULATE THEIR AVERAGE, AND THEN COMPUTE
   THE DEVIATION OF EACH NUMBER ABOUT THE AVERAGE *)

VAR n,count : integer;
    sum,average,deviation : real;
    x : ARRAY [1..100] OF real;

BEGIN
   BEGIN (* Read in the numbers and calculate the average *)
      write(' How many numbers will be averaged? ');
      readln(n);
      writeln;
      sum := 0;
```

(Program continues on next page)

```
        FOR count := 1 TO n DO
           BEGIN
              write(' i= ',count:3,'      x= ');
              readln(x[count]);
              sum := sum + x[count]
           END;
        average := sum/n;
        writeln(' The average is ',average);
        writeln;
     END;   (* calculate average *)

  BEGIN (* Calculate the deviations about the average *)
     FOR count := 1 TO n DO
        BEGIN
           deviation := x[count] - average;
           write(' i= ',count:3,'      x= ',x[count]);
           writeln('      d= ',deviation)
        END
  END   (* calculate deviations *)
END.
```

Notice the manner in which this program is modularized. There are no procedures or functions in the program. Rather, the main block consists of two compound statements, each with its own distinct purpose. Each compound statement is identified with its own comments. This method is convenient for certain short, simple programs such as this.

Now suppose that the program is executed using the following five numerical values: $x[1] = 3.0$, $x[2] = -2.0$, $x[3] = 12.0$, $x[4] = 4.4$, $x[5] = 3.5$. The interactive entering of the data will appear as follows. (The user's responses are underlined.)

```
How many numbers will be averaged? 5

i=   1      x= 3.0
i=   2      x= -2.0
i=   3      x= 12.0
i=   4      x= 4.4
i=   5      x= 3.5
```

As soon as all of the data have been entered, the following output will be generated.

```
The average is  4.1800000E+00

i=   1      x=  3.0000000E+00     d= -1.1800000E+00
i=   2      x= -2.0000000E+00     d= -6.1800000E+00
i=   3      x=  1.2000000E+01     d=  7.8200000E+00
i=   4      x=  4.4000000E+00     d=  2.2000000E-01
i=   5      x=  3.5000000E+00     d= -6.8000000E-01
```

Arrays are particularly useful in situations where the individual data items must be ordered with respect to one another. For example, some applications require that certain data items be compared with one another and then some action taken, depending on the outcome of the comparison. In such situations the array index provides a convenient way to order the data items.

EXAMPLE 9.5 Reordering a List of Numbers

Consider the well-known problem of rearranging a list of n numbers into a sequence of algebraically increasing values. The program is to be written in such a manner that unnecessary storage will not be used. Therefore the program will contain only one array—a one-dimensional, real array called x—which will be reordered one element at a time.

The procedure will begin by scanning the entire array for the smallest number, and then interchanging this number with the first number in the array so that the smallest number will be at the top of the list. Next the remaining $n-1$ numbers will be scanned for the smallest, which will be exchanged with the second number so that the second-smallest number will be second in the list. Then the remaining $n-2$ numbers will be scanned for the smallest, which will be interchanged with the third number, and so on, until the entire array has been rearranged. This will require a total of $n-1$ passes through the array, though the length of each scan will become progressively smaller with each pass.

In order to find the smallest number for each pass, we sequentially compare each number in the array, x[i], with the starting number, x[loc], where loc is an integer variable that is used to "tag" one of the array elements. If x[i] is smaller than x[loc], we interchange the two numbers; otherwise we leave the two numbers in their original positions. Once this procedure has been applied to the entire array, the first number in the array will be the smallest. We then repeat the entire procedure $n-2$ times, for a total of $n-1$ passes. (Thus, the value assigned to loc will take on the successive values $1, 2, \ldots, n-1$.)

The only remaining question is how the two numbers are interchanged. We first temporarily save the value of x[loc] for future reference. Then we assign the current value of x[i] to x[loc]. Finally, we assign the *original* value of x[loc], which had been saved, to x[i]. The interchange is now complete.

The strategy described above can be incorporated into a Pascal procedure called interchange, as shown below.

```
PROCEDURE interchange;

(* Interchange array elements from smallest to largest *)

BEGIN
   FOR loc := 1 TO n-1 DO
      FOR i := loc + 1 TO n DO
         IF x[i] < x[loc] THEN
            BEGIN
               temp := x[loc];
               x[loc] := x[i];
               x[i] := temp
            END
END;
```

In this procedure we assume that loc, i and n are integer-type variables whose values range from 1 to 100. Also, we assume that temp is a real-type variable that is used for temporary storage of x[loc]. Note that the procedure utilizes nested FOR - TO structures.

Now let us consider the overall program strategy, as shown in the following outline.

1. Read in the size of the array, n.

2. Read in the n array elements, in response to interactive prompts.

3. Rearrange the numbers within the array by accessing procedure interchange.

4. Write out the rearranged values.

Here is the entire Pascal program.

```
    PROGRAM reorder;

    (* REORDER AN ARRAY OF REAL NUMBERS FROM SMALLEST TO LARGEST *)

    VAR n,i,loc : 1..100;
        x : ARRAY [1..100] OF real;
        temp : real;

    PROCEDURE interchange;
    (* Interchange array elements from smallest to largest *)
    BEGIN
        FOR loc := 1 TO n-1 DO
            FOR i := loc + 1 TO n DO
                IF x[i] < x[loc] THEN
                    BEGIN
                        temp := x[loc];
                        x[loc] := x[i];
                        x[i] := temp
                    END
    END;   (* interchange *)

    BEGIN    (* main action block *)
        write('How many numbers are there? ');
        readln(n);
        writeln;
        FOR i := 1 TO n DO
            BEGIN
                write('x[',i:3,']= ? ');
                readln(x[i])
            END;
        interchange;
        writeln;
        writeln('Rearranged Data:');
        writeln;
        FOR i := 1 TO n DO
            writeln('x[',i:3,']= ',x[i]:4:1);
    END.
```

Execution of the program begins with an interactive data entry session. A typical data entry session is shown below. (The user's responses are shown underlined.)

```
How many numbers are there? 5

x[  1] = ? 4.7
x[  2] = ? -2.3
x[  3] = ? 12.9
x[  4] = ? 8.8
x[  5] = ? 6.0
```

The program then rearranges the five input quantities and generates the following output.

```
x[  1] = -2.3
x[  2] =  4.7
x[  3] =  6.0
x[  4] =  8.8
x[  5] = 12.9
```

Some applications can be enhanced through the use of an enumerated-type index, as shown in the following example.

EXAMPLE 9.6

Here is a portion of a Pascal program that defines an integer-type one-dimensional array with an enumerated-type index.

```
TYPE color = (red,white,blue,yellow,green);
VAR index  : color;
    values : ARRAY [color] OF integer;
```

Notice that `values` is defined as a 5-element array. Each element will represent an integer quantity.

If we wanted to write out the value of each element, we might include the following structure somewhere within the program.

```
FOR index := red TO green DO writeln(values[index]);
```

The array elements themselves can also be of an enumerated type, as illustrated in the following example.

EXAMPLE 9.7

Here is a variation of the situation described in Example 9.6. Suppose that `values` is a 100-element array of type `color`. Then the Pascal program might include the following type definition and variable declaration.

```
TYPE color = (red,white,blue,yellow,green);
VAR values : ARRAY [1..100] OF color;
```

Now each of the array elements will take on one of the values `red`, `white`, `blue`, `yellow` or `green`. The index values will be integers ranging from 1 to 100.

Many applications involve the use of strings. In ANSI Pascal, we represent a string as a one-dimensional array of type char. The technique is illustrated in the following example.

EXAMPLE 9.8 Names and Addresses

Here is a simple Pascal program that allows a name and address to be entered and stored within the computer and then displayed. We will assume that each name, street address and city address does not exceed 60 characters. Hence, we will introduce three 60-element, char-type arrays, called `name`, `street` and `city`, respectively. Each string need not, however, contain 60 characters. Rather, we will enter successive characters into each array until an end of line is encountered. The standard function `eoln` will be used for this purpose. Thus, we will continue to read characters from each line, until the function `eoln` returns the value `true`. (Note that `eoln` will automatically become `false` when a new line is begun.)

Let us count the number of characters in each array so that we will know how many characters (array elements) to write out later in the program. We will refer to these character counters as `namecount`, `streetcount` and `citycount`, respectively.

Here is the entire Pascal program. Note that the program consists essentially of two procedures - `readin`, which causes the input data to be entered into the computer, and `writeout`, which then displays the data. Observe the prompts for name, street and city that are included within `readin`.

```
    PROGRAM namesandaddresses1;

    (* ENTER AND DISPLAY A NAME AND ADDRESS (STREET AND CITY) *)

    VAR count,namecount,streetcount,citycount : 0..60;
        name,street,city : ARRAY [1..60] OF char;


    PROCEDURE readin;
    (* Read a name and address into the computer *)
    BEGIN
       write('Name:    ');
       count := 0;
       REPEAT
          count := count + 1;
          read(name[count])
       UNTIL eoln;
       namecount := count;
       readln;

       write('Street: ');
       count := 0;
       REPEAT
          count := count + 1;
          read(street[count])
       UNTIL eoln;
       streetcount := count;
       readln;

       write('City:    ');
       count := 0;
       REPEAT
          count := count + 1;
          read(city[count])
       UNTIL eoln;
       citycount := count;
       readln
    END;   (* readin *)


    PROCEDURE writeout;
    (* Display a name and address *)
    BEGIN
       FOR count := 1 TO namecount DO write(name[count]);
       writeln;
       FOR count := 1 TO streetcount DO write(street[count]);
       writeln;
       FOR count := 1 TO citycount DO write(city[count])
    END;   (* writeout *)


    BEGIN   (* main action block *)
       readin;
       writeln;
       writeout
    END.
```

Execution of the program results in the following input dialog. (The user's input is again underlined.)

```
Name:   Susan H. Gottfried
Street: 129 Old Suffolk Drive
City:   Monroeville, PA 15146
```

Once the input data have been entered, the program writes out the name, street and city, as shown below.

```
Susan H. Gottfried
129 Old Suffolk Drive
Monroeville, PA 15146
```

Keep in mind that this program can be used as a starting point for many other more complex (and more interesting) programs. For example, many business applications (e.g., mailing lists, payrolls, accounts receivables) require names, addresses and related data to be entered into the computer, modified in some way, and later written out.

String input/output is much simpler in Turbo Pascal, owing to the use of string-type variables. The following example illustrates this point. We will see how individual characters within a string-type variable can be manipulated later in this chapter.

EXAMPLE 9.9 Names and Addresses (Turbo Pascal version)

Here is a Turbo Pascal program that reads and displays a name and address, as in the last example.

```
PROGRAM namesandaddresses2;

(* ENTER AND DISPLAY A NAME AND ADDRESS (STREET AND CITY) *)

VAR name,street,city : string;

PROCEDURE readin;
(* Read a name and address into the computer *)
BEGIN
   write('Name:   ');
   readln(name);

   write('Street: ');
   readln(street);

   write('City:   ');
   readln(city)
END;   (* readin *)

PROCEDURE writeout;
(* Display a name and address *)
BEGIN
   writeln(name);
   writeln(street);
   writeln(city)
END;   (* writeout *)

BEGIN   (* main action block *)
   readin;
   writeln;
   writeout
END.
```

Notice that this program is much simpler than the corresponding program presented in Example 9.8, because of the use of the string-type variables `name`, `street` and `city`. In particular, note that the REPEAT-UNTIL loops in the last example have been replaced by simple `readln` statements, and the FOR-TO loops have been replaced by `writeln` statements. (Remember that the use of string-type variables is *not* supported in ANSI Pascal.)

When this program is executed it behaves in exactly the same manner as the program presented in the previous example.

9.2 MULTIDIMENSIONAL ARRAYS

Pascal supports multidimensional as well as single-dimensional arrays. The use of multidimensional arrays can be very helpful in many different types of applications.

We have already seen that a one-dimensional array can be thought of as a list (i.e., a single column) of data items. The multidimensional array provides a natural extension of this idea. Thus, we can think of a two-dimensional array as a *table* of data items, consisting of rows and columns. The first dimension (i.e., the first index) might refer to the row number, and the second dimension (the second index) to the column number. Similarly, a three-dimensional array might be thought of as a collection of tables, like pages in a book.

Suppose, for example, that `table` is a two-dimensional array containing m rows and n columns. The individual array elements would be `table[1,1]`, `table[1,2]`, . . . , `table[1,n]`, `table[2,1]`, `table[2,2]`, . . . , `table[2,n]`, . . . , `table[m,1]`, `table[m,2]`, . . . , `table[m,n]`. Thus, the entire array can be visualized as shown in Fig. 9.2.

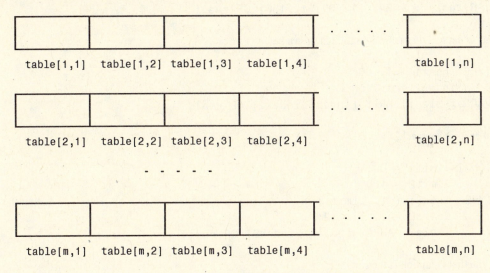

Fig. 9.2

Regardless of its dimensionality, an array always consists of a collection of data items of the same type. All of the data items can be collectively referred to by a single identifier (i.e., a common array name). An individual array element (i.e., a single data item) can be referred to by specifying the array name, followed by appropriate values for the indices (subscripts), enclosed in square brackets and separated by commas.

EXAMPLE 9.10

A Pascal program contains a two-dimensional, real-type array called `table`. This array will represent a table of numbers containing a maximum of 60 rows and 150 columns. Therefore the first index will range from 1 to 60, and the second index from 1 to 150.

Suppose we want to access the array element in the third row and the seventh column. This data item can be referenced simply by writing `table[3,7]`. Similarly, we can refer to the array element in the `ith` row and the `jth` column as `table[i,j]`, where `i` and `j` are integer-type variables that are used as indices. Therefore, if `i` is assigned a value of 12 and `j` is assigned a value of 5, `table[i,j]` will refer to the array element in the fifth column of the twelfth row.

A multidimensional array definition can be included within a variable declaration, in the same manner as a one-dimensional array. However, a separate index type must be specified for each of the array dimensions. Hence an array definition can be written as

```
VAR array name : ARRAY [index 1 type, index 2 type, . . . ,index n type] OF type
```

The index types can be ordinal, simple types (i.e., integer, char, boolean or enumerated) or subranges. They need not all be of the same type. On the other hand, the array elements themselves must all be of the same type, though they can be of *any* type, including structured types.

EXAMPLE 9.11

Consider once again the two-dimensional, real-type array `table`, described in the previous example. This array can be defined in the following manner.

```
VAR table : ARRAY [1..60, 1..150] OF real;
```

Another way to express this same definition is shown below.

```
TYPE index1 = 1..60;
     index2 = 1..150;
VAR  table : ARRAY [index1,index2] OF real;
```

Here is still another approach.

```
CONST limit1 = 60;
      limit2 = 150;
TYPE  index1 = 1..limit1;
      index2 = 1..limit2;
VAR   table : ARRAY [index1,index2] OF real;
```

Obviously, the first definition is the simplest.

Note that both indices are subranges of type integer, but the array elements themselves are of type real.

Many applications that involve the use of multidimensional arrays require nested loops, one loop for each dimension. Thus, an application that is oriented toward processing the elements in a table might make use of two loops, one within another. The outer loop might be used to process each of the individual rows, and the inner loop to process the columns within each row. The manner in which this is accomplished is illustrated in the next example.

EXAMPLE 9.12 Table Manipulation

Now let us write an interactive Pascal program that will read a table of real numbers into the computer and store them in a two-dimensional array, calculate the sum of the numbers in every row and every column and then display the table, along with the calculated row sums and the column sums.

Let us begin by defining the following variables.

   `table` = the two-dimensional, real array containing the given table and the calculated sums

   `nrows` = an integer variable indicating the number of rows in the given table

   `ncols` = an integer variable indicating the number of columns in the given table

      `row` = an integer counter that indicates the row number

      `col` = an integer counter that indicates the column number

We will assume that the size of the table will not exceed 10 rows and 10 columns. We will add one additional row and one additional column within the array, however, so that we will have a place to store the row sums and the column sums. Thus, the row sums will be placed in the rightmost column (i.e., column number `ncols + 1`), and the column sums will appear in the bottom row (i.e., row `nrows + 1`). We will therefore define `table` to be a two-dimensional, real array with a maximum of 11 rows and 11 columns.

Let us employ a modular structure in the development of the program, with separate procedures for reading in the data, calculating the row sums, calculating the column sums and writing out the final table. These procedures will be called `readinput`, `rowsums`, `columnsums` and `writeoutput`, respectively.

The logic required for each procedure is straightforward, though it should be noted that a double loop will be required within each of the procedures. For example, in order to read in the original table, we will have to provide the following double loop.

```
FOR row := 1 TO nrows DO
   BEGIN
      FOR col := 1 TO ncols DO read(table[row,col]);
      writeln
   END
```

The `writeln` statement is required in order to skip to the next line.

Similarly, the following loop is required in order to calculate each of the row sums.

```
FOR row := 1 TO nrows DO
   BEGIN
      table[row,ncols+1] := 0;
      FOR col := 1 to ncols DO
         table[row,ncols+1] := table[row,ncols+1] + table[row,col]
   END
```

Similar double-loop structures can be used to calculate the column sums and to write out the final table.

Here is the complete Pascal program.

```
PROGRAM table1;

(* READ IN A TABLE OF NUMBERS, SUM THE COLUMNS WITHIN EACH ROW,
   AND THEN SUM THE ROWS WITHIN EACH COLUMN *)

VAR row,col : 1..11;
    nrows,ncols : 1..10;
    table : ARRAY [1..11, 1..11] OF real;
```

(*Program continues on next page*)

```
PROCEDURE rowsums;
(* Add the columns within each row *)
BEGIN
    FOR row := 1 TO nrows DO
        BEGIN
            table[row,ncols+1] := 0;
            FOR col := 1 to ncols DO
                table[row,ncols+1] := table[row,ncols+1] + table[row,col]
        END
END;    (* rowsums *)

PROCEDURE columnsums;
(* Add the rows within each column *)
BEGIN
    FOR col := 1 TO ncols DO
        BEGIN
            table[nrows+1,col] := 0;
            FOR row := 1 TO nrows DO
                table[nrows+1,col] := table[nrows+1,col] + table[row,col]
        END
END;    (* columnsums *)

PROCEDURE readinput;
(* Read the elements of the table *)
BEGIN
    write(' How many rows? (1..10) ');
    readln(nrows);
    writeln;
    write(' How many columns? (1..10) ');
    readln(ncols);
    writeln;
    FOR row := 1 TO nrows DO
        BEGIN
            writeln(' Enter data for row no. ',row:2);
            FOR col := 1 TO ncols DO read(table[row,col]);
            writeln
        END
END;    (* readinput *)

PROCEDURE writeoutput;
(* Display the table and the corresponding sums *)
BEGIN
    writeln(' Original table, with row sums and column sums:');
    writeln;
    FOR row := 1 TO nrows + 1 DO
        BEGIN
            FOR col := 1 to ncols + 1 DO write(table[row,col]:6:1);
            writeln
        END
END;    (* writeoutput *)

BEGIN    (* main action block *)
    readinput;
    rowsums;
    columnsums;
    writeoutput
END.
```

Suppose the program will be used to process the following table of numbers.

2.5	−6.3	14.7	4.0
10.8	12.4	−8.2	5.5
−7.2	3.1	17.7	−9.1

When the program is executed, the following dialog will take place. (The user's responses are underlined.)

```
How many rows? (1..10) 3

How many columns? (1..10) 4

Enter data for row no.  1
2.5 -6.3 14.7 4.0

Enter data for row no.  2
10.8 12.4 -8.2 5.5

Enter data for row no.  3
-7.2 3.1 17.7 -9.1
```

The program will then calculate the row sums and the column sums and generate the following output

```
Original table, with row sums and column sums:

 2.5  -6.3  14.7   4.0  14.9
10.8  12.4  -8.2   5.5  20.5
-7.2   3.1  17.7  -9.1   4.5
 6.1   9.2  24.2   0.4   0.0
```

From this output, we can see that the sum of the elements in the first row is 14.9 (i.e., 2.5 − 6.3 + 14.7 + 4.0 = 14.9). Similarly, the sum of the elements in the first column is 6.1 (i.e., 2.5 + 10.8 − 7.2 = 6.1), and so on.

The indices in a multidimensional array need not all be of the same type. The only restriction is that each index be of some ordinal, simple type.

EXAMPLE 9.13

Some additional multi-array declarations are shown below.

```
TYPE color = (red,white,blue,yellow,green);
     index = 1..100;
VAR sample : ARRAY [color,index] OF boolean;
```

Thus one of the elements of `sample` might be `sample[white,25]`. Another might be `sample[green,66]`. Since `sample` is a boolean array, the values assigned to the individual elements will be boolean; i.e., their values will be either `true` or `false`.

Recall that an array may be of any type, including a structured type. Therefore, it is possible to define a one-dimensional array whose elements are themselves one-dimensional arrays (all having the same dimensionality), of the same type as the first array. The result of such an array definition is equivalent to an ordinary two-dimensional array.

EXAMPLE 9.14

Let us define a one-dimensional, char-type array called `codes`, whose elements are one-dimensional, char-type arrays. We will assume that `code` has a maximum of 25 elements, and that each element is a 50-element array. The array definition can be written as

```
VAR codes : ARRAY [1..25] OF ARRAY [1..50] OF char;
```

This is equivalent to defining an ordinary two-dimensional, char-type array. Thus, we can alternatively write

```
VAR codes : ARRAY [1..25, 1..50] OF char;
```

Each of these declarations defines a table having a maximum of 25 rows, with as many as 50 char-type elements within each row.

The individual array elements can also be accessed two different ways. For example, the element in row `i` and column `j` can be accessed as

```
code[i][j]16395
```

or as

```
code[i,j].
```

Similarly, row `i` (i.e., the entire row) can be accessed as

```
code[i].
```

Therefore, the element in row 12, column 20 can be accessed by writing either `code[12][20]` or `code[12,20]`. Also, all of the elements in row 12 can be accessed simply by writing `code[12]`.

In most applications it is more convenient to utilize multidimensional array elements using the original method, as in Example 9.12, rather than the method described above.

9.3 OPERATIONS WITH ENTIRE ARRAYS

There are certain types of operations that can be carried out with an entire array, thus affecting all of the array elements in the same manner. In particular, we can define array types, assign arrays to one another, and pass arrays as parameters to procedures or functions. Let us consider each of these features in some detail.

Some programs make use of several different arrays of the same type and dimensionality. In such cases it is convenient to define a single array type, and then declare the individual arrays as variables of this type.

In general terms, an array type definition can be expressed as

```
TYPE array name = ARRAY [index 1 type, index 2 type, . . . ,index n type] OF type
```

where the index types and the array data type have the same meaning as in an array-type variable declaration (see Section 9.2).

EXAMPLE 9.15

Suppose that `group1` and `group2` are two-dimensional integer-type arrays, each having a maximum of 25 rows and 50 columns. These arrays can be defined in the following manner.

```
TYPE table = ARRAY [1..25, 1..50] OF integer;
VAR group1,group2 : table;
```

Thus, `table` is a user-defined structured type (specifically, an integer-type, two-dimensional array with a maximum of 25 rows and 50 columns). The variables `group1` and `group2` are declared to be of type `table`. Hence, `group1` and `group2` will each be an integer-type, two-dimensional array with a maximum of 25 rows and 50 columns.

The variable declarations need not have the same scope as the type definition. For example, the type might be defined within the main block, and certain of the array-type variable declarations might appear immediately thereafter. The remaining variable declarations might then appear in a procedure or a function.

Sometimes it is desirable to assign all of the elements of one array to the corresponding elements of another array, where both arrays are of the same type and the same dimensionality. This can be accomplished with a single assignment statement, thus avoiding the need to assign each element individually within some type of looping structure.

EXAMPLE 9.16

Consider once again the two integer-type arrays, `group1` and `group2`, defined in the previous example. Suppose that all of the elements of `group1` have already been read into the computer, and we now wish to assign these elements to the corresponding elements of `group2`. This can be accomplished simply by writing

```
group2 := group1;
```

Note that this single assignment statement is equivalent to a nested double loop; i.e.,

```
FOR row := 1 TO 25 DO
    FOR col := 1 TO 50 DO
        group2[row,col] := group1[row,col];
```

Obviously, the single assignment statement is much simpler.

It is *not* possible, however, to include entire arrays in numeric or boolean expressions. Therefore, if a, b and c are array-type variables, a statement such as

```
c := a + b;
```

would not be permitted .

Similarly, an entire array cannot be read into the computer with a single `read` or `readln` statement. Thus, a loop structure is required in order to read in multiple array elements. In general, the same restriction applies to writing an entire array with a single `write` or `writeln` statement.

An entire array *can* be passed to a procedure or a function as an actual parameter. Note, however, that the corresponding formal parameter (within the procedure or function) must be associated with a recognized data type—in this case, an array type. Therefore, the array type must be explicitly defined within a block that encloses the procedure or function definition.

A convenient way to satisfy this requirement is to define a global array type, as described at the start of this section. The actual array-type parameters and the corresponding formal parameters can then be declared as members of this array type as required within the program. This approach is illustrated in the next example.

EXAMPLE 9.17 Adding Two Tables of Numbers

Suppose we read two tables of integers into the computer, calculate the sums of the corresponding elements, i.e.,

```
c[i,j] = a[i,j] + b[i,j]
```

and then write out the new table containing these sums. We will assume that all of the tables contain the same number of rows and columns, which do not exceed 20 rows and 30 columns.

Let us make use of the following variable definitions.

table = a two-dimensional integer array type having a maximum of 20 rows and 30 columns

a,b,c = two-dimensional arrays of type table

nrows = an integer variable indicating the actual number of rows in each table

ncols = an integer variable indicating the actual number of columns in each table

row = an integer counter that indicates the row number

col = an integer counter that indicates the column number

Let us employ a modular structure similar to that used in Example 9.12. Thus, we will define one procedure for reading the data into a table, another for summing all of the elements, and a third for writing out the new table containing the calculated sums. We will call these procedures readinput, computesums and writeoutput, respectively.

The actual program, shown below, is quite straightforward.

```
PROGRAM table2;

(* READ IN TWO TABLES OF INTEGERS, CALCULATE THE SUMS OF THEIR RESPECTIVE
   ELEMENTS, AND WRITE OUT THE RESULTING TABLE CONTAINING THE SUMS *)

TYPE table = ARRAY [1..20,1..30] OF integer;
VAR  a,b,c : table;
     row,nrows : 1..20;
     col,ncols : 1..30;

PROCEDURE readinput(VAR t : table);
(* Read the elements of one table *)
BEGIN
   FOR row := 1 TO nrows DO
      BEGIN
         writeln(' Enter data for row no. ',row:2);
         FOR col := 1 TO ncols DO read(t[row,col]);
         writeln
      END
END;   (* readinput *)


PROCEDURE computesums(t1,t2 : table; VAR t3 : table);
(* Sum the elements of two similar tables *)
BEGIN
   FOR row := 1 TO nrows DO
      FOR col := 1 TO ncols DO
         t3[row,col] := t1[row,col] + t2[row,col]
END;   (* computesums *)
```

(Program continues on next page)

```
        PROCEDURE writeoutput(t : table);
        (* Write out the elements of a table *)
        BEGIN
            writeln(' Sums of the elements:');
            writeln;
            FOR row := 1 TO nrows DO
                BEGIN
                    FOR col := 1 TO ncols DO write(t[row,col]:4);
                    writeln
                END
        END;    (* writeoutput *)

        BEGIN    (* main action block *)
            write(' How many rows? (1..20) ');
            readln(nrows);
            writeln;
            write(' How many columns? (1..30) ');
            readln(ncols);
            writeln;
            writeln(' First table:');
            writeln;
            readinput(a);
            writeln(' Second table:');
            writeln;
            readinput(b);
            computesums(a,b,c);
            writeoutput(c)
        END.
```

This program contains several noteworthy characteristics. First, notice that the program contains an array type definition, called `table`. Three variables `a`, `b` and `c` within the main block are declared to be arrays of type `table`. In addition, the procedures contain array-type parameters that are also declared to be of type `table`.

Notice that the array-type parameter `t` in procedure `readinput` is a *variable* parameter. This allows the elements of `t` to be returned from the procedure to the main block. On the other hand, the array-type variable `t` in `writeoutput` is a *value* parameter, since the elements of `t` that are transferred to this procedure need not be returned to the main block.

The remaining procedure, `computesums`, utilizes both value array-type parameters and variable array-type parameters. In particular, the first two parameters (`t1` and `t2`) are value parameters, since they represent input data to the procedure. The third parameter (`t3`) is a variable parameter, since it represents information that must be returned to the main block.

Now suppose that the program is used to sum the following two tables of numbers.

First Table					Second Table			
1	2	3	4		10	11	12	13
5	6	7	8		14	15	16	17
9	10	11	12		18	19	20	21

Execution of the program will first generate the following dialog, in order to enter the data. (Once again, the user's responses are underlined.)

```
How many rows? (1..20) 3

How many columns? (1..30) 4

First table:

Enter data for row no.  1
1 2 3 4

Enter data for row no.  2
5 6 7 8

Enter data for row no.  3
9 10 11 12

Second table:

Enter data for row no.  1
10 11 12 13

Enter data for row no.  2
14 15 16 17

Enter data for row no.  3
18 19 20 21
```

The program will then sum all of the respective elements and produce the following output.

```
Sums of the elements:

11  13  15  17
19  21  23  25
27  29  31  33
```

It is easy to verify that these are indeed the correct sums.

9.4 PACKED ARRAYS

In ANSI Pascal, some types of arrays can be defined so that they utilize the computer's memory more efficiently by "packing" the data items close together. This feature allows a greater quantity of information to be stored in a given anount of memory. (Turbo Pascal does not support this feature.)

In order to utilize array packing, we must include the reserved words PACKED ARRAY in the type specification; i.e.,

```
VAR array name : PACKED ARRAY [index 1 type,
                               index 2 type, . . . , index n type] OF type
```

This feature is most effective with array elements of type char, boolean or enumerated, or with subrange-type data.

On the other hand, the storage economy gained by packing may be offset by a loss in computing speed. Thus any program that utilizes a packed array involves a potential tradeoff between these two factors. For a given program, it is not clear which method is most advantageous. This distinction will generally vary from one application to another.

There are certain circumstances under which packing can be beneficial, both from a standpoint of storage economy and computing speed. This tends to be true in programs that include a large number of array assignments (i.e., assigning the elements of one array to another), or procedure or function calls in which arrays are passed as value parameters.

EXAMPLE 9.18

Consider once again the two-dimensional, boolean-type array called `sample`, which we defined in Example 9.13. If we are working with standard ANSI Pascal, we can declare `sample` to be a packed array. The array declaration will appear as follows.

```
TYPE color = (red,white,blue,yellow,green);
     index = 1..100;
VAR sample : PACKED ARRAY [color,index] OF boolean;
```

This declaration will cause the elements of `sample` to be packed into less memory than the corresponding declaration shown in Example 9.13.

ANSI Pascal includes two standard procedures, `pack` and `unpack`, that are used to convert unpacked arrays into packed arrays and vice versa. In particular, the standard procedure `pack` will transfer some or all elements of an unpacked array into a packed array. The syntax is

```
pack(unpacked array name, index, packed array name);
```

where *index* refers to the first element of the unpacked array to be transferred.

Once this procedure is accessed the transfer operation will continue until all elements of the packed array have been filled. The unpacked array (the source array) must contain enough elements beyond element *index* so that all elements within the packed array (the target array) can be filled.

EXAMPLE 9.19

Consider the following two arrays in an ANSI Pascal program.

```
VAR unpacked : ARRAY [1..20] OF char;
    packed   : PACKED ARRAY [1..20] OF char;
```

The statement

```
pack(unpacked,1,packed);
```

will cause each element of `unpacked` (starting at position 1) to be transferred to the corresponding location within `packed`. Thus,

```
packed[1] := unpacked[1];
packed[2] := unpacked[2];
. . . . .
packed[20] := unpacked[20];
```

The standard procedure unpack will transfer the elements of a packed array to to an unpacked array, beginning with element *index* of the unpacked array. The syntax is

```
unpack(packed array name, unpacked array name, index);
```

The transfer operation will continue until all elements of the packed array have been transfered. The unpacked array (i.e., the target array) must have enough elements beyond element *index* so that all elements within the packed array (the source array) can be transferred.

EXAMPLE 9.20

Consider the following two ANSI Pascal arrays.

```
VAR packed   : PACKED ARRAY [1..13] OF char;
    unpacked : ARRAY [1..20] OF char;
```

Suppose that packed contains the following 13 characters.

```
North America
```

Then the statement

```
unpack(packed,unpacked,5);
```

will result in the following assignments.

```
unpacked[5] := packed[1];        (hence unpacked[5] = 'N')
unpacked[6] := packed[2];        (hence unpacked[6] = 'o')
. . . . .
unpacked[17] := packed[13];      (hence unpacked[17] = 'a')
```

The remaining elements of unpacked will be undefined.

There is one restriction that must be observed when using packed arrays. Namely, that individual packed-array elements cannot be passed to a procedure or a function as actual parameters. Entire arrays can, however, be passed in the usual manner.

Remember that Turbo Pascal does not support packed arrays.

9.5 STRINGS AND STRING VARIABLES

Let us now turn our attention to the relationship between strings and arrays, in both standard ANSI Pascal and Turbo Pascal.

In ANSI Pascal, an *n*-character string is actually a one-dimensional, *n*-element packed array of type char.

EXAMPLE 9.21

Suppose an ANSI Pascal program contains the following constant definition.

```
CONST title = 'The Super-Duper Computer Company';
```

The identifier title represents a 32-element packed array of type char.

In ANSI Pascal, a char-type packed array may be considered a *string variable*. Thus,

```
PACKED ARRAY [1..n] OF char
```

is a string variable data type. Such variables can be used to represent strings of length n. (Do not confuse these string variables with the string variables defined in Turbo Pascal, which are much more robust. More about this later.)

EXAMPLE 9.22

Suppose an ANSI Pascal program contains the following variable declaration.

```
VAR heading : PACKED ARRAY [1..14] OF char;
```

The identifier `heading` is a string variable, since it represents a 14-element packed array of type char.

ANSI Pascal includes some special packed-array operations that can only be utilized with strings or string variables. For example, an *n*-element string can be assigned to an *n*-element string variable by means of an ordinary assignment statement. (Note that this single operation involves the assignment of a sequence of array elements to an entire array.)

EXAMPLE 9.23

Consider once again the packed array `heading`, defined in the previous example. Since `heading` is a 14-element string variable, we can assign any 14-character string to `heading`; i.e.,

```
heading := 'Dallas Cowboys';
```

We can, of course, also assign one string variable to another, provided both variables contain the same number of elements. (Recall that this feature applies to *all* arrays, as described in Section 9.3.)

EXAMPLE 9.24

An ANSI Pascal program contains the following variable declarations.

```
VAR factory,warehouse : PACKED ARRAY [1..11] OF char;
```

The identifiers `factory` and `warehouse` are string variables, since they both represent packed arrays of type char. Also, note that both variables are defined as 11-element arrays. Hence, one array can be assigned to the other.

Now suppose that the program contains the following string assignment.

```
factory := 'Seattle, WA';
```

Then at some later point in the program we can assign this same string to another 11-element string variable. For example,

```
warehouse := factory;
```

Thus, `warehouse` will also represent the string `'Seattle, WA'`.

Strings of equal length can be compared with one another by means of the relational operators. In ANSI Pascal such comparisons can be carried out between two string constants, two string variables, or a string constant and a string variable. In each case, we will be creating a boolean expression that is either true or false.

When relational operators are used with strings or string variables, the operators = and <> denote equivalence or lack of equivalence, respectively. The remaining four operators, < , <= , > and >= , refer to the ordering of the characters within each string, as defined by the character code.

EXAMPLE 9.25

Consider the following ANSI Pascal string-variable declarations.

```
TYPE colors = PACKED ARRAY [1..5] OF char;
VAR  c1,c2,c3 : colors;
```

Now suppose that the string variables are assigned the following string values.

```
c1 := 'black';
c2 := 'white';
c3 := 'green';
```

Several boolean expressions involving these variables are shown below. The corresponding values of the expressions are also given.

Boolean Expression	Value	
c1 < c2	true	(because 'b' < 'w')
c3 < c2	true	(because 'g' < 'w')
c1 > 'brown'	false	(because 'l' < 'r')
'gross' > c3	true	(because 'o' > 'e')

It should be understood that the use of an entire array as an operand in a boolean expression is valid only if the array represents a string variable. Such comparisons are not allowed with other types of arrays.

In ANSI Pascal another special feature associated with string variables involves the use of the write and writeln statements. String variables can be included within these statements, thus causing entire strings (i.e., all elements within the packed arrays) to be written out without the need for loop structures.

EXAMPLE 9.26

A portion of an ANSI Pascal program is shown below.

```
VAR factory : PACKED ARRAY [1..11] OF char;
 . . . . .
BEGIN
   . . . . .
   factory := 'Seattle, WA';
   . . . . .
   writeln(' Factory Location: ',factory);
   . . . . .
END.
```

Notice that the `writeln` statement contains both a string constant and a string variable.

When this program is executed, the following output will be produced.

```
Factory Location: Seattle, WA
```

In ANSI Pascal a string variable is the *only* type of array that can be included in a `write` or `writeln` statement in this manner. Moreover, a similar capability is *not* available when using the `read` or `readln` statement, even with string variables. Therefore strings must be entered into the computer on a character-by-character basis, using some type of loop structure.

EXAMPLE 9.27

A portion of a Pascal program is shown below.

```
VAR factory : PACKED ARRAY [1..11] OF char;
    i : 1..11;
. . . . .
BEGIN
    . . . . .
    FOR i := 1 TO 11 DO read(factory[i]);
    writeln;
    . . . . .
    writeln(' Factory Location: ',factory);
    . . . . .
END.
```

Note the distinction between the input and the output statements in this example. Also, notice the differences between this example and the previous example.

The ability to define and manipulate string variables opens the door to a broad class of important, comprehensive programming applications. Some indication is given in the following example.

EXAMPLE 9.28 A Pig Latin Generator

Pig Latin is an encoded form of English that is often used by children as a game. A pig Latin word is formed from an English word by transposing the first sound (usually the first letter) to the end of the word, and then adding the letter "a." Thus, the word "cat" becomes "atca," "Pascal" becomes "ascalPa," "pigLatin" becomes "igLatinpa," and so on.

Let us write an ANSI Pascal program that will accept a line of English text and then print out the corresponding text in pig Latin. We will assume that each textual message can be typed on one 80-column line, with a single blank space between successive words. (Actually, we will require that the *pig Latin* message not exceed 80 characters. Therefore the original message must be somewhat less than 80 characters, since the corresponding pig Latin message will be lengthened by the addition of the letter "a" after each word.) For simplicity, we will transpose only the first letter (not the first sound) of each word. Also, we will ignore any special consideration that might be given to capital letters and to punctuation marks.

The overall computational strategy will be straightforward, consisting of the following major steps.

1. Initialize all arrays (string variables) by assigning blank spaces to all of the elements.

2. Read in an entire line of text (several words).

3. Determine the number of words in the line, by counting the number of single blank spaces that are followed by a nonblank space.

4. Rearrange the words into pig Latin, on a word-by-word basis, as follows:

    (a) locate the end of each word.

    (b) transpose the first letter to the end of the word.

    (c) add an "a" to the end of each modified word.

5. Write out the entire line of pig Latin.

We will continue this procedure repetitiously, until the computer reads a line of text whose first three letters are "end."

In order to implement this strategy we will make use of two "pointers," called p1 and p2, respectively. The first pointer (p1) will indicate the position of the *beginning* of a particular word within the original line of text. The second pointer (p2) will indicate the *end* of the word. Note that the character in the column preceding column number p1 will be a blank space (except for the first word). Also, the character in the column beyond column number p2 will be a blank space.

Let us again employ a modular approach in the development of this program. Before discussing each of the modules, however, we define the following program variables.

english = a string variable (i.e., a packed array of type char) that represents the original line of text

latin = a string variable that represents the new line of text (i.e., the pig Latin)

flag = a boolean variable that will remain true until the word "end" is entered, thus allowing the program to execute repetitiously.

words = an integer-type variable that indicates the number of words in the given line of text

n = an integer-type variable that is used as a word counter ($n = 1, 2, \ldots,$ words)

count = an integer-type variable that is used as a character counter within each line (count $= 0, 1, 2, \ldots, 80$)

These variables will be used in conjunction with the integer-type variables p1 and p2 discussed earlier.

Now let us return to the overall program outline presented above. The first step, array initialization, can be carried out in a straightforward manner with the following procedure.

```
PROCEDURE initialize;
(* initialize the arrays with blank spaces *)
BEGIN
    FOR count := 1 TO 80 DO
        english[count] := ' ';
        latin := english
END;
```

Step 2 can also be carried out with a simple procedure. This procedure will contain a conditional loop (a WHILE - DO structure) that will continue to read characters until an end-of-line is detected (i.e., until the function eoln becomes true). This sequence of characters will become the elements of the string variable english. Here is the entire procedure.

```
PROCEDURE readinput;
(* read one line of English *)
BEGIN
    count := 0;
    WHILE NOT eoln DO
        BEGIN
            count := count +1;
            read(english[count])
        END;
    readln
END;
```

Step 3 of the overall outline is equally straightforward. We simply scan the original line for occurrences of single blank spaces followed by nonblank characters. The word counter (`words`) is then incremented each time such a single blank space is encountered. Here is the word-count routine.

```
PROCEDURE countwords;
(* scan the line and count the number of words *)
BEGIN
    words := 1;
    FOR count := 1 TO 79 DO
        IF (english[count] = ' ') AND (english[count + 1] <> ' ')
            THEN words := words + 1
END;
```

Now let us consider steps 4 and 5 of the overall program outline. These steps are really the heart of the program. They can easily be combined into one procedure, since step 5 requires only a single statement. On the other hand, step 4 is rather involved since it requires three separate, though related, operations.

We must first identify the end of each word, by finding the first blank space beyond `p1`. We then assign the characters that make up the word to `latin`, with the first character at the end of the word. This must be handled carefully, since the new line of text will be longer than the original line (because of the additional a's). Hence, the characters in the first pig Latin word will occupy locations `p1` to `p2+1`. The characters in the second word will occupy locations `p1+1` to `p2+2` (note that these are new values of `p1` and `p2`), and so on. These rules can be generalized as follows.

First, for word number n, transfer all characters except the first from the original line to the new line. This can be accomplished by writing

```
FOR count := p1 TO p2 - 1 DO
    latin[count + (n - 1)] := english[count + 1];
```

The last two characters (i.e., the first character in the original word plus the letter "a") can then be added in the following manner.

```
latin[p2 + (n-1)] := english[p1];
latin[p2 + n] := 'a';
```

We then reset the value of `p1`, i.e.,

```
p1 := p2 + 2
```

in preparation for the next word.

This entire group of calculations is repeated for each word in the original line. The new line, containing the pig Latin equivalent of the original line, is then written out.

Here is the procedure that accomplishes all of this.

```
PROCEDURE rearrangewords;
(* rearrange each word into pig Latin, then write out the entire line *)
BEGIN
    p1 := 1;
    FOR n := 1 TO words DO
        BEGIN
```

(Program continues on next page)

```
                (* locate end of word *)
                count := p1;
                WHILE english[count]  <> ' ' DO count := count + 1;
                p2 := count - 1;

                (* transpose first letter and add 'a' *)
                FOR count := p1 TO p2 - 1 DO
                    latin[count + (n - 1)] := english[count + 1];
                latin[p2 + (n - 1)] := english[p1];
                latin[p2 + n] := 'a';
                p1 := p2 + 2
            END;
        writeln(latin)
    END;
```

We now turn our attention to the main block. This portion of the program is nothing more than an initial message, followed by a REPEAT - UNTIL structure that allows for repetitious program execution, until the word "end" is detected as the first word in the English text . Specifically, we begin by assigning the value true to flag, and then change this value to false once "end" has been detected within the loop. An IF - THEN structure will be placed within the loop to test for this condition. The looping action will then terminate once flag becomes false.

The entire ANSI Pascal program is shown below. Note that several comments have been added to the procedures presented earlier.

```
    PROGRAM pigLatin;
    (* ENTER A LINE OF ENGLISH TEXT AND CONVERT IT TO PIG LATIN *)
    (* Word pointers: p1 -> beginning of word
                      p2 -> end of word        *)

    TYPE line = PACKED ARRAY [1..80] OF char;
    VAR english,latin : line;
        p1,p2,count,n,words : integer;
        flag : boolean;

    PROCEDURE initialize;
    (* initialize the arrays with blank spaces *)
    BEGIN
        FOR count := 1 TO 80 DO
            english[count] := ' ';
        latin := english
    END;   (* initialize *)

    PROCEDURE readinput;
    (* read one line of English *)
    BEGIN
        count := 0;
        WHILE NOT eoln DO
            BEGIN
                count := count + 1;
                read(english[count])
            END;
        readln
    END;   (* readinput *)
```

```
PROCEDURE countwords;
(* scan the line and count the number of words *)
BEGIN
    words := 1;
    FOR count := 1 TO 79 DO
        IF (english[count] = ' ') AND (english[count + 1] <> ' ')
            THEN words := words + 1
END;   (* countwords *)

PROCEDURE rearrangewords;
(* rearrange each word into pig Latin, then write out the entire line *)
BEGIN
    p1 := 1;
    FOR n := 1 TO words DO
        BEGIN

            (* locate end of word *)
            count := p1;
            WHILE english[count]  <> ' ' DO count := count + 1;
            p2 := count - 1;

            (* transpose first letter and add 'a' *)
            FOR count := p1 TO p2 - 1 DO
                latin[count + (n - 1)] := english[count + 1];
            latin[p2 + (n - 1)] := english[p1];
            latin[p2 + n] := 'a';
            p1 := p2 + 2
        END;
    writeln(latin)
END;   (* rearrangewords *)

BEGIN   (* main action block *)
    writeln('Pig Latin Generator');
    writeln;
    writeln('Type ''end'' when finished');
    writeln;
    flag := true;
    REPEAT   (* process a line of text *)
        initialize;
        readinput;
        IF (english[1] = 'e') AND (english[2] = 'n') AND
            (english[3] = 'd') THEN flag := false;
        countwords;
        rearrangewords
    UNTIL flag = false
END.
```

Notice that this program includes the assignment of one entire array to another (in procedure `initialize`) as well as the assignment of individual array elements (in `readinput` and `rearrangewords`). Also, note that an entire string variable (i.e., an entire packed array) is written out with a single `writeln` statement in procedure `rearrangewords`. The corresponding input operation must, of course, be carried out on an element-by-element basis, as in procedure `readinput`.

Now consider what happens when the program is executed. Here is a typical interactive session, in which the user's responses are underlined.

```
Pig Latin Generator

Type 'end' when finished

Pascal is a popular structured programming language
ascalPa sia aa opularpa tructuredsa rogrammingpa anguagela

baseball is the great American pastime, though
aseballba sia heta reatga mericanAa astime,pa houghta

though there are many who prefer football
houghta hereta reaa anyma howa referpa ootballfa

please do not sneeze in the computer room
leasepa oda otna neezesa nia heta omputerca oomra

end
ndea
```

Note that the program does not include any special accommodations for punctuation marks, upper-case letters, or double-letter sounds (e.g., "th," "sh," etc.). These refinements are left as exercises for the reader.

Turbo Pascal supports a much broader class of string manipulation operations. We have already seen that Turbo Pascal categorizes string data as a separate data type (see Section 3.5). We have also seen that string-type data can be read in and written out of the computer using the read, readln, write and writeln statements, as with any other scalar data type (see Chap. 4). In addition, strings can be assigned to string variables, irrespective of the length of the strings, and strings and string variables of different lengths can be compared with one another.

EXAMPLE 9.29

Here is a Turbo Pascal program that reads in two strings, not necessarily of the same length, compares them, assigns the lower-order string (as defined by the character code) to a third string variable, and then displays this newly assigned string variable.

```
PROGRAM strings;
(* Turbo Pascal string manipulation *)
VAR str1,str2,str3 : string;

BEGIN
   write('String 1: ');
   readln(str1);
   write('String 2: ');
   readln(str2);
   IF (str1 < str2) THEN str3 := str1
                    ELSE str3 := str2;
   write('Lower-order string: ');
   writeln(str3)
END.
```

Note that this program reads, compares, assigns and displays string variables whose lengths are unspecified.

When the program is executed an interactive dialog, such as that shown below, is generated. The user's responses are again underlined.

```
String 1: blue
String 2: red
Lower-order string: blue
```

Note that blue precedes red because 'b' precedes 'r', even though blue contains more characters than red.

In Turbo Pascal, individual characters within a string can be accessed as separate array elements. Thus, if city is the name of a string, city[1] refers to the first character, city[2] the second character, and so on.

EXAMPLE 9.30

The following Turbo Pascal program accesses individual characters within a string. The program reads in a string whose length is unspecified, then displays the number of characters, the first character and the last character.

```
program string_chars;
(* string manipulation in Turbo Pascal *)
VAR str : string;
      n : integer;

BEGIN
    write('String: ');
    readln(str);
    n := length(str);
    writeln('Length: ',n,' characters');
    writeln('First character: ',str[1]);
    writeln('Last character: ',str[n])
END.
```

Note that this program utilizes the Turbo Pascal standard function length to determine the number of characters in the string.

When the program is executed, the following dialog is generated. Again, the user's response is underlined.

```
String: yellow
Length: 6 characters
First character: y
Last character: w
```

9.6 VARIABLE-LENGTH ARRAY PARAMETERS

We have already seen that entire arrays can be passed to a procedure or function provided the actual parameters and the corresponding formal parameters are of the same explicit type and hence contain the same number of elements (see Section 9.3, and particularly Example 9.16). In some applications, however, it may be desirable for a procedure or function to include a formal parameter whose maximum number of elements is unspecified in absolute terms. This feature allows the procedure or function to be accessed from several different places, with actual parameters that are of a different size at each point of access.

In ANSI Pascal, formal array parameters of variable length can be included within a procedure or function, though they must be declared in a special way. Such parameters are known as *formal conformant array parameters*. Their corresponding actual parameters are called *actual conformant array parameters*.

The use of conformant array parameters can enhance the generality of an ANSI Pascal program. On the other hand, the syntactical requirements associated with their use is rather complicated. Beginning programmers may therefore choose to avoid their use until they are comfortable with other forms of parameter passing. (*Note*: Some versions of Pascal, including Turbo Pascal do *not* support conformant array parameters.)

Let us first consider one-dimensional conformant array parameters. The manner in which they are defined will depend on whether they are value parameters or variable parameters, as illustrated in the following examples.

EXAMPLE 9.31

Suppose `sample` is an ANSI Pascal procedure that makes use of a variable formal array parameter called `list`, which is of type real. The procedure header would then be written as follows.

```
PROCEDURE sample (VAR list : ARRAY [first..last : integer] OF real);
```

Thus we see that `list` is a one-dimensional, real-type array whose index values will be integers ranging from `first` to `last`. The numerical values of `first` and `last` will be determined by the corresponding actual parameter, which must also be a one-dimensional, real-type array with an integer-type index.

Consider, for example, the one-dimensional, real-type array `item`, whose declaration appears in the main program block; i.e.,

```
VAR item : ARRAY [1..100] OF real;
```

Now suppose that `item` is an actual parameter that is passed to `sample`, i.e.,

```
sample(item);
```

In this situation `first` will take on a value of 1, and `last` a value of 100. Hence, `list` will be treated as a 100-element, real-type array during this procedure access.

If the elements of `list` are modified within the procedure, then these modified array elements will be returned to `item`, as is always the case with a variable formal parameter.

EXAMPLE 9.32

In this example we see a skeletal outline of an ANSI Pascal program that includes a function that presumably counts the number of words in a line of text. For illustrative purposes, let us make use of a value conformant array parameter within the function.

```
PROGRAM dummy;
TYPE length = 1..80;
     words  = 1..20;
VAR heading : PACKED ARRAY [1..12] OF char;
    message : PACKED ARRAY [1..80] OF char;
    n1,n2   : words;
```

(Outline continues on next page)

```
FUNCTION count (text : PACKED ARRAY [start..stop : length] OF char) : words;
BEGIN
    . . . . .
    count := . . .
END;

BEGIN (* main action statements *)
. . . . . .
    n1 := count(heading);
    . . . . . .
    n2 := count(message);
    . . . . .
END.
```

This example includes several features that require some explanation. First, within function `count`, `text` is considered a 12-element packed array during the initial function reference, and an 80-element packed array during the second function reference. In each case the function will return an integer whose value lies somewhere between 1 and 20. (This assumes that each line of text will contain at least 1 and not more than 20 words.)

Next, the packed arrays `heading` and `message`, which are used as actual parameters in the function references, are legitimate string variables. (We assume that the strings represented by these variables have been read into the computer, or otherwise assigned, prior to the function references.) However, the formal value parameter `text` (i.e., the value conformant array parameter) is *not* considered to be a string variable. Hence the special properties of string variables discussed in Section 9.5 cannot be utilized within the function. This restriction applies to all packed arrays of type char that are used as conformant array parameters.

Conformant array parameters can be multidimensional as well as one-dimensional. In general the same rules apply, though there is one restriction that concerns the use of packing. Specifically, only the innermost dimension (i.e., the last dimension) can be packed. Furthermore, if packing is to be used in this manner, then the conformant array parameter must be defined as an array of packed arrays, as illustrated below.

EXAMPLE 9.33

Consider the following ANSI Pascal procedure header, which makes use of a two-dimensional conformant array parameter.

```
PROCEDURE sample (page : ARRAY [first..last : integer]
                                OF PACKED ARRAY [c1..cn : integer] OF char);
```

Note that `page` is a value conformant array parameter whose elements are individual characters. It can therefore be thought of as a page of text, where the first index represents the line number and the second index represents the character position within a given line. Also, notice that both indices are of type integer, even though the array elements themselves are of type char.

There are certain restrictions that must be observed when using conformant array parameters. We have already discussed two such restrictions; namely, that a packed array of type char cannot be treated as a string variable within the procedure or function to which it has been passed (see Example 9.32), and that packing can be employed only with the innermost dimension of a multidimensional array. An additional restriction concerns the passing of a conformant array parameter to another procedure or function. In such situations the formal parameter within the secondary module must be defined as a *variable* conformant array parameter rather than a *value* formal array parameter.

EXAMPLE 9.34

The skeletal outline of an ANSI Pascal program is shown below.

```
PROGRAM nothing;
VAR item : ARRAY [1..100] OF real;

FUNCTION largest (VAR numbers : ARRAY [start..stop : integer] OF real) : real;
BEGIN
   . . . . .
   largest := . . .
END;

PROCEDURE process (VAR list : ARRAY [first..last : integer] OF real);
VAR count : real;
BEGIN
   . . . . .
   count := largest(list);
   . . . . .
END;

BEGIN (* main block *)
   . . . . .
   process(item);
   . . . . .
END.
```

In this example the 100-element, real array item is passed to procedure process. The corresponding formal parameter is a variable conformant array parameter, called list. Within process, this array is passed to the function largest. The corresponding formal parameter in largest is also a variable conformant array parameter, called numbers.

Note that the conformant array parameter within process (i.e., list) later becomes an actual parameter, when the function largest is referenced. Therefore numbers (the formal parameter within largest) must be defined as a *variable* conformant array parameter rather than a *value* conformant array parameter.

There is another restriction that must be observed when two or more conformant array parameters are defined together. In such a situation, the corresponding actual parameters in any single reference must be of the same type. Adherence to this restriction is illustrated in the next example.

EXAMPLE 9.35 Adding Two Tables of Numbers

Let us consider once again a program for adding two tables of numbers, originally given in Example 9.17. Now, however, we present an ANSI Pascal program that utilizes conformant array parameters to represent the tables within the program modules.

Here is the entire program.

```
PROGRAM table3;

(* READ IN TWO TABLES OF INTEGERS, CALCULATE THE SUMS OF THEIR RESPECTIVE
   ELEMENTS, AND WRITE OUT THE RESULTING TABLE CONTAINING THE SUMS *)

(* THIS PROGRAM MAKES USE OF CONFORMANT ARRAY PARAMETERS *)
```

```
VAR  a,b,c : ARRAY [1..20,1..30] OF integer;
     row,nrows : 1..20;
     col,ncols : 1..30;

PROCEDURE readinput (VAR t : ARRAY [firstrow..lastrow : integer;
                                    firstcol..lastcol : integer] OF integer);
(* Read the elements of one table *)
BEGIN
   FOR row := 1 TO nrows DO
      BEGIN
         writeln(' Enter data for row no. ',row:2);
         FOR col := 1 TO ncols DO read(t[row,col]);
         writeln
      END
END;   (* readinput *)

PROCEDURE computesums (VAR t1,t2,t3 : ARRAY [firstrow..lastrow : integer;
                                    firstcol..lastcol : integer] OF integer);
(* Sum the elements of two similar tables *)
BEGIN
   FOR row := 1 TO nrows DO
      FOR col := 1 TO ncols DO
         t3[row,col] := t1[row,col] + t2[row,col]
END;   (* computesums *)

PROCEDURE writeoutput (t : ARRAY [firstrow..lastrow : integer;
                                    firstcol..lastcol : integer] OF integer);
(* Write out the elements of a table *)
BEGIN
   writeln(' Sums of the elements:');
   writeln;
   FOR row := 1 TO nrows DO
      BEGIN
         FOR col := 1 TO ncols DO write(t[row,col]:4);
         writeln
      END
END;   (* writeoutput *)

BEGIN   (* main action block *)
   write(' How many rows? (1..20) ');
   readln(nrows);
   writeln;
   write(' How many columns? (1..30) ');
   readln(ncols);
   writeln;
   writeln(' First table:');
   writeln;
   readinput(a);
   writeln(' Second table:');
   writeln;
   readinput(b);
   computesums(a,b,c);
   writeoutput(c)
END.
```

It is interesting to compare this ANSI Pascal version of the program with the earlier version given in Example 9.17. Note, for example, that a type definition is not included in the present version. Rather, the array specifications are included with the variable declarations. Of greater significance is the fact that all of the procedures utilize conformant array parameters as formal parameters. Two of the procedures, `readinput` and `computesums`, make use of variable conformant array parameters, whereas the third procedure, `writeoutput`, utilizes a value conformant array parameter. Note that three conformant array parameters, `t1`, `t2` and `t3`, are defined together in procedure `computesums`. Also note that the corresponding reference to `computesums` within the main block contains three actual parameters (`a`, `b` and `c`) that are all of the same type, as required.

Before leaving this section we again remind the reader that the use of conformant array parameters is somewhat complicated and may therefore be inappropriate for beginning programmers. Moreover, some versions of Pascal, including Turbo Pascal, do not support the use of conformant array parameters. Even if this feature is available, however, some discretion should be exercised in its use.

Review Questions

9.1   What are the four different structured data types?

9.2   What are the particular characteristics of an array as a structured data type?

9.3   Suggest a practical way to visualize a one-dimensional array.

9.4   What is meant by an array element? What data types can be used as array elements?

9.5   What is meant by an index (or subscript)? What data types can be used for an index? (Compare with the answer to the previous question.)

9.6   How can an individual array element be accessed?

9.7   Explain how an array can be defined within the variable declaration part of a program.

9.8   Summarize the rules for utilizing an array element within an expression, assignment statement, read/write statement, etc. How can the indices be written? What restrictions apply to the manner in which the indices are written?

9.9   Can enumerated data items be used as array elements?

9.10   Explain how an array can be used to represent a string in ANSI Pascal. Does this technique also work in Turbo Pascal?

9.11   Suggest a practical way to visualize a two-dimensional array.

9.12   Summarize the rules for defining a multidimensional array as a part of a variable declaration. Must the indices all be of the same data type?

9.13   Summarize the rules for referencing a multidimensional array element.

9.14   Explain why some applications of multidimensional arrays require nested loops. What is the purpose of each loop?

9.15   Describe how a two-dimensional array can be expressed as a one-dimensional array whose individual elements are one-dimensional arrays. Can this concept be extended to arrays of higher dimensionality?

9.16   Describe how several arrays of the same type can be declared by first defining an array type and then declaring the individual arrays to be variables of this type. Must all of the arrays declared in this manner have the same scope?

9.17   How can all of the elements of one array be collectively assigned to the corresponding elements of another array with a single assignment statement? What restrictions apply to the two arrays?

9.18   Can an entire array appear in a numeric or boolean expression?

9.19   Can an entire array be read into the computer with a single `read` or `readln` statement?

9.20   Can an entire array be written out of the computer with a single `write` or `writeln` statement?

9.21   What restrictions apply to the passing of an entire array to a procedure or a function?

9.22   Describe a convenient way to pass an entire array to a procedure or a function.

9.23   Can a single array element be passed to a procedure or a function?

9.24   What is a packed array? How do packed arrays differ from ordinary arrays?

9.25   Are packed arrays supported in all versions of Pascal? Explain.

9.26   What possible advantages and disadvantages are associated with the use of packed arrays?

9.27   For what types of applications are packed arrays particularly advantageous?

9.28   Can a packed array be unpacked? Can an unpacked array be packed? Explain.

9.29   Summarize the rules associated with the use of the standard procedures `pack` and `unpack`.

9.30   Can an entire packed array be passed to a procedure or a function?

9.31   Can a single packed array element be passed to a procedure or a function?

9.32   What is a string variable in ANSI Pascal? In ANSI Pascal, what is the relationship between packed arrays and string variables?

9.33   Describe the special ANSI Pascal packed-array operations that can only be utilized with strings or string variables.

9.34   Summarize the differences between ANSI Pascal and Turbo Pascal in the interpretation and processing of string variables.

9.35   How are the relational operators interpreted when they are used to connect strings or string variables to form boolean expressions? In particular, how are the operators <, <=, > and >= interpreted?

9.36   In ANSI Pascal, what is a conformant array parameter? What purpose does it serve?

9.37   Are conformant array parameters supported in all versions of Pascal? Explain.

9.38   Summarize the rules for defining one-dimensional conformant array parameters. Distinguish between value conformant array parameters and variable conformant array parameters.

9.39   Summarize the rules for defining multidimensional conformant array parameters. Compare with the rules for one-dimensional conformant array parameters.

9.40   Can packing be utilized with a multidimensional conformant array parameters? Explain fully.

9.41   Suppose a packed array of type char is passed to a procedure or a function as a conformant array parameter. Can this array be treated as a string variable within the procedure or function?

9.42   Suppose that a formal conformant array parameter within a given procedure is to be passed to another procedure. (That is, the formal conformant array parameter becomes an actual conformant array parameter which is passed to the secondary procedure.)   In what way must the formal conformant array parameter be defined within the secondary procedure?

9.43   Suppose that two or more formal conformant array parameters are defined together within a procedure header. What condition must be satisfied by the corresponding actual conformant array parameters?

Problems

9.44   Describe the meaning of each of the following array declarations.

(*a*)   `VAR values : ARRAY [0..100] OF real;`

(*b*)   `TYPE days = (sun,mon,tues,wed,thurs,fri,sat);`
       `VAR calories : ARRAY [days] OF integer;`

(*c*)   `TYPE colors = (blue,brown,gray,green,black);`
       `        size   = (small,medium,large);`
       `VAR coats : ARRAY [size] OF color;`

(*d*)   `VAR parts : ARRAY ['A'..'Z', 1..10000] OF integer;`

(*e*)   `TYPE days = (sun,mon,tues,wed,thurs,fri,sat);`
       `VAR sunshine : PACKED ARRAY [1..365] OF days;`

9.45   Write a variable declaration, and any required type declarations, to define each of the following arrays.

(*a*)   A one-dimensional, real-type array called `list`, whose index may take on integer values ranging from −10 through +10.

(*b*)   A one-dimensional array called `sunshine` of type `days`. The array elements may take on the values `sun`, `mon`, `tues`, `wed`, `thurs`, `fri` and `sat`. The index may take on integer values ranging from 1 through 365.

(*c*)   A two-dimensional, integer-type array called `coats`, whose first index may take on the values `blue`, `brown`, `gray`, `green` and `black`, and whose second index may take on the values `small`, `medium` and `large`.

(d) Repeat the previous problem, writing the array declaration as a one-dimensional array of one-dimensional arrays.

(e) A two-dimensional, char-type array called `tally`, whose first index ranges from 1 to `max1`, and whose second index ranges from 1 to `max2`. Define `max1` and `max2` to be constants whose values are 2000 and 5000, respectively.

(f) A three-dimensional, boolean-type array called `symbol`, whose first index may take on the integers 1 through 12, whose second index may take on the integers 1 through 20 and whose third index may take on the integers 0 through 5.

(g) A one-dimensional, packed array called `name`, whose index may take on the integers 1 through 80.

(h) A two-dimensional, char-type packed array called `page`, whose first index may take on the integers 1 through 66 and whose second index may take on the integers 1 through 80. Define `page` as a one-dimensional array of one-dimensional packed arrays.

9.46 The following skeletal outlines illustrate the use of arrays and/or array elements in typical programming situations. Describe the purpose of each outline.

(a)
```
PROGRAM sample;
VAR square : ARRAY [1..100] OF integer;
    count  : 1..100;

BEGIN
    . . . . .
  FOR count := 1 TO 100 DO square[count] := sqr(count);
    . . . . .
END.
```

(b)
```
PROGRAM sample;
VAR table : ARRAY [1..20, 1..8] OF real;
    i,m : 1..20;
    j,n : 1..8;

BEGIN
    . . . . .
  readln(m,n);
  FOR i := 1 TO m DO
    BEGIN
       FOR j := 1 TO n DO read(table[i,j]);
       writeln
    END;
    . . . . .
  FOR i := 1 TO m DO
    BEGIN
       FOR j := 1 TO n DO write(table[i,j]);
       writeln
    END
END.
```

(c)
```
     PROGRAM sample;
     VAR value : ARRAY [0..100] OF real;
        index,max : 0..100;

     BEGIN
         . . . . .
        readln(max);
         . . . . .
        value[0] := 0;
        FOR index := max DOWNTO 1 DO
          BEGIN
             value[index] := index MOD 8;
             IF value[index] < 5.0 THEN value[0] := value[0] + value[index]
          END;
         . . . . .
     END.
```

(d)
```
     PROGRAM sample;
     TYPE color = (red,white,blue,yellow,green);
     VAR foreground : PACKED ARRAY [1..5] OF color;
        background : ARRAY [1..5] OF color;
        index : 1..5;

     BEGIN
         . . . . .
        FOR index := 1 TO 5 DO background[index] := . . .;
         . . . . .
        pack(background,1,foreground);
         . . . . .
     END.
```

This program outline refers to ANSI Pascal.

(e)
```
     PROGRAM sample;
     VAR city,office : PACKED ARRAY [1..3] OF char;
        order : 1..maxint;

     BEGIN
         . . . . .
        city := 'CHI';
         . . . . .
        readln(order);
        IF order < 100 THEN office := city
                    ELSE IF order < 1000 THEN office := 'NYC'
                                          ELSE office := 'ATL';
         . . . . .
        writeln(office);
         . . . . .
     END.
```

This program outline also refers to ANSI Pascal. Note that that city and office are string variables.

(*f*)
```
     PROGRAM sample;
     VAR list1 : ARRAY [1..40] OF integer;
         list2 : ARRAY [1..80] OF integer;

         PROCEDURE sort(VAR items : ARRAY [first..last : integer] OF integer);
         VAR . . .;    (* local variables *)
         BEGIN
           . . . . .
           (* process the elements of items *)
           . . . . .
         END;

         BEGIN    (* main action statements *)
           . . . . .
           (* read elements of list1 *)
           . . . . .
           sort(list1);
           . . . . .
           (* read elements of list2 *)
           . . . . .
           sort(list2);
           . . . . .
         END.
```

This program outline refers to ANSI Pascal. Note that list1 and list2 are integer-type arrays that differ in size.

Programming Problems

9.47 Modify the program given in Example 9.5 so that the numbers are rearranged into a sequence of algebraically decreasing values (i.e., from largest to smallest). Test the program using the data given in Example 9.5.

9.48 Modify the program given in Example 9.5 so that any one of the following rearrangements can be carried out:

(*a*) Smallest to largest, by magnitude

(*b*) Smallest to largest, algebraic

(*c*) Largest to smallest, by magnitude

(*d*) Largest to smallest, algebraic

Include a menu that will allow the user to select which rearrangement will be used each time the program is executed. Test the program using the following 10 values.

4.7	−8.0
−2.3	11.4
12.9	5.1
8.8	−0.2
6.0	−14.7

9.49   Modify the program given in Example 9.8 so that it utilizes packed arrays and variable-length array parameters. Test the program using your own name and address.

9.50   Modify the program given in Example 9.17 to calculate the differences rather than the sums of the corresponding elements in two tables of integer numbers. Test the program using the data given in Example 9.17.

9.51   Modify the pig Latin generation program given in Example 9.28 so that it can accommodate punctuation marks, uppercase letters and double-letter sounds.

9.52   Write a Turbo Pascal version of the pig Latin generator given in Example 9.28

9.53   Write a Pascal program that will enter a line of text, store it in a packed array, and then write it out backward. Allow the length of the line to be unspecified (terminated by pressing the ENTER key), but assume that it will not exceed 80 characters.

Test the program with any line of text of your own choosing. Compare with the program given in Example 7.20, which makes use of a recursive procedure rather than an array. Which approach is better?

9.54   Presented below are several related programming problems that make use of the following set of student exam grades [see Probs. 6.50 (*k*) through (*m*)]. Use arrays to solve each problem.

Student Name	Exam Scores (percent)					
Adams	45	80	80	95	55	75
Brown	60	50	70	75	55	80
Davis	40	30	10	45	60	55
Fisher	0	5	5	0	10	5
Hamilton	90	85	100	95	90	90
Jones	95	90	80	95	85	80
Ludwig	35	50	55	65	45	70
Osborne	75	60	75	60	70	80
Prince	85	75	60	85	90	100
Richards	50	60	50	35	65	70
Smith	70	60	75	70	55	75
Thomas	10	25	35	20	30	10
Wolfe	25	40	65	75	85	95
Zorba	65	80	70	100	60	95

(*a*)   Write an interactive Pascal program that will accept each student's name and exam grades as input, determine an average grade for each student, and then display the name, the individual exam grades and the calculated average. (Hint: Note that each name is followed by a blank space.) Make the program as general as possible.

(*b*)   Modify the program written for the above problem to allow for unequal weighting of the individual exam grades. In particular, assume that each of the first four exams contributes 15 percent to the final score, and each of the last two exams contributes 20 percent.

(*c*)   Extend the program written for the previous problem so that an overall class average is determined in addition to the individual student averages.

(d) Extend the program written for the previous problem so that the deviation of each student's average about the overall class average will be determined. Display the class average, followed by each student's name, exam grades, final score, and deviation about the class average. Be sure that the output is logically organized and clearly labeled.

9.55 Write a Pascal program that will produce a table of values of the equation

$$y = 2 e^{-0.1t} \sin 0.5t$$

where t varies between 0 and 60. Allow the size of the t-increment to be entered as an input parameter.

9.56 Write a Pascal program that will generate a table of compound interest factors, F/P, where

$$F/P = (1 + i/100)^n$$

In this formula F represents the future value of a given sum of money, P represents its present value, i represents the annual interest rate, expressed as a percentage, and n represents the number of years.

Let each row in the table correspond to a different value of n, with n ranging from 1 to 30 (hence 30 rows). Let each column represent a different interest rate. Include the following interest rates: 4, 4.5, 5, 5.5, 6, 6.5, 7, 7.5, 8, 8.5, 9, 9.5, 10, 11, 12 and 15 percent (hence a total of 16 columns). Be sure to label the rows and columns appropriately.

9.57 Write an ANSI Pascal program that will rearrange a list of words into alphabetical order. To do so, enter the words into a two-dimensional packed array of type char, with each row representing one complete word. The rows can then be rearranged in the same manner that a list of numbers is rearranged from smallest to largest (see Example 9.5).

Use the program to rearrange the names given below. Be careful with the first initials.

Washington	Taylor	Harrison, B.	Kennedy
Adams, J.	Fillmore	McKinley	Johnson, L. B.
Jefferson	Pierce	Roosevelt, T.	Nixon
Madison	Buchanan	Taft	Ford
Monroe	Lincoln	Wilson	Carter
Adams, J. Q.	Johnson, A.	Harding	Reagan
Jackson	Grant	Coolidge	Bush
Van Buren	Hayes	Hoover	Clinton
Harrison, W. H.	Garfield	Roosevelt, F. D.	
Tyler	Arthur	Truman	
Polk	Cleveland	Eisenhower	

9.58 Consider the following foreign currencies and their equivalents to one U.S. dollar.

British pound:	0.65 pounds per U.S. dollar
Canadian dollar:	1.3 dollars per U.S. dollar
Dutch guilder:	1.8 guilders per U.S. dollar
French franc:	5.5 francs per U.S. dollar
German mark:	1.6 marks per U.S. dollar
Italian lira:	1500 lira per U.S. dollar
Japanese yen:	110 yen per U.S. dollar
Mexican peso:	3.1 pesos per U.S. dollar
Swiss franc:	1.5 francs per U.S. dollar

Write an interactive, menu-driven Pascal program that will accept two different currencies and return the value of the second currency per one unit of the first currency. (For example, if the two currencies are Japanese yen and Mexican pesos, the program will return the number of Mexican pesos equivalent to one Japanese yen.) Use the data given above to carry out the conversions. Design the program so that it executes repetitively, until an ending condition is selected from the menu.

9.59   Consider the following list of countries and their capitals.

Canada	Ottawa
China	Peking
England	London
France	Paris
India	New Delhi
Israel	Jerusalem
Italy	Rome
Japan	Tokyo
Mexico	Mexico City
Russia	Moscow
United States	Washington

Write an interactive Pascal program that will that will accept the name of a country as input and write out the corresponding capital, and vice versa. Design the program to execute repetitiously, until the word End is entered as input.

9.60   Write a complete Pascal program for each of the problems presented below. Include the most appropriate types of arrays for each problem. Be sure to modularize each program, label the output clearly, and make use of natural data types and efficient control structures.

(a)   Suppose we are given a table of integers, A, having m rows and n columns, and a list of integers, X, having n elements. We wish to generate a new list of integers, Y, that is formed by carrying out the following operations.

$$Y[1] = A[1,1]*X[1] + A[1,2]*X[2] + \cdots + A[1,N]*X[N]$$
$$Y[2] = A[2,1]*X[1] + A[2,2]*X[2] + \cdots + A[2,N]*X[N]$$
$$\cdots \cdots$$
$$Y[M] = A[M,1]*X[1] + A[M,2]*X[2] + \cdots + A[M,N]*X[N]$$

Write out the input data (i.e., the values of the elements A and X), followed by the values of the elements of Y.

Use the program to process the following data.

$$A = \begin{bmatrix} 1 & 2 & 3 & 4 & 5 & 6 & 7 & 8 \\ 2 & 3 & 4 & 5 & 6 & 7 & 8 & 9 \\ 3 & 4 & 5 & 6 & 7 & 8 & 9 & 10 \\ 4 & 5 & 6 & 7 & 8 & 9 & 10 & 11 \\ 5 & 6 & 7 & 8 & 9 & 10 & 11 & 12 \\ 6 & 7 & 8 & 9 & 10 & 11 & 12 & 13 \end{bmatrix} \qquad X = \begin{bmatrix} 1 \\ -8 \\ 3 \\ -6 \\ 5 \\ -4 \\ 7 \\ -2 \end{bmatrix}$$

(b)   Suppose that A is a table of real numbers having k rows and m columns, and B is a table of real numbers having m rows and n columns. We wish to generate a new table, C, where each element of C is determined by

$$C[i, j] = A[i,1]*B[1, j] + A[i,2]*B[2, j] + \cdots + A[i, m]*B[m, j]$$

where $i = 1, 2, \ldots, k$ and $j = 1, 2, \ldots, n$. Write out the elements of A, B and C. Be sure that everything is clearly labeled.

Use the program to process the following set of data.

$$A = \begin{bmatrix} 2 & -1/3 & 0 & 2/3 & 4 \\ 1/2 & 3/2 & 4 & -2 & 1 \\ 0 & 3 & -9/7 & 6/7 & 4/3 \end{bmatrix} \qquad B = \begin{bmatrix} 6/5 & 0 & -2 & 1/3 \\ 5 & 7/2 & 3/4 & -3/2 \\ 0 & -1 & 1 & 0 \\ 9/2 & 3/7 & -3 & 3 \\ 4 & -1/2 & 0 & 3/4 \end{bmatrix}$$

(c)   Consider a sequence of real numbers, x_i, $i = 1, 2, \ldots, m$. The mean is defined as

$$\bar{x} = \frac{(x_1 + x_2 + \cdots + x_m)}{m}$$

the deviation about the mean is

$$d_i = (x_i - \bar{x}), \qquad i = 1, 2, \ldots, m$$

and the standard deviation is

$$s = \sqrt{\frac{(d_1^2 + d_2^2 + \cdots + d_m^2)}{m}}$$

Read in the first m elements of a one-dimensional real array. Calculate the sum of these elements, the mean, the deviations, the standard deviation, the algebraic maximum and the algebraic minimum. Use the program to process the following set of data.

27.5	87.0
13.4	39.9
53.8	47.7
29.2	8.1
74.5	63.2

Repeat the computation for k different lists of numbers. Calculate the overall mean, the overall standard deviation, the absolute (largest) maximum and the absolute (algebraically smallest) minimum.

(d)   Suppose we are given a set of tabulated values for y vs. x, i.e.,

$$y_0 \quad y_1 \quad y_2 \quad \cdots \quad y_n$$
$$x_0 \quad x_1 \quad x_2 \quad \cdots \quad x_n$$

and we wish to obtain a value of y at some x that lies between two of the tabulated values. This problem is commonly solved by *interpolation*, i.e., by passing a polynomial $y(x)$ through n points such that $y(x_0) = y_0$, $y(x_1) = y_1$, $\ldots$, $y(x_n) = y_n$ and then evaluating y at the desired value of x.

A common way to carry out the interpolation is to use the *Lagrange form* of the interpolation polynomial. To do this we write

$$y(x) = f_0(x)*y_0 + f_1(x)*y_1 + \cdots + f_n(x)*y_n$$

where $f_i(x)$ is a polynomial such that

$$f_i(x) = \frac{(x - x_0)(x - x_1)\cdots(x - x_{i-1})(x - x_{i+1})\cdots(x - x_n)}{(x_i - x_0)(x_i - x_1)\cdots(x_i - x_{i-1})(x_i - x_{i+1})\cdots(x_i - x_n)}$$

Notice that $f_i(x_i) = 1$ and $f_i(x_j) = 0$, where x_j is a tabulated value of x different from x_i. Therefore we are assured that $y(x_i) = y_i$.

Write a Pascal program to read in n pairs of data, where n does not exceed 10, and then obtain an interpolated value of y at one or more specified values of x. Use the program to obtain interpolated values of y at $x = 13.7$, $x = 37.2$, $x = 112$ and $x = 147$ from the data listed below. Determine how many tabulated pairs of data are required in each calculation in order to obtain a reasonably accurate interpolated value for y.

$y = 0.21073$	$x = 0$
0.37764	10
0.45482	20
0.49011	30
0.50563	40
0.49245	50
0.47220	60
0.43433	80
0.33824	120
0.19390	180

9.61 The following problems are concerned with games of chance (gambling games). Each problem requires use of a random number generator, such as that described in Example 7.18. Each program requires the use of an array. In addition, the programs should be interactive and they should be modularized.

(a) Write a Pascal program that will simulate a game of blackjack between two players. Note that the computer will not be a participant in this game, but will simply deal the cards to each player and then provide each player with one or more "hits" (additional cards) when requested.

The cards are dealt in order, first one card to each player, then a second card to each player. Additional hits may then be requested.

The object of the game is to obtain 21 points, or as many points as possible without exceeding 21 points, on each hand. A player is automatically disqualified if his or her hand exceeds 21 points. Picture cards count 10 points, and an ace can count either 1 point or 11 points. Thus a player can obtain 21 points (blackjack!) if he or she is dealt an ace and either a picture card or a 10. If the player has a low score with his (her) first two cards he (she) may request one or more hits, as long as his (her) total score does not exceed 21.

A random number generator should be used to simulate the dealing of the cards. Be sure to include a provision that the same card is not dealt more than once.

(b) Roulette is played with a wheel containing 38 different squares along its circumference. Two of these squares, numbered 0 and 00, are green; 18 squares are red, and 18 are black. The red and black squares alternate in color, and are numbered 1 through 36 in a random order.

A small marble is spun within the wheel, which eventually comes to rest within a groove beneath one of the squares. The game is played by betting on the outcome of each spin, in any one of the following ways.

1. By selecting a single red or black square, at 35-to-1 odds. (Thus, if a player were to bet $1.00 and win, he or she would receive a total of $36.00 — the original $1.00, plus an additional $35.00.)

2. By selecting a color, either red or black, at 1-to-1 odds. (Thus if a player chose red on a $1.00 bet, he or she would receive $2.00 if the marble came to rest beneath any red square.)

3. By selecting either the odd or the even numbers (excluding 0 and 00), at 1-to-1 odds.

4. By selecting either the low 18 or the high 18 numbers at 1-to-1 odds.

The player will automatically lose if the marble comes to rest beneath one of the green squares (0 or 00).

Write an interactive Pascal program that will simulate a roulette game. Allow the players to select whatever type of play they wish by choosing from a menu. Then print the outcome of each game followed by an appropriate message indicating whether each player has won or lost.

(c) Write an interactive Pascal program that will simulate a game of BINGO. Print each letter-number combination as it is drawn (generated). Be sure that no combination is drawn more than once. Remember that each of the letters B-I-N-G-O corresponds to a certain range of numbers, as indicated below.

> B:　　　1 – 15
> I :　　　16 – 30
> N:　　　31 – 45
> G:　　　46 – 60
> O:　　　61 – 75

Each player will have a card with five columns, labeled B-I-N-G-0. Each column will contain 5 numbers, within the ranges indicated above. No two players will have the same card. The first player to have one entire row of numbers drawn (either vertically, horizontally or diagonally) wins. *Note*: the center position of each card is sometimes covered before the game begins (a "free" call). Also, the game is sometimes played such that a player must have *all* of the numbers on his or her card drawn before he or she can win.

9.62 Write an interactive Pascal program that will encode or decode a line of text. To encode a line of text, proceed as follows.

1. Convert each character, including blank spaces, to its ASCII equivalent.

2. Generate a positive random integer. Add this integer to the ASCII equivalent of each character. (The same random integer will be used for the entire line of text.)

3. Suppose that N1 represents the lowest permissible value in the ASCII code, and N2 represents the highest permissible value. If the number obtained in step 2 above (i.e., the original ASCII equivalent plus the random integer) exceeds N2, then subtract the largest possible multiple of N2 from this number, and add the remainder to N1. Hence the encoded number will always fall between N1 and N2, and will therefore always represent some ASCII character.

4. Print the characters that correspond to the encoded ASCII values.

The procedure is reversed when decoding a line of text. Be certain, however, that the same random integer is used in decoding as was used in encoding.

Chapter 10

Records

In the last chapter we studied the array — a structured data type in which all elements must be of the same type. We now turn our attention to an equally important structured data type — the *record* — whose constituent elements need not be the same. Thus, we can refer collectively to a set of data items that differ among themselves in type. The individual data items are said to occupy *fields* within the record.

10.1 DEFINING A RECORD

The easiest way to define a record is to include the definition as a part of a variable declaration. This allows us to declare an individual record-type variable, just as we declared simple-type variables and array-type variables.

The general form of a record-type variable declaration is

VAR *record name* : RECORD *field 1*; *field 2*; . . .;*field n* END

where *field 1* represents the first field declaration, *field 2* represents the second field, and so on. Each field declaration is written in a manner that is similar to an individual variable declaration; i.e.,

field name : *type*

where *field name* is an identifier that represents the name of the field, and *type* is the data type of the data item that will occupy the field.

Note that the individual fields within the record are separated by semicolons.

EXAMPLE 10.1

Suppose a customer record consists of an integer-type customer number, a customer account designation which is of type char, and a customer balance which is a real number. Let us represent the customer record with a record-type variable called `customer`. The variable declaration is shown below.

```
VAR customer : RECORD
    custno : integer;
    custtype : char;
    custbalance : real
END;
```

Notice that the record consists of an integer-type field called `custno`, a char-type field called `custtype` and a real-type field called `custbalance`.

The individual field declarations need not always be written on separate lines, as in this example. However, they are often written in this manner to enhance readibility.

Fig. 10.1 shows a schematic diagram illustrating the composition of the customer record.

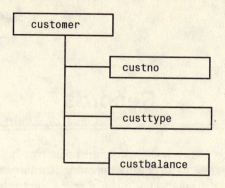

Fig. 10.1

Another way to define a record, which is frequently more useful than a variable declaration, is to define a record *type*. Then individual variables can be declared to be of this type. (Notice the analogy with the methods that are used to define arrays, described in the last chapter.) In general form, a record type definition is written as

TYPE *record name* = RECORD *field 1*; *field 2*; . . .;*field n* END

where the meaning of the individual items is the same as described above.

EXAMPLE 10.2

Consider once again the customer record described in the previous example. Let us now define a record type called account, and a corresponding variable called customer, as before. This can be accomplished by writing

```
TYPE account = RECORD
                 custno : integer;
                 custtype : char;
                 custbalance : real
              END;
VAR customer : account;
```

This accomplishes the same thing as the variable declaration shown in Example 10.1. The present approach is more general, however, because it will allow us to introduce additional record-type variables if we wish.

The individual fields can be associated with user-defined data types and subrange types as well as standard data types. Moreover, the field types can be structured as well as scalar. Hence, an individual field may be an array or another record.

EXAMPLE 10.3

Here is a variation of the record definition shown in Example 10.2.

```
TYPE status = (current,overdue,delinquent);
     account = RECORD
                 custno : 1..9999;
                 custtype : status;
                 custbalance : real
              END;
VAR customer : account;
```

Now the customer number is a subrange-type data item, and the customer type is an enumerated-type data item.

Note that the enumerated data type (`status`) must be defined before it can be referenced in the record declaration.

EXAMPLE 10.4

Now let us add the customer's name to the above record. In ANSI Pascal, we define an additional field that represents a packed array of type char. Therefore, the entire record definition becomes

```
TYPE status = (current,overdue,delinquent);
     account = RECORD
                   custname : PACKED ARRAY [1..80] OF char;
                   custno : 1..9999;
                   custtype : status;
                   custbalance : real
               END;
  VAR customer : account;
```

A variation of this record definition, which is somewhat more general, is given below.

```
TYPE status = (current,overdue,delinquent);
     line = PACKED ARRAY [1..80] OF char;
     account = RECORD
                   custname : line;
                   custno : 1..9999;
                   custtype : status;
                   custbalance : real
               END;
  VAR customer : account;
```

This variation allows other string-type information to be defined very easily, either within the current record or in other parts of the program. Thus, if we wanted to add an address field to `customer`, we could write

```
TYPE status = (current,overdue,delinquent);
     line = PACKED ARRAY [1..80] OF char;
     account = RECORD
                   custname : line;
                   custaddress : line;
                   custno : 1..9999;
                   custtype : status;
                   custbalance : real
               END;
  VAR customer : account;
```

In Turbo Pascal we can enter the customer's name and address simply as string-type fields. Thus, the same record definition would be written in Turbo Pascal as

```
TYPE status = (current,overdue,delinquent);
     account = RECORD
                   custname : string;
                   custaddress : string;
                   custno : 1..9999;
                   custtype : status;
                   custbalance : real
               END;
  VAR customer : account;
```

EXAMPLE 10.5

Let us now add a last-payment date to our customer record. This can best be accomplished by representing the date as a separate record and then including this date record as one of the fields in customer, as illustrated in Fig. 10.2. Thus our record declaration, in Turbo Pascal, now becomes

```
TYPE status = (current,overdue,delinquent);
     date = RECORD
                month : 1..12;
                day : 1..31;
                year : 1900..2100
            END;
     account = RECORD
                   custname : string;
                   custaddress : string
                   custno : 1..9999;
                   custtype : status;
                   custbalance : real;
                   lastpayment : date
               END;
VAR customer : account;
```

Notice that the record account now contains another record, lastpayment, as one of its fields. Also, we see that account contains two strings (custname and custaddress), a subrange type (custno), an enumerated data type (custtype) and a standard data type (custbalance). This example thus illustrates the flexibility that is inherent in record definitions.

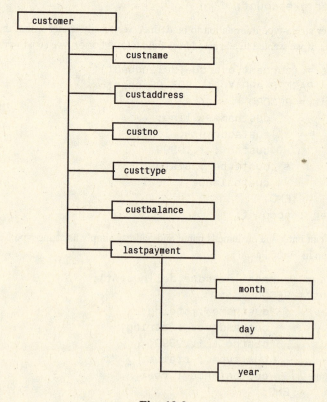

Fig. 10.2

A record can also be an individual data item in another structured data type, such as an array. Thus we can define arrays whose elements are records, records whose elements (or some of whose elements) are arrays, and so on.

EXAMPLE 10.6

Here is an example of an array whose elements are records. In particular, let us define an array called events, whose individual elements are dates, as defined in the previous example.

```
TYPE date = RECORD
                 month : 1..12;
                 day : 1..31;
                 year : 1900..2100
             END;
VAR events : ARRAY [1..100] OF date;
```

Thus, we have a one-dimensional array (i.e., a list) that can contain as many as 100 different dates. Notice that events is defined as a variable, not a data type.

Once a single record type has been defined, we can declare several different variables as records of that type. This feature is illustrated in the following example.

EXAMPLE 10.7

Consider the record account, defined in Example 10.5. We can now declare the variables preferred and regular to be records of this type. Thus,

```
TYPE status = (current,overdue,delinquent);
     date = RECORD
                  month : 1..12;
                  day : 1..31;
                  year : 1900..2100
              END;
     account = RECORD
                    custname : string;
                    custaddress : string;
                    custno : 1..9999;
                    custtype : status;
                    custbalance : real;
                    lastpayment : date
                END;
  VAR preferred,regular : account;
```

ANSI Pascal permits records to be packed, just as arrays can be packed. This allows a record to be stored more compactly, though accessing the individual data items within the record will take longer.

Record packing is accomplished by writing PACKED RECORD instead of RECORD in the record type definition, as illustrated in the following example.

EXAMPLE 10.8

Consider once again the record-type `account`, originally defined in Example 10.2. In ANSI Pascal we can redefine `account` as a packed record, as follows.

```
TYPE account = PACKED RECORD
                    custno : integer;
                    custtype : char;
                    custbalance : real
               END;
VAR customer : account;
```

Thus, the variable `customer` will represent a packed record of type `account`.

Record packing, like array packing, involves a tradeoff between execution speed and memory requirements. However, this feature is not as widely used as array packing. As a rule it is used only in applications that emphasize the copying of entire records, rather than the more common applications where individual record elements are manipulated. Rember that some versions of Pascal, including Turbo Pascal, do not support packed records (or packed arrays).

Finally, it should be mentioned that each record is considered a separate entity with respect to its field definitions. Thus, each field within a given record must have a unique name, but the same field name can be used in different records. In other words, the scope of a field identifier is confined to the particular record within which it is defined.

EXAMPLE 10.9

Two different record types, `one` and `two`, are defined below.

```
TYPE one = RECORD
                a : real;
                b : integer;
                c : char
           END;
     two = RECORD
                a : char;
                b,c : real
           END;
```

In this example the individual field names `a`, `b` and `c` are duplicated between the records, but the associated data types are different. Thus, field `a` refers to a real-type field within `one`, but a char-type field within `two`, and so on. This is permissible, since the scope of each set of field definitions is confined to its respective record. Also, note that the field names are distinct within each record, as required.

10.2 PROCESSING A RECORD

Now that we have seen how records are defined, let us turn our attention to the use of records, or record components, in typical programming situations.

The simplest type of record processing operation involves the assignment of one entire record to another. This requires that both records be of the same type.

EXAMPLE 10.10

The skeletal outline of a Turbo Pascal program involving the assignment of one record to another is shown below. (Notice that this outline utilizes the record definitions originally presented in Example 10.7.)

```
TYPE status = (current,overdue,delinquent);
     date = RECORD
                month : 1..12;
                day : 1..31;
                year : 1900..2100
            END;
     account = RECORD
                   custname : string;
                   custaddress : string;
                   custno : 1..9999;
                   custtype : status;
                   custbalance : real;
                   lastpayment : date
               END;
VAR preferred,regular : account;

BEGIN
   . . . . .
   preferred := regular;
   . . . . .
END.
```

In this example we see that the record `regular` is assigned to `preferred`. This is possible because `regular` and `preferred` are both records of type `status` and therefore have the same composition. It is, of course, assumed that the elements of `regular` have been entered into the computer or otherwise defined prior to the assignment statement.

It is much more common to process record elements individually rather than processing entire records collectively. To do so, we must be able to access the individual record elements. This is accomplished by forming a *field designator*, which is a combination of a record-type variable name and a field name; i.e.,

```
variable name.field name
```

(Note the period between the two names.)

EXAMPLE 10.11

Consider once again the record-type variables `preferred` and `regular`, defined in Example 10.10. The individual data items within each of these records are referred to with field designators such as `preferred.custname`, `regular.custno` and `regular.lastpayment`.

For example, `preferred.custname` and `preferred.custaddress` represent string variables, `preferred.custno` represents an integer quantity whose value is bounded between 1 and 9999, and `preferred.custtype` represents one of the enumerated simple quantities `current`, `overdue` or `delinquent`. Also, `preferred.custbalance` represents a real quantity, and `preferred.lastpayment` represents an enclosed record whose individual fields can take on the values defined by the record `date` (more about this in the next example). Similar field descriptions apply to the elements of `regular`.

If a field represents a structured data item, then the individual elements of that field can be accessed by including the structured data element in the field designator. Thus, if a field represents an array, an individual array element can be accessed by writing

```
variable name.field name[index values]
```

Similarly, if a field represents an enclosed record, an individual element of the enclosed record can be accessed as

```
variable name.field name.sub-field name
```

where *sub-field* refers to one field within the enclosed record.

EXAMPLE 10.12

Consider once again the record-type variables `preferred` and `regular`, defined in Example 10.10. The field designator `preferred.custname[12]` refers to the twelfth character in the first field of `preferred` (i.e., the twelfth character in the string `custname`).

Similarly, the field designator `regular.lastpayment.month` refers to the first integer quantity in the last field of `regular` (i.e., the quantity in the first field in the enclosed record `lastpayment`). This quantity must be an integer whose value falls within the subrange `1..12`, as defined by the record-type `date`.

The individual record elements can be utilized in the same manner as ordinary variables. The particular features (and restrictions) that apply to each element are determined by the data type of that element. Thus, if a record element represents a simple-type quantity, then it can appear in an assignment statement, within an expression, within a control structure, within an I/O statement, as a parameter within a procedure or function reference, etc., subject to the restrictions that apply to that particular data type.

Similarly, if a record element represents a structured data type (e.g., an array or another record), then it can be utilized in the same manner as other structured data items of the same type. (However, ANSI Pascal imposes the following special restriction: an element of a packed record cannot be passed to a procedure or function if the corresponding formal parameter is a variable parameter.)

EXAMPLE 10.13

Several unrelated statements that make use of individual record elements are shown below. All of the record elements conform to the record definitions and record-type variable declarations given in Example 10.10. Type compatibility is assumed throughout.

```
regular.custbalance := 0;

regular.custbalance := regular.custbalance - payment;

preferred.custname := regular.custname;

writeln(regular.custname, regular.custaddress);

average := (preferred.custbalance + regular.custbalance)/2;

newbalance := round(preferred.balance);

IF preferred.custname[1] = '*'
   THEN preferred.custtype := current;

IF regular.lastpayment.month < 6
   THEN writeln(regular.custno, regular.custbalance)
   ELSE preferred := regular;
```

Some applications require that a sequence of records be stored and processed in some particular order. In such situations it is often convenient to define a one-dimensional array whose elements are records. A particular record can then be accessed as

array name[*index value*]

and an individual record element as

array name[*index value*].*field name*

EXAMPLE 10.14

Here is an example of an array (i.e., a list) containing 100 records.

```
TYPE account = RECORD
                    custno : integer;
                    custtype : char;
                    custbalance : real
                END;
VAR customer : ARRAY [1..100] OF account;
```

Thus, `customer[23]` refers to the twenty-third record. Furthermore, `customer[23].custbalance` refers to the third data item in the twenty-third record (i.e., the current balance for the twenty-third customer).

EXAMPLE 10.15

Here is a more complicated example of several one-dimensional arrays whose elements are records. (Turbo Pascal is assumed.)

```
TYPE status = (current,overdue,delinquent);
     date = RECORD
                month : 1..12;
                day : 1..31;
                year : 1900..2100
            END;
     account = RECORD
                    custname : string;
                    custaddress : string;
                    custno : 1..9999;
                    custtype : status;
                    custbalance : real;
                    lastpayment : date
                END;
VAR preferred,regular : ARRAY [1..100] OF account;
```

In this example, `preferred[5]` refers to the fifth record in the first array, and `regular[82].custname` refers to the customer name in the eighty-second record of the second array. Similarly, `regular[14].lastpayment.year` refers to the year of the last payment for (i.e., the third item in the enclosed record) in the fourteenth record of the second array.

EXAMPLE 10.16

Here are several unrelated statements that make use of individual record elements defined in the preceding example.

```
regular[82].custbalance := 0;

preferred[i].custbalance :=

preferred[i].custbalance – payment;

writeln(regular[15].custname, regular[15].custaddress);

IF preferred[count].custname[1] ='*'
   THEN preferred[count].custtype := current;

IF regular[i].lastpayment.month < 6
   THEN writeln(regular[i].custno, regular[i].custbalance)
   ELSE preferred[i] := regular[i];
```

In these examples the variables i and count are assumed to be integer-type variables that have been assigned appropriate values earlier in the program.

10.3 THE WITH STRUCTURE

Many programs require that different elements of the same record be manipulated at various places within the program. The need to specify several different field designators can become tedious, however, and may reduce the overall readability of the program. In such situations the WITH structure allows the record name to be omitted from the field designators.

The general form of the WITH structure is

```
WITH record name DO statement
```

or, if two or more records are to be included within the structure,

```
WITH record 1 name, record 2 name, . . . , record n name DO statement
```

The statement part of the structure refers to any action statement, which may itself be structured. Within this statement, any reference to an element contained in one of the specified records need not include the record name.

EXAMPLE 10.17

Consider the following declarations.

```
TYPE date = RECORD
                month : 1..12;
                day : 1..31;
                year : 1900..2100
            END;
VAR birthday : date;
```

One way to update the values of birthday is to write

```
    BEGIN
        birthday.month := 5;
        birthday.day := 13;
        birthday.year := 1966
    END;
```

It is easier, however, to write

```
    WITH birthday DO BEGIN month := 5; day := 13; year := 1966 END;
```

Both statements accomplish the same thing.

EXAMPLE 10.18

Here is another example that illustrates the use of the WITH structure. This example makes use of the declarations first presented in Example 10.7. These declarations are repeated in the Turbo Pascal program outline presented below.

```
    TYPE status = (current,overdue,delinquent);
    date = RECORD
                month : 1..12;
                day : 1..31;
                year : 1900..2100
            END;
    account = RECORD
                    custname : string;
                    custaddress : string;
                    custno : 1..9999;
                    custtype : status;
                    custbalance : real;
                    lastpayment : date
                END;
    VAR preferred,regular : account;

    BEGIN
        . . . . .
        WITH regular DO
            BEGIN
                . . . . .
                custno := 1262;
                lastpayment.day := 8;
                . . . . .
                IF custbalance = 0 THEN custtype := current
                                   ELSE custtype := overdue;
                . . . . .
            END;
        . . . . .
    END.
```

Note that all of the field references within the WITH structure refer to elements of `regular`. If it were necessary to refer to an element of `preferred`, then the entire field designation (e.g., `preferred.custbalance`) would have to be specified.

EXAMPLE 10.19

Here is a Turbo Pascal program outline that makes use of the record-type array declarations given in Example 10.15.

```
     TYPE status = (current,overdue,delinquent);
          date = RECORD
                     month : 1..12;
                     day : 1..31;
                     year : 1900..2100
                 END;
          account = RECORD
                        custname : string;
                        custaddress : string;
                        custno : 1..9999;
                        custtype : status;
                        custbalance : real;
                        lastpayment : date
                    END;
     VAR i : 1..100;
         preferred,regular : ARRAY [1..100] OF account;

     BEGIN
        . . . . .
        FOR i := 1 TO 100 DO
           WITH regular[i] DO
               BEGIN
                   . . . . .
                   custno := i + 1200;
                   lastpayment.day := 8;
                   . . . . .
                   IF custbalance = 0 THEN custtype := current
                                       ELSE custtype := overdue;
                   . . . . .
               END;
        . . . . .
     END.
```

Compare this example with the outline shown in Example 10.18.

If the WITH statement includes two or more record-type variable names having the same field names, then a possible ambiguity arises as to which record is referred to when a field is accessed within the structure. This ambiguity is resolved as follows.

The multi-record WITH structure

```
    WITH record 1 name, record 2 name, . . . , record n name DO statement
```

is equivalent to the following nested structure.

```
    WITH record 1 name DO
       WITH record 2 name DO
           . . . . .
              WITH record n name DO statement
```

If a field name is common to two or more of the specified records, its scope is confined to the innermost record within the nest. Any reference to a field with the same name but associated with another record must include the record name as a part of the field designation.

EXAMPLE 10.20

A skeletal Pascal program outline is shown below.

```
VAR first  : RECORD a,b,c : integer END;
    second : RECORD c,d,e : integer END;
BEGIN
   . . . . .
   WITH first, second DO
      BEGIN
         a := 1;
         b := 2;
         first.c := 3;
         c := 4;
         d := 5;
         e := 6
      END;
   . . . . .
END.
```

Notice that c is a field name that is common to both records. Thus, a reference to c within the WITH structure will automatically refer to second.c, since second is the innermost record name. In order to refer to first.c within this structure, we must specify the entire field designator.

The above structure causes the following values to be assigned to the fields named c.

```
first.c := 3                     second.c := 4
```

The WITH structure should be used freely in situations to which it applies. Its use contributes to overall program clarity, and in some situations may also improve the computational efficiency of the program.

EXAMPLE 10.21 A Customer Billing System

Consider a simple customer billing system in which customer records are entered into the computer, each customer's balance is updated to reflect current payments and a new balance is computed. In addition, we will calculate and then display the current status of each customer, based upon the customer's previous balance and the amount of the current payment.

Each account will be considered to be current unless:

(a) The current payment is greater than zero but less than 10 percent of the previous outstanding balance. In this case the account will be considered overdue.

(b) There is an outstanding balance and the current payment is zero, in which case the account will be considered delinquent.

Let us write a Turbo Pascal program to support this billing system. Suppose each customer record contains the following items of information: name, street address, city and state, account number, account status (current, overdue or delinquent), previous balance, current payment, new balance and payment date. The appropriate record declarations are shown below.

```
TYPE status = (current,overdue,delinquent);
     date = RECORD
                month : 1..12;
                day : 1..31;
                year : 1900..2100
            END;
     account = RECORD
                   name : string;
                   street : string;
                   city : string;
                   custno : 1..9999;
                   custtype : status;
                   oldbalance : real;
                   newbalance : real;
                   payment : real;
                   paydate : date
               END;
```

For convenience, all records will be stored as elements of a one-dimensional array. Therefore the overall program strategy will be as follows.

1. Specify the number of accounts (i.e., the number of records) to be processed.

2. For each record, read in the following items:

    (a) name

    (b) street

    (c) city

    (d) account number

    (e) previous balance

    (f) current payment

    (g) payment date

3. After all of the records have been read into the computer, process each record in the following manner:

    (a) Compare the current payment with the previous balance and determine the appropriate account status.

    (b) Calculate the new account balance by subtracting the current payment from the previous balance (a negative balance will indicate a credit).

4. After all of the records have been processed, display the following information for each record:

    (a) name

    (b) account number

    (c) street

    (d) city

    (e) old balance

    (f) current payment

    (g) new balance

    (h) account status

Let us write the program in a modular manner, with a separate procedure to read the input data, to process the data and to display the results. Each procedure is straightforward and does not require further elaboration. The main block will simply enter the number of records and then access the appropriate procedures.

Here is the entire Turbo Pascal program.

```
PROGRAM customers;

(* CUSTOMER BILLING SYSTEM ILLUSTRATING THE USE OF RECORDS *)

TYPE status = (current,overdue,delinquent);
     date = RECORD
                month : 1..12;
                day : 1..31;
                year : 1900..2100
            END;
     account = RECORD
                   name : string;
                   street : string;
                   city : string;
                   custno : 1..9999;
                   custtype : status;
                   oldbalance : real;
                   newbalance : real;
                   payment : real;
                   paydate : date
               END;
VAR customer : ARRAY [1..10] OF account;
    i,n : 1..10;


PROCEDURE readinput;
(* Read input data for each record *)
VAR space : char;
BEGIN
    FOR i := 1 TO n DO
        WITH customer[i] DO
            BEGIN
                writeln;
                writeln('Customer no. ',i:3);
                write('   Name:   ');
                readln(name);
                write('   Street: ');
                readln(street);
                write('   City:   ');
                readln(city);
                write('   Account number: ');
                readln(custno);
                write('   Previous balance: ');
                readln(oldbalance);
                write('   Current payment: ');
                readln(payment);
                write('   Payment date (mm dd yyyy): ');
                WITH paydate DO
                    read(month,space,day,space,year);
                    readln
                END
    END;   (* readinput *)
```

```
PROCEDURE processdata;
(* Determine status and calculate a new balance for each record *)
BEGIN
   FOR i := 1 TO n DO
      WITH customer[i] DO
         BEGIN
            custtype := current;
            IF (payment > 0) AND (payment < 0.1*oldbalance)
               THEN custtype := overdue;
            IF (oldbalance > 0) AND (payment = 0)
               THEN custtype := delinquent;
            newbalance := oldbalance - payment
         END
END;   (* processdata *)

PROCEDURE writeoutput;
(* Display current information for each record *)
BEGIN
   FOR i := 1 TO n DO
      WITH customer[i] DO
         BEGIN
            writeln;
            write('Name:    ',name);
            writeln('   Account number: ',custno:4);
            writeln('Street: ',street);
            writeln('City:    ',city);
            writeln;
            write('Old balance: ',oldbalance:7:2);
            write('   Current payment: ',payment:7:2);
            writeln('   New balance: ',newbalance:7:2);
            writeln;
            write('Account status: ');
            CASE custtype OF
               current    : writeln('CURRENT');
               overdue    : writeln('OVERDUE');
               delinquent : writeln('DELINQUENT')
            END;
            writeln
         END
END;   (* writeoutput *)

BEGIN   (* main action statements *)
   writeln('CUSTOMER BILLING SYSTEM');
   writeln;
   write('How many customers are there? ');
   readln(n);
   readinput;
   processdata;
   writeoutput
END.
```

Notice that a WITH structure is included in each of the procedures.

Now suppose the program is used to process 4 fictitious customer records. The input dialog is shown below, with the user's responses underlined.

```
CUSTOMER BILLING SYSTEM

How many customers are there? 4

Customer no.    1
    Name:    Richard L. Warren
    Street: 123 Mountain Boulevard
    City:    Denver, CO
    Account number: 4208
    Previous balance: 247.88
    Current payment: 25.00
    Payment date (mm dd yyyy): 6 14 1993

Customer no.    2
    Name:    Janet Davis
    Street: 4383 Lakeview Drive
    City:    Beachwood, OH
    Account number: 2219
    Previous balance: 135.00
    Current payment: 135.00
    Payment date (mm dd yyyy): 8 10 1993

Customer no.    3
    Name:    Mort Singer
    Street: 1787 Oceanview Lane
    City:    San Francisco, CA
    Account number: 8452
    Previous balance: 387.42
    Current payment: 35.00
    Payment date (mm dd yyyy): 7 4 1993

Customer no.    4
    Name:    Phyllis Smith
    Street: 1140 Massachusetts Avenue
    City:    Boston, MA
    Account number: 711
    Previous balance: 260.00
    Current payment: 0
    Payment date (mm dd yyyy): 11 27 1993
```

The program then generates the following output data, in response to the above input.

```
Name:    Richard L. Warren   Account number: 4208
Street: 123 Mountain Boulevard
City:    Denver, CO

Old balance: 247.88   Current payment:   25.00   New balance:  222.88

Account status: CURRENT
```

```
Name:     Janet Davis    Account number: 2219
Street: 4383 Lakeview Drive
City:     Beachwood, OH


Old balance:  135.00   Current payment:  135.00   New balance:     0.00


Account status: CURRENT



Name:     Mort Singer   Account number: 8452
Street: 1787 Oceanview Lane
City:     San Francisco, CA


Old balance:  387.42   Current payment:   35.00   New balance:  352.42


Account status: OVERDUE



Name:     Phyllis Smith   Account number:   711
Street: 1140 Massachusetts Avenue
City:     Boston, MA


Old balance:  260.00   Current payment:    0.00   New balance:  260.00


Account status: DELINQUENT
```

From a practical standpoint, the nature of this example is somewhat unrealistic. In particular, it makes little sense to enter an entire customer record, perform a simple calculation and then write out the updated record without maintaining a permanent copy of the new information on an auxiliary storage device. In the next chapter we will see how the customer records can be permanently maintained in a data file, thus eliminating the need to reenter the data whenever an update is required.

10.4 VARIANT RECORDS

So far we have only considered records whose composition remains invariant throughout the program. It is also possible, however, to define a record whose composition (or a portion thereof) may vary within the program, depending on the value that is assigned to some particular field within the record (the *tag field*). Such a variable-type record is known as a *variant record* (or the *variant part* of a record).

The general form of a record type definition containing both a fixed part and a variant part is

```
TYPE record name = RECORD
                      fixed field 1;
                      fixed field2;
                      . . . . .
                      CASE tag field idenfifier : type OF
                         case label 1 : variant field list 1;
                         case label 2 : variant field list 2;
                         . . . . .
            END
```

Each variant field list is expressed in the form of a *field enumeration*; i.e.,

```
(variant field 1; variant field 2; . . . , variant field n)
```

The tag field must be associated with an ordinal data type that has been previously defined. Each value of this ordinal type must appear once (and only once) as a case label, in the subsequent variant part of the record definition. The active part of the record will then consist of those fields that correspond to some particular case label, as assigned to the tag field identifier.

There can be only one variant part in any record, and it must always follow the fixed part of the record.

EXAMPLE 10.22

Here is a Turbo Pascal record definition that contains both a fixed part and a variant part.

```
TYPE item = (stereo,tv);
     stock = RECORD
                 stockno : 1..20000;
                 supplier : string;
                 quantity : integer;
                 CASE itemtype : item OF
                     stereo : (power : 1..1000);
                         tv : (tubesize : 1..25; color : char)
             END;
VAR stockitem,backorder : stock;
```

The record type is called `stock`. Its fixed part consists of the fields `stockno`, `supplier` and `quantity`, and its variant part will either consist of the field `power` or the fields `tubesize` and `color`, depending on the value that is assigned to the tag-field identifier `itemtype`. In particular, if `stereo` is assigned to `itemtype`, then the variant part of the record will consist of the field `power`, but if `tv` is assigned to `itemtype`, then the variant part will consist of the fields `tubesize` and `color`.

Note that we have included a declaration for two record-type variables — `stockitem` and `backorder`. Each of these variables represents a record of type `inventory`.

The individual variant record elements and the tag field identifier can be accessed in the same manner as the individual fixed record elements, by writing

```
variable name.field name
variable name.field name.sub-field name
```

or

```
variable name.field name [index values]
```

depending upon the particular data type of the individual record element.

EXAMPLE 10.23

Several unrelated statements that make use of individual record elements are shown below. All of the statements refer to elements of the record-type variables defined in Example 10.22.

```
stockitem.stockno := 12345;
```

```
backorder.quantity := 15;

stockitem.itemtype := stereo;

stockitem.power := 150;

writeln(backorder.stockno,backorder.power);

IF stockitem.quantity < 24 THEN
    BEGIN
        writeln(stockitem.supplier);
        writeln(stockitem.tubesize,stockitem.color)
    END;
```

Some of the statements utilize fixed fields, whereas others utilize variant fields. The last two statements include references to both fixed and variant fields. Also, note that a value is assigned to the tag-field identifier in the third statement.

Example 10.22 illustrates certain features that are required of all variant records. First, the field names within a record, including the variant field names, must be unique. (In some applications there is the temptation to use the same field name in two or more variant field lists.) Furthermore, an appropriate value must be assigned to the tag field identifier if an individual variant field is accessed. Thus, if `stockitem.power` is accessed in Example 10.22, then `stockitem.itemtype` must represent `stereo`.

The WITH structure can be used with variant-type records, just as with fixed-type records (see Section 10.3). This tends to reduce the likelihood of errors as well as improve the overall readibility of the program.

EXAMPLE 10.24

Suppose we wish to update certain fields within the record `stockitem`, defined in Example 10.22. This can easily be accomplished using the WITH structure, as shown below.

```
WITH stockitem DO
    BEGIN
        quantity := quantity - sales;
        IF quantity < O THEN backorder.quantity := -quantity;
        IF itemtype = stereo THEN writeln(power)
                             ELSE writeln(tubesize,color)
    END;
```

This example includes the use of a fixed field (`quantity`), the tag field (`itemtype`), and several variable fields (`power`, `tubesize` and `color`). Also, notice the reference to one field within another record (`backorder`). This field reference is written in its complete form (i.e., as `backorder.quantity`), since the WITH statement does not apply to this record.

There are several variations of the general record format that should be mentioned. For example, it is possible to define a record that does not contain a fixed part. Moreover, a variant field list can be empty if desired. This is indicated by an empty set of parentheses following the appropriate case label. Both of these situations are illustrated in the next example.

EXAMPLE 10.25

Consider the following variant record definition.

```
      TYPE status = (single,married,divorced,widowed);
           background = RECORD
                              CASE maritalstatus : status OF
                                  single               : ();
                                  married              : (children : 0..10);
                                  divorced,widowed : (remarried : boolean)
                        END;
      VAR employees : ARRAY [1..100] OF background;
```

In this example `employees` is a one-dimensional array whose elements are records of type `background`. Notice that this particular record definition does not include a fixed part. Also, notice that the first variant field list (corresponding to the case label `single`), is empty, and the last variant field list corresponds to two different case labels, `divorced` and `widowed`.

The nature of this example suggests that a fixed record part could also be included, consisting of a name, address, employee number, etc. You can easily add these fields as an exercise.

Another situation that requires some discussion is the presence of the tag-field identifier within the record definition. Strictly speaking, the presence of the tag-field identifier is not essential. If it is not present, the active variant fields will be determined implicitly by the particular variant field that is accessed. Thus, a reference to a particular variant field will activate a particular case label; all variant fields associated with this case label will then become active. Good programming practice suggests, however, that this feature generally not be used, particularly by beginners.

EXAMPLE 10.26

Consider the following Turbo Pascal program outline.

```
      TYPE item = (stereo,tv);
           stock = RECORD
                          stockno : 1..20000;
                          supplier : string;
                          quantity : integer;
                          CASE item OF
                              stereo : (power : 1..1000);
                                  tv : (tubesize : 1..25; color : char)
                    END;
      VAR stockitem,backorder : stock;
      BEGIN
         WITH stockitem DO
             BEGIN
                 . . . . .
                 tubesize := 19;
                     color := 'Y';
                 . . . . .
             END
      END.
```

Notice that the record definition includes the tag-field type (i.e., `item`), but not the tag-field identifier. Thus, the references to `tubesize` and `color` within the main action block imply that the second variant field list is active (i.e., that which corresponds to the case label `tv`).

Although a given record can have only one fixed part and one variant part, it is possible to include one variant definition within another. Thus we can create nested variant fields within a single record.

EXAMPLE 10.27

Here is a variation of the record definition shown in Example 10.22.

```
TYPE item = (stereo,tv);
     style = (portable,stationary);
     stock = RECORD
                 stockno : 1..20000;
                 supplier : string;
                 quantity : integer;
                 CASE itemtype : item OF
                     stereo : (power : 1..1000);
                         tv : (tubesize : 1..25;
                               color : char;
                               CASE size : style OF
                                   portable : (weight  : 1..100;
                                               voltage : 1..220);
                                   stationary : ())
              END;
     VAR stockitem,backorder : stock;
```

Notice the second variant field list, corresponding to the case label `tv`. This field list now includes another variant definition, which depends upon the value assigned to the tag-field identifier `size`. If `size` represents `portable`, then the variant field list `tv` will contain the fields `tubesize`, `color`, `weight` and `voltage`. On the other hand, if `size` represents `stationary`, then `tv` will contain only the fields `tubesize` and `color`.

Observe that the innermost variant definition has its own unique tag field (`size`), which is associated with its own enumerated data type (`style`). Also, notice the empty variant field list corresponding to the nested case label `stationary`. And finally, note that the variant fields associated with `tv` follow the fixed fields, as required.

It should be understood that a new group of variant fields will become active whenever a new value is assigned to the tag-field identifier. Moreover, if the tag-field identifier is not present, then a new group of variants will become active as a result of a reference to a nonactive variant field. Any inadvertent (and unwanted) change in the active variant fields must therefore be avoided. You must be particularly cautious of this potential problem in programs that employ procedures or functions.

In order to minimize the likelihood of such errors, a change of variant is not permitted under the following circumstances.

1. Within a WITH structure if a variant field name appears in the WITH statement.

2. Whenever a variant field has been passed to a procedure or function as an actual variable parameter.

Moreover, a tag-field identifier cannot be passed to a procedure or function as an actual variable parameter.

EXAMPLE 10.28 Inventory Control

Let us now develop a simple inventory control system, similar to the customer billing system shown in Example 10.21. Now, however, we will make use of records that contain both a fixed part and a variant part.

Specifically, consider a system that keeps track of two types of merchandise — stereos and television sets. The following information will periodically be entered into the computer: stock number (a nonnegative integer), item type ('s' for stereo, 't' for TV), the supplier's name, the original (previous) inventory level (a nonnegative integer), and the current change in inventory level (an integer that is unrestricted in sign). In addition, some descriptive information will be added for each item, the nature of which will depend on the type of item. For a stereo, the power level (an integer ranging from 1 to 1000) will be entered. For a TV, an indication of whether the set is portable ('y' or 'n', respectively), the tube size (an integer ranging from 1 to 25) and an indication of whether or not it is a color TV ('y' or 'n'). Also, if the set is portable, the weight (1..100) and the voltage (1..220) will be entered.

The appropriate record declarations, written in Turbo Pascal, are shown below.

```
TYPE item = (stereo,tv);
     style = (portable,stationary);
     stock = RECORD
                 stockno : 0..20000;
                 supplier : string;
                 quantity : integer;
                 CASE itemtype : item OF
                     stereo : (power : 1..1000);
                         tv : (tubesize : 1..25;
                               color : char;
                               CASE size : style OF
                                   portable : (weight : 1..100;
                                               voltage : 1..220);
                                   stationary : ())
             END;
VAR stockitem,backorder : ARRAY [1..100] OF stock;
```

Notice that the record-type stock contains nested variant parts. Also, notice that we have defined two different arrays — stockitem and backorder — that contain records of type stock. The former (stockitem) will contain the inventory records as entered into the computer; backorder will contain information only for those items that are backordered (i.e., for which there is a shortage).

The overall strategy will consist of the following two steps:

1.   Read all of the input data for each record and adjust the inventory level accordingly.

2.   After all of the records have been read into the computer and the inventory levels have been adjusted, display the records showing the adjusted inventory levels.

Rather than specify the number of records in advance, as we did with the billing system shown in Example 10.21, let us continue to enter new records until a value of zero is entered for the stock number. Thus, the main action block will appear as follows.

```
BEGIN
    writeln('I N V E N T O R Y   C O N T R O L   S Y S T E M');
    writeln;
    writeln('           D A T A   I N P U T');
    writeln;
    writeln(' When finished, enter 0 for the stock number');
    writeln;
    i := 0;
    REPEAT
        i := succ(i);
        readinput;
    UNTIL stockitem[i].stockno = 0;
    n := pred(i);
    IF n > 0 THEN writeoutput
END.
```

Note that i is an integer record counter whose value ranges from 0 to n, where n is the total number of records entered. (The last value of i will be assigned to n.) Also, readinput is a procedure that reads data into the computer and adjusts the inventory level, whereas writeoutput is a procedure that displays the adjusted data.

The procedure readinput will be interactive, with a number of appropriate conversational prompts. The programming is straightforward, though perhaps a bit long. Thus, we have

```
PROCEDURE readinput;

(* Enter input data for one record *)

BEGIN
    WITH stockitem[i] DO
        BEGIN
            writeln;
            write('Stock no.: ');
            readln(stockno);
            IF stockno > 0 THEN
                BEGIN
                    write('Item type (s/t): ');
                    readln(designator);
                    IF (designator = 's') OR (designator = 'S')
                        THEN BEGIN (* stereo *)
                                itemtype := stereo;
                                write('Power level: ');
                                readln(power)
                            END
                        ELSE BEGIN (* tv *)
                                itemtype := tv;
                                write('Portable TV? (y/n) ');
                                readln(designator);
                                IF (designator = 'y') OR (designator = 'Y')
                                    THEN BEGIN
                                            size := portable;
                                            write('Weight: ');
                                            readln(weight);
                                            write('Voltage: ');
                                            readln(voltage)
                                        END
                                    ELSE size := stationary;
                                write('Tube size: ');
                                readln(tubesize);
                                write('Color: (y/n) ');
                                readln(color)
                            END;
                    write('Supplier: ');
                    readln(supplier);
                    write('Original inventory level:  ');
                    readln(quantity);
                    write('Change in inventory level: ');
                    readln(change);
                    quantity := quantity + change;
```

(Program continues on next page)

```
                      IF quantity < 0 THEN
                         BEGIN
                            backorder[i] := stockitem[i];
                            backorder[i].quantity := abs(quantity);
                            quantity := 0
                         END
              END    (* IF stockno > 0 *)
        END    (* WITH stockitem[i] *)
   END;   (* readinput *)
```

In this procedure `designator` is a global char-type variable that identifies the type of input, and `change` is a global integer-type variable that represents the change in the inventory level. Notice that `change` can take on values that are either positive or negative, depending on whether the inventory is being replenished or depleted. Also, notice that this procedure is written to accommodate only one record at a time (since it is not known in advance how many records will be entered into the computer).

Another noteworthy feature of `readinput` is the fact that the inventory is updated as soon as it has been entered. If the adjusted inventory level is negative, then the information is transferred from `stockitem[i]` to `backorder[i]`, and the shortage is stored as a positive value. The use of `backorder[i]` is not essential and in fact adds little to the program except to suggest how such pairs of corresponding records might be maintained in a more comprehensive and realistic program (more about this later).

Now let us consider the procedure `writeoutput`. This procedure need not be interactive, and it can process all n records at one time. Thus, we can write

```
PROCEDURE writeoutput;

(* Display output data for all records *)

BEGIN
   writeln;
   writeln('I N V E N T O R Y    C O N T R O L    S Y S T E M');
   writeln;
   writeln('    C U R R E N T    I N V E N T O R Y');
   writeln;
   FOR i := 1 TO n DO
      WITH stockitem[i] DO
         BEGIN
            writeln;
            writeln('Stock no.: ',stockno:5);
            CASE itemtype OF
               stereo : writeln('Stereo: ',power:4,' watts');
                   tv : BEGIN
                           IF size = portable
                              THEN write('Portable ');
                           IF (color = 'y') OR (color = 'Y')
                              THEN write('Color TV')
                              ELSE write('B & W TV');
                           writeln('    ',tubesize:2,'-inch tube');
                           IF size = portable THEN
                              BEGIN
                                 write('Weight: ',weight:3,' pounds      ');
                                 writeln('Voltage: ',voltage:3,' volts')
                              END
                        END    (* tv *)
            END;    (* CASE itemtype *)
```
                        (Program continues on next page)

```
                        writeln('Supplier: ',supplier);
                        IF quantity > 0
                            THEN writeln('Present inventory: ',quantity:3)
                            ELSE writeln('Quantity backordered: ',
                                                        backorder[i].quantity:3);
                        writeln
                END    (* WITH stockitem[i] *)
        END;    (* writeoutput *)
```

Note that one field of `backorder[i]` is written out in the event that the adjusted inventory indicates a shortage.
   Here is the entire program, written in Turbo Pascal.

```
    PROGRAM inventory;

    (* INVENTORY CONTROL SYSTEM, ILLUSTRATING THE USE OF VARIANT RECORDS *)

    TYPE item = (stereo,tv);
         style = (portable,stationary);
         stock = RECORD
                     stockno : 0..20000;
                     supplier : string;
                     quantity : integer;
                     CASE itemtype : item OF
                         stereo : (power : 1..1000);
                             tv : (tubesize : 1..25;
                                   color : char;
                                   CASE size : style OF
                                       portable : (weight : 1..100;
                                                   voltage : 1..220);
                                       stationary : ())
                 END;
    VAR stockitem,backorder : ARRAY [1..100] OF stock;
        designator : char;
        i,n,change : integer;


    PROCEDURE readinput;

    (* Enter input data for one record *)

    BEGIN
        WITH stockitem[i] DO
            BEGIN
                writeln;
                write('Stock no.: ');
                readln(stockno);
                IF stockno > 0 THEN
                    BEGIN
                        write('Item type (s/t): ');
                        readln(designator);
                        IF (designator = 's') OR (designator = 'S')
                            THEN BEGIN (* stereo *)
                                    itemtype := stereo;
                                    write('Power level: ');
                                    readln(power)
                                 END
```

(Program continues on next page)

```
                    ELSE BEGIN (* tv *)
                            itemtype := tv;
                            write('Portable TV? (y/n) ');
                            readln(designator);
                            IF (designator = 'y') OR (designator = 'Y')
                                THEN BEGIN
                                            size := portable;
                                            write('Weight: ');
                                            readln(weight);
                                            write('Voltage: ');
                                            readln(voltage)
                                     END
                                ELSE size := stationary;
                            write('Tube size: ');
                            readln(tubesize);
                            write('Color: (y/n) ');
                            readln(color)
                       END;
                write('Supplier: ');
                readln(supplier);
                write('Original inventory level:  ');
                readln(quantity);
                write('Change in inventory level: ');
                readln(change);
                quantity := quantity + change;
                IF quantity < 0 THEN
                    BEGIN
                        backorder[i] := stockitem[i];
                        backorder[i].quantity := abs(quantity);
                        quantity := 0
                    END
           END   (* IF stockno > 0 *)
     END   (* WITH stockitem[i] *)
END;   (* readinput *)


PROCEDURE writeoutput;

(* Display output data for all records *)

BEGIN
   writeln;
   writeln('I N V E N T O R Y   C O N T R O L   S Y S T E M');
   writeln;
   writeln('      C U R R E N T   I N V E N T O R Y');
   writeln;
   FOR i := 1 TO n DO
      WITH stockitem[i] DO
         BEGIN
             writeln;
             writeln('Stock no.: ',stockno:5);
```

(Program continues on next page)

```
              CASE itemtype OF
                  stereo : writeln('Stereo: ',power:4,' watts');
                      tv : BEGIN
                               IF size = portable
                                  THEN write('Portable ');
                               IF (color = 'y') OR (color = 'Y')
                                  THEN write('Color TV')
                                  ELSE write('B & W TV');
                               writeln('   ',tubesize:2,'-inch tube');
                               IF size = portable THEN
                                  BEGIN
                                     write('Weight: ',weight:3,' pounds      ');
                                     writeln('Voltage: ',voltage:3,' volts')
                                  END
                           END    (* tv *)
                  END;   (* CASE itemtype *)
                  writeln('Supplier: ',supplier);
                  IF quantity > 0
                     THEN writeln('Present inventory: ',quantity:3)
                     ELSE writeln('Quantity backordered: ',
                                                    backorder[i].quantity:3);
                  writeln
            END    (* WITH stockitem[i] *)
  END;   (* writeoutput *)


BEGIN   (* main action statements *)
   writeln('I N V E N T O R Y   C O N T R O L   S Y S T E M');
   writeln;
   writeln('            D A T A   I N P U T');
   writeln;
   writeln('  When finished, enter 0 for the stock number');
   writeln;
   i := 0;

   (* read input records *)

   REPEAT
      i := succ(i);
      readinput;
   UNTIL stockitem[i].stockno = 0;
   n := pred(i);

   (* write output records *)

   IF n > 0 THEN writeoutput
END.
```

Now suppose the program is used to process three illustrative records. The input dialog would appear as follows. (The user's responses are again underlined.)

INVENTORY CONTROL SYSTEM

DATA INPUT

When finished, enter 0 for the stock number

Stock no.: <u>12417</u>
Item type (s/t): <u>s</u>
Power level: <u>150</u>
Supplier: <u>House of Audio</u>
Original inventory level: <u>200</u>
Change in inventory level: <u>-12</u>

Stock no.: <u>912</u>
Item type (s/t): <u>t</u>
Portable TV? (y/n) <u>n</u>
Tube size: <u>23</u>
Color: (y/n) <u>y</u>
Supplier: <u>Ace Radio & TV</u>
Original inventory level: <u>8</u>
Change in inventory level: <u>72</u>

Stock no.: <u>644</u>
Item type (s/t): <u>t</u>
Portable TV? (y/n) <u>y</u>
Weight: <u>25</u>
Voltage: <u>110</u>
Tube size: <u>12</u>
Color: (y/n) <u>n</u>
Supplier: <u>Campus Electronics</u>
Original inventory level: <u>12</u>
Change in inventory level: <u>-15</u>

Stock no.: <u>0</u>

In the above dialog, the computer supplies the prompts, and the user then enters the requested information. Notice that the input dialog continues until a value of 0 is entered for the stock number.

The following output is generated by the program in response to the preceding input data.

INVENTORY CONTROL SYSTEM

CURRENT INVENTORY

Stock no.: 12417
Stereo: 150 watts
Supplier: House of Audio
Present inventory: 188

Stock no.: 912
Color TV   23-inch tube
Supplier: Ace Radio & TV
Present inventory: 80

```
Stock no.:    644
Portable B & W TV    12-inch tube
Weight:  25 pounds    Voltage: 110 volts
Supplier: Campus Electronics
Quantity backordered:    3
```

You are again reminded that this program, like the customer billing system presented in Example 10.21, is oversimplified in the sense that it does not save the inventory records permanently within a data file. All realistic inventory control systems do, in fact, include such permanent storage capabilities. Individual records can then be retrieved from the file, modified, written out, saved, etc. We will see how this can be accomplished in the next chapter. It should be clear that the present example is intended only to show how record-type data can be processed in Pascal.

Review Questions

10.1   What is the principal difference between a record and an array?

10.2   What is meant by a field? What is the relationship between a field and a record?

10.3   Summarize the rules for defining a record type.

10.4   Summarize the rules for defining a record-type variable. Compare with your answer to the previous problem.

10.5   Which data types can be associated with the individual data items within a field?

10.6   For what type of application would it be desirable for a record element to be an array? Explain.

10.7   For what type of application would it be desirable for an array element to be a record? Explain and compare with your answer to the previous problem.

10.8   In ANSI Pascal, how can a record be packed? What are the advantages and disadvantages to utilizing packed records? Are packed records available in all versions of Pascal?

10.9   Can two different records utilize the same field name? Explain.

10.10   Can an entire record be assigned to another record? What restrictions apply to this type of an assignment?

10.11   In what ways can individual record elements be utilized within a Pascal program?

10.12   What is a field designator? How is a field designator written? How is it used?

10.13   Suppose an individual record element is a structured data item. How can one element of that data item be accessed?

10.14   What is the purpose of the WITH structure?

10.15   Summarize the rules for writing the WITH structure. Can multiple record names be included in a single WITH structure?

10.16   Suppose a single WITH statement includes several record-type variables with a common field name. Which record will be accessed when a field is accessed within the structure? How can a field having the same name but belonging to another record be accessed?

10.17 Cite several advantages to using the WITH structure wherever it is appropriate to do so.

10.18 What is meant by the variant part of a record? How does the variant part differ from the fixed part?

10.19 Must each record have a variant part? Must it have a fixed part?

10.20 Summarize the rules for defining a record having both a fixed part and a variant part. Contrast the variant definition with the CASE structure described in Chapter 6.

10.21 Can a record have more than one variant part?

10.22   If a record includes a variant part, where must the variant part be located?

10.23 What is a tag field? What is its purpose?

10.24 What data types can be associated with a tag field?

10.25 Must a tag field be present in every variant record? Explain.

10.26 How can individual elements within the variant part of a record be accessed? What restrictions apply to the access of such variant fields?

10.27 Can the WITH structure be used with variant-type records?

10.28 How can an empty variant field list be defined? Why might this be a desirable thing to do?

10.29 How can variant parts be nested within a single record?

10.30 Is a change of variant allowed within a WITH structure if a variant field name appears in the WITH statement?

10.31 What restrictions must be observed when a variant field is passed to a procedure or a function as a parameter?

10.32 Can a tag-field identifier be passed to a procedure or function as an actual variable parameter? Explain.

Problems

10.33 Write appropriate record and variable declarations for each of the following situations.

(a) Define a record-type variable called `sample`, consisting of the following three fields:
1. A subrange field called `first`, whose value may range from 1 to 100.
2. A real field called `second`.
3. A boolean field called `third`.

(b) Define a record type called `demo`, consisting of the fields described in part *(a)* above. Then define two variables, called `demo1` and `demo2`, of type `demo`.

(c) In ANSI Pascal define a data type called `line`, consisting of an 80-element, char-type packed array. Then define a record type called `personal` that consists of three fields of type `line`, called `name`, `street` and `city`, respectively. Finally, define a 500-element array called `employee`, whose elements are records of type `personal`.

(d) Define a Turbo Pascal record type called `personal` that consists of three string-type fields, called `name`, `street` and `city`, respectively. Then define a 500-element array called `employee`, whose elements are records of type `personal`. Compare your answer with that for part (c) above.

(e) In ANSI Pascal define an enumerated type called `color`, consisting of the items `red`, `green` and `blue`. Then define a packed record type called `sample`, consisting of the following three fields:

1. A field called `first`, of type `color`.

2. A subrange field called `second`, whose value may range from 1 to 132.

3. A char-type field called `third`.

Finally, define a variable of type `sample` called `trial`.

(f) How might the definitions described in part (e) above be written in Turbo Pascal?

(g) Define an enumerated type called `color`, consisting of the items `red`, `green` and `blue`. Then define a record type called `sample`, consisting only of a variant part whose tag-field identifier is called `select` and is of type `color`. The variant will include the following field lists:

1. A field list labeled `red`, consisting of the following fields:

    (i) A subrange field called `first`, whose value may range from 100 to 199.

    (ii) A subrange field called `second`, whose value may range from 200 to 299.

2. A field list labeled `green`, consisting of a single subrange field called `third` whose value may range from 300 to 399.

3. A field list labeled `blue`, consisting only of an empty field.

Finally, define a 500-element array called `demo`, whose individual elements are records of type `sample`.

(h) Define an enumerated type called `color`, consisting of the items `red`, `green` and `blue`, and another enumerated type called `texture`, consisting of the items `coarse` and `fine`. Then define a record type called `sample`, consisting of a fixed part and a variant part. The fixed part will include the following two fields:

1. A field called `first`, of type `color`.

2. A subrange field called `second`, whose value may range from 1 to 132.

The variant part will include a tag-field of type `color` (but no tag-field identifier), and the following three field lists:

1. A field list labeled `red`, consisting of the following fields:

    (i) A subrange field called `first`, whose value may range from 100 to 199.

    (ii) A subrange field called `second`, whose value may range from 200 to 299.

2. A field list labeled `green`, consisting only of an empty field.

3. A field list labeled `blue`, whose single field is itself a variant. This variant will include a tag-field of type `texture` (but no tag-field identifier), and the following two field lists:

    (i) A field list labeled `coarse`, consisting of a single subrange field called `third`, whose value may range from 300 to 399.

    (ii) A field list labeled `fine`, consisting only of an empty field.

Finally, define two 99-element arrays of type `sample`, called `demo1` and `demo2`, respectively.

10.34 The following skeletal outlines illustrate the use of records and/or record elements in typical programming situations. Describe the purpose of each outline. Also, describe any features that may be unique to certain versions of Pascal.

(*a*)
```
PROGRAM sample;
TYPE personal = RECORD
                       name,street,city : string;
                 END;
VAR employee : personal;

BEGIN

   . . . . .
   (* enter input data *)

   . . . . .
   writeln(employee.name);
   writeln(employee.street);
   writeln(employee.city);
   . . . . .

END.
```

(*b*)
```
PROGRAM sample;
TYPE line = PACKED ARRAY [1..80] OF char;
     personal = RECORD
                       name,street,city : line
                 END;
VAR employee : ARRAY [1..500] OF personal;
    count : 1..500;

BEGIN

   . . . . .
   (* enter input data *)

   . . . . .
   FOR count := 1 TO 500 DO
      BEGIN
          writeln(employee[count].name);
          writeln(employee[count].street);
          writeln(employee[count].city)
      END;
   . . . . .

END.
```

(*c*)
```
PROGRAM sample;
TYPE  personal = RECORD
      name,street,city : string
END;
VAR employee : ARRAY [1..500] OF personal;
    count,total : 1..500;

BEGIN

   . . . . .
   (* enter input data *)
   . . . . .
```

(*Outline continues on next page*)

```
              FOR count := 1 TO total DO
                 WITH employee[count] DO
                    BEGIN
                       writeln(name);
                       writeln(street);
                       writeln(city)
                    END;
           . . . . .
        END.


(d)   PROGRAM sample;
      TYPE line = PACKED ARRAY [1..80] OF char;
           personal = RECORD
                             name,street,city : line
                      END;
      VAR customer,employee : ARRAY [1..500] OF personal;
          i,j,total : 1..500;

      BEGIN
         . . . . .
         (* enter input data *)
         . . . . .
         FOR i := 1 TO total DO
            WITH customer[i] DO
               FOR j := 1 TO total DO
                  IF name = employee[j].name THEN
                     BEGIN
                        writeln(name);
                        writeln(street);
                        writeln(city)
                     END;
         . . . . .
        END.


(e)   PROGRAM sample;
      TYPE status = (single,married,divorced,widowed);
           background = RECORD
                             name,address : string;
                             employeeno : 1..9999;
                             CASE maritalstatus : status OF
                                single : ();
                                married : (children : 0..10);
                                divorced,widowed : (remarried : boolean)
                      END;
      VAR employees : ARRAY [1..100] OF background;
          count,total : 1..100;

      BEGIN
         . . . . .
         (* enter input data *)
         . . . . .
         FOR count := 1 TO total DO
```

(Outline continues on next page)

```
           WITH employees[count] DO
              BEGIN
                 writeln(name);
                 writeln(address);
                 writeln(employeeno:4);
                 IF maritalstatus = married THEN writeln(children:2);
                 IF ((maritalstatus = divorced) OR
                     (maritalstatus = widowed)) AND
                     (remarried = true) THEN writeln('Remarried')
              END;
         . . . . .
      END.
```

Programming Problems

10.35 Modify the customer billing program given in Example 10.21 so that any of the following reports can be displayed:

   (a)   Status of all customers (now generated by the program).

   (b)   Status of overdue and delinquent customers only.

   (c)   Status of delinquent customers only.

   Include a provision for generating a menu when the program is executed, from which the user may choose which report will be displayed. Have the program return to the menu after generating each report, thus allowing for the possibility of displaying several different reports.

10.36 Modify the inventory control program given in Example 10.28 so that any of the following reports can be displayed:

   (a)   Complete inventory list (now generated by the program).

   (b)   List of all backordered items.

   (c)   List of all stereos now in stock.

   (d)   List of all television sets now in stock.

   (e)   List of all color television sets now in stock.

   (f)   List of all black-and-white television sets now in stock.

   (g)   List of all portable television sets now in stock.

   Begin by generating a menu when the program is executed, allowing the user to select a particular report. Have the program return to this menu after generating each report, so that multiple reports can be displayed if desired.

10.37 Rewrite each of the following Pascal programs so that it makes use of a record-type data structure.

   (a)   The depreciation program presented in Examples 6.17 and 7.12.

   (b)   The program given in Example 8.10, for calculating the number of days between two dates.

   (c)   The program for reading and displaying names and addresses, presented in Example 9.8.

10.38 Modify the Pascal program given in Example 9.8 so that it reads several different names and addresses into the computer, rearranges them in alphabetical order, and then displays the alphabetized list. Include a record-type data structure within the program.

10.39 Modify the pig Latin generator presented in Example 9.28 so that it will accept multiple lines of text. Represent each line of text with a separate record. Include the following three fields within each record:

(a)   The original line of text.

(b)   The number of words within the line.

(c)   The modified line of text (i.e., the pig Latin equivalent of the original text).

Include the enhancements described in Prob. 9.51 (i.e., provisions for punctuation marks, upper-case letters and double-letter sounds).

10.40 For each of the following programming problems, write a complete Pascal program that makes use of a record-type data structure.

(a)   The student-exam averaging problem described in Prob. 9.54(a).

(b)   The more comprehensive version of the student-exam averaging problem described in Prob. 9.54(d).

(c)   The currency conversion problem described in Prob. 9.58.

(d)   The problem of matching the names of countries with their corresponding capitals (see Prob. 9.59).

(e)   The text encoding/decoding problem as described in Prob. 9.62, but extended to accommodate multiple lines of text.

10.41 Write a complete Pascal program that will accept the following information for each team in a baseball or a football league:

(a)   Team name, including the city (e.g., "Pittsburgh Steelers").

(b)   Number of wins.

(c)   Number of losses.

For a baseball team, add the following information:

(a)   Number of hits (season total).

(b)   Number of runs.

(c)   Number of errors.

(d)   Number of extra-inning games.

Similarly, add the following information for a football team:

(a)   Number of ties.

(b)   Number of touchdowns.

(c)   Number of field goals.

(d)   Total yards gained (season total).

(e)   Total yards given up to opponents.

Enter this information for all of the teams in the league. Then reorder and print the list of teams according to their win/loss records, using the reordering technique described in Example 9.5.

Utilize a record-type data structure that includes a fixed part and a variant part. Maintain all of these records within an array.

Test the program using a current set of team statistics. (Ideally, the program should be tested using both baseball and football statistics.)

Chapter 11

Files

We now turn our attention to another important structured data type — the *file*. A file may consist of a series of *records*, all of which have the same structure, or it may consist of unstructured streams of information, such as lines of text. Unlike other structured data types, files can be stored on auxiliary storage devices such as a floppy disks, hard disks or magnetic tapes. Thus, the file structure allows us to store information permanantly and access that information whenever necessary. Many important applications require this capability.

11.1 PRELIMINARIES

In general, there are two kinds of files that can be generated and accessed by a computer program: *permanent files* and *temporary files*. Permanent files are stored on auxiliary memory devices and therefore preserved after the program has completed its execution. The contents of a permanent file (i.e., the individual file components) can be accessed and/or modified, either by the program that created the file or by some other program, at any time. In Pascal, permanent files are referred to as *external files*.

Temporary files, on the other hand, are stored within the computer's main memory. A temporary file is lost as soon as the the program that created the file has completed its execution. Thus, temporary files are less useful (and less common) than permanent files. Temporary files are referred to as *internal files* in Pascal.

All files, whether permanent or temporary, can be organized in one of two different ways — *sequential* and *random*. In a sequential file all of the file components are stored sequentially, one after the other. In order to access a particular component it is necessary to start at the beginning and search through the entire file, until the desired component has been found. This type of access can be very slow, particularly if the file is large. Sequential files are relatively easy to create, however, and they are the only kind of file that can be used with certain types of storage media (e.g., magnetic tape).

In a random access file any component can be accessed directly, without proceeding through the entire file from the beginning. (Random access files are also known as *direct access* files, which is actually a more descriptive name.) Files of this type offer much faster access to individual file components than sequential files, though they are more difficult to create and maintain.

ANSI Pascal supports only sequential files, though many implementations of the language, including Turbo Pascal, also support random access files. In this book we will confine our attention to sequential files, in order to keep the discussion as broadly based as possible.

11.2 DEFINING A SEQUENTIAL FILE

Sequential files are very useful because their components can be array or record types as well as scalar-type data. One way to define a sequential file is through a variable declaration. The general form of such a declaration is

```
VAR file name : FILE OF type
```

where *file name* is an identifier that represents the name of the file and *type* refers to the data type of the individual file components. The file components must all be of the same type. They can be of any type, simple or structured, but they cannot be file-type components. Thus, a file cannot be embedded within another file.

EXAMPLE 11.1

Shown below is a sequential file definition in which each file component is a simple, char-type data item.

```
VAR symbols : FILE OF char;
```

EXAMPLE 11.2

Now consider a sequential file definition in which each component is a two-dimensional real array.

```
TYPE table = ARRAY [1..50,1..20] OF real;
VAR data : FILE OF table;
```

EXAMPLE 11.3

Here is an example of a sequential file definition in ANSI Pascal in which the file components are records.

```
TYPE status = (current,overdue,delinquent);
    account = RECORD
                  custname : PACKED ARRAY [1..80] OF char;
                  custno : 1..9999;
                  custtype : status;
                  custbalance : real
              END;
    VAR customers : FILE OF account;
```

Each record contains a char-type packed array (i.e., a string variable), an integer quantity, an enumerated data type and a real quantity.

Now consider a more general approach to the definition of sequential files. We can first define a file type, and then declare one or more file variables to be of this type. (We also used this approach to define arrays and records.) The general form of this kind of file definition is

```
TYPE name = FILE OF type
```

where *type* now refers to the data type of each file component. This data type must have been defined previously.

EXAMPLE 11.4

Here is an example of a sequential file definition in Turbo Pascal in which two different files are defined to have the same record-type components. (Note the use of the string data type, which is not supported in ANSI Pascal.)

```
        account = RECORD
                     custname : string;
                     custno : 1..9999;
                     custtype : status;
                     custbalance : real
                  END;
        customers = FILE OF account;
    VAR oldcustomers,newcustomers : customers;
```

Thus, `oldcustomers` and `newcustomers` are both sequential files of type `customers`. The components of each file are records of type `account`.

Notice that the length of a file is never specified as a part of the file definition. This situation differs from that of other structured data types, where the number of components is either explicitly (in the case of arrays) or implicitly (as with records) specified within the data-type definition. As a rule, the maximum length of a file is determined only by the physical capacity of the medium on which it is stored.

In ANSI Pascal, external files can be passed to a Pascal program as parameters. This is accomplished by including the names of the external files in the program header, enclosed in parentheses and separated by commas. This parameter specification is in addition to the required file definitions, which must be included within the main program block. (We have not used external file parameters earlier in this book because their use is optional and generally inconsistent with Turbo Pascal programming style.)

ANSI Pascal includes two standard (predeclared) external files, `input` and `output`, which direct character-type information from an input device and to an output device, respectively. These file names can be included in the program header if they will be accessed by a program. Since they are standard language features, however, these two files need not be defined within the program.

EXAMPLE 11.5

Suppose an ANSI Pascal program makes use of the external file `customers`, described in Example 11.3. A skeletal outline of this program is shown below.

```
    PROGRAM sample(input,output,customers);
    TYPE status = (current,overdue,delinquent);
        account = RECORD
                     custname : PACKED ARRAY [1..80] OF char;
                     custno : 1..9999;
                     custtype : status;
                     custbalance : real
                  END;
    VAR customers : FILE OF account;

    BEGIN   (* main action statements *)
       . . . . .
       (* process the records within customers *)
       . . . . .
    END.
```

Note that the files `input`, `output` and `customers` are included in the program header, enclosed in parentheses. This is followed by a definition of the nonstandard file `customers`, within the declaration part of the main block. Note that the standard files `input` and `output` are not defined explicitly within the program.

Turbo Pascal does not make use of external files that are passed to the program as parameters. If they are present, they are ignored.

EXAMPLE 11.6

Here is a Turbo Pascal version of the program outline shown in Example 11.5.

```
PROGRAM sample;
TYPE status = (current,overdue,delinquent);
     account = RECORD
                    custname : string;
                    custno : 1..9999;
                    custtype : status;
                    custbalance : real
               END;
VAR customers : FILE OF account;

BEGIN   (* main action statements *)
   . . . . .
   (* process the records within customers *)
   . . . . .
END.
```

Notice that the program does not include any file names as parameters within the program header. Also, note the use of the string data type for custname.

11.3 CREATING A SEQUENTIAL FILE

When creating a sequential file in ANSI Pascal, the first step is to open the file for writing. To do so, we use the standard procedure rewrite. Thus, we begin with the statement

```
rewrite(file);
```

where *file* is the name of the file.

If the specified file is being is being created for the first time, then the rewrite statement simply establishes the beginning of the file. If the file already exists with the given name, however, then the effect of the rewrite statement is to *erase all of the existing information within the existing file* and then establish the beginning of the new file.

Once the file has been opened, we can actually write the data items to the file with the write statement. The file name must be included within the write statement, as follows:

```
write(file, data item);
```

where *data item* represents the data item whose value (or values, in the case of a structured data item) will be written to the file.

EXAMPLE 11.7 Creating a File of Customer Records

Here is an ANSI Pascal program that creates a file called customers. The components of this file will be customer records. The number of records need not be known in advance. The user simply continues to enter data until a value of 9999 is detected for the customer number, signifying the end of the data. Note that we now include the standard file identifiers, input and output, in the program header for illustrative purposes.

```
          PROGRAM createfile(input,output,customers);
          (* CREATE A FILE OF CUSTOMER RECORDS *)
          TYPE account = RECORD
                              custno : 1..9999;
                              custbalance : real;
                          END;
          VAR customeracct : account;
              customers: FILE OF account;

          BEGIN
              rewrite(customers);                     (* open the file *)

              WITH customeracct DO
                 BEGIN
                    write('Customer Number: ');
                    readln(custno);                   (* first record *)
                    WHILE custno < 9999 DO
                       BEGIN
                          write('Customer Balance: ');
                          readln(custbalance);

                          write(customers,customeracct);  (* write record to file *)

                          writeln;
                          write('Customer Number: ');
                          readln(custno)              (* next record *)
                       END
                 END;
          END.
```

Notice that the individual data items are read in separately, but entire records are written to the file. Also, notice that the file is opened via the rewind statement before any data are actually written to the file.

We have already seen that Turbo Pascal does not require reference to any external file names in the program header. However, Turbo Pascal does require that the internal file name be associated with an external file identifier before the file is accessed by any other statement. This is accomplished with the assign statement which, in general terms, is written as

```
assign(file, 'file identifier')
```

where *file* is the internal file name and *file identifier* is an external file identifier at the operating system level (i.e., the file name that is recognized by the operating system after exiting the Turbo Pascal environment). Note that the *file identifier* is written as a string, enclosed in apostrophes.

After all of the information has been written to a Turbo Pascal file, the file should be closed with the close statement. This statement is written simply as

```
close(file)
```

where *file* represents the internal file name.

Beginning programmers often forget to add the close statement at the end of a Turbo Pascal program. In such cases the file will automatically be closed at the end of the program execution. Thus, the close statement is not absolutely essential. However, good programming practice suggests that it always be included at the end of any Turbo Pascal program in which a file has been opened.

EXAMPLE 11.8 Creating a File of Customer Records

Here is a Turbo Pascal version of the program presented in Example 11.7.

```
PROGRAM createfile;
(* CREATE A FILE OF CUSTOMER RECORDS *)
TYPE account = RECORD
                   custno : 1..9999;
                   custbalance : real;
               END;
VAR customeracct : account;
    customers: FILE OF account;

BEGIN
   assign(customers,'sample.dat');
   rewrite(customers);                    (* open the file *)

   WITH customeracct DO
     BEGIN
        write('Customer Number: ');
        readln(custno);                   (* first record *)
        WHILE custno < 9999 DO
          BEGIN
             write('Customer Balance: ');
             readln(custbalance);

             write(customers,customeracct);  (* write record to file *)

             writeln;
             write('Customer Number: ');
             readln(custno)               (* next record *)
          END
     END;

   close(customers)
END.
```

Notice that the internal file name customers is associated with the external file sample.dat. This association is established before the file is opened. The file is then closed after all of the data items (all of the customer records) have been written to the file.

When entering structured file components (e.g. records), it may be desirable to enter the individual data items for each structured component through a procedure. In such cases the data items are read into the procedure and then transferred to the calling portion of the program by means of a variable parameter, which is of the same type as the structured file component. Accessing the procedure will therefore cause the data items within one structured file component to be entered into the computer. After the procedure has been accessed, the file component (i.e., the parameter in the procedure access) can be written to the file. The details are illustrated in the following example.

EXAMPLE 11.9 Creating a File of Customer Records

Here is another version of the Turbo Pascal program presented in Example 11.8. In the present program, the individual data items for each customer record are entered through a procedure called readinput.

```
      PROGRAM createfile;
      (* CREATE A FILE OF CUSTOMER RECORDS *)
      TYPE account = RECORD
                          custno : 1..9999;
                          custbalance : real;
                    END;
      VAR customeracct : account;
          customers: FILE OF account;

      PROCEDURE readinput(VAR info : account);
      BEGIN
         WITH info DO
            BEGIN
               write('Customer Number: ');
               readln(custno);
               if custno < 9999 THEN
                  BEGIN
                     write('Customer Balance: ');
                     readln(custbalance);
                     writeln
                  END
            END
      END;

      BEGIN
         assign(customers,'sample.dat');
         rewrite(customers);
         readinput(customeracct);

         WHILE customeracct.custno < 9999 DO
            BEGIN
               write(customers,customeracct);
               readinput(customeracct)
            END;

         close(customers)
      END.
```

A single `write` statement can contain multiple data items if we wish. Thus, a more general form of the write statement is

> write(*file*, *data item 1*, *data item 2*, . . . , *data item n*);

ANSI Pascal permits the data items to be written as expressions, though some versions of the language restrict the data items to variables. Turbo Pascal includes these restrictions.

EXAMPLE 11.10 Creating a File of Squares and Square Roots

Here is a Turbo Pascal program that generates a file containing the first 100 integers, their squares and their square roots.

```
      PROGRAM squares;
      (* GENERATE A FILE CONTAINING 100 SQUARES AND SQUARE ROOTS *)

      VAR data : FILE OF real;
          v,v1,v2 : real;
          count : 1..100;
```

```
     BEGIN
        assign(data,'squares.dat');
        rewrite(data);
        FOR count := 1 TO 100 DO
           BEGIN
              v := count;          (* convert to real *)
              v1 := sqr(v);
              v2 := sqrt(v);
              write(data,v,v1,v2)
           END;
        close(data)
     END.
```

Note that the `write` statement includes three data items: the integer (expressed as a real quantity), its square and its square root. Thus, the data file contains all real quantities.

11.4 READING A SEQUENTIAL FILE

The process of reading a sequential file is essentially a mirror image of the process of creating a sequential file. The first step is to open the file for reading and locate the beginning of the file. This is accomplished with standard procedure `reset`, which is written as

        reset(*file*);

where *file* is the file name. (In Turbo Pascal the `reset` statement must be preceded by an `assign` statement, as described in Section 11.3.)

When the file is opened, the standard end-of-file function

        eof(*file*)

will be set to `false` if the file contains one or more components, and `true` otherwise. This function allows us to detect the end of a file when reading multiple file components.

Once the file has been opened in the read mode, we use the `read` statement to read the individual file components. The read statement is written as

        read(*file*, *input variable*);

where *input variable* refers to the input variable to which the incoming file component will be assigned.

EXAMPLE 11.11 Reading a File of Customer Records

Here is a Turbo Pascal program that reads the file `sample.dat`, created by the Turbo Pascal program shown in Example 11.8 (or Example 11.9).

```
     PROGRAM readfile;
     (* READ A FILE CONTAINING CUSTOMER RECORDS *)
     TYPE account = RECORD
                       custno : 1..9999;
                       custbalance : real
                    END;
     VAR customeracct : account;
         customers : FILE OF account;
```

```
          BEGIN
             assign(customers,'sample.dat');
             reset(customers);
             WITH customeracct DO
                WHILE NOT eof(customers) DO
                   BEGIN
                       read(customers,customeracct);
                       writeln('Customer Number: ',custno:5);
                       writeln('Customer Balance: ',custbalance:4:0);
                       writeln
                   END;
             close(customers)
          END.
```

The main action block begins by associating the internal file name `customers` with the external identifier `sample.dat` and then opens the file for reading via the `reset` statement. The program then proceeds to read an individual record from the file and display its contents on the screen. This process continues until an end-of-file condition has been detected in the file being read (i.e., `customers`).

Notice that the `eof` function is used to detect the end-of-file condition in the file being read. This function was first introduced in Section 4.4. Also, note that the program reads an entire record, not individual record components, with a single `read` statement. This is analogous to the use of the `write` statement in Examples 11.8 and 11.9.

Multiple data items can be included in the `read` statement if desired. Thus, the `read` statement can be written as

> read(*file*, *input variable 1*, *input variable 2*, . . . , *input variable n*);

The data items that are read from the file are assigned to the corresponding input variables.

EXAMPLE 11.12 Reading a File of Squares and Square Roots

In Example 11.10 we saw a Turbo Pascal program that generates a file containing a sequence of integers, their squares and their square roots. Here is a Turbo Pascal program that will read this file and display the file contents on the screen. The overall program logic is similar to that in Example 11.11.

```
          PROGRAM squares;
          (* READ A FILE CONTAINING SQUARES AND SQUARE ROOTS *)
          VAR v,v1,v2 : real;
              data    : FILE OF real;

          BEGIN
             assign(data,'squares.dat');
             reset(data);
             WHILE NOT eof(data) DO
                BEGIN
                    read(data,v,v1,v2);
                    writeln(v:7:2,v1:10:2,v2:7:2)
                END;
             close(data)
          END.
```

This program is more general than its counterpart in Example 11.10, since it is not restricted to a file of predetermined size. Also, note the appearance of multiple variables in the `read` statement.

11.5 UPDATING A SEQUENTIAL FILE

Within a single ANSI Pascal program a sequential file can be treated as either an input file or an output file, but not both. (Note, however, that a particular file can be treated as an input file in one program and an output file in another.) Thus, it is not possible to read a file component, modify the file component, and then write the modified component back to the original file. Similarly, it is not possible to read a file to the end and then write additional records onto that file.

These restrictions tend to complicate the process of updating an existing file. A file can still be updated in a relatively straightforward manner, however, by utilizing *two* files within the program. The file containing the original information (the "old" file) will be treated as an input file. The updated file (the "new" file) will receive some information from the old file and some from the keyboard (or some other input source). The new file will therefore be treated as an output file.

To update the old file, we carry out the following steps for each component within the file.

1. Read the file component into the computer's memory and determine whether or not this particular component must be updated. To do so, we will compare some key data item, such as a customer number, with a value that has been entered from the keyboard. (This new value will indicate the next component to be updated.)

    (*a*) If the current file component does not require updating, then copy it directly to the new file.

    (*b*) If updating is required, then the new information is entered from the keyboard and merged with the old information. The modified file component is then written to the new file and another data item (e.g., another customer number) is entered from the keyboard, indicating which file component must be modified next.

2. This scheme is repeated until all file components have been read from the old file (i.e., until the end of file has been reached).

3. If additional file components must be appended to the original file, they are entered from the input device at this time. Each new file component is written to the new file as it is entered.

For this scheme to work properly, the new information must be entered sequentially from the input device, in the correct order. The order must conform to that in which the file components are stored within the original file. For example, if the file components are customer records that are stored by ascending customer number, then the new information must also be entered by ascending customer number.

EXAMPLE 11.13 Copying a File

The following ANSI Pascal program causes the components of a file called `oldfile` to be copied to a file called `newfile`.

```
PROGRAM sample(newfile,oldfile);
(* COPY THE CONTENTS OF ONE FILE TO ANOTHER *)
TYPE account = RECORD
                  custno : 1..9999;
                  oldbalance : real;
                  newbalance : real;
                  payment : real;
               END;
VAR newfile,oldfile : FILE OF account;
    newaccount,oldaccount : account;
```

(Program continues on next page)

```
BEGIN   (* main action block *)
   reset(oldfile);
   rewrite(newfile);
   WHILE NOT eof(oldfile) DO
      BEGIN
         read(oldfile,oldaccount);
         newaccount := oldaccount;
         write(newfile,newaccount)
      END
END.
```

Actually, it is not necessary to include two separate record-type variables, `newaccount` and `oldaccount`, within this program outline. One such variable would have been sufficient. Thus, the main action block could have been written

```
BEGIN   (* main action block *)
   reset(oldfile);
   rewrite(newfile);
   WHILE NOT eof(oldfile) DO
      BEGIN
         read(oldfile,newaccount);
         write(newfile,newaccount)
      END
END.
```

Though not absolutely necessary, the use of two different variables does emphasize the manner in which the individual file components are transferred from one file to another. This is particularly significant if the contents of `oldaccount` were to be modified in some way before being transferred to `newaccount`.

EXAMPLE 11.14 Appending to a File

Let us now consider the process of appending one or more new components to an existing file. We will again read each file component within `oldfile` and transfer it to `newfile`. After all of the existing old components have been transferred, the new components will be entered from the keyboard. This process will continue until a value of 9999 has been entered for the variable `custno`.

Here is an ANSI Pascal program outline. (We again include the standard file identifiers, `input` and `output`, in the program header for illustrative purposes.)

```
PROGRAM sample(input,output,oldfile,newfile);
(* TRANSFER THE CONTENTS OF ONE FILE TO ANOTHER,
   THEN APPEND ADDITIONAL FILE COMPONENTS TO THE NEW FILE *)
TYPE account = RECORD
                  custno : 1..9999;
                  oldbalance : real;
                  newbalance : real;
                  payment : real;
               END;
VAR newfile,oldfile : FILE OF account;
    newaccount : account;
    custno : 1..9999;
```

(Program continues on next page)

```
      PROCEDURE readinput(VAR newaccount : account);
      (* enter input data for one record *)
      BEGIN
         . . . . .
         (* enter input data from the keyboard for each record *)
         . . . . .
      END;

      BEGIN    (* main action block *)
         reset(oldfile);
         rewrite(newfile);

         (* transfer the old records *)

         WHILE NOT eof(oldfile) DO
            BEGIN
               read(oldfile,newaccount);
               write(newfile,newaccount)
            END;

         (* enter the new records *)

   write('Customer number: ');
   readln(custno);
   WHILE custno < 9999 DO
      BEGIN
         readinput(newaccount);
         write(newfile,newaccount);
         write('Customer number: ');
         readln(custno)
      END;
   END.
```

Notice that each new file component (each new record) is passed from procedure readinput to the main part of the program as a variable-type parameter.

In Turbo Pascal we can read from and write to the same file within a single program. For most applications, however, this strategy represents poor programming practice, since an error in writing to the file may corrupt the original file. This would be particularly disastrous if the old file contains the only source of data. The use of two different files is much safer, since an error in writing to the new file would not affect the data contained in the old file.

EXAMPLE 11.15 Updating a File

Here is an outline of a Turbo Pascal program that reads successive file components from oldfile, updates them if necessary, and then copies the components to newfile. The updating of various components will continue until a value of 9999 has been entered for custno. Any components remaining in oldfile will then be transferred directly to newfile, without any opportunity for updating.

Note that all of the components of oldfile will be transferred to newfile. Some will be updated, however, and others will be transferred without change.

In order for this scheme to work properly, it is essential that the successive values of custno be entered in ascending order. This will assure that the sequence of changes conform to the order in which the corresponding components are stored in oldfile.

```
        PROGRAM sample;
        (* READ SUCCESSIVE FILE COMPONENTS FROM A DATA FILE, UPDATE EACH COMPONENT IF
            NECESSARY, AND THEN WRITE THE COMPONENT TO A NEW DATA FILE *)
        TYPE account = RECORD
                              custno : 1..9999;
                              oldbalance : real;
                              newbalance : real;
                              payment : real;
                         END;
        VAR newfile,oldfile : FILE OF account;
            newaccount,oldaccount : account;
            custno : 1..9999;

        BEGIN   (* main action statements *)
            assign(oldfile,'old.dat');
            assign(newfile,'new.dat');
            reset(oldfile);
            rewrite(newfile);
            write('Customer number: ');
            readln(custno);
            WHILE NOT eof(oldfile) DO
                BEGIN
                    read(oldfile,oldaccount);
                    newaccount := oldaccount;
                    IF (custno < 9999) AND (oldaccount.custno = custno) THEN
                        BEGIN
                            . . . . .
                            (* accept appropriate input from the keyboard and
                                make changes in a file component as required *)
                            . . . . .
                            write('Customer number: ');
                            readln(custno)
                        END;   (* IF custno *)
                    write(newfile,newaccount)
                END   (* WHILE NOT eof *);
            close(oldfile);
            close(newfile)
        END.
```

EXAMPLE 11.16 Updating a Customer Billing System

Let us now consider a complete Turbo Pascal program that will allow us to update a data file at regular intervals. The file will contain the records that make up a customer billing system.

We will examine all of the records during each update. This will allow recent payments to be credited to the account of any customer with an outstanding balance. The status of the account can then be changed accordingly. The update will include a recording of the most recent payment and the payment date, a calculation of the new balance and a determination of each customer's status.

Suppose each record contains the following information: customer name, account number (i.e., customer number), previous balance, new balance, current payment and payment date. The appropriate record declarations are shown below. (Note that the record declarations are similar to those given in Example 10.21.)

```
TYPE date = RECORD
                month : 1..12;
                day : 1..31;
                year : 1900..2100
           END;
     account = RECORD
                  name : string;
                  custno : 1..9999;
                  oldbalance : real;
                  newbalance : real;
                  payment : real;
                  paydate : date
               END;
```

The status of each customer's account will be considered current unless there is an outstanding balance, in which case the status of the account will depend on the size of the most recent payment. The following rules will apply (as in Example 10.21).

1. If the current payment is greater than zero but less than 10 percent of the previous outstanding balance, the account will be considered overdue.

2. If the current payment is zero, the account will be considered delinquent.

Each file update will proceed sequentially on a record-by-record basis. The overall strategy will be as follows.

1. Read a record from the old data file.

2. Display the customer's name, account number and previous balance on the screen. Then display a prompt for the current payment.

3. Update the record by entering the current payment amount and the current payment date.

4. Determine the new balance and the current account status, and display them on the screen.

5. Write the record to the new data file (regardless of whether or not the record has been updated).

6. Continue this procedure until all of the records in the old data file have been processed (i.e., until an end-of-file has been detected in the old data file).

Here is the entire Turbo Pascal program.

```
PROGRAM billing;

(* UPDATE CUSTOMER RECORDS AND CREATE A NEW FILE *)

TYPE date = RECORD
                month : 1..12;
                day : 1..31;
                year : 1900..2100
           END;
     account = RECORD
                  name : string;
                  custno : 1..9999;
                  oldbalance : real;
                  newbalance : real;
                  payment : real;
                  paydate : date
               END;
     datafile = FILE OF account;
VAR newfile,oldfile : datafile;
    newaccount,oldaccount : account;
    count : 1..9999;
    space : char;
```

```
      PROCEDURE update(VAR custaccount : account);

      (* UPDATE A RECORD *)

      BEGIN
         WITH custaccount DO
            BEGIN
               writeln('Customer Number: ',count);
               write('Name: ',name);
               writeln('      Account Number: ',custno:4);
               writeln('Balance: ',oldbalance:7:2);
               payment := 0;
               write('Current Payment: ');
               readln(payment);
               IF payment > 0 THEN
                  BEGIN
                     write('Payment Date (mm dd yyyy): ');
                     WITH paydate DO
                        readln(month,space,day,space,year);
                     newbalance := oldbalance - payment
                  END;
               writeln('New Balance: ',newbalance:7:2);
               write('Account status: ');
               IF payment >= 0.1*oldbalance
                  THEN writeln('CURRENT')
                  ELSE IF payment > 0 THEN writeln('OVERDUE')
                                     ELSE writeln('DELINQUENT');
               writeln
            END    (* WITH custaccount *)
      END;

      BEGIN    (* main action block *)
         assign(oldfile,'old.dat');
         assign(newfile,'new.dat');
         reset(oldfile);
         rewrite(newfile);
         count := 1;
         space := ' ';
         writeln('CUSTOMER BILLING SYSTEM - FILE UPDATE');
         writeln;

         BEGIN        (* update the old file *)
            WHILE NOT eof(oldfile) DO
               BEGIN
                  read(oldfile,oldaccount);
                  update(oldaccount);
                  newaccount := oldaccount;
                  write(newfile,newaccount);
                  count := count + 1
               END    (* WHILE NOT eof(oldfile) *)
         END;   (* file update *)

         close(oldfile);
         close(newfile)
      END.
```

Notice that this program reads an old file whose external identifier is old.dat, and creates a new file with the external identifier new.dat.

Now suppose the program is used to process a small data file containing 4 records. The interactive dialog generated by the update procedure is shown below. (Note that the user's responses are underlined.)

```
CUSTOMER BILLING SYSTEM - FILE UPDATE

Customer Number: 1
Name: Richard L. Warren      Account Number: 4208
Balance:  247.88
Current Payment: 25.00
Payment Date (mm dd yyyy): 6 14 1993
New Balance:  222.88
Account Status: CURRENT


Customer Number: 2
Name: Janet Davis     Account Number: 2219
Balance:  135.00
Current Payment: 135.00
Payment Date (mm dd yyyy): 8 10 1993
New Balance:  0.00
Account Status: CURRENT


Customer Number: 3
Name: Mort Singer      Account Number: 8452
Balance:  387.42
Current Payment: 35.00
Payment Date (mm dd yyyy): 7 4 1993
New Balance:  352.42
Account Status: CURRENT


Customer Number: 4
Name: Phyllis Smith       Account Number: 711
Balance:  260.00
Current Payment: 0.00
New Balance:  260.00
Account Status: DELINQUENT
```

Once the program execution has been completed, `old.dat` should be deleted or archived and `new.dat` should be renamed as `old.dat`. This will allow the newly created data file to be updated in the future.

In this example we have assumed that `old.dat` exists, though we have not discussed how it might be generated initially. We leave this as an exercise for the reader (see Prob. 11.46 at the end of this chapter).

In some situations we may wish to transfer an entire file to a procedure as a parameter. To do so, the file must be passed as a *variable* parameter. (Note the similarity to passing a structured file *component* to a procedure, as discussed in Section 11.3.) This avoids the need to generate a copy of a lengthy file, as would be required if the file were passed as a value parameter.

11.6 TEXT FILES

Pascal also supports another type of file, known as a *text file*. This is a file of type char, with end-of-line designations interspersed at various places to distinguish one line of text from another. (Typically, an end-of-line designation will consist of a line feed followed by a carriage return.) Thus, a text file consists of multiple lines of character-type data.

The characters on any given line may be grouped (i.e., separated by blank spaces), and the individual groups of characters can be interpreted in one of several different ways. For example, a group of digits can be interpreted as an integer or a real quantity. The manner in which a character group is interpreted will be determined by the corresponding data item in the associated `read` or `write` statement (more about this later).

A text file is defined by declaring a file identifier (i.e., a variable representing the file name) to be of type `text`. Formally, the declaration can be expressed as

```
VAR name : text
```

where *name* is an identifier that represents the name of the text file. Multiple file names can be included in a single declaration.

EXAMPLE 11.17

Suppose a Pascal program must make use of the text files `oldtext` and `newtext`. The file definitions will appear as follows.

```
VAR oldtext,newtext : text;
```

Notice that it is not necessary to write `FILE OF text` within the declaration.

The standard procedures `reset` and `rewrite` can be used with text files, just as they are used with other types of files. Thus, the statement

```
reset(file);
```

prepares the file for reading. Moreover, the standard function

```
eof(file)
```

is set to an appropriate value (`true` if the file is empty, `false` otherwise) when the file is reset. Note that we have used this function in several of the examples presented earlier in this chapter.

Similarly, the statement

```
rewrite(file);
```

will prepares the file for writing by erasing any text already in the text file and then establishing the beginning of the text file.

Turbo Pascal also includes an `append` statement; i.e.,

```
append(file);
```

This statement permits new data to be appended to (i.e., to be written at the end of) an existing text file.

Most programs that make use of text files utilize the standard procedures `read`, `readln`, `write` and `writeln`. Let us consider how these procedures are utilized with text files.

If the statement

```
read(file, input variable);
```

refers to a text file, the action will depend upon the type of the input variable. If the input variable is a char-type variable, then a character will be read from the file and assigned to the input variable in the usual manner. If the input variable is of type integer or type real, however, then a sufficient number of consecutive characters will be read to allow construction of a complete integer or real quantity. This quantity will then be assigned to the input variable.

Multiple input variables may appear in a single `read` statement. In such situations, the statement will be interpreted as a sequence of `read` statements, each containing a single input variable. Thus, the statement

```
read(file, input variable 1, input variable 2, . . . , input variable n);
```

will be interpreted as

```
BEGIN
    read(file, input variable 1);
    read(file, input variable 2);
    . . . . .
    read(file, input variable n)
END;
```

If the variables represent consecutive numerical quantities, then the separation of one numerical quantity from another will be based upon the detection of preceding blanks or line control characters, as discussed in Chap. 4 (see Section 4.2).

The `readln` statement is similar to the `read` statement. In this case, however, a single `readln` statement will cause reading to continue until an end-of-line designation (`eoln`) has been encountered. Thus, any *subsequent* read or readln will begin on the next line.

Moreover, a `readln` statement that contains multiple input variables, such as

```
readln(file, input variable 1, input variable 2, . . ., input variable n);
```

will be interpreted as

```
BEGIN
    read(file, input variable 1, input variable 2, . . ., input variable n);
    readln(file)
END;
```

The standard function

```
eoln(file)
```

is often used when reading from a text file. This function returns the value `false` unless the current character in the file is an end-of-line indicator. Thus, the function `eoln` remains false until an end-of-line has been detected, which causes it to become true. The function again becomes false whenever some other character is examined, after an end-of-line has been detected.

Now let us turn our attention to the `write` and `writeln` statements. If the statement

```
write(file, output item)
```

is used with a text file, the action taken will depend upon the exact nature of the output item. If the output item is of type char (e.g., a constant or a char-type variable), then the character will be written to the file. If, however, the output item represents some other data type (e.g., a boolean variable, or a numeric constant, variable or expression), then the value of the output item will be converted into its constituent characters. These characters will then automatically be written to the text file.

Multiple output items may appear in a single `write` statement. Such a statement will be interpreted as a sequence of `write` statements, each containing a single output item. Hence, the statement

```
write(file, output item 1, output item 2, . . . , output item n);
```

will be interpreted as

```
    BEGIN
        write(file, output item 1);
        write(file, output item 2);
              . . . . .
        write(file, output item n)
    END;
```

The writeln statement

```
    writeln(file);
```

causes an end-of-line designation to be written to the file. Hence, any subsequent output to the text file will begin on the next line. Furthermore, the statement

```
    writeln(file, output item 1, output item 2, . . . , output item n);
```

will be interpreted as

```
    BEGIN
        write(file, output item 1, output item 2, . . . , output item n);
        writeln(file)
    END;
```

thus allowing multiple output items to be placed on one line, followed by an end-of-line designation.

EXAMPLE 11.18 Transferring Data Between Text Files

Here is a simple Turbo Pascal program that transfers the contents of one text file to another on a line-by-line basis.

```
    PROGRAM filetransfer;
    (* TRANSFER TEXT FROM ONE TEXT FILE TO ANOTHER ON A LINE-BY-LINE BASIS *)
    VAR oldtext,newtext : text;
        x : char;
        y : integer;
        z : real;

    BEGIN
        assign(oldtext,'text1.dat');
        assign(newtext,'text2.dat');
        reset(oldtext);
        rewrite(newtext);

        WHILE NOT eof(oldtext) DO
           BEGIN
              WHILE NOT eoln(oldtext) DO
                 BEGIN     (* transfer one line of text *)
                    read(oldtext,x,y,z);
                    write(newtext,x,y,z)
                 END;
              readln(oldtext);
              writeln(newtext)
           END;

        close(oldtext);
        close(newtext)
    END.
```

Note that the the two text files are called `oldtext` and `newtext`, respectively. The corresponding external file identifiers are `text1.dat` and `text2.dat`. Within `oldtext`, each line contains a char-type data item, an integer-type data item and a real-type data item. After `newtext` has been created, it will have the same internal structure as `oldtext`.

The inner WHILE - DO loop causes the text in one line of `oldtext` to be read and written to `newtext`. The transfer takes place one character at a time, for any given line of text. Following this WHILE - DO loop is a `readln` statement, which prepares the program to read the next line of `oldtext`, and then a `writeln` statement, which places an end-of-line designation on the current line of `newtext`.

The outer WHILE - DO loop causes the action to be repeated on a line-by-line basis, until an end-of-file designation has been detected in `oldtext`.

The two standard files `input` and `output`, which we have utilized in various programming examples throughout this book, are actually text files. When reading from or writing to one of these standard text files, it is not necessary to include the file name as a parameter within the `read` or `write` statement. If the file parameter is not specified, then either `input` or `output` is assumed, as required.

The following procedures and functions are always assumed to apply to the standard `input` file if a file parameter is not explicitly included in the procedure or function reference: `read`, `readln`, `eof` and `eoln`. Similarly, the procedures `write`, and `writeln` are always assumed to apply to the standard `output` file if a file parameter is not explicitly included. Moreover, `input` and `output` are automatically initialized and closed, so that the standard procedures `assign`, `reset`, `rewrite` and `close` are not needed with these files. (Remember that `assign` and `close` are Turbo Pascal procedures that are not included in standard ANSI Pascal.)

EXAMPLE 11.19 Entering and Saving a Text File

Here is a Turbo Pascal program that allows several lines of text to be entered from an input device and stored in a text file called `newfile`. (Note that the text file's external designation will be `text3.dat`.)

```
PROGRAM entertext;
(* ENTER TEXT FROM THE KEYBOARD AND STORE IN A TEXT FILE, LINE-BY-LINE *)

VAR newtext : text;
    x : char;

BEGIN
   assign(newtext,'text3.dat');
   rewrite(newtext);

   WHILE NOT eof DO
      BEGIN
         WHILE NOT eoln DO
            BEGIN    (* enter and store one line of text *)
               read(x);
               write(newtext,x)
            END;
         readln;
         writeln(newtext)
      END;

   close(newtext)
END.
```

When this program is executed, an unspecified number of lines can be entered from the keyboard and stored in `newtext`. To terminate the execution, an end-of-file designation will have to be entered from the keyboard. The exact nature of this designation will vary from one operating system to another, though CTRL-Z (pressing the control key and the letter Z simultaneously) is frequently used for this purpose.

It should be understood that a text file need not be created under program control, as in the preceding example. Any text editor or word processor can be used to create a text file. Moreover, the contents of an existing text file can be viewed or printed at the operating system level.

EXAMPLE 11.20 Encoding and Decoding Text

We now consider a more interesting application involving the use of text files. Let us develop a Turbo Pascal program that will encode and decode multiple lines of text. The program will include a menu, which will allow any one of the following actions to be taken:

1. Enter text from the keyboard, encode the text and store the encoded text in a text file.

2. Retrieve the encoded text and display it in its encoded form.

3. Retrieve the encoded text, decode it, and then display the decoded text.

4. End the computation.

The entire text may consist of several lines. These lines will be preserved as the text is encoded, stored, decoded and displayed. However, the actual encoding and decoding will occur on a character-by-character basis.

In order to encode and decode the text, the user must enter a single-character "key." (The program will prompt for this if menu items 1 or 3 are selected.) Each character will be encoded by adding its numerical code to the numerical code for the key, and then determining the character represented by the sum; i.e.,

```
z := chr(ord(x) + ord(key))
```

where z represents the encoded character that is equivalent to the original character x.

When adding the two numerical codes together, care must be taken that the sum not exceed 127, since this is the largest value for a character code (assuming the standard ASCII character set). Therefore, if the value of z exceeds 127, its value must be adjusted by subtracting 127 from the sum. Thus, we can write

```
y := ord(x) + ord(key);
IF y > 127 THEN y := y - 127;
z := chr(y);
```

This scheme works well and is easy to implement. It should be understood, however, that certain values for z will result in unprintable characters (e.g., line feeds, carriage returns, "beeps," etc.), though these characters will be placed in the encoded text. Thus, the encoded text may appear very erratic when it is displayed.

The encoded text can be decoded by reversing the above process; i.e.,

```
y := ord(z) - ord(key);
IF y < 0 THEN y := y + 127;
x := chr(y);
```

When decoding the text it is essential that we use the same value of key as was used to encode the original text. Otherwise the decoded text will be garbled.

Here is a skeletal outline of the entire program, illustrating the overall computational strategy.

```
PROGRAM encode;

TYPE features = 1..4;

VAR code : text;
x,z,key : char;
y : -127..254;
choice : features;

PROCEDURE menu(VAR choice : features; VAR key : char);
BEGIN
   . . . . .
   (* generate a menu, return the user's choice
      and a value for the key, if appropriate *)
   . . . . .
END;

BEGIN   (* main action statements *)
   assign(code,'code.dat');
   choice := 1;
   WHILE choice <> 4 DO
      menu(choice,key);
      CASE choice OF
      1 : BEGIN
             rewrite(code);
             . . . . .
             (* enter text, encode and store *)
             . . . . .
          END;

      2,3 : BEGIN
             reset(code);
             . . . . .
             (* retrieve encoded text, decode (choice = 2) and display *)
             . . . . .
          END;

       4 : ;

      END   (* CASE *)
   END;   (* WHILE loop *)
   close(code)
END.
```

The overall strategy is staightforward, based upon the use of a CASE structure to implement whatever choice is returned from the menu. Upon completion of each major activity (i.e., each pass through the CASE structure), the program returns to the menu for another selection until a choice of 4 has been requested.

The completeTurbo Pascal program is shown below. Within this program, procedure menu provides the necessary input/output statements to generate the menu and, if the user chooses options 1 or 3, prompts for a single-character key. Notice that this procedure employs two variable parameters: choice, which is of type features, and key, which is of type char.

When the program is executed, the data input will continue until an end-of-file marker is entered from the keyboard. The manner with which this is accomplished will vary from one operating system to another. We will assume that the control character CTRL-Z is used for this purpose.

```pascal
PROGRAM encode;

(* ENTER TEXT FROM AN INPUT DEVICE, ENCODE IT, STORE THE ENCODED TEXT
   IN A TEXT FILE AND DISPLAY THE TEXT, EITHER ENCODED OR DECODED *)

TYPE features = 1..4;

VAR code : text;
    x,z,key : char;
    y : -127..254;
    choice : features;

PROCEDURE menu (VAR choice : features; VAR key : char);

(* Generate a menu and return the user's choice *)

BEGIN
   writeln;
   writeln('E N C O D I N G / D E C O D I N G   T E X T');
   writeln;
   writeln('Program Features:');
   writeln;
   writeln('  1 - Enter text, encode and store');
   writeln;
   writeln('  2 - Retrieve encoded text and display');
   writeln;
   writeln('  3 - Retrieve encoded text, decode and display');
   writeln;
   writeln('  4 - End computation');
   writeln;
   write('Please enter your selection (1, 2, 3 or 4) -> ');
   readln(choice);
   writeln;
   IF (choice = 1) OR (choice = 3) THEN
      BEGIN
         write('Please enter the key (one character) -> ');
         readln(key);
         writeln
      END
END;    (* menu *)

BEGIN    (* main action statements *)
   assign(code,'code.dat');
   choice := 1;

   WHILE choice <> 4 DO
      BEGIN
         menu(choice,key);
         CASE choice OF
```

(Program continues on next page)

```
                1 : BEGIN    (* enter text, encode and store *)
                      rewrite(code);
                      writeln('Enter text:');
                      writeln;
                      WHILE NOT eof DO
                          BEGIN
                              WHILE NOT eoln DO
                                  BEGIN
                                      read(x);
                                      y := ord(x) + ord(key);
                                      IF y > 127 THEN y := y - 127;
                                      z := chr(y);
                                      write(code,z)
                                  END;
                              readln;
                              writeln(code)
                          END;  (* NOT eof *)
                      reset(input)   (* eof = false *)
                  END;

            2,3 : BEGIN    (* retrieve encoded text, decode and display *)
                      reset(code);
                      WHILE NOT eof(code) DO
                          BEGIN
                              WHILE NOT eoln(code) DO
                                  BEGIN
                                      read(code,z);
                                      IF choice = 2
                                          THEN x := z
                                          ELSE BEGIN
                                                  y := ord(z) - ord(key);
                                                  IF y < 0 THEN y := y + 127;
                                                  x := chr(y)
                                              END;
                                      write(x)
                                  END;   (* NOT eoln *)
                              readln(code);
                              writeln
                          END   (* NOT eof *)
                  END;

              4 : ;

          END   (* CASE *)
      END;   (* WHILE choice <> 4 *)

  writeln;
  writeln('Goodbye, Have a Nice Day!');
  close(code)
END.
```

The main block consists essentially of a CASE structure with four different selections. The first selection, corresponding to choice = 1, provides the instructions for entering multiple lines of data, and encoding and storing each line on a character-by-character basis. Notice that the encoded characters are written to text file code (recognized externally as `code.dat`). After the data entry has been completed, the text file `input` is reset so that the `eof` condition is once again false.

If `choice` has a value of 2 or 3, then the text file `code` is reset and the encoded text is read from it on a character-by-character basis. If choice = 2, the encoded text is written directly to the output device. Otherwise (if choice = 3), the characters are decoded as they are read and then written to the output device.

When the program is executed, the following menu is generated:

```
E N C O D I N G / D E C O D I N G   T E X T

Program Features:

  1 - Enter text, encode and store

  2 - Retrieve encoded text and display

  3 - Retrieve encoded text, decode and display

  4 - End computation

Please enter your selection (1, 2, 3 or 4) ->
```

If a value of 1 or 3 is entered for the selection, then the following prompt will be generated for the key:

```
Please enter the key (one character) ->
```

Now suppose the user elects to enter several lines of text. The user would first enter a value of 1 for the selection. Suppose the user then enters the character C for the key, followed by the text

```
All digital computers, regardless of their size, are
basically electronic devices that can transmit, store and
manipulate information (i.e., data).
<ctrl-Z>
```

(The characters `<ctrl-Z>` at the end of the text represent the end-of-file marker.) This information will be encoded, one character at a time, and then stored in text file `code.` Following this, the main menu will reappear.

If the user now selects the second choice, the following encoded data will be read from text file `code` and displayed.

```
♣00c(-+-8%0c'31498)67oc6)+%6(0)77c3*c8,)-6c7->)oc%6)
&%7-'%00=c)0)'8632-'c():-')7c8,%8c'%2c86%271-8oc7836)c%2(
1%2-490%8)c-2*361%8-32ck-q)qoc(%8%1q
```

This, of course, is the encoded version of the text entered above.

Now suppose the user selects the third choice. A prompt for the key will again appear. The user must respond by entering a C, the same key that was used to encode the text. Once the key has been entered, the encoded data will again be read from text file code, decoded on a character-by-character basis, and then displayed as follows.

```
All digital computers, regardless of their size, are
basically electronic devices that can transmit, store and
manipulate information (i.e., data).
```

Thus, the original text is again reconstructed.

If the incorrect key is entered in response to the prompt, the text will be decoded incorrectly and garbled text will appear. Suppose, for example, that the user entered the character B instead of C as the key. Then the following garbled text would appear in place of the correctly decoded text.

```
Bmm!ejhjubm!dpnqvufst-!sfhbsemftt!pg!uifjs!tj{f-!bsf
cbtjdbmmz!fmfduspojd!efwjdft!uibu!dbo!usbotnju-!tupsf!boe
nbojqvmbuf!jogpsnbujpo!)j/f/-!ebub*/
```

Finally, suppose the user elects to end the computation by choosing the last selection on the menu. Then the message

    `Goodbye, Have a Nice Day!`

will appear and the computation will end.

11.7 PRINTING OUTPUT DATA

In most contemporary computing environments the standard output device is a TV monitor or some other type of display device. However, some applications require "hard copy" (printed) output. One way to accomplish this is to direct the desired output to a text file and then print the contents of the text file after the program execution has been completed. A more straightforward procedure, however, is to print the desired output directly while the program is executing. To do so, the printer is considered to be an external file identifier for a text file. Any output that is directed to this file is then printed as it is being written, under program control. The procedure is illustrated in the following example.

EXAMPLE 11.21 Printing Output Data

In this example we present a Turbo Pascal program that will read, display and print customer records from a file such as that created in Example 11.16.

```
PROGRAM printfile;

(* READ, DISPLAY AND PRINT A DATA FILE *)

TYPE date = RECORD
                month : 1..12;
                day : 1..31;
                year : 1900..2100
            END;
     account = RECORD
                   name : string;
                   custno : 1..9999;
                   oldbalance : real;
                   newbalance : real;
                   payment : real;
                   paydate : date
               END;
     datafile = FILE OF account;

VAR oldfile : datafile;
    newfile : text;
    newaccount : account;
    count : 1..9999;
    filename : string;

BEGIN   (* main action block *)
    writeln('CUSTOMER BILLING FILE');
    writeln;
    write('FILE NAME: ',filename);
    readln(filename);
    writeln;
```

```
        assign(oldfile,filename);
        assign(newfile,'prn');              (* 'prn' is the printer *)
        reset(oldfile);
        rewrite(newfile);
        count := 1;

    WITH newaccount DO
        BEGIN
            WHILE NOT eof(oldfile) DO
                BEGIN
                    read(oldfile,newaccount);

                    (* display the record on the monitor *)

                    writeln('Customer Number: ',count:4);
                    writeln('Name: ',name);
                    writeln('Account Number: ',custno:4);
                    writeln('Old Balance: ',oldbalance:7:2);
                    writeln('Current Payment: ',payment:7:2);
                    writeln('New Balance: ',newbalance:7:2);
                    write('Payment Date: ');
                    WITH paydate DO
                        writeln(month:2,day:3,year:5);
                    writeln;
                    write('Press any key to continue');
                    readln;
                    writeln;

                    (* print the record *)

                    writeln(newfile,'Customer Number: ',count:4);
                    writeln(newfile,'Name: ',name);
                    writeln(newfile,'Account Number: ',custno:4);
                    writeln(newfile,'Old Balance: ',oldbalance:7:2);
                    writeln(newfile,'Current Payment: ',payment:7:2);
                    writeln(newfile,'New Balance: ',newbalance:7:2);
                    write(newfile,'Payment Date: ');
                    WITH paydate DO
                        writeln(newfile,month:2,day:3,year:5);
                    writeln(newfile);

                    count := count + 1
                END
        END;

    close(oldfile);
    close(newfile)
END.
```

This program includes a number of interesting features. Notice, for example, that oldfile is not associated with any particular external file. Rather, the external file identifier is entered from the keyboard and assigned to the string variable filename when the program is executed. This string variable is then associated with oldfile in the usual manner, via an assign statement.

Notice also that newfile is associated with the external file identifier prn. Within this operating system, prn is understood to represent a printer. Thus, newfile is associated with a printer rather than an actual data file, and any data that is directed to newfile will actually be printed on the printer. Finally, note that newfile is a text file, though oldfile is a file of type account.

Now suppose we execute this program to display the file new.dat, which was created during file update in Example 11.16. The on-screen dialog would appear as shown below. (The user's responses are underlined.)

```
CUSTOMER BILLING FILE

FILE NAME: new.dat

Customer Number:    1
Name: Richard L. Warren
Account Number: 4208
Old Balance:  247.88
Current Payment:  25.00
New Balance:  222.88
Payment Date:  6 14 1993

Press any key to continue_

Customer Number:    2
Name: Janet Davis
Account Number: 2219
Old Balance:  135.00
Current Payment: 135.00
New Balance:    0.00
Payment Date:  8 10 1993

Press any key to continue_

Customer Number:    3
Name: Mort Singer
Account Number: 8452
Old Balance:  387.42
Current Payment:  35.00
New Balance:  352.42
Payment Date:  7  4 1993

Press any key to continue_

Customer Number:    4
Name: Phyllis Smith
Account Number:  711
Old Balance:  260.00
Current Payment:   0.00
New Balance:  260.00
Payment Date:  1  1 1900

Press any key to continue_
```

The printed "hard copy" is shown below.

```
Customer Number:      1
Name: Richard L. Warren
Account Number: 4208
Old Balance:  247.88
Current Payment:   25.00
New Balance:  222.88
Payment Date:  6 14 1993

Customer Number:      2
Name: Janet Davis
Account Number: 2219
Old Balance:  135.00
Current Payment:  135.00
New Balance:     0.00
Payment Date:  8 10 1993

Customer Number:      3
Name: Mort Singer
Account Number: 8452
Old Balance:  387.42
Current Payment:   35.00
New Balance:  352.42
Payment Date:  7  4 1993


Customer Number:      4
Name: Phyllis Smith
Account Number:  711
Old Balance:  260.00
Current Payment:    0.00
New Balance:  260.00
Payment Date:  1  1 1900
```

Review Questions

11.1   What are the principal characteristics of a file? How does a file differ from other structured data types?

11.2   What is the difference between a permanent file and a temporary file? What are permanent files referred to in Pascal?

11.3   What is the difference between an external file and an internal file?

11.4   What is the difference between an sequential file and a random file? What are the advantages and disadvantages of each?

11.5   What is another name for a random access file? Which name is more descriptive? Explain.

11.6   What kinds of files are supported by ANSI Pascal? What additional files are supported by Turbo Pascal?

11.7   Summarize the rules for defining a sequential file type.

11.8   Summarize the rules for defining a file-type variable. Compare with your answer to the previous question.

11.9   What data types can be associated with individual file components?

11.10   What restrictions apply to the maximum permissible length of a file? Do these restrictions also apply to other structured data types?

11.11   How are external files passed to or from an ANSI Pascal program? Syntactically, how is this accomplished?

11.12   How are external files passed to or from a Turbo Pascal program? Compare with your answer to the previous question.

11.13   What is the first step when creating a new file in ANSI Pascal? How is this accomplished?

11.14   What is the first step when creating a new file in Turbo Pascal? How is this accomplished? Compare with your answer to the previous question.

11.15   In Turbo Pascal, what should be done once all information has been read from or written to a file?

11.16   What is the effect of the `rewrite` statement on a new file? What is its effect on an existing file?

11.17   What is the purpose of the `write` statement?

11.18   What kinds of output items can be included in a `write` statement? Can multiple output items be included in a single `write` statement?

11.19   Suppose a file consisting of structured components is being created. How can the individual data items for each component be entered into the computer and written to the file? Must all of these data items be of the same type?

11.20   How can a structured file component be passed as a parameter between a procedure and the main action block?

11.21   In ANSI Pascal, how can an existing file be prepared for reading? What additional step is required in Turbo Pascal?

11.22   What is the effect of the `reset` statement?

11.23   When a file is being read, how can the end of the file be detected?

11.24   What is the purpose of the `read` statement?

11.25   What kinds of input items can be included in a `read` statement? Can multiple variables be included in a single `read` statement?

11.26   Can a single Pascal program read information from a file and then append new information to that same file?

11.27   Summarize the steps that are generally taken when updating an existing file.

11.28   Can a file be transferred to a procedure or a function as a value parameter? Explain.

11.29   What is a text file? How do text files differ from other types of files?

11.30   How are the characters on a single line of a text file interpreted?

11.31 How is a text file defined?

11.32 Can the standard file-oriented procedures such as `reset, rewrite, eof,` etc. be utilized with a text file?

11.33 What is the purpose of the special Turbo Pascal `append` procedure?

11.34 What is the purpose of the `readln` statement when reading a text file? How does this statement differ from the `read` statement? Can the `readln` statement be used with all types of files?

11.35 Suppose that a `read` or a `readln` statement contains a variable that is of type integer or real. How will the corresponding characters in the text file be interpreted?

11.36 What is the purpose of the standard function `eoln`? Compare with the standard function `eof`.

11.37 What is the purpose of the `writeln` statement when writing to a text file? How does this statement differ from the `write` statement? Can the `writeln` statement be used with all types of files?

11.38 Suppose that a `write` or a `writeln` statement contains a variable or an expression that is of some simple type other than char. How will the corresponding characters in the text file be interpreted?

11.39 Outline the manner in which the contents of a text file can be transferred to another text file, preserving the line-by-line organization of the original file.

11.40 How do the predeclared text files `input` and `output` differ from other text files?

11.41 Describe the simplifications that are permissible when one of the predeclared text files is used with the standard file-oriented procedures and functions, such as `read`, `write`, `eof` and `eoln`.

11.42 Is the `reset` statement required when preparing to read an `input` file? Is `rewrite` required with an `output` file?

Problems

11.43 Write a file definition for each of the situations shown below.

  (*a*) Define a variable called `data`, which refers to a file consisting of integer-type components.

  (*b*) Define two variables called `sales` and `costs`, which refer to files consisting of real-type components.

  (*c*) Define a data type called `acctno`, which refers to the integers 1 through 9999. Then define a file-type variable called `accounts` whose components are integers of type `acctno`.

  (*d*) Define a data type called `color`, which refers to the enumerated data items `red`, `green` and `blue`, and a data type called `sample`, which refers to a record having the following three fields:
   (*i*)   `first`, an enumerated data item of type color.
   (*ii*) `second`, a subrange data item consisting of the integers 1 through 132.
   (*iii*) `third`, a char-type data item.
   Then define a file-type variable called `data` whose components are records of type `sample`.

(e) Define the data types color and sample, as in the preceding problem. In addition, define a data type called list, which refers to a 100-element array whose elements are records of type sample. Then define a file-type variable called data whose components are arrays of type list.

(f) Define two text files called oldstuff and newstuff.

11.44 Determine the purpose of each of the following ANSI Pascal programs.

(a)
```pascal
PROGRAM sample(input,data);
TYPE line = PACKED ARRAY [1..80] OF char;
     personal = RECORD
                    name : line;
                    address : line;
                    phone : line
                END;
VAR data : FILE OF personal;
    nameandaddress : personal;

PROCEDURE readline(VAR info : line);
VAR count : 1..80;
BEGIN
   FOR count := 1 TO 80 DO read(info[count]);
   readln
END;

BEGIN
   rewrite(data);
   WITH nameandaddress DO
      BEGIN
         readline(name);
         WHILE (name[1] <> 'e') AND (name[2] <> 'n')
                           AND (name[3] <> 'd') DO
            BEGIN
               readline(address);
               readline(phone);
               write(data,nameandaddress);
               readline(name)
            END
      END
END.
```

[See also Prob 11.44(e)]

(b)
```pascal
PROGRAM sample(output,data);
TYPE line = PACKED ARRAY [1..80] OF char;
     personal = RECORD
                    name : line;
                    address : line;
                    phone : line
                END;
VAR data : FILE OF personal;
    nameandaddress : personal;
```

```
          BEGIN
              reset(data);
              WITH nameandaddress DO
                  WHILE NOT eof(data) DO
                      BEGIN
                          read(data,nameandaddress);
                          writeln(name);
                          writeln(address);
                          writeln(phone);
                          writeln
                      END
          END.


  (c)  PROGRAM sample(data1,data2);
       TYPE line = PACKED ARRAY [1..80] OF char;
            personal = RECORD
                              name : line;
                              address : line;
                              phone : line
                       END;
       VAR data1,data2 : FILE OF personal;
           nameandaddress : personal;

       BEGIN
          reset(data1);
          rewrite(data2);
          WHILE NOT eof(data1) DO
              BEGIN
                  read(data1,nameandaddress);
                  write(data2,nameandaddress)
              END
       END.


  (d)  PROGRAM sample(input,data);
       TYPE line = PACKED ARRAY [1..80] OF char;
            personal = RECORD
                              name : line;
                              address : line;
                              phone : line
                       END;
       VAR count : 1..80;
           newname : line;
           data : FILE OF personal;
           nameandaddress : personal;

       BEGIN
          reset(data);
          FOR count := 1 TO 80 DO read(newname[count]);
              REPEAT
                  read(data,nameandaddress)
              UNTIL nameandaddress.name = newname
       END.
```

(e)
```
    PROGRAM sample(input,data);
      TYPE line = PACKED ARRAY [1..80] OF char;
      VAR name,address,phone : line;
          data : text;

      PROCEDURE readline(VAR info : line);
      VAR count : 1..80;
      BEGIN
         FOR count := 1 TO 80 DO read(info[count]);
         readln
      END;

      BEGIN
         rewrite(data);
         readline(name);
         WHILE (name[1] <> 'e') AND (name[2] <> 'n') AND (name[3] <> 'd') DO
            BEGIN
               readline(address);
               readline(phone);
               write(data,name,address);
               writeln(data,phone);
               readline(name)
            END
      END.
```

[See also Prob. 11.44(a)]

11.45 Convert each of the following ANSI Pascal programs to Turbo Pascal.

(a)   The program given in Prob. 11.44(a).

(b)   The program given in Prob. 11.44(b).

(c)   The program given in Prob. 11.44(e).

Programming Problems

11.46 Write a complete Pascal program that will generate the old data file shown in Example 11.16. Run the program, creating a data file for use in the next problem.

11.47 Modify the customer billing program given in Example 11.16 by adding the following features.

(a)   Specify each record to be updated by entering the customer number from the keyboard, rather than attempting to update all records for which there is a current outstanding balance. (See the program outline shown in Example 11.15.)

(b)   Include a provision for increasing the outstanding balance (i.e., adding new charges) during the current billing period. Again, determine which records will be updated in this manner by entering the appropriate customer numbers from the keyboard.

Use the program to process the data file created in the last program, together with the following new charges.

Customer	New Charge
Janet Davis	$245.00
Mort Singer	88.50

11.48 Modify the encoding and decoding program given in Example 11.20 so that a multi-digit key can be entered, with successive digits being used for each successive line. For example, if a 3-digit key is entered, use the first digit to encode/decode the first line of text, the second digit for the second line, and the third digit for the third line. If there are more lines of text than there are digits in the key, then apply the given digits repeatedly; i.e., use the first digit for the fourth line, the second digit for the fifth line, etc.

Test the program using several lines of text of your choice.

11.49 Modify the craps game simulator given in Example 7.18 so that it simulates a specified number of games and saves the outcome of each game in a text file. At the end of the simulation, read the text file to determine the percentage of wins and losses that the player has experienced.

Test the program by simulating 100 consecutive games. Use the results to estimate the odds of winning in craps.

11.50 Modify the pig Latin generator presented in Example 9.28 so that multiple lines of text can be entered from the keyboard. Save the entire English text in a text file, and save the corresponding pig Latin in another text file.

Include within the program a provision for generating a menu that will allow the user to select any one of the following features.

(a) Enter new text, convert to pig Latin and save. (Save both the original text and the pig Latin, as described above.)

(b) Read previously entered text from a text file and display.

(c) Read the pig Latin equivalent of previously entered text and display.

(d) End the computation.

Test the program using several arbitrary lines of text.

11.51 Modify the inventory control system described in Example 10.28 so that it utilizes a data file containing the individual records. Include provisions for carrying out any of the following operations.

(a) Add a new record.

(b) Modify an existing record (including changes in descriptive information as well as inventory adjustments).

(c) Delete a record.

(d) Generate a complete list of all items presently in stock.

(e) End the computation.

Allow the individual operations to be selected from a menu. Test the program using the sample data given in Example 10.28.

11.52 Write a complete Pascal program that will generate a data file containing the student exam data presented in Prob. 9.54. Let each file component be a record containing the name and exam scores for a single student. Run the program, creating a data file for use in the next problem.

11.53 Write a file-oriented Pascal program that will process the student exam scores given in Prob. 9.54. Read the data from the data file created in the previous problem. Then create a report containing the name, exam scores and average grade for each student.

11.54 Extend the program written for Prob. 11.53 so that an overall class average is determined, followed by the deviation of each student's average from the class average. Write the output onto a new data file. Then display the output in the form of a printed "hard copy" report. Be sure that the report is logically organized and clearly labeled.

11.55 Write an interactive, file-oriented program that will maintain a list of names, addresses and telephone numbers in alphabetical order (by last name). Place the information associated with each name in a separate file. Include a menu that will allow the user to select any of the following features.

    (*a*)   Add a new record.

    (*b*)   Delete a record.

    (*c*)   Modify an existing record.

    (*d*)   Retrieve and display an entire record that corresponds to a given name.

    (*e*)   Generate a complete list of all names, addresses and telephone numbers.

    (*f*)   End computation.

Be sure to rearrange the records whenever a new record is added or an existing record is deleted, so that the records are always maintained in alphabetical order.

11.56 Write a program that will generate a data file containing the list of countries and their corresponding capitals given in Prob. 9.59. Place the name of each country and its corresponding capital in a separate record. Run the program, creating a data file for use in the next problem.

11.57 Write an interactive, menu-driven program that will access the data file generated in the preceding problem and then allow one of the following operations to be carried out.

    (*a*)   Determine the capital of a specified country.

    (*b*)   Determine the country whose capital is specified.

    (*c*)   End the computation.

11.58 Extend the program written for Prob. 11.57 to include the following additional features.

    (*a*)   Add a new record.

    (*b*)   Delete a record. Be sure that the list of countries is maintained in alphabetical order whenever a record is added or deleted.

11.59 Write a complete Pascal program that can be used as a simple line-oriented text editor. This program must have the following capabilities:

    (*a*)   Enter several lines of text and store in a text file.

    (*b*)   List the text file.

    (*c*)   Retrieve and display a particular line, determined by line number.

    (*d*)   Insert n lines.

    (*e*)   Delete n lines.

    (*f*)   Save the newly edited text and end the computation.

       Each of these tasks should be carried out in response to a one-letter command, preceded by a dollar sign. The *retrieve* command should be followed by an unsigned integer to indicate which line should be retrieved. Also, the *insert* and *delete* commands can be followed by an optional unsigned integer if several consecutive lines are to be inserted or deleted.

       Each command should appear on a line by itself, thus providing a means of distinguishing commands from lines of text. (Note that a command line will begin with a dollar sign, followed by a single-letter command, an optional unsigned integer, and an end-of-line designation.)

       The following commands are recommended.

           $E – Enter new text.

           $L – List the entire text.

           $F*k* – Find (retrieve) line number *k*.

In – Insert n lines after line number k.

Dn – Delete n lines after line number k.

S – Save the edited text and end computation.

11.60 Extend the sports-team program described in Prob. 10.41 so that the team information is maintained in a data file rather than an array. Each file component should be a record containing the data for one team. Include provisions for

(*a*)   Entering new records (adding new teams).

(*b*)   Updating existing records.

(*c*)   Deleting records (removing teams).

(*d*)   Generating a summary report for all of the teams in the league.

Chapter 12

Sets

In Pascal we formally define a *set* as a collection of ordered, simple data items that are all of the same type. Thus, a set may be a collection of integers or characters or enumerated data items.

In order to utilize the set concept, we must first define a set type. We can then declare set-type variables whose individual values are elements of that set type. In fact a single set-type variable can represent any number of set elements, including none. This capability offers us a simple way to determine if an entity or an event falls into one or more predefined categories.

12.1 DEFINING A SET TYPE

We begin by associating a group of ordered, simple-type data items with a data type using a TYPE definition, as we have done earlier. This data type will be known as the *base type*. We can therefore establish the base type as

```
TYPE base type = (data item 1, data item 2, . . . ,data item n)
```

or

```
TYPE base type = first data item .. last data item
```

The set type that we wish to define is then introduced in terms of the base type; i.e.,

```
set type = SET OF base type
```

Thus, the set type will refer to the same collection of data items as the base type.

Once a set type has been defined we can declare a set-type variable in the following manner.

```
VAR set name : set type
```

or, if several different set-type variables are desired,

```
VAR set name 1, set name 2, . . . ,set name n : set type
```

Each of these set-type variables can represent some subset of the elements within the base type.

EXAMPLE 12.1

Consider the following declarations.

```
TYPE sizes = (small,medium,large);
     shirtsizes = SET OF sizes;
VAR shortsleeve,longsleeve : shirtsizes;
```

In this example sizes is the base type, consisting of the enumerated data items small, medium and large. The set type is shirtsizes. Note that shirtsizes is defined in terms of the base type sizes. Finally, shortsleeve and longsleeve are set-type variables of type shirtsizes.

334

We can, if we wish, define several different set types from the same base type. However, most simple applications do not require this much complexity.

EXAMPLE 12.2

Here is a variation of the set-type definitions given in Example 12.1.

```
TYPE sizes = (small,medium,large);
     shirtsizes,dresssizes = SET OF sizes;
VAR shortsleeve,longsleeve : shirtsizes;
    shorthem,longhem : dresssizes;
```

Notice that `shirtsizes` and `dresssizes` are both set types of base type `sizes`. Also, note that `shortsleeve` and `longsleeve` are set-type variables of type `shirtsizes`, and that `shorthem` and `longhem` are set-type variables of type `dresssizes`.

We can also define a set type in terms of a standard, ordered simple type (e.g., integer or char), or a subrange of a standard, ordered simple type. In such situations the standard data type, or its subrange, becomes the base type.

EXAMPLE 12.3

Each of the following set types is defined in terms of a standard, ordered simple type or a corresponding subrange.

```
TYPE numbers = SET OF integer;

TYPE digits = SET OF 0..9;

TYPE numchars = SET OF '0'..'9';

TYPE lowercase = SET OF 'a'..'b';
```

Notice that the second set type defines sets of integers, whereas the third defines sets of characters.

12.2 CONSTRUCTING A SET

Now let us turn out attention to the construction of individual sets. Such sets can then be assigned to corresponding set-type variables. They can also be used as operands in certain kinds of boolean expressions (more about this later).

A set can consist of any number of elements from the associated base set. The set is constructed by writing the individual elements consecutively, enclosed in square brackets and separated by commas. Thus, an individual set will appear as

```
[set element 1, set element 2, . . . , set element n]
```

The included elements are known as the *members* of the set.

A set can consist of only one element, and it is also possible to construct a set that does not contain any elements. This is known as an *empty* (or *null*) *set*. It is written as [ ].

EXAMPLE 12.4

Shown below are several sets that can be constructed from the base type `sizes`, defined in Example 12.1.

```
[small,medium,large]

[medium,large]

[large,small]

[medium]

[]
```

The set members need not be ordered, as illustrated by the third set. Also, notice that the last set is empty.

Some of the set members can be represented by variables, provided these variables represent elements of the proper base type. Moreover, if some of the set members are consecutive set elements, they may be represented as a subrange; i.e., as

first consecutive element .. last consecutive element

EXAMPLE 12.5

Here are some additional sets that are constructed from the base type `sizes` and several corresponding variables.

```
TYPE sizes = (small,medium,large);
     shirtsizes = SET OF sizes;
VAR shirt,blouse : sizes;

[small..large]

[shirt]

[shirt,blouse]

[medium,large,blouse]
```

Note that the variables used in this example are simple-type variables. They are *not* set-type variables, as described in the last section.

A set element may not be included in a set more than once. It is possible, however, that a single element will indirectly (and perhaps unintentionally) be specified two or more times, particularly if the set specification includes both explicit set elements and variables. (A variable may represent a set element that has already been specified, thus resulting in unwanted duplication.) In such situations the repeated specification will be ignored.

EXAMPLE 12.6

Consider the set presented in the last example; i.e.,

```
[medium,large,blouse]
```

Recall that `medium` and `large` are elements of the base type `sizes`, but `blouse` is a *variable* of type `sizes`. If either `medium` or `large` is assigned to `blouse`, then that element will be repeated within the set. The set will therefore be interpreted as having only two members: `medium` and `large`. If `blouse` represents `small`, however, then the set will have three members: `small`, `medium` and `large`.

Similar problems can arise if some of the set elements are expressed as a subrange. If the first element and the last element in the subrange are the same, then the subrange will be interpreted as a single element. Moreover, if the first element and the last element are different but in the wrong order (i.e., if the first element comes after the last element), then the set will be considered to be empty.

EXAMPLE 12.7

Now consider the set

```
[shirt .. blouse]
```

where `shirt` and `blouse` are variables of type `sizes`, as declared in Example 12.5. If `shirt` and `blouse` represent the same base-type element (e.g., `medium`), then the set will contain only one member, the element `medium`. Furthermore, if `shirt` represents an element that comes *after* `blouse` in the base type (e.g., if `shirt` represents `large` and `blouse` represents `small`), then the set will be considered empty.

Once a set has been constructed, it can be assigned to a set-type variable. This is accomplished in the usual manner, by writing

```
variable name := [set element 1, set element 2, . . . , set element n]
```

It should be understood that the set appearing on the right-hand side is regarded as a single-valued data item. This data item must be of the same set type as the variable to which it is assigned.

EXAMPLE 12.8

The following skeletal outline illustrates set assignment within a Pascal program.

```
PROGRAM sample;
TYPE sizes = (small,medium,large);
     shirtsizes = SET OF sizes;
VAR shortsleeve,longsleeve : shirtsizes;

BEGIN
   . . . . .
   shortsleeve := [small,large];
   . . . . .
   longsleeve := [small,medium,large];
   . . . . .
END.
```

12.3 OPERATIONS WITH SETS

There are three different operations that can be carried out with sets, each of which results in the creation of a new set. We refer to the resultants of these operations (i.e., the newly created sets) as the *union*, the *intersection*, and the *set difference* of the original two sets, respectively.

Each set operation requires two operands (i.e., two sets) of the same type. The resultant will then be of the same type as the operands.

The union of two sets is a new set that contains all of the members of the original two sets. The + operator is used to indicate this operation, as illustrated below.

EXAMPLE 12.9

This example illustrates the union of two sets.

```
PROGRAM sample1;
TYPE sizes = (small,medium,large);
     shirtsizes = SET OF sizes;
VAR shortsleeve,longsleeve : shirtsizes;

BEGIN
   . . . . .
   shortsleeve := [small] + [large];
   . . . . .
   longsleeve := [small,medium] + [small,large];
   . . . . .
END.
```

The first assignment statement causes the union of the two sets [small] and [large] to be assigned to the set-type variable shortsleeve. Therefore shortsleeve will represent the set

   [small,large]

Similarly, the second assignment statement causes the set-type variable longsleeve to represent the set

   [small,medium,large]

The intersection of two sets is a set whose members are common to both of the original sets. We use the operator * to denote this operation.

EXAMPLE 12.10

The intersection of two sets is illustrated below.

```
PROGRAM sample2;
TYPE sizes = (small,medium,large);
     shirtsizes = SET OF sizes;
VAR shortsleeve,longsleeve : shirtsizes;

BEGIN
   . . . . .
   shortsleeve := [small,medium] * [medium,large];
   . . . . .
   longsleeve := [small] * [medium,large];
   . . . . .
END.
```

The first assignment statement causes the intersection of the two sets [small,medium] and [medium,large] to be assigned to the set-type variable shortsleeve. Therefore, shortsleeve will represent the set

   [medium]

The second assignment statement causes the set-type variable longsleeve to represent the empty set [], since the two operands do not contain any common members.

The set difference of two sets is a set whose members are in the first set but not in the second. This operation is denoted by the operator − , as seen below.

EXAMPLE 12.11

This example illustrates the operation of set difference.

```
PROGRAM sample3;
TYPE sizes = (small,medium,large);
     shirtsizes = SET OF sizes;
VAR shortsleeve,longsleeve : shirtsizes;

BEGIN
   . . . . .
   shortsleeve := [small,medium] − [small,large];
   . . . . .
   longsleeve := [small,medium,large] − [medium];
   . . . . .
END.
```

The first assignment statement causes the difference of the two sets [small,medium] and [small,large] to be assigned to the set-type variable shortsleeve. Therefore, shortsleeve will represent the set

[medium]

The second assignment statement causes the set

[small,large]

to be assigned to the set-type variable longsleeve.

These set operations are often combined with set assignment statements to modify the values of set-type variables. This is particularly true of the union and set difference operations.

EXAMPLE 12.12

Shown below are several set assignment statements that involve the use of set operations. The variables shortsleeve and longsleeve are assumed to be set-type variables, as defined in the previous examples.

```
shortsleeve := shortsleeve + [medium];

longsleeve := longsleeve − [small];

shortsleeve := longsleeve + [large];

shortsleeve := longsleeve * [small,medium];
```

The first statement causes the element medium to be added to the set represented by the set variable shortsleeve. (If medium is already a member of the set, then this statement will have no effect on the set.)

The purpose of the second statement is to remove the element small from the set represented by the variable longsleeve (unless small is not originally present, in which case the statement has no effect).

In the third statement, large is added to the set represented by longsleeve, and the new set is assigned to the variable shortsleeve. Note that longsleeve is unchanged.

Finally, the last statement causes the common members of the set represented by longsleeve and the set [small,medium] to be assigned to the variable shortsleeve.

12.4 SET COMPARISONS

Four of the six relational operators can be used with sets to form boolean-type expressions. These four operators, and their interpretation when used with sets, are summarized below.

Operator	Interpretation	
=	Set equality	(both operands contain the same members, in any order)
<>	Set inequality	(the operands do not contain exactly the same members)
<=	Set inclusion	(each member of the first set is included within the second set)
>=	Set inclusion	(each member of the second set is included within the first set)

When utilizing any of these operators, both operands must be of the same type.

EXAMPLE 12.13

Several boolean expressions involving sets are shown below. In each expression, assume that the set members are elements of the enumerated data type

```
sizes = (small,medium,large)
```

which was first introduced in Example 12.1.

Expression	Value
[small,large] = [small,medium,large]	false
[small,large] = [large,small]	true
[small,medium,large] = [small..large]	true
[small,medium] <> [medium]	true
[small] <= [small..large]	true
[small,medium] <= [small,large]	false
[small..large] <= [large]	false
[] <= [small..large]	true
[small,medium,large] >= [medium,large]	true
[medium,large] >= [medium,large]	true
[medium] >= [small,medium]	false

Note that the null set is always contained within any other set. Hence, an expression such as

```
[] <= [small,large]
```

will always be true.

The relational operators <= and >= have somewhat different interpretations with sets than with other types of operands. In particular, if S1 and S2 are both sets, it is possible that the expressions S1 <= S2 and S1 >= S2 will both be false for certain values of the operands. This cannot happen with other types of operands.

EXAMPLE 12.14

Suppose we have two sets that are mutually exclusive, such as [small] and [large]. Then the boolean expressions

        [small] <= [large]

and

        [small] >= [large]

will both be false.

When carrying out set comparisons, the elements within a set can be expressed as variables whose base type includes the set members. Moreover, a comparison may be carried out between a set and a set-type variable of the same base type.

EXAMPLE 12.15

The outline of a Turbo Pascal program is shown below.

```
PROGRAM sample4;
TYPE letters = SET OF char;
VAR used,unused : letters;
    alpha : char;
    line : string;

BEGIN
    . . . . .
    FOR alpha := 'A' TO 'z' DO
       IF [alpha] <= used THEN write(alpha);
    . . . . . .
    WHILE NOT ([line[1]] <= ['E','e']) DO
       BEGIN
          . . . . .
       END;
    . . . . .
END.
```

In the first action statement (i.e., the FOR - TO statement), the set containing the value of alpha is compared with the value of used. Note that alpha is a char-type variable, so that [alpha] is a set which contains a single, char-type element. Also, used is a set-type variable of base type char. Thus we are comparing sets whose elements are of the same base type (i.e., we are comparing sets whose elements are characters).

The FOR - TO loop considers all characters ranging from uppercase A (ASCII value 65) to lowercase z (ASCII value 122). This assures that all of the characters in the alphabet will be included in the comparison.

In the second action statement (the WHILE - DO statement), the set containing the value of line[1] is compared with the the set ['E','e']. Recall that line[1] is an element of an array of type char. Therefore [line[1]] will be a set containing a single element of type char. The set with which it is compared, ['E','e'], contains two members, also of type char. Hence we are comparing two sets whose elements are of the same base type.

This program can easily be converted to ANSI Pascal by declaring line to be a char-type packed array; i.e.,

        line : PACKED ARRAY [1..80] OF char;

The following example presents a complete Turbo Pascal program that includes the use of sets.

EXAMPLE 12.16 Analyzing a Line of Text

Suppose we want to enter a line of text into the computer and then determine which letters of the alphabet are included within that line. This can easily be accomplished through the use of sets.

Let us write a Turbo Pascal program to solve this problem. Our overall strategy will be to read in a line of text, analyze the line by determining which letters are present, and then write out all of the letters that have been found. We will consider both upper-case and lower-case letters, but not other kinds of characters (e.g., punctuation).

We begin with the following declarations:

```
TYPE letters = SET OF char;
VAR used,unused : letters;
    count,charcount : 0..80;
    alpha : char;
    line : string;
```

The set-type variables `used` and `unused` will represent the set of used and the set of unused letters, respectively. Also, `line` will represent the actual line of text.

Given these declarations, the main action block might appear as

```
BEGIN
    readinput;   (* read a line of text *)
    used := [];
    unused := ['A'..'Z','a'..'z'];
    FOR count := 1 TO charcount DO
       IF [line[count]] <= unused THEN
          BEGIN
             used := used + [line[count]];
             unused := unused - [line[count]]
          END;
    writeoutput   (* display the results of the analysis *)
END.
```

The statements `readinput` and `writeoutput` are references to procedures that read in the line of text and display the results of the analysis, respectively. Also, the integer variable `charcount` represents the number of characters entered into the computer.

Once the line of text has been entered, the set-type variables `used` and `unused` are initialized by assigning a null set to `used`, and a set containing all upper- and lowercase letters to `unused`. We then scan the line of text on a character-by-character basis. If the character being examined is an unused letter (i.e., if the set `[line[count]]` is contained within the set `unused`), then `used` and `unused` are updated by adding the current letter to `used` and removing it from `unused`. The updating is accomplished by writing

```
used := used + [line[count]];
```

```
unused := unused - [line[count]];
```

The results of the analysis are then displayed on the screen.

This strategy will work nicely for a single line of text, but if we want to analyze multiple lines of text the program will have to be restarted for each new line. Let us therefore modify the main action block so that it runs repetitively, until the word `end` is entered at the beginning of a new line. Hence, the main action block will be modified to read

```
     BEGIN
        readinput;    (* read a line of text *)
        WHILE NOT (([line[1]] <= ['E','e']) AND ([line[2]] <= ['N','n'])
                                       AND ([line[3]] <= ['D','d'])) DO
        BEGIN
           used := [];
           unused := ['A'..'Z','a'..'z'];
           FOR count := 1 TO charcount DO
              IF [line[count]] <= unused THEN
                 BEGIN
                    used := used + [line[count]];
                    unused := unused - [line[count]]
                 END;
           writeoutput;    (* display the results of the analysis *)
           readinput       (* read the next line *)
        END
     END.
```

The WHILE - DO structure allows the computation to continue until a new line of text contains an e in the first column, an n in the second column and a d in the third column. Notice that the use of set comparisons within this structure allows a convenient way to test for both upper- and lowercase letters.

The procedure used to enter a line of text, readinput, begins by initializing line so that it contains only blank spaces. It then reads the actual text, overwriting the initial blanks. The reading will continue until an end-of-line designation has been detected. The number of characters entered will then be assigned to charcount. Here is the entire procedure.

```
     PROCEDURE readinput;
     (* read a line of text *)
     BEGIN
        FOR count := 1 TO 80 DO line[count] := ' ';
        writeln('Please enter a line of text below');
        count := 0;
        WHILE NOT eoln DO
           BEGIN
              count := count + 1;
              read(line[count])
           END;
        readln;
        charcount := count
     END;
```

To display the results of the analysis, we simply loop through all of the letters of the alphabet (upper- and lowercase), and write out those letters that are members of the set used. The entire procedure can be written as

```
     PROCEDURE writeoutput;
     (* display an analysis of a line of text *)
     BEGIN
        writeln;
        write('Letters used:');
        FOR alpha := 'A' TO 'z' DO
           IF [alpha] <= used THEN write(' ',alpha);
        writeln;
        writeln
     END;
```

Recall that `alpha` is a char-type variable. Therefore `[alpha]` and `used` both represent sets whose elements are of type `char`.

Now let us put all of the pieces together to form a complete Turbo Pascal program, as shown below.

```
PROGRAM lettersused;

(* READ A LINE OF TEXT AND DETERMINE WHICH LETTERS ARE PRESENT *)

TYPE letters = SET OF char;
VAR used,unused : letters;
    count,charcount : 0..80;
    alpha : char;
    line : string;

PROCEDURE readinput;
(* read a line of text *)
BEGIN
   FOR count := 1 TO 80 DO line[count] := ' ';
      writeln('Please enter a line of text below');
      count := 0;
      WHILE NOT eoln DO
         BEGIN
            count := count + 1;
            read(line[count])
         END;
      readln;
      charcount := count
END;

PROCEDURE writeoutput;
(* display an analysis of a line of text *)
BEGIN
   writeln;
   write('Letters used:');
   FOR alpha := 'A' TO 'z' DO
     IF [alpha] <= used THEN write(' ',alpha);
   writeln;
   writeln
END;

BEGIN   (* main action block *)
   readinput;
   WHILE NOT ((([line[1]] <= ['E','e']) AND ([line[2]] <= ['N','n'])
                                    AND ([line[3]] <= ['D','d'])) DO
      BEGIN
         used := [];
         unused := ['A'..'Z','a'..'z'];
         FOR count := 1 TO charcount DO
            IF [line[count]] <= unused THEN
               BEGIN
                  used := used + [line[count]];
                  unused := unused - [line[count]]
               END;
         writeoutput;
         readinput
      END
END.
```

Suppose the program is used to process the following line of text.

```
Pascal is a structured programming language derived from ALGOL-60
```

Execution of the program would then generate the following dialog. (The user's responses are shown underlined.)

```
Please enter a line of text below
Pascal is a structured programming language derived from ALGOL-60

Letters used: A G L O P a c d e f g i l m n o p r s t u v

Please enter a line of text below
end
```

12.5 MEMBERSHIP TESTING

Pascal also includes an additional relational operator, IN, which is used to form boolean expressions. This operator can be used only with set-type operands. It is particularly useful, since it allows us to determine whether or not a value is contained within a set (i.e., whether or not the value is a member of the set).

Formally, the IN operator must be used in the following manner to create boolean-type expressions:

```
set element IN set
```

The expression will be true if the first operand is a member of the second, and false otherwise. Both operands must correspond to the same base type. The first operand may be an individual set element, or a variable or expression representing a set element. The second operand is generally a set or a set-type variable.

EXAMPLE 12.17

Consider the following variation on the set declarations presented in Example 12.1.

```
TYPE sizes = (small,medium,large);
     shirtsizes = SET OF sizes;
VAR shortsleeve,longsleeve : shirtsizes;
    mysize : sizes
```

Several boolean expressions that illustrate the use of the IN operator are shown below.

```
medium IN [small,medium,large]

medium IN [small,large]

mysize IN [small,medium]

mysize IN shortsleeve
```

The first expression is true and the second is false. The value of the third expression, however, will depend on the value that is assigned to mysize. If mysize represents small or medium, then the expression will be true. Otherwise, it will be false.

Similarly, the value of the last expression will depend on the values that are assigned to `mysize` and to `shortsleeve`. If `mysize` represents an element that is a member of the set represented by `shortsleeve`, then the expression will be `true`; otherwise it will be `false`.

For example, suppose that `mysize` represents the value `large`. The expression will be `true` if `shortsleeve` represents any of the following sets:

```
[small,medium,large]

[small,large]

[medium,large]

[large]
```

But the expression will be `false` for all other values of `shortsleeve`.

Membership testing is frequently used in conjunction with various control structures within a Pascal program. This allows us to carry out various logical operations selectively, only if certain set-type membership conditions are satisfied.

EXAMPLE 12.18

The skeletal outline of a Turbo Pascal program is shown below.

```
PROGRAM sample5;
TYPE letters = SET OF char;
VAR vowels,consonants : letters;
    count,charcount,vowelcount,conscount : 0..80;
    line : string;

BEGIN
    vowels := ['A','E','I','O','U','a','e','i','o','u'];
    consonants := ['A'..'Z','a'..'z'] - vowels;
    . . . . .
    vowelcount := 0;
    conscount := 0;
    . . . . .
    (* count the number of characters and assign to charcount *)
    . . . . .
    FOR count := 1 TO charcount DO
       BEGIN
           IF line[count] IN vowels
              THEN vowelcount := vowelcount + 1;
           IF line[count] IN consonants
              THEN conscount := conscount + 1
       END;
    . . . . .
END.
```

The first two statements assign values to the set-type variables `vowels` and `consonants`. The two IF statements (within the FOR - TO structure) then test to see if the current value of the string element `line[count]` is a member of the sets represented by `vowels` and `consonants`.

It is instructive to compare this outline with the skeletal outline shown in Example 12.15. In the present example we are testing to see if a single data item is a member of a set. In the earlier example, however, we tested to see if one set was contained within another. Note that base-type compatibility is required in both examples.

A complete Pascal program that makes use of membership testing is presented in the next example.

EXAMPLE 12.19 Number of Vowels in a Line of Text

Let us now develop a Turbo Pascal program that will perform the following functions:

1. Enter a line of text into the computer.
2. Determine the total number of characters (including blank spaces and punctuation) within the line.
3. Determine the total number of vowels and the total number of consonants within the line.
.4. Write out the total number of characters, the number of vowels and the number of consonants.

We will write the program so that it will execute repetitively, until the word end is entered at the beginning of a new line. We will allow end to be entered in either uppercase or lowercase letters.

We begin by introducing the following declarations:

```
TYPE letters = SET OF char;
VAR vowels,consonants : letters;
    count,charcount,vowelcount,conscount : 0..80;
    line : string;
```

The set-type variables vowels and consonants will represent the sets of vowels and consonants, respectively. Both upper- and lowercase letters will be included in each set. The integer variables charcount, vowelcount and conscount will represent the total number of characters in the line of text (including blank spaces and punctuation), the number of vowels, and the number of consonants, respectively. And finally, the string variable line will represent the actual line of text.

Now let us consider the main action block. If we include a provision for repetitive program execution, the main block can be written as follows.

```
BEGIN
    vowels := ['A','E','I','O','U','a','e','i','o','u'];
    consonants := ['A'..'Z','a'..'z'] - vowels;
    readinput;
    WHILE NOT ((line[1] IN ['E','e']) AND (line[2] IN ['N','n'])
                                       AND (line[3] IN ['D','d'])) DO
        BEGIN
            vowelcount := 0;
            conscount := 0;
            FOR count := 1 TO charcount DO
                BEGIN
                    IF line[count] IN vowels
                        THEN vowelcount := vowelcount + 1;
                    IF line[count] IN consonants
                        THEN conscount := conscount + 1
                END;
            writeoutput;
            readinput
        END
END.
```

The first two statements establish the values for the set-type variables vowels and consonants, respectively. These values will be used as standards for membership testing and therefore will not change throughout the program.

Following the set assignments we see the statement readinput. This is a reference to a procedure that causes the line of text to be read into the computer and the total number of characters to be counted.

Now consider the WHILE - DO structure, which is actually the heart of the program. The structure begins by assigning an initial value of zero to the counters vowelcount and conscount. The program then examines the entire line of text on a character-by-character basis. If a given character is a vowel (more precisely, if a given character is a member of the set of characters assigned to vowels), the vowel counter (vowelcount) is incremented by 1. Similarly, if a given character is a consonant, the consonant counter (conscount) is incremented by 1.

The results of the analysis are then displayed by accessing the procedure writeoutput, and a new line of text is entered into the computer via procedure readinput. This cycle is repeated until the word end is entered at the beginning of a new line of text.

The procedure that is used to read in a new line of text and determine the total number of characters can be written as follows:

```pascal
PROCEDURE readinput;
(* read a line of text *)
BEGIN
   writeln('Please enter a line of text below');
   count := 0;
   WHILE NOT eoln DO
      BEGIN
         count := count + 1;
         read(line[count])
      END;
   readln;
   charcount := count
END;
```

This procedure is straightforward and does not require further discussion.

The output procedure, writeoutput, is equally straightforward. This procedure merely displays the final values of the three counters, charcount, vowelcount and conscount. We can therefore write this procedure as

```pascal
PROCEDURE writeoutput;
(* display an analysis of a line of text *)
BEGIN
   writeln;
   writeln('Number of characters: ',charcount:2);
   writeln('Number of vowels    : ',vowelcount:2);
   writeln('Number of consonants: ',conscount:2);
   writeln
END;
```

Here is the complete Turbo Pascal program.

```pascal
PROGRAM charactercount;

(* COUNT THE TOTAL NUMBER OF CHARACTERS, THE NUMBER OF VOWELS
   AND THE NUMBER OF CONSONANTS APPEARING IN A LINE OF TEXT *)

TYPE letters = SET OF char;
VAR vowels,consonants : letters;
```

```
            count,charcount,vowelcount,conscount : 0..80;
            line : string;
        PROCEDURE readinput;
        (* read a line of text *)
        BEGIN
            writeln('Please enter a line of text below');
            count := 0;
            WHILE NOT eoln DO
                BEGIN
                    count := count + 1;
                    read(line[count])
                END;
            readln;
            charcount := count
        END;

        PROCEDURE writeoutput;
        (* display an analysis of a line of text *)
        BEGIN
            writeln;
            writeln('Number of characters: ',charcount:2);
            writeln('Number of vowels    : ',vowelcount:2);
            writeln('Number of consonants: ',conscount:2);
            writeln
        END;

        BEGIN    (* main action block *)
            vowels := ['A','E','I','O','U','a','e','i','o','u'];
            consonants := ['A'..'Z','a'..'z'] - vowels;
            readinput;
            WHILE NOT ((line[1] IN ['E','e']) AND (line[2] IN ['N','n'])
                                            AND (line[3] IN ['D','d'])) DO
                BEGIN
                    vowelcount := 0;
                    conscount := 0;
                    FOR count := 1 TO charcount DO
                        BEGIN
                            IF line[count] IN vowels
                                THEN vowelcount := vowelcount + 1;
                            IF line[count] IN consonants
                                THEN conscount := conscount + 1
                        END;
                    writeoutput;
                    readinput
                END
        END.
```

Now consider what happens when this program is executed. Suppose, for example, that we enter the following lines of text.

```
Pascal is a structured programming language derived from ALGOL-60
end
```

Execution of the program would then result in the final dialog. (Note that the user's responses are underlined.)

```
Please enter a line of text below
Pascal is a structured programming language derived from ALGOL-60

Number of characters: 65
Number of vowels    : 20
Number of consonants: 34

Please enter a line of text below
end
```

Review Questions

12.1   What are the principal characteristics of a set? How does a set differ from an array? How does it differ from a record?

12.2   What is meant by a base type? How is a base type defined?

12.3   What is meant by a set type? How does a set type differ from a base type? How is a set type defined?

12.4   What types of data can be included within a set?

12.5   Can several different set types be defined having the same base type?

12.6   What is the purpose of a set-type variable? What kind of data item is represented by a set-type variable?

12.7   Summarize the rules for constructing a set.

12.8   What is the minimum number of elements that must be present in a set?

12.9   When constructing a set, must the individual set elements be specified in any particular order?

12.10 What restrictions apply to the use of set-type variables when constructing a set?

12.11 When constructing a set, can consecutive set elements be expressed as a subrange?

12.12 When constructing a set, what happens if the same set element is specified more than once?

12.13 Suppose a set specification consists of a single subrange, and the subrange specification is written in the wrong order. How will this be interpreted? Explain.

12.14 Summarize the rules for assigning a set to a set-type variable. What restrictions apply with regard to type compatibility?

12.15 What is meant by the union of two sets? How can this operation be carried out in Pascal? What restrictions apply to the operands?

12.16 What is meant by the intersection of two sets? How is this operation carried out in Pascal? What restrictions apply to the operands?

12.17 What is meant by the difference of two sets? How is this operation carried out in Pascal? What restrictions apply to the operands?

12.18 Which relational operators can be used with set-type operands? What are the relational operators used for? How is each interpreted?

12.19 What is meant by membership testing? How is membership testing carried out in Pascal?

12.20 What kinds of operands can be used with the relational operator IN? Compare with the use of other relational operators with set-type operands.

Problems

12.21 Write appropriate set definitions and variable declarations for each of the situations described below.

(*a*) Define `vowels` and `consonants` to be set-type variables which refer to a set of type `char`.

(*b*) Define `caps` to be a set-type variable that refers to the set of the uppercase letters `'A'` through `'Z'`.

(*c*) Define a subrange data type called `capitals` which refers to the uppercase letters `'A'` through `'Z'`. Then define a set-type variable called `caps` which is of type `capitals`.

(*d*) Define a subrange data type called `capitals` which refers to the uppercase letters `'A'` through `'Z'`. Then define a set called `uppers` which is of type `capitals`. Finally, define a variable called `caps` which is of type `uppers`.

(*e*) Define a set-type variable called `movement` which refers to the set whose members are `north`, `south`, `east` and `west`.

(*f*) Define an enumerated data type called `compass` which refers to the data items `north`, `south`, `east` and `west`. Then define a set-type variable called `movement` which refers to a set of type `compass`.

(*g*) Define an enumerated data type called `compass` which refers to the data items `north`, `south`, `east` and `west`. Then define a set-type called `direction` which refers to a set of type `compass`. Finally, define two variables called `nextmove` and `lastmove` which are of type `direction`.

12.22 Determine which elements are included in each of the sets given below, based upon the following declarations.

```
TYPE weekdays = (sun,mon,tue,wed,thu,fri,sat);
     days = SET OF weekdays;
```

(*a*) `[mon..fri]`

(*b*) `[mon..fri] + [wed]`

(*c*) `[mon..fri] - [wed]`

(*d*) `[fri..mon] + [wed]`

(*e*) `[tue] - [mon..sat]`

(*f*) `[sun..wed] * [tue..sat]`

12.23 Determine the outcome of each of the assignment statements shown below, based upon the following declarations.

```
TYPE weekdays = (sun,mon,tue,wed,thu,fri,sat);
     days = SET OF weekdays;
VAR workdays,restdays : days;
    today : weekdays;
```

   (a)   `workdays := [mon,wed..sat] + [sun];`

   (b)   `restdays := [tue,thu];`
```
. . . . .
workdays := [mon..sat] - restdays;
```

   (c)   `workdays := [];`
```
FOR today := mon TO thu DO
workdays := workdays + [today];
restdays := workdays * [thu..sat];
```

12.24 Determine the value of each boolean expression given below, based upon the following declarations.

```
TYPE weekdays = (sun,mon,tue,wed,thu,fri,sat);
days = SET OF weekdays;
VAR  workdays,restdays : days;
today : weekdays;
```

   (a)   `[sun,sat] = [sun..sat]`

   (b)   `[tues,fri] >= []`

   (c)   `[mon,wed,fri] <= [mon..fri]`

   (d)   `[fri,mon..wed] = [mon,wed,fri]`

   (e)   `workdays := [mon..fri];`
```
. . . . .
workdays <> [mon,tue,wed,thu,fri]
```

   (f)   `today := fri;`
```
restdays := [fri,sat,sun];
. . . . .
[today] <= restdays
```

   (g)   `mon IN [mon,wed,fri]`

   (h)   `sun IN [sun..sat]`

   (i)   `sat IN [mon,wed,fri]`

   (j)   `today := wed;`
```
. . . . .
today IN [mon,wed,fri]
```

   (k)   `today := sat;`
```
workdays := [mon..fri];
. . . . .
today IN workdays
```

12.25 Determine which elements are included in each of the sets given below, based upon the following declarations.

```
TYPE notes = (do,re,mi,fa,so,la,ti);
     song = SET OF notes;
```

(a)   [re..la]

(b)   [do..fa] + [re..la]

(c)   [do..fa] - [re..la]

(d)   [do..fa] * [re..la]

(e)   [do..fa] - [la..re]

(f)   [re,fa,so] - [re..la]

(g)   [re,fa,so] * []

(h)   [do,re,mi] + [re]

12.26 Determine the outcome of each of the assignment statements shown below, based upon the following declarations.

```
TYPE notes = (do,re,mi,fa,so,la,ti);
     song  = SET OF notes;
VAR ballad,disco : song;
    tone : notes;
```

(a)   ballad := [do..fa] * [re,fa];

(b)   disco := [do..fa] - [mi];

(c)   tone := ti;
       . . . . .
       ballad := [re..fa,la] + [tone];

(d)   disco := [do,mi,so];
       . . . . .
       ballad := disco + [re,ti];

(e)   disco := [];
       FOR tone := la DOWNTO re DO
       disco := disco + [tone];

12.27 Determine the value of each of the boolean expressions given below, based upon the following declarations.

```
TYPE coins = (penny,nickel,dime,quarter,half,dollar);
     change = SET OF coins;
VAR money : coins;
    wine,whiskey,song : change;
```

(a)   [penny,nickel] <= [penny,quarter]

(b)   [nickel,dime,quarter] = [nickel..quarter]

(c)   [penny..dollar] = [dollar..penny]

    (*d*)   `[nickel..quarter] >= [dime,quarter]`

    (*e*)   `[half..nickel] <> []`

    (*f*)   `dollar IN [penny..dollar]`

    (*g*)   `money := dollar;`
            `. . . . .`
            `[money] <= [penny..dollar]`

    (*h*)   `money := dollar;`
            `. . . . .`
            `money IN [penny..dollar]`

    (*i*)   `wine := [penny,nickel,dime];`
            `. . . . .`
            `dollar IN wine`

    (*j*)   `whiskey := [penny,nickel,dime];`
            `. . . . .`
            `dime IN whiskey`

    (*k*)   `wine := [penny,nickel,dime];`
            `song := [dime..dollar];`
            `. . . . .`
            `dime IN wine * song`

    (*l*)   `money := penny;`
            `song := [dime..dollar];`
            `. . . . .`
            `money IN song`

Programming Problems

12.28 Write an ANSI Pascal version of the program given in Example 12.16.

12.29 Modify the program given in Example 12.16 in the following ways:

    (*a*)   Utilize membership testing within the program (i.e., replace the boolean expressions with equivalent expressions that make use of the IN operator).

    (*b*)   Determine which nonletter characters (i.e., digits, punctuation marks, etc.) are present, in addition to which letters are present.

    (*c*)   Write out the following four lists after analyzing each line:

        1.   The letters that are included in the given line of text.

        2.   The nonletter characters that are included in the given line of text.

        3.   The letters that are <u>not</u> included within the text.

        4.   The nonletter characters that are not included.

    Test the program using several lines of input which you have chosen.

12.30 Write an ANSI Pascal version of the program given in Example 12.19.

12.31 Extend the program given in Example 12.19 to include the following features.

    (*a*)   Count the number of times each vowel appears within the line of text.

(b)   Determine the number of words within the line. (*Hint:* count the number of blank spaces within the line.)

(c)   Determine the average length of each word within the line.

Test the program using several lines of your own input.

12.32 Write an interactive Pascal program that will convert a date, entered in the form mm-dd-yy (example: 4-12-69) into an integer that indicates the number of days beyond January 1, 1960, using the method described in Prob. 6.50(*s*). Include error checks in the program, so that an incorrectly entered date will be detected and an appropriate error message generated. Utilize a set-type data structure for the error-check routine.

12.33 Rewrite the interactive tic-tac-toe program described in Prob. 7.49(*i*) so that it includes an error-checking routine for the input data. This routine should check for illegal moves and incorrect responses to the input prompts. Utilize a set-type data structure for this purpose.

12.34 Write an interactive Pascal program that makes use of the set-type data structure for each of the following gambling games:

(a)   The interactive blackjack game, described in Prob. 9.61(*a*).

(b)   The interactive roulette game, described in Prob. 9.61(*b*).

(c)   The interactive BINGO game, described in Prob. 9.61(*c*).

(Remember that the set-type data structure offers a convenient way to carry out error-checking, membership testing, and sampling without replacement.)

12.35 Rewrite the pig Latin generator described in Prob. 9.51 so that it makes use of a set-type data structure when testing for punctuation marks, upper-case letters and double-letter sounds. Is the use of a set the best way to implement each of these tests?

12.36 Prob. 9.54 describes a programming application in which the exam scores for each student in a Pascal programming course are averaged and an overall class average is determined. Now suppose that five numerical ranges are defined in such a manner that the overall class average falls in the middle of the third category. Each student could then be given a letter grade, determined by the particular range that contains the student's average score. Thus, the first (highest) range would represent A's, the second would represent B's, etc.

One way to construct the individual numerical ranges is as follows. Let CA represent the overall class average. Calculate the quotient

$$Q = (100 - CA)/3$$

Then calculate the ranges as

first range	(A):	$(CA + 2Q)$	to	100
second range	(B):	$(CA + Q)$	to	$(CA + 2Q)$
third range	(C):	$(CA - Q)$	to	$(CA + Q)$
fourth range	(D):	$(CA - 2Q)$	to	$(CA - Q)$
fifth range	(F):	below $(CA - 2Q)$		

Thus, if the overall class average were 70 percent, Q would equal $(100 - 70)/3 = 10$, and the ranges would be

A:	90 to 100	D:	50 to 60
B:	80 to 90	F:	below 50
C:	60 to 80		

Write an interactive Pascal program that will implement this strategy, assuming equal weighting of all exams. Include both record-type and set-type data structures in your program. Test the program using the data given in Prob. 9.54.

12.37 Here is an interesting technique for obtaining a list of prime numbers that fall within the interval ranging from 2 to n.

(*a*)   Generate an ordered list of integers ranging from 2 to n.

(*b*)   For some particular integer, i, within the list, carry out the following operations:

    1.   Write out the integer, thus adding it to the list of primes.

    2.   Remove all succeeding integers that are multiples of i.

(*c*)   Repeat part (*b*) for each successive value of i, beginning with $i = 2$ and ending with the last remaining integer.

This method is often referred to as the *sieve of Eratosthenes.*

Write a Pascal program that uses this method to determine the primes that are contained in a list of numbers ranging from 1 to n, where n is an input quantity. Utilize a set-type data structure within the program.

12.38 An employment agency wishes to maintain a computerized list of currently available positions. Within this list, each position will be described by the monthly salary and one or more attributes that characterize the position.

When the agency is approached by a person seeking a position, descriptive information about that person will be entered into the computer and compared with the attributes that characterize the available positions. A list will then be generated of all positions with a sufficiently high monthly salary and attributes that match those of the prospective employee.

The following attributes are used to characterize the required job skills:

Attribute	Job Skill
A	Accounting
B	Business
C	Computer science
D	Dental technology
E	Engineering/technical
F	Food service
M	Medical technology
P	Personnel administration
R	Receptionist
S	Sales
T	Typing/word processing
U	Unskilled labor

Several attributes are also required to indicate the required educational level. They are

Attribute	Educational Level
C	College
H	High school
P	Postgraduate
V	Vocational

Write a Pascal program that can accommodate the needs of the agency. Use a set-type data structure to carry out the matching.

Test the program using the following data:

Positions Available

Position Number	Monthly Salary, $	Required Job Skills	Education Level
1	$625	U	H
2	1350	A,T	C
3	900	S	C
4	2400	E,B	P
5	450	F	H
6	1100	P,T	H
7	1700	D,T,R	H
8	2000	M	V

Potential Employees

Client Number	Minimum Req'd Salary	Job Skills	Education Level
1	$800	R,T	H
2	1200	A,C,T	C
3	2000	E,B,C	P
4	400	U	H
5	800	S,P,T	C

12.39 Modify the program written for the above problem so that information describing the available positions is stored in a data file. Utilize a record-type data structure to represent each of the available positions. Include provisions for adding records, deleting records, changing records and listing all records.

12.40 A university wishes to create an automated registration procedure for its students. Each department will utilize its own desktop computer and its own database for this purpose. The database will contain a list of all courses that the student must take in order to graduate, and the corresponding prerequisites. This list of courses will be stored in a data file.

The courses should be taken in numerical order, except that students cannot register for a course unless they have taken (and passed) all of the required prerequisites. This situation becomes somewhat complicated by the fact that some students fail a course and are therefore thrown out of sequence, and some students transfer into a program of study and therefore have not taken all of the prerequisites.

Write a Pascal program that will allow each student in a given department to register for 3 new courses each term, choosing from the courses that are listed in the data file. (Assume that all of the courses listed will be offered each term.) The courses should be selected in their proper numerical sequence, except that students cannot register for courses unless they have successfully completed all of the prerequisites. Use a set-type data structure to carry out the selection.

Test your program using the following sample data (the prerequisites for each course are shown in parentheses following the course number).

Courses

101	201 (101)	301 (204)	401 (301)
102	202	302 (102,202)	402 (302)
103	203 (106)	303	403
104 (101)	204 (201)	304 (301)	404 (304)
105 (102)	205	305 (302)	405 (205)
106	206 (102,203)	306	406 (102,306)

Student Records

Name	Courses Taken
Smith	101,103
Brown	101,102,103,104,105,202
Richardson	101,102,103,104,105,106,201,203,204
Davis	101,102,104,105,201,203,204,206,301,304
Thomas	101,102,103,104,105,106,201,202,203,204, 205,206,302,303,305,306,402,405

Chapter 13

Lists and Pointers

In Chaps. 9 through 12 we were concerned with several different structured data types; namely, the array, the record, the file and the set. Though each of these data types has its own unique features, they share certain common characteristics. For example, the maximum number of components within an array, a record or a set (and hence the required amount of memory) is specified within the data declaration, and remains unchanged throughout the program. Furthermore, the individual components within a particular structured data type are arranged in a fixed order with respect to one another. (This is true of all structured data types, including files.) These characteristics tend to restrict the utility of the structured data types for certain kinds of applications.

In particular, some applications require the use of *lists*, whose components are linked together by means of *pointers*. Such lists are therefore referred to as *linked lists*. Linked lists are used, for example, in the construction of compilers, operating systems and database management systems. Therefore, we now turn out attention to the use of linked lists within Pascal.

13.1 PRELIMINARIES

The basic idea of a linked list is that each individual component within the list includes a pointer that indicates where the next component can be found. Therefore, the relative order of the components can easily be changed simply by altering the pointers. In addition, individual components can easily be added to or removed from the list, again by altering the pointers. Hence a linked list is not confined to some maximum number of components — it can expand and contract in size as its host program is executed.

EXAMPLE 13.1

Fig. 13.1(*a*) illustrates a linked list consisting of three components. Each component consists of two data items — an enumerated value (a color), and a pointer that references the next component within the list. Thus the first component has the value red, the second green and the third blue. The beginning of the list is indicated by a separate pointer, which is labeled start. Also, the end of the list is indicated by the value NIL (more about this later).

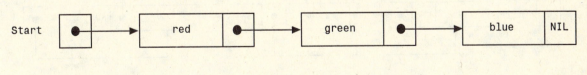

Fig. 13.1(*a*)

Now let us add another component, whose value is white, between red and green. To do so we merely change the pointers, as illustrated in Fig. 13.1(*b*).

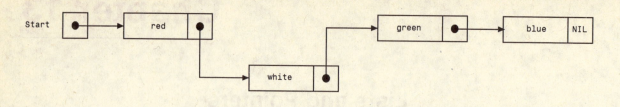

Fig. 13.1(*b***)**

If we now choose to delete the component whose value is green, we simply change the pointer associated with the second component, as shown in Fig. 13.1(*c*).

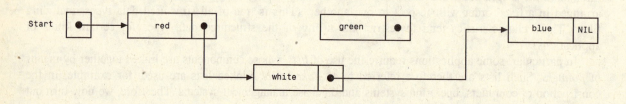

Fig. 13.1(*c***)**

There are several different kinds of linked structures, including *linear* linked lists (in which the components are all linked together in some sequential manner), linked lists with multiple pointers (permitting forward and backward traversal through the list), *circular* lists (linear lists having no beginning and no ending) and *trees* (in which the components are arranged in a hierarchical structure). We have already seen an illustration of a linear linked list in Example 13.1. Some other kinds of linked lists are shown in the next example.

EXAMPLE 13.2

In Fig. 13.2 we see a linear linked list that is similar to that shown in Fig. 13.1(*a*). Now, however, we see that there are *two* pointers associated with each component — a *forward* pointer and a *backward* pointer. This double set of pointers allows us to traverse the list in either direction; i.e., from beginning to end, or from end to beginning.

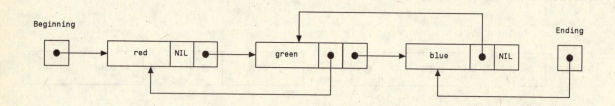

Fig. 13.2

Now consider the list shown in Fig. 13.3. This list is similar to that shown in Fig. 13.1(*a*), except that the last data item (blue) points to the first data item (red). Hence, this list has no beginning and no ending. Such lists are referred to as *circular* lists.

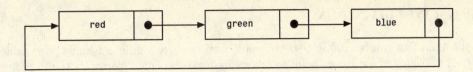

Fig. 13.3

Finally, in Fig. 13.4(*a*) we see an example of a *tree*. Trees consist of *nodes* and *branches*, arranged in some hierarchical manner that indicates a corresponding hierarchical structuring of the data. (A *binary tree* is a tree in which every node has no more than two branches.)

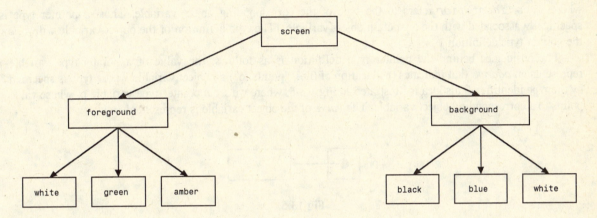

Fig. 13.4(*a*)

In Fig. 13.4(*a*) the root node has the value `screen`, and the associated branches lead to the nodes whose values are `foreground` and `background`, respectively. Similarly, the branches associated with `foreground` lead to the nodes whose values are `white`, `green` and `amber`, and the branches associated with `background` lead to the nodes whose values are `black`, `blue` and `white`.

Fig. 13.4(*b*) illustrates the manner in which pointers are used to construct the tree.

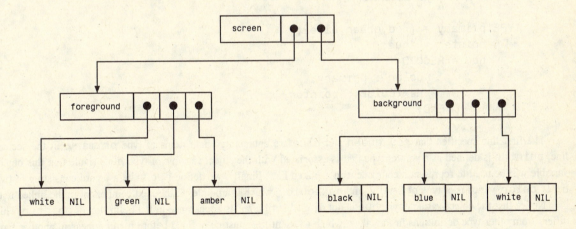

Fig. 13.4(*b*)

Pascal does not treat each linked structure as a separate data type. Rather, Pascal supports a single data type — the *pointer* — that allows various kinds of linked structures to be constructed from a common set of rules.

13.2 POINTER TYPE DEFINITIONS

In applications that involve linked lists, we must work with two different kinds of variables: *pointer variables* (i.e., variables whose values point to other variables) and *object variables* (i.e., variables that are "pointed to"). Careful attention must be given to the type definition that is associated with each kind of variable. This is particularly true of the *pointer type*, i.e., the type definition that will be used to declare pointer-type variables.

In general terms, a pointer type definition is written as

```
TYPE pointer type = ^type identifier
```

where `type identifier` refers to the type of the corresponding object variable. Thus, a pointer type is specifically associated with the type of an object variable. (The type definition of the object variable will *follow* the pointer type definition.)

The basic idea behind the pointer type definition is as follows: the value of a pointer-type variable represents an *address* that indicates the location of (i.e., "points to") an object variable whose type is specified by the type identifier. This idea is illustrated in Fig. 13.5, where we see a pointer-type variable p, whose value points to a corresponding object variable. The *value* of the object variable is represented by v.

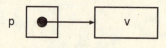

Fig 13.5

The object variable is usually defined as a record that is a component within the linked list. The last field in the record will generally be a pointer-type data item that indicates the location of the next record. Thus, the pointer provides a link between the current record and its successor.

EXAMPLE 13.3

Consider the following type definitions.

```
TYPE primary = (red,green,blue);
     pointer = ^hue;
     hue = RECORD
               color : primary;
               nextcolor : pointer
           END;
```

The first line specifies that `red`, `green` and `blue` are enumerated data items of type `primary`. In the second line, `pointer` is defined as a pointer type that is associated with the object variable of type `hue`. (Note that this object variable will be used to represent a component in a linked list.) Finally, we define `hue` to be a record consisting of two fields: `color`, which is of type `primary`, and `nextcolor`, which is a pointer to the next component in the linked list.

Notice that the object-variable type `hue` is not defined until *after* its appearance in the definition of `pointer`. This differs from other type definitions in Pascal, in which an identifier must be defined before it can appear in another type definition.

Since a pointer type can only be defined in terms of a corresponding object-variable type, we say that the pointer type is *bound* to its object-variable type.

13.3 VARIABLE DECLARATIONS

Pointer-type variables are declared in the conventional manner, i.e.,

    VAR *pointer name* : *type*

where *pointer name* refers to a pointer-type variable and *type* is a pointer type. This declaration will create a *static* (conventional) variable whose value will point to an object variable (e.g., a component within a linked list).

On the other hand, object variables are *not* declared in the conventional manner, since object variables are created and destroyed *dynamically*, i.e., as the program is being executed. Hence, object variables must be declared within those portions of the program that contain the action statements. Such declarations are carried out differently than the variable declarations that we have encountered previously.

To create a dynamic object variable, we utilize the standard procedure new, by writing

    new(*pointer name*)

This statement creates a new object variable whose type is defined in the formal type definitions. The pointer whose name appears in the new statement will automatically point to this new variable. The object variable will have the same name as the pointer variable. However, the object variable is written with a circumflex (^) after its name, so that it can be distinguished from the corresponding pointer variable.

EXAMPLE 13.4

Consider the following skeletal outline of a Pascal program.

```
PROGRAM sample;
TYPE primary = (red,green,blue);
     pointer = ^hue;
     hue = RECORD
                color : primary;
                nextcolor : pointer
           END;
VAR foreground,background : pointer;

BEGIN   (* main action block *)
   . . . . .
   new(foreground);
   . . . . .
END.
```

The type definitions are repeated from Example 13.3. Following these type definitions, the variables foreground and background are declared to be pointer-type variables. Note that foreground and background are static variables whose values can be assigned in the conventional manner.

On the other hand, the new statement within the main action block creates a dynamic object variable of type hue, which will be called foreground^. Moreover, the corresponding pointer variable foreground will automatically point to foreground^.

Note that the object variable foreground^ is a record-type variable comprised of two fields. Hence, foreground^.color will represent an enumerated value of type primary, and foreground^.nextcolor will represent a pointer that will point to the next object variable.

13.4 OPERATIONS WITH POINTER VARIABLES AND OBJECT VARIABLES

There are two kinds of operations that can be carried out with pointer variables and object variables. These are *assignment* and *comparison*. Both kinds of operations must be carried out with like operands, i.e., pointers must be assigned to or compared with other pointers, and object variables must be assigned to or compared with other object variables.

Let us first consider assignment. Suppose that p1 and p2 are both pointer variables of the same type. Then we can assign the value of p1 to p2 by writing

```
p2 := p1
```

Similarly, suppose that p1^ and p2^ are both object variables containing a pointer-type field called next. Then we can write assignment statements such as

```
p2 := p1^.next

p2^.next := p1

p2^.next := p1^.next
```

In each case, we are assigning the value of one pointer variable to another pointer variable (provided, of course, that the object variables have already been created prior to each assignment).

A pointer variable can also be made to point to nothing, by assigning the special value NIL to the variable. (Note that NIL is a reserved word in Pascal.) Hence, if we did not want p1 to point to anything, we would write

```
p1 := NIL
```

We will see uses for this feature later in this chapter.

Observe that we have now seen two different ways to assign values to pointer variables. One way is to use the traditional assignment statement, as we have done above. The other is to make use of the standard procedure new, as described in the last section. (Remember that a value is automatically assigned to a pointer variable when a corresponding object variable is created via the new statement.)

Object variables can also be assigned to one another, provided they are of the same type. Thus, we can write

```
p2^ := p1^
```

This will cause the value of each field within p1^ to be assigned to the corresponding field within p2^. Such assignments can be carried out with individual fields of object variables as well as entire object variables.

EXAMPLE 13.5

Consider the following declarations, which are repeated from the previous example.

```
TYPE primary = (red,green,blue);
     pointer = ^hue;
     hue = RECORD
               color : primary;
               nextcolor : pointer
           END;
VAR foreground,background : pointer;
```

If the object variables `foreground^` and `background^` have both been created (via the `new` statement), then all of the following will be valid pointer assignments.

```
foreground := background

background := NIL

foreground := background.nextcolor

foreground^.nextcolor := background

foreground^.nextcolor := background^.nextcolor
```

We can also assign some or all values of `foreground^` to `background^`. Thus, we can write

```
background^ := foreground^

background^.color := foreground^.color
```

And finally, we can assign an enumerated value to a field of the same type in one of the object variables. For example,

```
foreground^.color := green
```

You should clearly understand the difference between assignments involving pointers and assignments involving object variables. To illustrate this point, suppose that the pointers p1 and p2 point to their respective object variables, as illustrated in Fig. 13.6(*a*). Then the assignment

```
p2 := p1
```

will cause p2 to point to the same object as p1, as shown in Fig. 13.6(*b*). On the other hand, the assignment

```
p2^ := p1^
```

will cause the values of the two object variables, p1^ and p2^, to be identical, as illustrated in Fig. 13.6(*c*). Note that both object variables now point to the same successor.

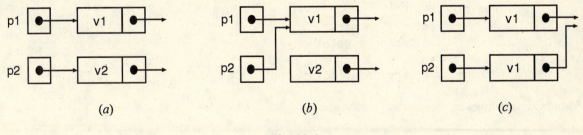

(*a*)   (*b*)   (*c*)

Fig. 13.6

Pointer variables can be compared by means of the two relational operators = and <> . This feature allows us to determine whether or not two pointer variables have the same value, or if a pointer variable has been assigned the value `NIL`.

EXAMPLE 13.6

Consider once again the declarations given in Example 13.4 and 13.5, i.e.,

```
TYPE primary = (red,green,blue);
     pointer = ^hue;
     hue = RECORD
                color : primary;
                nextcolor : pointer
            END;
VAR foreground,background : pointer;
```

Shown below are several statements that involve comparisons among the pointer variables foreground and background. (These examples are intended to illustrate syntax; they are not related.)

```
IF foreground = background THEN foreground := NIL

WHILE foreground <> background DO

REPEAT
    . . . . .
UNTIL background = foreground^.nextcolor

IF background = NIL THEN foreground^.color := red
```

Object variables can also be compared for equality provided they are of the same type. Such comparisons can involve entire variables, or individual fields. If individual fields are compared, then they must also be of the same type.

EXAMPLE 13.7

Here are some examples of comparisons among object variables or individual fields within object variables. We again make use of the declarations provided in the earlier examples, i.e.,

```
TYPE primary = (red,green,blue);
     pointer = ^hue;
     hue = RECORD
                color : primary;
                nextcolor : pointer
            END;
VAR foreground,background : pointer;
```

Some valid comparisons are shown below:

```
IF foreground^ = background^ THEN foreground := NIL

IF foreground^.color <> blue THEN foreground^.color := blue

WHILE background^.color <> foreground^.color DO
```

13.5 CREATING AND DESTROYING DYNAMIC VARIABLES

We now turn our attention to some typical programming situations that require pointer variables and their corresponding object variables. We will see that the use of pointer variables allows us to create and destroy object variables dynamically; i.e., as the program is being executed.

In order to illustrate the manner in which object variables are created and destroyed dynamically, we will work with a common type of linked list in which each component points to its predecessor. Thus, the second component points to the first, the third points to the second, and so on, as illustrated in Fig. 13.7. This scheme is called *last-in, first-out* (LIFO), since the last component to enter the list will be the first to leave.

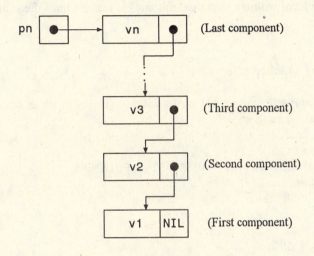

Fig. 13.7

The linked list will be created by reading in each new component and then linking that component to its predecessor. Suppose, for example, that `item` is a pointer-type variable whose corresponding object variable, `item^`, contains two fields: a string variable called `item^.name`, and a pointer called `item^.next`. The pointer will provide a link to the previously entered component, whose location will be indicated by a pointer-type variable called `pointer`.

In order to create the first component, we generate a dynamic variable called `item`, read in a value for `item^.name` and set `item^.next` to NIL. This will represent the component at the bottom of the list. The variable `pointer` is then made to point to this component, so that a predecessor can be identified when the next component is entered. Thus, the first component is created by writing

```
new(item);
readname(item^.name);
item^.next := NIL;
pointer := item;
```

where `readname` is a procedure that reads in `item^.name`. Note that `item^.name` can be entered on a character-by-character basis (ANSI Pascal) or as a single string-type data item (Turbo Pascal).

These steps are then repeated for each successive component, except that `item^.next` is made to point to its predecessor by assigning to it the current value of `pointer`. Thus,

```
new(item);
readname(item^.name);
item^.next := pointer;
pointer := item;
```

This group of statements must be placed within some type of loop (e.g., a WHILE - DO structure) so that it can be repeated for each successive component within the list.

The list can be displayed by traversing from top to bottom (last component to first). Initially, pointer will indicate the location of the last (most recent) component. Therefore we can display the entire list simply by repeating the following three statements for each component in the list.

```
item := pointer;
writeln(item^.name);
pointer := item^.next;
```

These statements must be placed within a loop that continues to execute until the value of pointer becomes NIL.

EXAMPLE 13.8 Creating a Linked List

Here is a complete Turbo Pascal program that creates and then displays a last-in first-out linked list, using the methods described in the preceding paragraphs.

```
PROGRAM makelist;
(* CREATE A LINKED LIST OF NAMES USING POINTERS *)
TYPE link = ^personal;
     personal = RECORD
                      name : string;
                      next : link
                 END;
VAR item,pointer : link;

PROCEDURE readname(VAR newname : link);
(* read a name into the computer *)
BEGIN
   write('New name: ');
   readln(newname^.name)
END;

BEGIN  (* main action block *)
   BEGIN    (* create the list *)
      new(item);
      readname(item);
      item^.next := NIL;
      pointer := item;
      WHILE NOT ((item^.name[1] IN ['E','e'])
            AND  (item^.name[2] IN ['N','n'])
            AND  (item^.name[3] IN ['D','d'])) DO
                BEGIN
                   new(item);
                   readname(item);
                   item^.next := pointer;
                   pointer := item
                END;
      pointer := item^.next
   END;   (* create list *)
```

```
        BEGIN   (* display the list *)
            writeln;
            WHILE pointer <> NIL DO
                BEGIN
                    item := pointer;
                    writeln(item^.name);
                    pointer := item^.next
                END;
        END    (* display list *)
    END.
```

This program includes a procedure called `readname`, which is used to read in a string-type data item. Note that `readname` makes use of a variable parameter called `newname`, which is of type `link`. Thus, the parameter is a pointer-type variable. The value that is returned by this procedure is a pointer to one of the items within the corresponding object variable (namely, `newname^.name`). Thus, we see that an object variable can implicitly be accessed within a procedure by transferring its associated pointer-type variable into (or out of) the procedure.

The main action block consists of two compound statements that create the linked list and display the list, respectively. The logic that is utilized within each of these statements is straightforward, in view of the discussion that preceded this example. Note, however, the WHILE - DO loop in the first compound statement. This loop causes new names to be entered repeatedly, until the word "end" is entered as a new name (in either upper or lowercase). Also, note that the parameter that is passed to `readname` is the pointer-type variable `item`.

Now suppose the program is utilized to create a linked list containing the following names:

Sharon, Gail, Susan, Marla, Marc, Amy, Megan.

The interactive dialog is shown below, followed by a listing of the newly creaged linked list. As before, the user's responses underlined.

```
New name: Sharon
New name: Gail
New name: Susan
New name: Marla
New name: Marc
New name: Amy
New name: Megan
New name: end

Megan
Amy
Marc
Marla
Susan
Gail
Sharon
```

Notice that the names are printed in reverse order, i.e., last-in first-out.

An additional component can easily be inserted into some designated location within an existing linked list. To do so we must read the new component, determine its intended location within the list, and then adjust a few pointers. For example, suppose `item` now represents the component to be added, and `pointer` indicates the component above (behind) the new component. The following two statements will allow the new component to be entered (again assumed to be `item^.name`):

```
new(item);
readname(item^.name);
```

The intended location of the new component can be determined by writing

```
readname(itemname);
pointer := last;
WHILE (pointer^.name <> itemname) AND
      (pointer^.next <> NIL) DO pointer := pointer^.next;
```

where `itemname` is a string variable that represents the new component's intended successor, and `last` is a pointer to the last component within the list.

Finally, the pointer adjustment proceeds as follows. If the new item is to be inserted at the *end* of the list, we write

```
item^.next := last;
last := item;
```

Otherwise, we write

```
item^.next := pointer^.next;
pointer^.next := item;
```

In each case, the pointer part of the new component is directed to its predecessor, and the (old) component that succeeds the newly added component is correctly readjusted.

The deletion of a component proceeds in much the same manner as an insertion. The actual deletion is carried out by means of the `dispose` statement, i.e.,

```
dispose(pointer name)
```

This statement is analogous to the `new` statement. Thus, `dispose` is a standard procedure that accepts a pointer-type variable as a parameter. Use of this procedure causes the object variable associated with the given pointer to be destroyed. Any subsequent reference to this variable (via another pointer) will then be undefined.

The overall strategy is as follows. We first locate the component to be deleted, then readjust a few pointers, and finally `dispose` of the component that is to be deleted. Thus,

```
readname(itemname);
IF last^.name = itemname
   THEN BEGIN   (* delete the last item *)
           item := last;
           last := item^.next;
           dispose(item)
        END
   ELSE BEGIN   (* find the item, then delete *)
           pointer := last;
           item := last^.next;
           WHILE (item^.name <> itemname) AND (item^.next <> NIL) DO
              BEGIN
                 pointer := item;
                 item := item^.next
              END;
           IF item^.name = itemname THEN
              BEGIN
                 pointer^.next := item^.next;
                 dispose(item)
              END
        END;
```

These statements can accommodate two different situations: deletion of the last component, and deletion of some other component. If the last component is to be deleted, then the pointer to the end of the list (`last`) is adjusted so that it points to the next component in the list, i.e.,

```
last := item^.next;
```

If some other component is to be deleted, then its successor is made to point to the next component in the list, i.e.,

```
pointer^.next := item^.next;
```

EXAMPLE 13.9 Processing a Linked List

In this example we expand on some of the ideas that were presented in Example 13.8. Specifically, we now present an interactive Turbo Pascal program that allows us to create a linked list, add a new component, or delete any component. The program will be menu-driven, to facilitate its use by a nonprogrammer. We will include a provision to display the list in reverse order (last component to first) after the selection of any menu item.

The program begins with the following type definitions and variable declarations.

```
TYPE link = ^personal;
     personal = RECORD
                      name : string;
                      next : link
                 END;
VAR item,pointer,last : link;
    choice : 1..4;
    itemname : string;
```

These definitions and declarations are similar to those presented in Example 13.8, though we have an additional pointer variable (`last`) and two new variables (`choice`, `itemname`) to accommodate the additional features in the present program.

Now consider the main action block. Let us place the generation of the menu and the action statements associated with each of the menu choices within separate procedures. The main action block will then consist of little more than a group of references to these procedures. Thus, we can write

```
BEGIN   (* main action block *)
   REPEAT
      menu;
      CASE choice OF
          1 : create;
          2 : add;
          3 : delete;
          4 :
      END
   UNTIL choice = 4
END.
```

Notice that we first access procedure `menu`, which causes a value of `choice` to be entered from the keyboard (`choice` can only take on the integer values 1, 2, 3 or 4). We then access an additional procedure, the choice of which depends upon the value that has been assigned to `choice`. This process is repeated until `choice` is assigned a value of 4, which indicates a stopping condition.

Now let us examine procedure menu. This is a very simple procedure, consisting only of input/output statements.

```
PROCEDURE menu;

(* display the main menu *)

BEGIN
    writeln;
    writeln;
    writeln('Main menu:');
    writeln;
    writeln('  1 - Create the linked list');
    writeln;
    writeln('  2 - Add a component');
    writeln;
    writeln('  3 - Delete a component');
    writeln;
    writeln('  4 - End');
    writeln;
    write('Enter your choice (1, 2, 3 or 4) -> ');
    readln(choice);
    writeln
END;
```

These statements could just as easily have been placed within the main action block. They were placed in a separate procedure in order to simplify the organization of the overall program logic.

The procedures that are used to create a new list, enter a name from the keyboard, and display the current list utilize essentially the same logic as the Pascal program given in Example 13.8. (Note, however, that the groups of statements required to create the list and to display the list have been moved from the main action block to individual subroutines.) Thus, the list can be created by accessing the following procedure:

```
PROCEDURE create;

(* create the linked list

    item    -> the new (most recent) component
    pointer -> the preceding component ('item' points to 'pointer')   *)

BEGIN
    new(item);
    write('New name: ');
    readname(item^.name);
    item^.next := NIL;
    pointer := item;
    WHILE NOT ((item^.name[1] IN ['E','e'])
          AND  (item^.name[2] IN ['N','n'])
          AND  (item^.name[3] IN ['D','d'])) DO
            BEGIN
                new(item);
                write('New name: ');
                readname(item^.name);
                item^.next := pointer;
                pointer := item
            END;
    last := item^.next;
    display
END;
```

Notice that the last component in the list is tagged with the pointer `last`. This will enable us to find the end of the list whenever we wish to display the list, to add a new component or to delete a component. Also, note that the new list will automatically be displayed after it has been created.

Procedure `readname`, which is accessed by the above procedure (and others as well), is written as

```
PROCEDURE readname(VAR name : string);

(* read a name into the computer *)

BEGIN
    name := ' ';
    read(name);
    readln
END;
```

This procedure is very similar to a procedure with the same name in Example 13.8. Note, however, that the present procedure utilizes a string variable as a variable-type parameter, whereas the previous version employed a pointer as a variable parameter. The present treatment of the variable parameter provides more generality, and therefore allows this procedure to be accessed by several other procedures (namely, `create`, `add` and `delete`).

The procedure used to display the list can be written as

```
PROCEDURE display;

(* display the complete list

    item    -> the current component to be displayed
    pointer -> the preceding component ('item' points to 'pointer')   *)

BEGIN
    writeln;
    pointer := last;
    WHILE pointer <> NIL DO
        BEGIN
            item := pointer;
            writeln(item^.name);
            pointer := item^.next
        END
END;
```

This procedure begins by locating the end of the list (`pointer := last;`), and then proceeds in the same manner as the program shown in Example 13.8.

The following procedure allows a component to be added to a linked list once the linked list has already been created.

```
PROCEDURE add;

(* add one component to the linked list

    pointer -> component below (i.e., pointing to) the new component
    item    -> the component to be added ('pointer' points to 'item')   *)

BEGIN
    new(item);
    write('New name: ');
    readname(item^.name);
    write('Place ahead of (press ENTER if new item is last): ');
```

```
        readname(itemname);
    IF itemname[1] = ' '
        THEN BEGIN   (* insert at end *)
                item^.next := last;
                last := item
             END
        ELSE BEGIN   (* find location, then insert *)
                pointer := last;
                WHILE (pointer^.name <> itemname) AND
                      (pointer^.next <> NIL) DO pointer := pointer^.next;
                item^.next := pointer^.next;
                pointer^.next := item
             END;
        display
    END;
```

This procedure first causes the new name, and then its location, to be entered from the keyboard. The procedure then follows the logic described earlier in this chapter, which allows an insertion either at the end of the list (i.e., at the top) or else at an appropriate place within the list. Notice that the new list is automatically displayed after an insertion has been made.

Now consider the procedure that is used to delete any one component from the list. This procedure can be written as

```
    PROCEDURE delete;

    (* delete one component from the linked list

        pointer -> component above (i.e., pointing to) component to be deleted
        item    -> component to be deleted ('pointer' points to 'item')   *)

    BEGIN
        write ('Name to be deleted: ');
        readname(itemname);
        IF last^.name = itemname
            THEN BEGIN   (* delete last item *)
                    item := last;
                    last := item^.next;
                    dispose(item)
                 END
            ELSE BEGIN   (* find item, then delete *)
                    pointer := last;
                    item := last^.next;
                    WHILE (item^.name <> itemname) AND
                          (item^.next <> NIL) DO
                        BEGIN
                            pointer := item;
                            item := item^.next;
                        END;
                    IF item^.name = itemname THEN
                        BEGIN
                            pointer^.next := item^.next;
                            dispose(item)
                        END
                 END;
        display
    END;
```

The logical details of this procedure have already been described earlier in this chapter. Note that the new list is automatically displayed after the deletion has been carried out.

The complete Turbo Pascal program is presented below:

```
PROGRAM linklist;

(* PROCESS A LINKED LIST (menu-driven program using pointers)    *)

TYPE link = ^personal;
     personal = RECORD
                      name : string;
                      next : link
                END;
VAR item,pointer,last : link;
    choice : 1..4;
    itemname : string;

PROCEDURE readname(VAR name : string);

(* read a name into the computer *)

BEGIN
   name := ' ';
   read(name);
   readln
END;

PROCEDURE display;

(* display the complete list

   item     -> the current component to be displayed
   pointer -> the preceding component ('item' points to 'pointer')   *)

BEGIN
   writeln;
   pointer := last;
   WHILE pointer <> NIL DO
      BEGIN
         item := pointer;
         writeln(item^.name);
         pointer := item^.next
      END
END;

PROCEDURE create;

(* create the linked list

   item     -> the new (most recent) component
   pointer -> the preceding component ('item' points to 'pointer')    *)

BEGIN
   new(item);
   write('New name: ');
   readname(item^.name);
   item^.next := NIL;
```

```
        pointer := item;
    WHILE NOT ((item^.name[1] IN ['E','e'])
           AND  (item^.name[2] IN ['N','n'])
           AND  (item^.name[3] IN ['D','d'])) DO
                 BEGIN
                     new(item);
                     write('New name: ');
                     readname(item^.name);
                     item^.next := pointer;
                     pointer := item
                 END;
    last := item^.next;
    display
END;


PROCEDURE add;

(* add one component to the linked list

    pointer -> component below (i.e., pointing to) the new component
    item    -> the component to be added ('pointer' points to 'item')   *)

BEGIN
    new(item);
    write('New name: ');
    readname(item^.name);
    write('Place ahead of (press ENTER if new item is last): ');
    readname(itemname);
    IF itemname[1] = ' '
       THEN BEGIN   (* insert at end *)
                item^.next := last;
                last := item
            END
       ELSE BEGIN   (* find location, then insert *)
                pointer := last;
                WHILE (pointer^.name <> itemname) AND
                      (pointer^.next <> NIL) DO pointer := pointer^.next;
                item^.next := pointer^.next;
                pointer^.next := item
            END;
    display
END;


PROCEDURE delete;

(* delete one component from the linked list

    pointer -> component above (i.e., pointing to) component to be deleted
    item    -> component to be deleted ('pointer' points to 'item')   *)

BEGIN
    write ('Name to be deleted: ');
    readname(itemname);
    IF last^.name = itemname
       THEN BEGIN   (* delete last item *)
```

```
                              item := last;
                              last := item^.next;
                              dispose(item)
                          END
                ELSE BEGIN   (* find item, then delete *)
                          pointer := last;
                          item := last^.next;
                          WHILE (item^.name <> itemname) AND
                                (item^.next <> NIL) DO
                            BEGIN
                              pointer := item;
                              item := item^.next;
                            END;
                          IF item^.name = itemname THEN
                            BEGIN
                              pointer^.next := item^.next;
                              dispose(item)
                            END
                END;
          END;
      display
END;


PROCEDURE menu;

(* display the main menu *)

BEGIN
   writeln;
   writeln;
   writeln('Main menu:');
   writeln;
   writeln('  1 - Create the linked list');
   writeln;
   writeln('  2 - Add a component');
   writeln;
   writeln('  3 - Delete a component');
   writeln;
   writeln('  4 - End');
   writeln;
   write('Enter your choice (1, 2, 3 or 4) -> ');
   readln(choice);
   writeln
END;


BEGIN   (* main action block *)
   REPEAT
      menu;
      CASE choice OF
         1 : create;
         2 : add;
         3 : delete;
         4 :
      END
   UNTIL choice = 4
END.
```

Now let us utilize this program to create a linked list containing the following cities: Boston, Chicago, Denver, New York, Pittsburgh, San Francisco. We will then add several additional cities and delete some other cities, thus illustrating all of the features of the program. We will maintain the list of cities in alphabetical order throughout the exercise. Therefore, we will enter the initial list backward, so that the cities will be displayed in the correct order. (Note that San Francisco will actually be at the beginning of the list, and Boston at the end.)

The entire interactive session is shown below. As usual, the user's responses are underlined.

```
Main menu:

1 - Create the linked list

2 - Add a component

3 - Delete a component

4 - End


Enter your choice (1, 2, 3 or 4) -> 1

New name: San Francisco
New name: Pittsburgh
New name: New York
New name: Denver
New name: Chicago
New name: Boston
New Name: end

Boston
Chicago
Denver
New York
Pittsburgh
San Francisco


Main menu:

1 - Create the linked list

2 - Add a component

3 - Delete a component

4 - End


Enter your choice (1, 2, 3 or 4) -> 2

New name: Atlanta
Place ahead of (press ENTER if new item is last): _
```

```
Atlanta
Boston
Chicago
Denver
New York
Pittsburgh
San Francisco


Main menu:

1 - Create the linked list

2 - Add a component

3 - Delete a component

4 - End


Enter your choice (1, 2, 3 or 4) -> 2

New name: Seattle
Place ahead of (press ENTER if new item is last): San Francisco

Atlanta
Boston
Chicago
Denver
New York
Pittsburgh
San Francisco
Seattle


Main menu:

1 - Create the linked list

2 - Add a component

3 - Delete a component

4 - End


Enter your choice (1, 2, 3 or 4) -> 3

Name to be deleted: New York

Atlanta
Boston
```

```
Chicago
Denver
Pittsburgh
San Francisco
Seattle


Main menu:

1 - Create the linked list

2 - Add a component

3 - Delete a component

4 - End


Enter your choice (1, 2, 3 or 4) -> 2

New name: Washington
Place ahead of (press ENTER if new item is last): Seattle

Atlanta
Boston
Chicago
Denver
Pittsburgh
San Francisco
Seattle
Washington


Main menu:

1 - Create the linked list

2 - Add a component

3 - Delete a component

4 - End


Enter your choice (1, 2, 3 or 4) -> 3

Name to be deleted: Atlanta

Boston
Chicago
Denver
Pittsburgh
```

```
San Francisco
Seattle
Washington
```

Main menu:

1 - Create the linked list

2 - Add a component

3 - Delete a component

4 - End

Enter your choice (1, 2, 3 or 4) -> 2

New name: Dallas
Place ahead of (press ENTER if new item is last): Chicago

```
Boston
Chicago
Dallas
Denver
Pittsburgh
San Francisco
Seattle
Washington
```

Main menu:

1 - Create the linked list

2 - Add a component

3 - Delete a component

4 - End

Enter your choice (1, 2, 3 or 4) -> 3

Name to be deleted: Washington

```
Boston
Chicago
Dallas
Denver
Pittsburgh
San Francisco
Seattle
```

```
Main menu:

1 - Create the linked list

2 - Add a component

3 - Delete a component

4 - End

Enter your choice (1, 2, 3 or 4) -> 4
```

Review Questions

13.1   What is a linked list?

13.2   What is a pointer? What is the relationship between pointers and linked lists?

13.3   How does a linked list differ from a sequential list, such as that found in a one-dimensional array? What advantages does the linked list offer?

13.4   How is the beginning of a linked list identified?

13.5   What is a linear linked list?

13.6   What is a circular linked list? How does a circular linked list differ from a linear linked list?

13.7   What is a tree? How do trees differ from linear linked lists?

13.8   What is a binary tree? How does a binary tree differ from other types of trees?

13.9   What are nodes and branches? With what type of data structure are nodes and branches associated?

13.10   What type of data structure is used to create linked structures in Pascal?

13.11   How is a pointer type defined in Pascal?

13.12   What structured data type is generally used to define an object variable? What is the reason for this choice?

13.13   Describe the manner in which pointer types and object variable types are related (bound) to one another.

13.14   How are pointer-type variables declared? In what part of a Pascal program do these declarations appear?

13.15   In general terms, how are object variables declared? Conceptually, how do object variable declarations differ from other kinds of variable declarations?

13.16   In what part of a Pascal program do object variable declarations appear? Compare with other types of variable declarations, and cite reasons for the differences.

13.17   What is the purpose of the new statement? What type of parameter is required?

13.18 Explain the relationship that is established between an object variable and its corresponding pointer variable.

13.19 How can the names of an object variable and its corresponding pointer variable be distinguished from one another?

13.20 Summarize the rules that apply to the assignment of one pointer variable to another.

13.21 How can a pointer variable be made to point to nothing?

13.22 Describe two different ways to assign values to pointer variables. What is the purpose of each type of assignment?

13.23 Summarize the rules that apply to the assignment of one object variable to another.

13.24 Can the individual fields within two different object variables be assigned to one another? What restrictions apply to this type of assignment?

13.25 Conceptually, how does the assignment of one pointer variable to another differ from the assignment of one object variable to another?

13.26 What kinds of comparisons can be carried out between pointer variables? Which operators can be used for this purpose?

13.27 What kinds of comparisons can be carried out between object variables? Can such comparisons be carried out with entire variables? Can they be carried out with individual fields? What restrictions apply to such comparisons?

13.28 How are the individual items within a last-in, first-out (LIFO) list linked to one other?

13.29 Describe the logic that is used to create new components within a LIFO list. In what order are the components entered? How are they linked?

13.30 Describe the logic that is used to display the components within a LIFO list. In what order are the components displayed?

13.31 Describe the logic that is used to insert a component into some designated location within a LIFO list. How are the pointers readjusted?

13.32 Describe the logic that is used to delete a component from a LIFO list. How are the pointers readjusted?

13.33 What is the purpose of the `dispose` statement? What type of parameter is required? Contrast with the `new` statement.

Problems

13.34 Write appropriate type definitions or variable declarations for each of the situations described below:

    (a) Define a pointer type called `link` whose corresponding object variable, `customer`, contains the following fields:

        (i)   `name` (20 characters)

        (ii) `acctno` (an integer ranging from 1 to 9999)

      (*iii*) balance (a real quantity)

      (*iv*) next (a pointer to the next record)

   (*b*) Declare two pointer variables of type link, called nextcustomer and lastcustomer, respectively.

   (*c*) Create and then destroy a dynamic variable corresponding to the pointer-type variable nextcustomer.

13.35 The following problems refer to the pointer-type variables, and their corresponding object variables, defined in the preceding problem.

   (*a*) Assign the value of the pointer in nextcustomer^ to the pointer variable lastcustomer.

   (*b*) Have the value of the pointer in nextcustomer^ point to nothing.

   (*c*) Assign each element of nextcustomer^ to its corresponding element in lastcustomer^.

   (*d*) Assign a balance of $287.55 to the nextcustomer whose account number is 1330.

   (*e*) Obtain a value of nextcustomer^.name by accessing a procedure called readinput. Include a description of readinput in your solution.

   (*f*) Outline a WHILE - DO structure that continues to execute as long as the value of nextcustomer is not NIL.

13.36 Shown below are several program outlines that involve the use of pointers and their corresponding object variables. Describe the purpose of each program.

   (*a*)
```
PROGRAM sample;
TYPE values = ARRAY [1..3] OF real;
     pointer = ^part;
     part = RECORD
                 dimension : values;
                 next : pointer
            END;
VAR workpart : pointer;

BEGIN    (* main action part *)
   . . . . .
   new(workpart);
   . . . . .
   dispose(workpart);
   . . . . .
END.
```

   (*b*) Assume this program is written in Turbo Pascal:

```
PROGRAM sample;
TYPE pointer = ^customer;
     customer = RECORD
                     name   : string;
                     street : string;
                     city   : string;
                     next   : pointer
                END;
VAR nameandaddress : pointer;
```

```
   BEGIN   (* main action block *)
      new(nameandaddress);
      . . . . .
      WITH nameandaddress^ DO
         BEGIN
            readln(name);
            readln(street);
            readln(city)
         END;
      . . . . .
   END.
```

(c)   Assume this program is written in ANSI Pascal:

```
PROGRAM sample;
TYPE line = PACKED ARRAY [1..40] OF char;
     pointer = ^customer;
     customer = RECORD
                    name   : line;
                    street : line;
                    city   : line;
                    next   : pointer
                END;
VAR nameandaddress : pointer;

PROCEDURE readinput (VAR item : line);
(* read a 40-character string *)
VAR count : 0..40;
BEGIN
   count := 0;
   WHILE NOT eoln DO
      BEGIN
         count := count + 1;
         read(item[count])
      END;
   readln
END;

BEGIN   (* main action block *)
   new(nameandaddress);
   . . . . .
   WITH nameandaddress^ DO
      BEGIN
         readinput(name);
         readinput(street);
         readinput(city)
      END;
   . . . . .
END.
```

(*d*)   Assume this program is written in Turbo Pascal:

```
PROGRAM sample;
TYPE pointer = ^customer;
     customer = RECORD
                     name   : string;
                     street : string;
                     city   : string;
                     next   : pointer
                END;
VAR nameandaddress : pointer;

PROCEDURE readinput (VAR personal : pointer);
(* read the name, street and city *)
BEGIN
   . . . . .
END;

PROCEDURE writeoutput (personal : pointer);
(* display the name, street and city *)
BEGIN
   . . . . .
END;

BEGIN   (* main action block *)
   new(nameandaddress);
   . . . . .
   readinput(nameandaddress);
   . . . . .
   writeoutput(nameandaddress);
   . . . . .
   dispose(nameandaddress);
   . . . . .
END.
```

(*e*)

```
PROGRAM sample;
TYPE values = ARRAY [1..3] OF real;
     pointer = ^part;
     part = RECORD
                 dimension : values;
                 next : pointer
            END;
VAR firstpart,nextpart : pointer;
    area,volume : real;

BEGIN   (* main action statements *)
   new(nextpart);
   . . . . .
   nextpart^.dimension[1] := 1.0;
   nextpart^.dimension[2] := 2.5;
   nextpart^.dimension[3] := 0.3;
   . . . . .
   nextpart^.next := firstpart;
   . . . . .
```

```
        WITH nextpart^ DO
            BEGIN
                area := dimension[1] * dimension[2];
                volume := area * dimension[3];
                IF dimension[1] <> dimension[3] THEN . . .
                                          ELSE . . .

            END;
        . . . . .
        IF nextpart^.next = NIL THEN . . .
                            ELSE . . . ;

        . . . . . .
        dispose(nextpart);
        . . . . .
    END.
```

Programming Problems

13.37 Modify the program given in Example 13.8 so that each component within the list (i.e., each record) contains a name, street address, and city/state/zip code. Place the name on one line, the street address on another line and the city/state/zip code on a third line.

Let the record consist of two fields. The first will be a two-dimensional array, with 3 rows and 80 columns, where each row represents a line of text. The second field will be a pointer to the next record.

13.38 Modify the program given in Example 13.9 so that it applies to each of the following linked structures.

(a) A linear linked list with two sets of pointers, one set pointing in the forward direction, the other set pointing backward.

(b) A circular linked list. Use a pointer variable to identify the beginning of the list.

(c) A *first-in, first out* (FIFO) linear linked list, as illustrated in Fig. 13.8.

(d) A binary tree with a specified number of levels. (Note that a systematic method for traversing the tree will be required.)

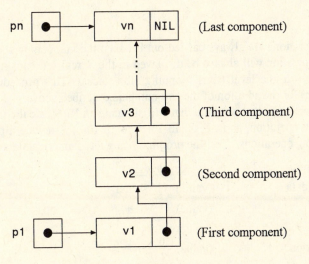

Fig 13.8

13.39 Write a complete Pascal program that will allow you to enter and maintain a computerized version of your family tree. Begin by specifying the number of generations (i.e., the number of levels). Then enter the names and nationalities in a hierarchical fashion. Include capabilities for modifying the tree and for adding new names (new nodes) to the tree. Also, include a provision for displaying the entire tree automatically after each update.

Test the program, beginning with one pair of your grandparents or, if known, one pair of great-grandparents.

13.40 An RPN calculator utilizes a scheme whereby each new numerical value is followed by the operation that is to be performed between the new value and its predecessor. (RPN stands for "reverse Polish notation.") Thus, adding two numbers, say 3.3 + 4.8, would require the following keystrokes:

$$3.3 \quad \text{<enter>}$$

$$4.8 \quad +$$

The sum, 8.1, would then be displayed in the calculator's single visible register.

RPN calculators make use of a *stack*, typically containing four registers (four components), as illustrated in Fig. 13.9. Each new number is entered into the X register, causing all previously entered values to be pushed up in the stack. If the T register was previously occupied, then the old number will be lost (it will be overwritten by the value that is pushed up from the Z register).

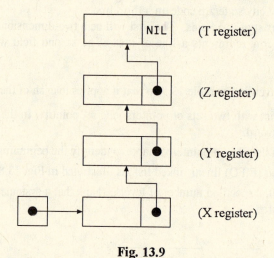

Fig. 13.9

Arithmetic operations are always carried out between the numbers in the X and Y registers. The result of such an operation will always be displayed in the X register, causing everything in the upper registers to drop down one level (thus "popping" the stack). This procedure is illustrated in Figs. 13.10(*a*) to 13.10(*c*) for the addition of the two numbers described above.

Write an interactive Pascal program that will simulate an RPN calculator. Display the contents of the stack after each operation, as in Figs. 13.10(*a*) to 13.10(*c*). Include a provision for carrying out each of the following operations. Test the program using any numerical data of your choice.

Operation	Keystrokes	
enter new data	(value)	<enter>
addition	(value)	+
subtraction	(value)	−
multiplication	(value)	*
division	(value)	/

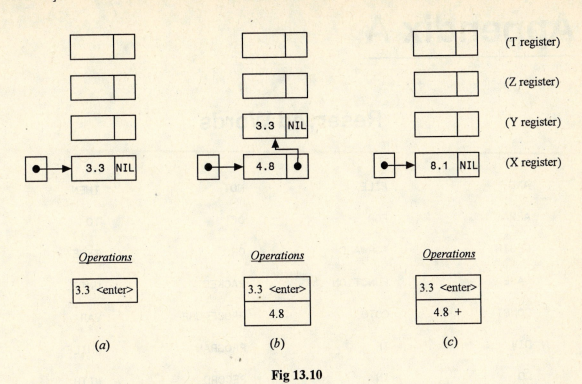

	(T register)
	(Z register)
	(Y register)
	(X register)

Operations

| 3.3 <enter> |

(a)

Operations

| 3.3 <enter> |
| 4.8 |

(b)

Operations

| 3.3 <enter> |
| 4.8 + |

(c)

Fig 13.10

Appendix A

Reserved Words

AND	FILE	NOT	THEN
ARRAY	FOR	OF	TO
BEGIN	FORWARD	OR	TYPE
CASE	FUNCTION	PACKED	UNTIL
CONST	GOTO	PROCEDURE	VAR
DIV	IF	PROGRAM	WHILE
DO	IN	RECORD	WITH
DOWNTO	LABEL	REPEAT	
ELSE	MOD	SET	
END	NIL	STRING*	

*Not included in ANSI Pascal.

Turbo Pascal includes some additional reserved words.

Appendix B

Standard Identifiers

abs	exp	pack	sqrt
append*	false	pred	succ
arctan	input	read	text
boolean	integer	readln	true
char	ln	real	trunc
chr	maxint	reset	unpack
cos	new	rewrite	write
dispose	odd	round	writeln
eof	ord	sin	
eoln	output	sqr	

*Not included in ANSI Pascal.

Turbo Pascal includes some additional standard identifiers.

Appendix C

Standard Procedures

Procedure	*Purpose*	*Reference*
append*	Prepare to add data to the end of a text file.	Sec. 11.6
assign*	Assign an external file identifier to an internal file name (prior to reading or writing data items).	Sec. 11.3
close*	Close a file after reading or writing all data.	Sec. 11.3
dispose	Delete a dynamic variable (delete a component in a linked list).	Sec. 13.5
new	Create a dynamic variable (create a component in a linked list).	Sec. 13.3
pack**	Create a dense storage of data items within the computer's memory.	Sec. 9.4
read	Read data items from the keyboard or from a data file.	Secs. 4.2, 11.4
readln	Read data items from the keyboard or from a data file, then skip to the next line.	Sec. 4.3
reset	Prepare a file for reading.	Secs. 11.4, 11.6
rewrite	Prepare a file for writing.	Secs. 11.3, 11.6
unpack**	Restore normal (sparse) storage of data items within the computer's memory.	Sec. 9.4
write	Write data items to the screen or to a data file.	Secs. 4.5, 11.3
writeln	Write data items to the screen or to a data file, then skip to the next line.	Sec. 4.6

*Not included in ANSI Pascal.

**Not included in Turbo Pascal.

Turbo Pascal includes additional standard procedures.

Appendix D

Standard Functions

Function	Purpose	Parameter Type	Result Type
abs(x)	Compute the absolute value of x.	integer or real	same as x
arctan(x)	Compute the arctangent of x.	integer or real	real
chr(x)	Determine the character represented by x.	integer	char
cos(x)	Compute the cosine of x (x in radians).	integer or real	real
eof(x)	Determine if an end-of-file has been detected.	file	boolean
eoln(x)	Determine if an end-of-line has been detected.	file	boolean
exp(x)	Compute e^x, where $e = 2.7182818...$ is the base of the natural (Naperian) system of logarithms.	integer or real	real
ln(x)	Compute the natural logarithm of x (x > 0).	integer or real	real
odd(x)	Determine if x is odd or even. (Return true if x is odd, false otherwise.)	integer	boolean
ord(x)	Determine the (decimal) integer that is used to encode the character x.	char	integer
pred(x)	Determine the predecessor of x.	integer, char or boolean	same as x
round(x)	Round the value of x to the nearest integer.	real	integer
sin(x)	Compute the sine of x (x in radians).	integer or real	real
sqr(x)	Compute the square of x.	integer or real	same as x
sqrt(x)	Compute the square root of x (x ≥ 0).	integer or real	real
succ(x)	Determine the successor to x.	integer, char or boolean	same as x

Function	*Purpose*	*Parameter Type*	*Result Type*
trunc(x)	Truncate x (i.e., drop the decimal part of x).	real	integer

Turbo Pascal includes additional standard functions.

Appendix E

Operators

The Pascal operators are summarized below, in their natural precedence (highest to lowest).

Precedence	_Operator(s)_
1 (highest)	NOT
2	* / DIV MOD AND
3	+ − OR
4 (lowest)	= <> < <= > >= IN

Within the same precedence group, successive operations are carried out from left to right.

Appendix F

Data Types

Data Type	Description	Reference
array	A collection of data items, all of the same type, that are referred to by the same name. Individual array elements (i.e., individual data items) are identified with integer *subscripts*.	Secs. 9.1, 9.2
boolean	Truth values that are either true or false.	Sec. 3.4
char	Single character enclosed in apostrophes. (Note that integer characters do *not* represent numerical values.)	Sec. 3.3
enumerated	An ordered sequence of identifiers. Enumerated data items are assigned integer values ranging from 0 to n-1, where n is the number of identifiers.	Sec. 8.2
file	A collection of data items that is typically stored on an auxiliary memory device.	Secs. 11.1, 11.2, 11.6
integer	Integer (whole-number) quantity.	Sec. 3.1
pointer	An address that indicates the location of an object variable within the computer's memory.	Secs. 13.2, 13.3
real	Numerical value including either a decimal point or an exponent, or both.	Sec. 3.2
record	A collection of data items whose individual data types may differ. Individual data items occupy *fields* within a record. Each field is given a unique name.	Secs. 10.1, 10.4
set	A collection of ordered, simple data items that are all of the same type.	Secs. 12.1, 12.2
string[*]	A sequence of characters enclosed in apostrophes.	Sec. 3.4
subrange	A portion of the original range of ordered, simple-type data (i.e., integer, char or boolean data).	Sec. 8.1

[*]Not included in ANSI Pascal.

Appendix G

Control Structures

Control Structure	General Form	Reference
assignment	*variable* := *expr*;	Sec. 3.9

Example:

```
area := 3.14159 * sqr(radius);
```

CASE	CASE *expression* OF	Sec. 6.7

```
CASE expression OF
    case label list 1 : statement 1;
    case label list 2 : statement 2;
    . . . . .
    case label list n : statement n;
```

Example:

```
CASE choice OF
   'R' : writeln(' RED ');
   'W' : writeln(' WHITE ');
   'B' : writeln(' BLUE ')
END;
```

FOR – TO – DO	FOR *ctrl var* := *val 1* TO *val 2* DO *statement*;	Sec. 6.4

Example:

```
sum := 0;
FOR count := 1 TO n DO
    sum := sum + count;
```

GOTO	GOTO *statement label*;	Sec. 6.8

Example:

```
    IF a <= 20 THEN GOTO 20;
    . . . . .
20 : writeln(x,y,z);
```

Control Structure	*General Form*	*Reference*
IF – THEN	IF *boolean expr* THEN *statement*;	Sec. 6.6

Example:

```
IF count <= n THEN count := count + 1;
```

IF – THEN – ELSE	IF *boolean expr* THEN *statement 1* ELSE *statement 2*;	Sec. 6.6

Example:

```
IF circle THEN
  BEGIN
     readln(radius);
     area := 3.14159 * sqr(radius);
     writeln('Area of circle = ',area)
  END
ELSE
  BEGIN
     readln(length, width);
     area := length * width;
     writeln('Area of rectangle = ',area)
  END;
```

REPEAT – UNTIL	REPEAT *statements* UNTIL *boolean expr*;	Sec. 6.3

Example:

```
sum := 0;
count := 1;
REPEAT
   sum := sum + count;
   count := count + 1
UNTIL count > n;
```

WHILE – DO	WHILE *boolean expr* DO *statement*;	Sec. 6.2

Example:

```
sum := 0;
count := 1;
WHILE count <= n DO
   BEGIN
      sum := sum + count;
      count := count + 1
   END;
```

Appendix H

The ASCII Character Set

ASCII Value	Character	ASCII Value	Character	ASCII Value	Character	ASCII Value	Character
0	NUL	32	(blank)	64	@	96	`
1	SOH	33	!	65	A	97	a
2	STX	34	"	66	B	98	b
3	ETX	35	#	67	C	99	c
4	EOT	36	$	68	D	100	d
5	ENQ	37	%	69	E	101	e
6	ACK	38	&	70	F	102	f
7	BEL	39	'	71	G	103	g
8	BS	40	(	72	H	104	h
9	HT	41	)	73	I	105	i
10	LF	42	*	74	J	106	j
11	VT	43	+	75	K	107	k
12	FF	44	,	76	L	108	l
13	CR	45	–	77	M	109	m
14	SO	46	.	78	N	110	n
15	SI	47	/	79	O	111	o
16	DLE	48	0	80	P	112	p
17	DC1	49	1	81	Q	113	q
18	DC2	50	2	82	R	114	r
19	DC3	51	3	83	S	115	s
20	DC4	52	4	84	T	116	t
21	NAK	53	5	85	U	117	u
22	SYN	54	6	86	V	118	v
23	ETB	55	7	87	W	119	w
24	CAN	56	8	88	X	120	x
25	EM	57	9	89	Y	121	y
26	SUB	58	:	90	Z	122	z
27	ESC	59	;	91	[	123	{
28	FS	60	<	92	\	124		
29	GS	61	=	93	]	125	}
30	RS	62	>	94	^	126	~
31	US	63	?	95	_	127	DEL

The first 32 characters and the last character are control characters. Usually, they are not displayed. However, some versions of Pascal (some computers) support special graphics characters for these ASCII values. For example, 001 may represent the character ☺, 002 may represent ☻, and so on.

399

Answers to Selected Problems

Chapter 1

1.28   (*a*)   Display a textual message.

          (*b*)   Calculate the area of a triangle.

          (*c*)   Calculate tax withheld and net pay after taxes.

          (*d*)   Determine the smaller of two numbers.

          (*e*)   Determine the smaller of two numbers using a function.

          (*f*)   Determine the smaller of two numbers using a procedure.

          (*g*)   Enter a known quantity of pairs of numbers. Determine the smallest number within each pair.

          (*h*)   Enter an unspecified quantity of pairs of numbers. Determine the smallest number within each pair.

          (*i*)   Enter an unspecified quantity of pairs of numbers. Determine the smallest number within each pair. Store all pairs of numbers internally. Then display each pair and identify which number is the smallest.

Chapter 2

2.42   (*a*)   Valid.

          (*b*)   Valid.

          (*c*)   `File` is a reserved word.

          (*d*)   Valid.

          (*e*)   Blank spaces are not allowed.

          (*f*)   Characters other than letters and digits are not allowed. (Some versions of Pascal do allow underscore characters.)

          (*g*)   The first character must be a letter. Also, hyphens are not allowed.

2.43   (*a*)   Valid, real.

          (*b*)   Commas are not allowed.

          (*c*)   Valid, real.

          (*d*)   The magnitude of the exponent may be too large.

          (*e*)   A digit must appear on each side of the decimal point.

          (*f*)   Illegal character.

          (*g*)   Valid, real.

          (*h*)   Valid, integer (may be too large in magnitude for some computers).

          (*i*)   Valid, real.

2.44   (*a*)   Valid.

          (*b*)   Double quotes cannot be used to surround a string.

          (*c*)   A single apostrophe cannot appear within a string.

          (*d*)   The right-hand apostrophe is missing.

          (*e*)   Valid.   (*g*) Valid.

          (*f*)   Valid.   (*h*) Valid.

2.45
```
CONST month = 'july';
      fica = '123-45-6789';
      price = '$95.00';      (or price = 95.00;)
      gross = 2500.00;
      partno = 48837;
      bound = 0.00391;
```

2.46
```
VAR period,status : char;
    terminal : boolean;
    index,row : integer;
    customer : string;
    clearance : real;
```

2.47 (a) This is an assignment statement, not an expression.

(b) Numerical or boolean, depending on the data type associated with `value`.

(c) Numerical.

(d) Boolean.

(e) Two successive operators are not permitted.

(f) Numerical.

(g) Boolean.

(h) Boolean.

2.48 (a) Simple (assignment statement).

(b) Structured (compound).

(c) Structured (repetitive).

(d) Structured (conditional).

(e) Simple (assignment).

(f) Simple (procedure access).

(g) Simple (unconditional transfer).

(h) Simple (assignment).

2.49 Probs. 2.48 (c) and 2.48 (f) access the `write` procedure. Prob. 2.48 (e) accesses the `sqrt` function.

Chapter 3

3.42 (a) Real   −0.3333333   (f) Integer   3

(b) Integer   −2   (g) Real   −0.4

(c) Real   0.3333333   (h) Real   −1.0

(d) Integer   −14   (i) Integer   3

(e) Real   0.03

3.43 (a) `vanillachocolatestrawberry`

(b) `vanilla, chocolate and strawberry`

(c) 9

(d) `chocoberry`   (f) 0

(e) 6   (g) `colat`

3.44	(a)	False		(e)	True
	(b)	True		(f)	False
	(c)	True		(g)	False
	(d)	True		(h)	True

3.45	(a)	4.667		(l)	2
	(b)	C		(m)	3
	(c)	101		(n)	−2
	(d)	9		(o)	−3
	(e)	d		(p)	2
	(f)	false		(q)	2
	(g)	11		(r)	−2
	(h)	f		(s)	−2
	(i)	true		(t)	<
	(j)	false		(u)	64
	(k)	true		(v)	g

3.46   (a)   DIV requires integer operands.

     (b)   Correct.

     (c)   An apostrophe is missing.

     (d)   Correct.

     (e)   An operator is missing in the denominator.

     (f)   Correct.

     (g)   The boolean operands must be enclosed in parentheses.

     (h)   Correct.

     (i)   The operands are incompatible.

     (j)   The parentheses are not balanced.

     (k)   This expression will result in a value that exceeds `maxint`.

     (l)   Consecutive operators are not allowed.

     (m)   The `odd` function requires an integer parameter.

     (n)   Correct.

3.47
```
VAR gross,net,tax : real;
    employee : integer;
    name : string;
    status,sex : char;
    exempt : boolean;
```

Chapter 4

4.31   This program reads one line of data (seven data items) from the input file, and writes three lines of data to the output file. The output data items will be labeled and formatted, and the lines of output will be double-spaced.

     The first line of output will contain two integers, each having a field width of 4 characters. The second line of output will contain three real numbers. The first two real numbers will each have a field width of 10 characters, with 2 characters to the right of the decimal point (2 decimals); the third real number will have a field width of 12 characters, with 4 characters to the right of the decimal point (4 decimals). The third line of output will contain the values of two char-type variables and one boolean variable. All values in this line will be labeled. The boolean quantity will have a field width of 5 characters.

4.32 (a)
```
read(i1,r3,c2);

or readln(i1,r3,c2);

or read(i1);
   read(r3);
   read(c2);
```

(b)
```
readln(i1,r1,r2,c1);
readln(i2,r3,c2);
```

The second `readln` statement could be replaced by a `read` statement, i.e.,

```
read(i2,r3,c2);
```

(c)
```
writeln(factor,' ',flag);
writeln;
writeln;
writeln(i1,i2,r1,r2,r3,c1,c2,b1);
```

The last `writeln` statement could be replaced by a `write` statement, i.e.,

```
write(i1,i2,r1,r2,r3,c1,c2,b1);
```

(d)
```
writeln('Factor=',factor,' Flag=',flag);
writeln;
writeln('i1=',i1,' r1=',r1,' r2=',r2,' c1=',c1);
writeln;
writeln('i2=',i2,' r3=',r3,' b1=',b1,' c2=',c2);
```

(e)
```
writeln(factor:5,' ',flag);
writeln;
writeln(i1:5, r1:10:3, r2:10:3,' ',c1);
writeln;
writeln(i2:5, r3:10:3, b1:7,' ',c2);
```

4.33
```
i1=10        i2=-817
r1=0.005     r2=4.66E+12        r3=2.7E-03
c1=A         c2= (blank space)
```

4.34
```
i1=10          i2=-63
r1=0.005       r2=4.66E+12      r3=17.7
c1= (blank space)  c2= (blank space)
```

4.35
```
12345 entry point
```
(blank line)
(blank line)
```
      -630     375 2.0800000E+01-4.7730000E+05 1.8500000E-04$5 false
```

4.36   `Factor=12345 Flag=entry point`
       (blank line)
       `i1=    -630 r1= 2.0800000E+01 r2=-4.7730000E+05 c1=$`
       (blank line)
       `i2=     375 r3= 1.8500000E-04 b1= false c2=5`

4.37   `12345 entry point`
       (blank line)
       `-630    20.800-477300.000 $`
       (blank line)
       `  375     0.000  false 5`

4.38   The two numerical values are 20 and −10, and the corresponding field widths are 6 and 4, respectively. Hence, the output will appear as

       `20 -10`

with four spaces preceding the first number and one space separating the two numbers.

4.39   The input data will be entered on five lines. One string will appear on the first line and another string on the second line. Three integers will appear on the third line and two real numbers will appear on the fourth line. The last line will contain four consecutive characters.

       The output will consist of four lines of data. The first line will contain the values of the two constants `flag` and `factor`. The second line will contain the first string, and the third line the second string. The third line will contain the current values of the three integer variables and the two real variables. The last line will contain the current values of the four char-type variables.

       A blank line will separate the first and second lines of output. Within each line, all of the individual output items will appear consecutively, without any separation, except for a blank space preceding each positive real value.

4.40   (*a*)   `str1=Smith, Robert`
           `str2=New York, NY`
           `i1=1    i2=2    i3=3    r1=4.0    r2=5.0`
           `c1=b    c2=l    c3=u    c4=e`

    (*b*)   `str1=red`
           `str2=green`
           `i1=1    i2=2    i3=3    r1=4.0    r2=5.0`
           `c1=b    c2=` (carriage return)   `c3=l    c4=` (carriage return)

    (*c*)   `str1=red    green    1    2    3    4    5    blue`

       All other variables will be undefined.

    (*d*)   `str1=red`
           `str2=green`
           `i1=1    i2=2    i3=3    r1=4.0    r2=5.0`
           `c1=y    c2=e    c3=l    c4=l`

4.41   `red 5.0000000000E-03`
       (blank line)
       `100-200-300 4.0044400000E+02-5.0055500000E+02`
       (blank line)
       `PINK`

4.42 `flag=red factor= 0.005`
(blank line)
`City: San Francisco   State: California`
`i1= 100 i2=-200 i3=-300 r1= 400.4 r2=-500.6`
(blank line)
`color=PINK`

4.43 (*a*) `readln(str1);`
`readln(str2);`
`readln(i1,i2,i3,r1,r2);`

The last statement (`readln`) can be replaced by a `read` statement.

(*b*) `readln(str1);`
`readln(str2);`
`readln(i1,r2,c3,c4);`

(*c*) `readln(i1,i2,i3);`
`readln(r1,r2);`
`readln(c1,c2,c3,c4);`

(*d*) `readln(str1);`
`readln(str2);`
`readln(i1);`
`readln(i2);`
`readln(i3);`
`readln(r1);`
`readln(r2);`
`readln(c1);`
`readln(c2);`
`readln(c3);`
`readln(c4);`

(*e*) `write(flag,factor:6:3,str1,' ',str2,i1:5,i2:5,i3:5,r1:9:3,r2:9:3);`
`writeln(' ',c1,' ',c2,' ',c3,' ',c4);`

(Other solutions are also possible.)

(*f*) `write(flag,factor:8:2,str1,' ',str2,i1:4,i2:4,i3:4,r1:8:2,r2:8:2);`
`writeln(' ',c1,' ',c2,' ',c3,' ',c4);`

(*g*) `writeln(flag,factor:6);`
`writeln;`
`writeln(c1,' ',c2,' ',c3,' ',c4);`
`writeln;`
`writeln(i1:5,i2:5,i3:5,r1:9:3,r2:9:3);`

(*h*) `writeln('flag=',flag,' factor=',factor);`
`writeln;`
`writeln('color=',c1,c2,c3,c4);`
`writeln;`
`write('i1=',i1:4,' i2=',i2:4,' i3=',i3:4);`
`writeln(' r1=',r1:8:3,' r2=',r2:8:3);`

```
(i)    writeln(flag,i1:5,r1:9:3,' ',c1,' ',c2);
       writeln;
       writeln;
       writeln(factor,i2:5,i3:5,r2:9:3,' ',c3,' ',c4);

(j)    writeln(flag,i1:5,r1,7:2,' ',c1,' ',c2);
       writeln;
       writeln;
       writeln(factor:7:2,i2:5,i3:5,r2:7:2,' ',c3,' ',c4);

(k)    writeln('flag=',flag);
       writeln('factor=',factor:12);
       writeln('string1: ',str1);
       writeln('string2: ',str2);
       writeln('i1=',i1:4);
       writeln('i2=',i2:4);
       writeln('i3=',i3:4);
       writeln('r1=',r1:12);
       writeln('r2=',r2:12);
       writeln('c1=',c1);
       writeln('c2=',c2);
       writeln('c3=',c3);
       writeln('c4=',c4);
```

4.44   SUM= 60 PRODUCT=   6000   (Note that there is one blank space before 60, two before 6000.)

Chapter 5

5.31   (*a*)   PROGRAM hello;

```
       (* display HELLO! at the beginning of a line *)

       BEGIN
          writeln('HELLO!')
       END.
```

(*b*)   Turbo Pascal version:

```
       PROGRAM friends;

       (* interactive HELLO program - Turbo Pascal*)

       VAR name : string;
       BEGIN
          write('HI, WHAT''S YOUR NAME? ');
          readln(name);
          writeln;
          writeln;
          writeln('WELCOME ',name);
          writeln('LET''S BE FRIENDS!')
       END.
```

Standard Pascal version, assuming a 5-character name:

```
PROGRAM friends;

(* interactive HELLO program *)

VAR c1,c2,c3,c4,c5,c6 : char;
BEGIN
   write('HI, WHAT''S YOUR NAME? ');
   readln(c1,c2,c3,c4,c5,c6);
   writeln;
   writeln;
   writeln('WELCOME ',c1,c2,c3,c4,c5,c6);
   writeln('LET''S BE FRIENDS!')
END.
```

(c)
```
PROGRAM celsius;

(* convert temperature from Fahrenheit to Celsius *)

VAR f,c : real;
BEGIN
   write('F= ');
   readln(f);
   c := (5/9)*(f-32);
   writeln('C=',c:7:2)
END.
```

(d)
```
PROGRAM piggybank;

(* piggy-bank problem *)

VAR n1,n2,n3,n4,n5 : integer;
    dollars : real;
BEGIN
   write('How many half-dollars? ');
   readln(n1);
   write('How many quarters? ');
   readln(n2);
   write('How many dimes? ');
   readln(n3);
   write('How many nickels? ');
   readln(n4);
   write('How many pennies? ');
   readln(n5);
   dollars := 0.5*n1 + 0.25*n2 + 0.1*n3 + 0.05*n4 + 0.01*n5;
   writeln;
   writeln('The piggy bank contains ',dollars:6:2,' dollars')
END.
```

Chapter 6

6.39 (a) true   (c) error (mixed data types)

     (b) true   (d) false

(e)   true   (h)   false

(f)   error (mixed data types)   (i)   false

(g)   true

6.40   (a)   A real-type variable cannot appear in a boolean expression.

    (b)   Correct.

    (c)   A real-type variable cannot be used as a control variable.

    (d)   Correct.

    (e)   Correct, provided b < c.

    (f)   The relative values of b and d are inconsistent.

    (g)   Correct.

    (h)   If flag remains true the REPEAT–UNTIL loop will continue indefinitely; otherwise, the WHILE–DO loop will execute only once, making it unnecessary.

    (i)   Correct.

    (j)   The selector cannot be a real-type expression; the labels cannot be real.

    (k)   Control cannot be transferred into a compound statement.

    (l)   Statement labels and case labels cannot be used interchangeably.

6.41   (a)
```
sum := 0;
i := 2;
WHILE i < 100 DO
    BEGIN
        sum := sum + i;
        i := i + 3
    END;
```

    (b)
```
sum := 0;
i := 2;
REPEAT
    sum := sum + i;
    i := i + 3
UNTIL i >= 100;
```

    (c)
```
sum := 0;
FOR i := 1 TO 33 DO
    BEGIN
        j := 3*i –1;
        sum := sum + j
    END;
```

6.42   In Turbo Pascal,

```
CASE color OF
    r,R : writeln(' RED');
    g,G : writeln(' GREEN');
    b,B : writeln(' BLUE');
ELSE
    writeln(' BLACK')
END;
```

In standard Pascal, if `flag` is a boolean-type variable,

```
flag := false;
CASE color OF
    r,R : BEGIN
                writeln(' RED');
                flag := true
            END;
    g,G : BEGIN
                writeln(' GREEN');
                flag := true
            END;
    b,B : BEGIN
                writeln(' BLUE');
                flag := true
            END
END;
IF flag = false THEN writeln(' BLACK');
```

6.43 (*a*)   0 5 15 30   (*e*)   1   3   6   9 13 18 22 27 33 40

               x = 30   x = 40

       (*b*)   1 2 3 4   (*f*)   2   5   9 13 18 24 29 35 39 42 50

               x = 4   x = 50

       (*c*)   1 2 3 4   (*g*)   0   1   3   5   8 12 15 19 24 30

               x = 4   x = 30

       (*d*)   1 0 3 2 7 6 13 12 21 20   (*h*)   0   0   2   4   5   9 10 14 14 20

               x = 20   x = 20

       (*i*)   1 3 5 7 9 12 14 17 20 23

               x = 23

Chapter 7

7.33 (*a*) Access the procedure `sample`.

      (*b*) Access the procedure `sample1`, with the parameters a, b and c as actual parameters.

      (*c*) Access the procedure `sample1`, with values of the expressions `a+b`, `2*x` and `sqr(c)` as actual parameters.

      (*d*) Access the function `demo` and assign its value to the variable z.

      (*e*) Assign the value of an expression to z. The expression consists of the value of a, plus 2 times the value returned by `demo`, minus 3.

      (*f*) Access the function `demo1`, with parameters a, b and c. Assign the value returned to z.

      (*g*) Access the function `demo1`, with values of the expressions `a+b`, `2*x` and `sqr(c)` as actual parameters. Add the value returned to the value of y and assign the sum to z.

      (*h*) Access the function `demo1`, with parameters a, b and c. If the value returned by `demo1` is less than the value of the variable `zstar`, assign the value returned by `demo1` to the variable z.

7.34 (*a*)   1 3 1   (*c*)   1 3 1

      (*b*)   1 3 3   (*d*)   1 3 3

(e)	3	6	4	1	
(f)	6	4	3	1	
(g)	3	2			
(h)	3	3			
(i)	2	4	5	9	
(j)	3	3	6	6	9
(k)	sum = 15				
(l)	sum = 25				

(m)	1.5E+01
	1.5E-01
	0.150
	15.000
(n)	z = 1.00
	z = 0.25
	z = 2.00
	z = 0.50

7.35 (a) $y = x_n + \sum_{i=1}^{n-1} x_i$ or $y_n = x_n + y_{n-1}$

(b) $y = \dfrac{(-1)^n x^n}{n!} + \sum_{i=0}^{n-1} \dfrac{(-1)^i x^i}{i!}$ or $y_n = (-1)^n x^n/n! + y_{n-1}$

(c) $p = f_n * \prod_{j=1}^{n-1} f_j$ or $p_n = f_n * p_{n-1}$

Chapter 8

8.19 (a) false   (d) false
(b) true   (e) true
(c) true   (f) true

8.20 (a) Miami   (e) 4
(b) Phoenix   (f) true
(c) 6   (g) false
(d) 4

8.21 (a) sundae is an enumerated variable of type flavors. It can take on the values vanilla, chocolate, ..., coconut.

(b) pint is a subrange variable of type flavors. It can take on the values vanilla, chocolate and strawberry.

(c) 4

(d) The enumerated data item cherry is assigned to cone.

(e) The ELSE clause will be executed if quart is assigned either vanilla or strawberry.

(f) conesize can take on the values small, medium and large.

(g) The enumerated data item medium has an equivalent value of 1. Hence, the action labeled medium will be taken if conesize represents a value of 1.

8.22 (a) color is an enumerated variable of type primary. It can take on the values yellow, cyan and magenta.

(b) Same as color.

(c) Yes, whatever new value is assigned to hue within proc1 will also be assigned to color within the main portion of the program (because hue is a variable parameter).

(d) 3

8.23 (*a*) The *characters* 0 through 9. (These are not numbers.)

(*b*) d1 is a subrange variable of type digits. It can take on the *characters* 0 through 9.

(*c*) 2

8.24 (*a*)
```
TYPE days = (sun,mon,tues,wed,thurs,fri,sat);
VAR days1 : mon..fri;
    days2 : sun..sat;
```

(*b*)
```
TYPE colors = (red,green,blue,white,black);
VAR highlight,foreground,background : colors;
    main : red..blue;
```

(*c*)
```
TYPE suits = (clubs,diamonds,hearts,spades);
     values = 1..12;
VAR cardtype : suits;
    cardvalue : values;
    count,n : 1..maxint;
```

(*d*)
```
PROGRAM sample(input,output);
TYPE wines = (chablis,sauterne,rose,burgundy,chianti);
VAR dinner : wines;
    cost : real;

    FUNCTION special(cost : real) : wines;
    BEGIN
       . . . . .
       special := . . .
    END;
```

Chapter 9

9.44 (*a*) values is a 101-element, one-dimensional array of type real. The index may take on integer values ranging from 0 through 100.

(*b*) calories is a 7-element, one-dimensional array of type integer. The index may take on the values sun, mon, tues, wed, thurs, fri and sat.

(*c*) coats is a 3-element, one-dimensional array of type color. The array elements may take on the values blue, brown, gray, green and black. The index may take on the values small, medium and large.

(*d*) parts is a two-dimensional array of type integer. The first index may take on the uppercase letters A through Z; the second index may take on integer values ranging from 1 through 10000.

(*e*) sunshine is a one-dimensional array of type days. The array elements may take on the values sun, mon, tues, wed, thurs, fri and sat. The index may take on integer values ranging from 1 through 365.

9.45 (*a*) `VAR list : ARRAY [-10..10] OF real;`

(b)   ```
       TYPE days = (sun,mon,tues,wed,thurs,fri,sat);
       VAR sunshine : ARRAY [1..365] OF days;
       ```

(c)    ```
       TYPE colors = (blue,brown,gray,green,black);
            size   = (small,medium,large);
       VAR coats : ARRAY [size,color] OF integer;
       ```

(d)   ```
       TYPE colors = (blue,brown,gray,green,black);
            size   = (small,medium,large);
       VAR coats : ARRAY [size] OF ARRAY [color] OF integer;
       ```

(e)    ```
       CONST max1 = 2000;
             max2 = 5000;
       TYPE range1 = 1..max1;
            range2 = 1..max2;
       VAR tally : ARRAY [range1,range2] OF char;
       ```

(f)   ```
       VAR symbol : ARRAY [1..12, 1..20, 0..5] OF boolean;
       ```

(g)    ```
       VAR name : PACKED ARRAY [1..80] OF char;
       ```

(h)   ```
       VAR page : ARRAY [1..66] OF PACKED ARRAY [1..80] OF char;
       ```

**9.46**  (a)    Each element of a 100-element integer array is assigned the square of its index.

(b)    The elements of a two-dimensional real array are read into the computer, on a row-by-row basis. Once all elements have been entered, the elements are written out (displayed) on a row-by-row basis. There can be as many as 20 rows and 8 columns. The actual number of rows and columns are read into the computer prior to reading the elements.

(c)    Some of the elements of a one-dimensional real array are assigned special values. Initially, a positive integer, not exceeding 100, is read into the computer and assigned to max. The first element of the array (value[0]) is then assigned an initial value of 0. Then the designated array elements are assigned the value index MOD 8, in reverse order (i.e., for index = max, max−1, . . ., 1). Note that the array elements will take on one the values 0, 1.0, . . ., 7.0. During this process (i.e., within the loop), the value assigned to the first element (value[0]) is increased by the value of the current element (value[index]) if the value of the current element is less than 5.0.

(d)    This outline involves two 5-element arrays, called foreground and background, respectively. However, foreground is a packed array whereas background is not. Each element of background is first assigned a value. Then each element of background is assigned to the packed array foreground.

(e)    In this outline, city and office are 3-element, char-type packed arrays (string variables). Initially, city is assigned the string 'CHI'. Then a positive integer value is entered and assigned to order. If this value is less than 100, the string originally assigned to city is assigned to office. Otherwise, if the value assigned to order is less than 1000, 'NYC' is assigned to office, and if the value assigned to order is equal to or greater than 1000, 'ATL' is assigned to office.

(f)    This outline involves the use of conformant array parameters. Within the main action block, procedure sort is accessed twice. The first time, a 40-element integer array (list1) is passed to sort. The second time, an 80-element integer array (list2) is passed to sort.
       ```

Chapter 10

10.33 (*a*)
```
         VAR sample : RECORD
                          first  : 1..100:
                          second : real;
                          third  : boolean
                      END;
```

(*b*)
```
         TYPE demo = RECORD
                          first  : 1..100:
                          second : real;
                          third  : boolean
                      END;
         VAR demo1,demo2 : demo;
```

(*c*)
```
         TYPE line = PACKED ARRAY [1..80] OF char;
              personal = RECORD
                              name,street,city : line
                          END;
         VAR employee : ARRAY [1..500] OF personal;
```

(*d*)
```
         TYPE personal = RECORD
                              name,street,city : string
                          END;
         VAR employee : ARRAY [1..500] OF personal;
```

(*e*)
```
         TYPE color = (red,green,blue);
              sample = PACKED RECORD
                                   first  : color;
                                   second : 1..132;
                                   third  : char
                      END;
         VAR trial : sample;
```

(*f*)
```
         TYPE color = (red,green,blue);
              sample = RECORD
                            first  : color;
                            second : 1..132;
                            third  : char
                        END;
         VAR trial : sample;
```

(*g*)
```
         TYPE color = (red,green,blue);
              sample = RECORD
                            CASE select : color OF
                                red   : (first  : 100..199;
                                         second : 200..299);
                                green : (third  : 300..399);
                                blue  : ()
                        END;
         VAR demo : ARRAY [1..500] OF sample;
```

```
(h)   TYPE color   = (red,green,blue);
           texture = (coarse,fine);
           sample  = RECORD
                           first  : color;
                           second : 1..132;
                           CASE color OF
                               red : (first : 100..199;
                                       second : 200..299);
                               green : ();
                               blue  : (CASE texture OF
                                           coarse : (third : 300..399);
                                              fine : ())
                        END;
               VAR demo1,demo2 : ARRAY [1..99] OF sample;
```

10.34 (a)   This Turbo Pascal program displays the values of the three string-type fields within the record called `employee`. (Note the use of the string data type; hence, Turbo Pascal.)

(b)   This ANSI Pascal program displays the values of the three fields within each record contained in the 500-element array called `employee`. (Note the use of char-type packed arrays to represent strings; hence, ANSI Pascal.)

(c)   This Turbo Pascal program displays the values of the three string-type fields within several of the records contained in the 500-element array called `employee`. The number of records processed is determined by the value assigned to the integer variable `total`. Note the use of the WITH structure, which simplifies the `writeln` statements.

(d)   This ANSI Pascal program displays the name, street and city of those customers (i.e., those records contained within the 500-element array called `customer`) whose name is the same as that of an employee (i.e., if `customer[i].name = employee[i].name`, where `employee` is another 500-element array whose elements are records). The number of records processed in each array is determined by the value assigned to the integer variable `total`. Note the use of a char-type packed array. Also, note the use of the WITH structure.

(e)   This Turbo Pascal program makes use of variant records. In this program the name, address and employee number of several different employees are displayed. In addition, if an employee is married, the number of children is displayed, and if a divorced or widowed employee has remarried, a message is displayed to that effect. The number of records processed is determined by the value assigned to the integer variable `total`. Note the use of the string data type (hence, Turbo Pascal). Also, note the use of the WITH structure.

Chapter 11

11.43 (a)   `VAR data : FILE OF integer;`

(b)   `VAR sales,costs : FILE OF real;`

(c)   `TYPE acctno = 1..9999;`
       `VAR accounts : FILE OF acctno;`

```
(d)   TYPE color = (red,green,blue);
          sample = RECORD
                        first : color;
                        second : 1..132;
                        third : char
                   END;
      VAR data : FILE OF sample;

(e)   TYPE color = (red,green,blue);
          sample = RECORD
                        first : color;
                        second : 1..132;
                        third : char
                   END;
          list = ARRAY [1..100] OF sample;
      VAR data : FILE OF list;

(f)   VAR oldstuff,newstuff : text;
```

11.44 (a) Enter a sequence of records from the keyboard and save in a file. Continue until end is entered for the name.

(b) Read a sequence of records from a file and display.

(c) Copy a sequence of records from one file to another.

(d) Enter a name from the keyboard. Then search a file for a record with the same name.

(e) Enter a sequence of names, addresses and phone numbers, and save in a text file. Continue until end is entered for the name.

11.45 (a)
```
PROGRAM sample;
TYPE personal = RECORD
                     name : string;
                     address : string;
                     phone : string
                END;
VAR data : FILE OF personal;
    nameandaddress : personal;

BEGIN
    assign(data,'records.dat');
    rewrite(data);
    WITH nameandaddress DO
       BEGIN
           readln(name);
           WHILE (name <> 'end') DO
              BEGIN
                  readln(address);
                  readln(phone);
                  write(data,nameandaddress);

                  readln(name)
              END
       END;
    close(data)
END.
```

```
(b)  PROGRAM sample;
     TYPE personal = RECORD
                          name : string;
                          address : string;
                          phone : string
                     END;
     VAR data : FILE OF personal;
         nameandaddress : personal;

     BEGIN
        assign(data,'records.dat');
        reset(data);
        WITH nameandaddress DO
           WHILE NOT eof(data) DO
              BEGIN
                 read(data,nameandaddress);
                 writeln(name);
                 writeln(address);
                 writeln(phone);
                 writeln
              END;
        close(data)
     END.


(c)  PROGRAM sample;
     VAR name,address,phone : line;
         data : text;

     BEGIN
        assign(data,'records.dat');
        rewrite(data);
        readln(name);
        WHILE (name <> 'end') DO
           BEGIN
              readln(address);
              readln(phone);
              write(data,name,address);
              writeln(data,phone);

              readln(name)
           END;
        close(data)
     END.
```

Chapter 12

12.21 (a) `VAR vowels,consonants : SET OF char;`

    (b) `VAR caps : SET OF 'A'..'Z';`

    (c) `TYPE capitals = 'A'..'Z';`
        `VAR caps : SET OF capitals;`

```
(d)  TYPE capitals = 'A'..'Z';
          uppers = SET OF capitals;
     VAR  caps : uppers;
(e)  VAR movement : SET OF (north,south,east,west);
(f)  TYPE compass = (north,south,east,west);
     VAR movement : SET OF compass;
(g)  TYPE compass = (north,south,east,west);
          direction = SET OF compass;
     VAR nextmove,lastmove : direction;
```

12.22 (a) `[mon,tue,wed,thu,fri]`

      (b) `[mon,tue,wed,thu,fri]`

      (c) `[mon,tue,thu,fri]`

      (d) `[wed]`

      (e) `[]`

      (f) `[tue,wed]`

12.23 (a) `workdays = [sun,mon,wed,thu,fri,sat]`

      (b) `workdays = [mon,wed,fri,sat]`

      (c) `workdays = [mon,tue,wed,thu]`
          `restdays = [thu]`

12.24	(a)	false	(g)	true	
	(b)	true	(h)	true	
	(c)	true	(i)	false	
	(d)	false	(j)	true	
	(e)	false	(k)	false	
	(f)	true			

12.25	(a)	`[re,mi,fa,so,la]`	(e)	`[do,re,mi,fa]`	
	(b)	`[do,re,mi,fa,so,la]`	(f)	`[]`	
	(c)	`[do]`	(g)	`[]`	
	(d)	`[re,mi,fa]`	(h)	`[do,re,mi]`	

12.26	(a)	`[re,fa]`	(d)	`[do,re,mi,so,ti]`	
	(b)	`[do,re,fa]`	(e)	`[re,mi,fa,so,la]`	
	(c)	`[re,mi,fa,la,ti]`			

12.27	(a)	false	(g)	true	
	(b)	true	(h)	true	
	(c)	false	(i)	false	
	(d)	true	(j)	true	
	(e)	false	(k)	true	
	(f)	true	(l)	false	

Chapter 13

13.34 (*a*)   ANSI Pascal solution:

```
TYPE link = ^customer;
     customer = RECORD
                     name : PACKED ARRAY [1..20] OF char;
                     acctno : 1..9999;
                     balance : real;
                     next : link
                END;
```

In Turbo Pascal, the first field could be defined as

```
                     name : string;
```

(*b*)   `VAR nextcustomer,lastcustomer : link;`

(*c*)
```
new(nextcustomer);
. . . . .
dispose(nextcustomer);
```

13.35 (*a*)   `lastcustomer := nextcustomer^.next;`

(*b*)   `nextcustomer^.next := NIL;`

(*c*)   `lastcustomer^ := nextcustomer^;`

(*d*)   `IF nextcustomer^.acctno = 1330 THEN nextcustomer^.balance := 287.55;`

or

```
WITH nextcustomer^ DO
   IF acctno = 1330 THEN balance := 287.55;
```

(*e*)   ANSI Pascal solution:

```
PROCEDURE readinput (VAR customer : link);
VAR count : 1..20;
BEGIN
   count := 1;
   WHILE NOT eoln DO
      BEGIN
         read(customer^.name);
         count := succ(count);
      END
END;

BEGIN    (* main action block *)
   . . . . .
   readinput(nextcustomer);
   . . . . .
END.
```

In Turbo Pascal, procedure `readinput` could simplified to

```
PROCEDURE readinput (VAR customer : link);
BEGIN
   readln(customer^.name);
END;
```

```
(f)    WHILE nextcustomer <> NIL DO
       BEGIN
          . . . . .
       END;
```

13.36 (*a*) Create and later dispose of a dynamic object variable. The object variable will be a record of type `part`.

(*b*) Create and enter data for a dynamic object variable of type `customer`.

(*c*) Create and enter data for a dynamic object variable of type `customer`.

(*d*) Create, enter data and display the contents of a dynamic object variable of type `customer`. Then dispose of the object variable.

(*e*) Create, process and then dispose of a dynamic object variable of type `part`.

Index

SCHAUM'S SOLVED PROBLEMS SERIES

- ■ **Learn the best strategies for solving tough problems in step-by-step detail**
- ■ **Prepare effectively for exams and save time in doing homework problems**
- ■ **Use the indexes to quickly locate the types of problems you need the most help solving**
- ■ **Save these books for reference in other courses and even for your professional library**

To order, please check the appropriate box(es) and complete the following coupon.

❑ **3000 SOLVED PROBLEMS IN BIOLOGY**
   ORDER CODE 005022-8/**$16.95 406 pp.**

❑ **3000 SOLVED PROBLEMS IN CALCULUS**
   ORDER CODE 041523-4/**$19.95 442 pp.**

❑ **3000 SOLVED PROBLEMS IN CHEMISTRY**
   ORDER CODE 023684-4/**$20.95 624 pp.**

❑ **2500 SOLVED PROBLEMS IN COLLEGE ALGEBRA & TRIGONOMETRY**
   ORDER CODE 055373-4/**$14.95 608 pp.**

❑ **2500 SOLVED PROBLEMS IN DIFFERENTIAL EQUATIONS**
   ORDER CODE 007979-x/**$19.95 448 pp.**

❑ **2000 SOLVED PROBLEMS IN DISCRETE MATHEMATICS**
   ORDER CODE 038031-7/**$16.95 412 pp.**

❑ **3000 SOLVED PROBLEMS IN ELECTRIC CIRCUITS**
   ORDER CODE 045936-3/**$21.95 746 pp.**

❑ **2000 SOLVED PROBLEMS IN ELECTROMAGNETICS**
   ORDER CODE 045902-9/**$18.95 480 pp.**

❑ **2000 SOLVED PROBLEMS IN ELECTRONICS**
   ORDER CODE 010284-8/**$19.95 640 pp.**

❑ **2500 SOLVED PROBLEMS IN FLUID MECHANICS & HYDRAULICS**
   ORDER CODE 019784-9/**$21.95 800 pp.**

❑ **1000 SOLVED PROBLEMS IN HEAT TRANSFER**
   ORDER CODE 050204-8/**$19.95 750 pp.**

❑ **3000 SOLVED PROBLEMS IN LINEAR ALGEBRA**
   ORDER CODE 038023-6/**$19.95 750 pp.**

❑ **2000 SOLVED PROBLEMS IN Mechanical Engineering THERMODYNAMICS**
   ORDER CODE 037863-0/**$19.95 406 pp.**

❑ **2000 SOLVED PROBLEMS IN NUMERICAL ANALYSIS**
   ORDER CODE 055233-9/**$20.95 704 pp.**

❑ **3000 SOLVED PROBLEMS IN ORGANIC CHEMISTRY**
   ORDER CODE 056424-8/**$22.95 688 pp.**

❑ **2000 SOLVED PROBLEMS IN PHYSICAL CHEMISTRY**
   ORDER CODE 041716-4/**$21.95 448 pp.**

❑ **3000 SOLVED PROBLEMS IN PHYSICS**
   ORDER CODE 025734-5/**$20.95 752 pp.**

❑ **3000 SOLVED PROBLEMS IN PRECALCULUS**
   ORDER CODE 055365-3/**$16.95 385 pp.**

❑ **800 SOLVED PROBLEMS IN VECTOR MECHANICS FOR ENGINEERS
   Vol I: STATICS**
   ORDER CODE 056582-1/**$20.95 800 pp.**

❑ **700 SOLVED PROBLEMS IN VECTOR MECHANICS FOR ENGINEERS
   Vol II: DYNAMICS**
   ORDER CODE 056687-9/**$20.95 672 pp.**

ASK FOR THE _SCHAUM'S_ SOLVED PROBLEMS SERIES AT YOUR LOCAL BOOKSTORE
OR CHECK THE APPROPRIATE BOX(ES) ON THE PRECEDING PAGE
AND MAIL WITH THIS COUPON TO:

McGRAW-HILL, INC.
ORDER PROCESSING S-1
PRINCETON ROAD
HIGHTSTOWN, NJ 08520

OR CALL
1-800-338-3987

_____

NAME (PLEASE PRINT LEGIBLY OR TYPE)

_____

ADDRESS (NO P.O. BOXES)

_____

CITY   **STATE**   **ZIP**

ENCLOSED IS   ☐ A CHECK   ☐ MASTERCARD   ☐ VISA   ☐ AMEX   (✓ ONE)

ACCOUNT # _____   **EXP. DATE** _____

SIGNATURE _____

MAKE CHECKS PAYABLE TO MCGRAW-HILL, INC. PLEASE INCLUDE LOCAL SALES TAX AND **$1.25** SHIPPING/HANDLING
PRICES SUBJECT TO CHANGE WITHOUT NOTICE AND MAY VARY OUTSIDE THE U.S.   FOR THIS
INFORMATION, WRITE TO THE ADDRESS ABOVE OR CALL THE **800** NUMBER.

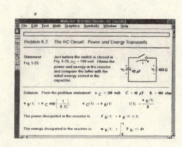